Programming Industrial Strength Windows

Shrink-Wrap your App!

Petter Hesselberg

R&D Books
Lawrence, Kansas 66046

R&D Books
CMP Media, Inc.
1601 W. 23rd Street, Suite 200
Lawrence, KS 66046
USA

Designations used by companies to distinguish their products are often claimed as trademarks. In all instances where R&D is aware of a trademark claim, the product name appears in initial capital letters, in all capital letters, or in accordance with the vendor's capitalization preference. Readers should contact the appropriate companies for more complete information on trademarks and trademark registrations. All trademarks and registered trademarks in this book are the property of their respective holders.

Copyright © 2000 by Petter Hesselberg, except where noted otherwise. Published by R&D Books, CMP Media, Inc. All rights reserved. Printed in the United States of America. No part of this publication may be reproduced or distributed in any form or by any means, or stored in a database or retrieval system, without the prior written permission of the publisher; with the exception that the program listings may be entered, stored, and executed in a computer system, but they may not be reproduced for publication.

The programs in this book are presented for instructional value. The programs have been carefully tested, but are not guaranteed for any particular purpose. The publisher does not offer any warranties and does not guarantee the accuracy, adequacy, or completeness of any information herein and is not responsible for any errors or omissions. The publisher assumes no liability for damages resulting from the use of the information in this book or for any infringement of the intellectual property rights of third parties that would result from the use of this information.

Cover art created by Robert Ward.

Distributed in the U.S. and Canada by:
Publishers Group West
1700 Fourth Street
Berkeley, CA 94710
1-800-788-3123
ISBN: 0-87930-605-X

Table of Contents

List of Listings..ix

Introduction...xiii
Who Should Read This Book?.......................................xv
The Source Code..xv
Acknowledgments...xvi
Legal Matters..xvii

Section I Background..........................1

Chapter 1 The Road Ahead.....................3
Destination: The Application......................................3
Roadbed: The Target Platform......................................4
Vehicle: The Programming Language.................................5

Chapter 2 Designing for Users.................9
Polite Applications..10
Robustness..11
Focused Design..12
The Windows Logo Program..12

Usability Testing. 12
The Unified File Model. 14

Chapter 3   Designing for Programmers 17
Programming Guiding Principles 17
Getting Your Priorities Straight 19
Global Variables Considered Harmful 21
Assert Your Sanity 21
Constantly on Guard 22
Use Destruction Constructively. 23
Programming Defensively. 31
Is Windows Object-Oriented?. 31

Chapter 4   The Mechanics of Subclassing 35
Subclassing Defined 35
Instance subclassing 36
Global Subclassing 39
Class Cloning 41
General Mechanism for Global Subclassing 43
General Mechanism for Instance Subclassing 46
The Window Class: Wrapping the HWND. 54

Section II   Foreground 63

Chapter 5   The Bare Bones. 65
The Major Organs 66
The Heart. 70
The Editor Class. 71
The Document Class. 76
The AbstractEditWnd Class. 82
Of Strings and PATHNAMEs 86

Chapter 6   Exceptions 93
Return Codes 94
Exceptions 95
Two-Stage Construction. 95
Global Object Constructor Exceptions. 96
The TextEdit Exception Classes 96
Converting Allocation Failures to Exceptions. 106
Recovering from Errors 106
Structured Exception Handling and C++ Exceptions 107

Chapter 7 Off the Launch Pad 111
Click, Drag, and Drop 111
Shell Integration 117
GUI Summary 118
The Console Connection 118
File Not Found 124
Read-Only 125
Other Anomalies 125
Command-Line Piping 127
Drag and Drop Revisited 128
Additional Switches 129
Accessing the Command Line. 130

Chapter 8 Child Windows 147
Window Creation 148
The Toolbar 148
The Status Bar 166

Chapter 9 The Main Window 179
Handling `WM_COMMAND` Messages 179
The Clipboard User Interface 180
Persistence in the Main Window 182
Drag and Drop 182
Menu Management 183
Communication Between TextEdit Instances 188
Changing User Settings 189
Notifications 189
The Editor Connection 189

Chapter 10 Customization and Persistence 223
Customizing Windows 223
Retrieving the Font 225
Customizing TextEdit 231
Long-Term Memory 232
The Registry Interface 234
MRU 248
RunOnce 255
Food for Persistent Thought 260

Chapter 11 Wait a Moment... 263
Changing the Cursor Image 265

Chapter 12 File I/O 269
Drive Type 270
SilentErrorMode 271
Opening Files 272
Reading and Writing Files 272
Copying the Original 275
Conversion 275
Saving 277
Conflict of Interest 278

Chapter 13 About Dialogs 299
What is a Dialog Box, Anyway? 299
The Dialog Class 300
The About Box 309
The Options Dialog 324
Enter with Care 325

Chapter 14 File Management 329
File Properties 329
Deleting Files 342
The Open File Dialog 346

Chapter 15 Search and Replace 367
Default Button Handling 368
Initializing the Dialog 371
Persistence 371
Text Not Found 372
The Relationship between Dialog and Main Window 373
Replacing Text 373

Chapter 16 Printing 395
DEVMODE and DEVNAMES 395
The Page Setup Dialog 400
The Print Dialog 404
Text Rendering and Pagination 409

Chapter 17 Changing Fonts 419
Subclassing the Font Common Dialog 420

Chapter 18 Going Abroad 425
Resource Files 427
Formatting Messages 429
Formatting Numbers 432
Formatting Dates, and Money, and... 436

Chapter 19 Meanwhile, in the Background 439
Threads in TextEdit 440
Starting Threads 440
Communication Between Threads 442

Chapter 20 Setup, and Down Again 443
Installation 445
Uninstall 460
Mea Culpa 480

Chapter 21 The End of the Road 481

Appendix A TextEdit Command Index 485

Appendix B Bibliography and Recommended Reading 489

Index 493

What's on the CD-ROM? 510

viii   Table of Contents

List of Listings

Listing 3.1 `AutoPtr.h` 26
Listing 3.2 `AutoArray.h` 27
Listing 3.3 `AutoHandle.h` 29
Listing 3.4 `PaintStruct.h` 30

Listing 4.1 `InstSub.rc` 37
Listing 4.2 `InstSub.cpp` 38
Listing 4.3 `GlobSub.cpp` 40
Listing 4.4 `Clone.cpp` 41
Listing 4.5 `GlobalSubclasser.h` 43
Listing 4.6 `GlobalSubclasser.cpp` 44
Listing 4.7 `InstanceSubclasser.h` 48
Listing 4.8 `InstanceSubclasser.cpp` 49
Listing 4.9 `Window.h` 55
Listing 4.10 `Window.cpp` 58

Listing 5.1 `WinMain.cpp` 67
Listing 5.2 `Editor.h` 71
Listing 5.3 `Document.h` 77
Listing 5.4 `AbstractEditWnd.h` 83

Listing 5.5 `String.h` 87
Listing 5.6 `common.h` 88

Listing 6.1 `Exception.h` 96
Listing 6.2 `Exception.cpp` 100
Listing 6.3 `handlers.cpp` 108

Listing 7.1 Exploring the Command Line 111
Listing 7.2 `createNewFile.cpp` 112
Listing 7.3 `getLongPathName.cpp` 120
Listing 7.4 `resolveName.cpp` 121
Listing 7.5 `activateOldInstance.cpp` 125
Listing 7.6 `ArgumentList.h` 130
Listing 7.7 `ArgumentList.cpp` 132
Listing 7.8 `init.cpp` 134

Listing 8.1 `Toolbar.h` 150
Listing 8.2 `Toolbar.cpp` 153
Listing 8.3 `Statusbar.h` 167
Listing 8.4 `Statusbar.cpp` 170

Listing 9.1 `menuUtils.h` 184
Listing 9.2 `menuUtils.cpp` 185
Listing 9.3 `mainwnd.h` 189
Listing 9.4 `mainwnd.cpp` 190

Listing 10.1 `MenuFont.h` 225
Listing 10.2 `MenuFont.cpp` 226
Listing 10.3 `Registry.h` 234
Listing 10.4 `Registry.cpp` 236
Listing 10.5 `persistence.h` 245
Listing 10.6 `MRU.h` 248
Listing 10.7 `MRU.cpp` 250
Listing 10.8 `reboot.cpp` 257

Listing 11.1 `WaitCursor.cpp` 265

Listing 12.1 `SilentErrorMode.h` 271
Listing 12.2 `FileMapping.h` 273

List of Listings

Listing 12.3 `FileMapping.cpp` 274
Listing 12.4 `Document.cpp` 278

Listing 13.1 `Dialog.h` 302
Listing 13.2 `Dialog.cpp` 304
Listing 13.3 `AboutDlg.cpp` 310
Listing 13.4 `HTML.h` 315
Listing 13.5 `HTML.cpp` 316

Listing 14.1 `PropertiesDlg.h` 332
Listing 14.2 `PropertiesDlg.cpp` 332
Listing 14.3 `DeleteDlg.h` 344
Listing 14.4 `DeleteDlg.cpp` 345
Listing 14.5 `openDlgCommon.cpp` 350
Listing 14.6 `openFile.cpp` 358

Listing 15.1 `dlgSubclasser.cpp` 369
Listing 15.2 `FindDlg.cpp` 377

Listing 16.1 `devMode.cpp` 396
Listing 16.2 `devNames.cpp` 398
Listing 16.3 `setupPage.cpp` 401
Listing 16.4 `printFile.cpp` 405
Listing 16.5 `print.cpp` 410

Listing 17.1 `FONT.DLG` 421
Listing 17.2 `FontDlg.cpp` 423

Listing 18.1 `formatMessage.cpp` 429
Listing 18.2 `formatNumber.cpp` 433

Listing 19.1 `threads.h` 441

Listing 20.1 `FileType.h` 446
Listing 20.2 `FileType.cpp` 448
Listing 20.3 `InstallDlg1.cpp` 452
Listing 20.4 `SetupDlg.cpp` 462

Introduction

"Error handling has been omitted for clarity."

Too many times have I read that sentence in a programming book or article. Not that there's anything inherently wrong with this; simplification is a legitimate teaching device. The problem is that the literature is terribly one-sided — it's a rare gem that says, "error handling has been included to show how it's done." Many programmers never learn how to handle errors and anomalies. Even more chilling, some never realize that the issue exists. The results are all around us; robustness and reliability are rarely considered defining characteristics of software.

This book gives you an understanding of what it takes to build industrial strength software — software that works reliably and robustly, software that doesn't get between the user and his task. It will not bestow software nirvana upon you; indeed, no book ever could. That unattainable state of grace can only be approached through experience; the most a book can do is to help you get the right, rather than the wrong, kind of experience. My highest hope is that the book will inspire you to *care* — about your users, about your profession, and about getting the details right.

The word *fragmentation* is descriptive of much current computer literature. Many books use minimalist examples to illustrate various APIs and subsystems, and rarely draw things together into a coherent whole. Again, this is not necessarily a Bad Thing — many excellent books use this approach.

Unfortunately, it is not enough. When you assemble those fragments to create a full-blown application, their interaction gives rise to an exponential increase in complexity, and a myriad of details must be considered. This aspect of software construction is rarely covered, and the literature is left with a hole large enough to drive a truck-full of bugs through. Sadly, bugs and inconsistencies often *are* considered defining characteristics of computer software.

In this book, I've taken a more holistic approach. I built it around the development of a single application called TextEdit. I did this with a considerable amount of trepidation, though — TextEdit doesn't have years of field-testing under its belt, so I worry that it will fail to work correctly.

One purpose of the book is to induce the same feeling of uneasiness in you. Anything that can go wrong will most certainly do so, one time or another; so preaches the Gospel according to Murphy. In software development, this often translates as "whatever users can do, some user will do," one time or another. Many developers suffer a failure of the imagination when confronted by this simple law of nature. In one application I tried recently, a numeric input field commendably refused to accept anything but digits. It did not object, however, when I *pasted* non-digits, realizing too late that it was in mortal danger: "Run-time error 13!" it cried, and expired.

This kind of glitch is not necessarily dishonorable; we all make mistakes. But listen to the reaction I got from the programmer when I reported it, "No, I'm not going to do anything about this. Nobody else has reported the problem, and *normal* people wouldn't do such a dumb thing anyway." *Idiot*, he didn't say.

Creating excellent software is difficult. No matter how hard you try, you will sometimes fail. The only sin is lack of trying; you owe it to yourself, as well as your users, to give it your best shot.

Usability comes in chunks of different granularity. On a high level, you have issues such as the overall conceptual model — the Unified File Model versus the current standard model, for example, which I'll cover in Chapter 2. On a lower level, you have issues such as where to place the widgets in a dialog box and how to label them. This level gets the most attention in Web design, for example. On the detail level, you have a huge number of issues concerning efficient "flow," i.e., smooth interaction. This concept is virtually unknown in Web design. Using default buttons correctly is one aspect of this that I'll return to several times throughout the book.

Efficient flow of information ought to receive much more consideration during software design, but the current state of the World Wide Web is proof that it rarely receives any consideration at all. Does the user really need that animated deodorant on his desk, or would your development effort be better spent ensuring that the user can get his work done efficiently and effectively, and that his data are never lost?

The book is divided into two parts of unequal size. Section I is called "Background," and does not concern itself much with TextEdit, but with general guiding principles for the design and implementation of computer programs. Section II is called "Foreground," and is the largest by far. It is mostly concerned with the implementation details of TextEdit.

Who Should Read This Book?

If you are a programmer with some knowledge of C++ and some Windows experience, this book is for you. If you don't know what a C++ class is, or if you have never heard of `WinMain` or window functions, you should read some introductory material first. This book doesn't cover the basics.

It does, however, cover many aspects of application design, target platform and implementation language selection, usability issues, and a myriad implementation details, including error handling and recovery, installation, internationalization, and registry handling. Along the way, I touch upon enough programming issues to make this book interesting for programmers at many levels of experience. Both neophytes and experienced Windows programmers will find things of interest here.

The book also has something to offer MFC programmers and even Visual Basic programmers — in short, all programmers working with Windows. Chapter 1 discusses the relationship between several approaches to Windows programming.

This is not a reference manual, but more of an exploratory trip into the nooks and crannies of the Windows API. If I don't exhaustively explain everything found along the way, you will at least learn something about what's out there, and can find the reference material for yourself — in the material included with your compiler or on the Internet.

The accompanying CD-ROM contains all the (approximately) 20,000 lines of source code that make up TextEdit. You may use them as you see fit in your own programming endeavors.

The Source Code

I won't describe my coding style in detail; you'll get the idea by looking at the source code. Here are a couple of specifics, though, just to give you a flavor:

- I always use braces with conditionals and loops, even if only a single statement is controlled. I started this practice after I had spent several hours hunting down a bug caused by indentation mismatch:

```
if ( x == y )
    ++x;
    --y;
```

I vowed that this bug would never bite me again, and it hasn't. Yet.

- When comparing for equality, I always put the constant (if any) on the left-hand side. In the past, I've been caught more than once by unintended assignments:

```
if ( variable = CONSTANT ) {
    ...
}
```

If you switch `variable` and `CONSTANT`, the assignment above generates a compilation error, as `CONSTANT` is not an l-value.

What these examples have in common is that they prevent bugs. Some aspects of coding style are matters of preference — it's unimportant whether you indent your code with three or four spaces. If you do not indent your code at all, however, it matters a great deal because such formatting fails to reflect the logical structure of the program.

Religious wars are fought over coding styles, and, curiously enough, the most intense battles are fought over insignificant details. I used to have a few pet hang-ups myself until I woke up one day and decided to do a thorough housecleaning. I completely revised my coding style, making conscious decisions at all points. As a result, I am now free of any religious hang-ups. (Some people will tell you that I've merely replaced old hang-ups with new ones. Pay them no heed; they are merely propagating vicious rumors spread by my enemies.)

All function and method names start with a lowercase character. This is a result of my exposure to Java; I found that I rather liked that convention. Preferences aside, the convention has practical advantages. First, it makes it easy to distinguish between class names and function names without resorting to the ugly C prefix for classes. Second, it avoids name clashes with the Windows API. The name space of `windows.h` and its underlings is a confused jumble where the documented name for a function is, as often as not, a macro resolving to either an ANSI or a Unicode version of the function. If, for example, a class had a method ostensibly named `GetWindowText`, the method would actually be named `GetWindowTextA` or `GetWindowTextW`, depending. The result of this renaming behind your back can be anything from simple confusion to outright compilation errors.

For a deeper discussion of coding styles, I recommend Steve McConnel's *Code Complete* (see Appendix B — Bibliography and Recommended Reading, page 490). In particular, pay attention to the way he clearly formulates *goals* for a set of coding conventions. For example, the code should clearly reflect the logical structure of the program, it should be readable, it should be maintainable (not necessarily the same thing), and it should prevent bugs.

I've made some compromises to fit the format of this book. Because I'm constrained by a maximum line length of 70 characters, some variable names are shorter than they would otherwise have been, and there is quite a number of extra line breaks. Also, indentations are spaces rather than the tab characters I normally use.

When I refer to a *method*, I invariably mean a non-static member function of some class. Everything else is a function.

The files on the companion CD-ROM are more up-to-date than those printed in the book, and the files maintained on R&D Books' ftp site are even more up-to-date. Go to `ftp.mfi.com/rdbooks/pub/Hesselberg.zip`; login as "anonymous" and no password is needed. As I write this, the first two versions are identical, and the third does not yet exist. I expect that to change by the time you read this.

TextEdit was developed using version 6 of Microsoft Visual C++. While the text reflects that fact on occasion, the book is meant to be compiler-independent. In particular, it is not a book about Visual C++.

Acknowledgments

The good will and helpful assistance of many people helped turn this book into reality. Ron Burk, editor of *Windows Developer's Journal*, has given me many a stimulating discussion on

Windows programming, and has bought numerous articles from me. Berney Williams, acquisitions editor at R&D Books, liked my proposal well enough to offer me a contract. Nils Øveraas, my boss at Andersen Consulting's Oslo office, approved of the project and gave me the time I needed to write.

Thanks to the above people, there is a book. Contributions from many others helped improve both the book and the TextEdit application. Ron Burk, Witold Sitek, and Alf Steinbach offered insights on C++ and the Windows API; Oddmund Møgedal and Tone Pettersen offered insights on usability. Paal Beyer, Anders Blehr, Frode Bonesvoll, Kjell Furnes, Henning Normann, Øyvind Pedersen, Leif Arne Roues, Simen Røkaas, Øyvind Sandvold, Nils Sandøy, Håvard Stenberg, and Frode Strand gave me feedback during the beta testing of TextEdit. Geir Regstad Aamodt did Win 2000 testing; Henrik Lund-Hanssen, Velitchko Koulichev, and Tone Pettersen commented on the text, as did my wife, Linda. Francis Daveronis helped with Greek, and Jean-Marc Delcourt helped with the French (what little there is of either). Mike Wallace did the technical editing, and Michelle Dowdy at R&D Books did the copyediting. Any remaining inaccuracies, errors, or omissions are my own responsibility.

On a more general note, I would like to thank my colleagues at Andersen Consulting's Oslo office for providing a generally stimulating work environment. I find it hard to conceive of a more interesting place to work.

Last, but by no means least, I thank my family — Linda, Håkon, Vegard, and Anders — for their support and encouragement while I was writing this book. I could not have done it without you.

Legal Matters

You may use all the source code in this book and on the accompanying CD for your own purposes, including commercial purposes. Neither the author, Andersen Consulting, nor R&D Books or CMP Media, Inc. is responsible for fitness of purpose or anything else.

Any customized version of TextEdit must be clearly marked as such.

Section I

Background

Chapter 1

The Road Ahead

This book is the story of a Windows application. I considered several alternatives for this application and eventually landed on TextEdit — a Notepad replacement with a twist in the usability department. This chapter explains the how, the why, and the wherefore.

Destination: The Application

Why did I end up with TextEdit as my sample program? One reason is its convenient size. On the one hand, it's large enough to illustrate how to build a non-trivial Windows application. On the other hand, it is small enough to fit in a reasonably-sized book. On the third hand, I wanted a Notepad replacement for my own use. For some editing tasks, speed is more important than power, and Notepad does start a lot faster than Word or Visual Studio. Every time I use it, however, I end up thinking, "I could do better than this!"

The actual editing of the text is delegated to a control. This taken care of, I can skip a great deal of that functional detail and concentrate on the mechanics of sewing up a Windows application.

I've seen Notepad described as "anemic," and that is apt. For example:
- Notepad has no toolbar and no status bar
- Notepad remembers little from one moment to the next — the only thing that comes to mind is your chosen font
- Notepad has no integration with standard input (see Chapter 7)

- Notepad lacks standard accelerator keys. (This has been fixed in the Notepad version delivered with Windows 98 and Windows 2000, but it sure didn't used to be)
- Notepad uses the standard edit control — a widget that's really beginning to show its age.

Notepad was never meant to be anything but a simple text editor, but I still feel that a couple of the roughest edges could have been filed off.

Is there anything good to say about Notepad? Simple though it is, it is at least reliable, and has never failed me in all the years I've been exposed to the thing. It also handles Unicode gracefully.

The most important reason why I want to replace Notepad is more fundamental: The entire conceptual model that Notepad presents to the end user is faulty. Admittedly, Notepad shares this problem with most current software, so I'm being a bit unfair, picking on Notepad like this.

I'll get back to that particular problem in the next chapter.

Roadbed: The Target Platform

TextEdit runs on a subset of Win32: Windows 95 or higher, and Windows NT 4.0 or higher. It does not run on any 16-bit version of Windows, or on Win32s, or on Windows NT versions prior to 4.0, or on Windows CE.

Why didn't I concentrate on the very latest versions of Windows? As I write this, Windows 98 has been out for a while, Windows NT 5 is in its beta 3 incarnation and has been renamed to Windows 2000 (or W2K, if you like). Well, Windows 95 and Windows NT 4.0 will remain in the mainstream for quite some time yet. Furthermore, backward compatibility is an important subject that you must consider for almost all real-life applications. It's a special form of platform independence, and I'll show you some techniques and attitudes for making your programs robust in the face of platform changes.

The Windows family of operating systems is as afflicted by Dancing Deodorant Syndrome (DDS) as any software product these days. New features and marketing frills are apparently given higher priority than bug fixing and conceptual soundness. While I'm as enamoured of cool stuff as the next programmer, I believe that cool stuff is better built on solid ground than on shifting sands.

Why not go all the way, then, and create an application that would work on 16-bit Windows as well as on 32-bit Windows? Even if I had chosen a "least common denominator" functionality, this would have been a major undertaking. Most of the book would have been devoted to cross-platform issues, with little space left over for my real agenda. I certainly didn't want to limit the functionality to what Win16 has to offer because this would have cut off too many desirable features.

Creating an application that *dynamically* takes advantage of the underlying system is still more difficult. TextEdit does this to an extent; it uses some Windows 95-specific and some Windows NT-specific APIs dynamically. Doing this on the scale required to cover the gap between Win16 and Win32 is definitely out of the book's scope.

There's a "political" side to it too — I don't believe in flogging a dead operating system. This doesn't mean that Win16 is dead, quite, but if you really need to create something cross-platform, the best way to go is usually to write a 16-bit application, then test it carefully on all target Win32-platforms.

Vehicle: The Programming Language

C, C++, Basic, Java — several programming languages are reasonable choices for writing Windows applications. Why C++?

Choosing C++ over C is a no-brainer. Even if you don't use a single object-oriented feature of C++, it is still a "better C" that lets you do function overloading and allows you to freely mix variable declarations and statements. The only *reasonable* reason ever to choose straight C is if you lack a C++ compiler for your platform — or if you're writing the control software for a new airplane.

See the discussion of MFC below also.

Visual Basic is a truly amazing piece of software; it certainly amazed me the first time I saw it. Nevertheless, I've found it to be of limited use in my work. Here are some of the reasons:

- The language is too limiting. Object-orientation really is a benefit, and Visual Basic does not offer it, advertising to the contrary.
- You're too shielded from the Windows API. Visual Basic "forms" are a peculiar variant of windows, a law unto themselves.
- Software distribution gets complicated because you have to distribute the VB runtime as well as your application.
- Performance is an issue. In a given case, this may or may not be a problem. Some, however, seem to think that performance issues are no longer critical because computers are getting faster and faster.

  This kind of thinking implies that we will do the same things with software next year as we did last year, and that simply isn't so. I'm writing this book on a laptop computer. It has a 300MHz Pentium II processor, 128MB of RAM and a 6.3GB hard disk. It was a high-end machine when I got it; now I suppose it's barely midrange, although it continues to serve me well.

  Yet Microsoft Word takes longer to start from my hard disk than did WordStar from a floppy on a Z80 I once owned (sometime back in the early Pleistocene). The point is that Word does enormously much more for me than WordStar ever did. "Slow" may be "fast enough" sometimes, but with real speed, you can design totally different UI paradigms.

  One project I was once involved in had a window with a list of items on the left-hand side and details about the selected item on the right-hand side. Whenever a new item was selected on the left, details would appear on the right. This is a common paradigm; the problem in this project was that retrieving the detail involved heavy network operations and could take up to one minute, during which time the application was completely unresponsive. The solution was to forego automatic updating, and instead add an explicit Update button to the window. A different UI paradigm.

  The Windows Explorer is somewhat more clever about updating its right-hand pane. It doesn't do this immediately after an item (folder) has been selected in the left-hand list, but (I think) starts a timer instead. The right-hand pane is updated when this timer fires. The timer is reset whenever the left-hand selection changes, and its interval is long enough that you can use the keyboard auto-repeat to arrow down the list without being held up by repeated updates.

The TextEdit Open File dialog uses this technique to update the preview window, as we shall see in Chapter 14.
- Visual Basic is easy to learn and to use. This is, of course, used as an argument in favor of Visual Basic, but there is a down side to it: even beginners can get something up and running very quickly. In the ensuing adrenaline rush, they run with the ball, adding functionality and cool doo-dads right and left. Being beginners, they do this with neither discipline nor structure, in an environment that allows you to spread your code all over the place, or rather under each button. Sooner than you would have thought possible, you have an unmaintainable mess.

A few years ago, I was on a project where we wrote the hard parts in C, using VB as glue to stick all the parts together. Most of the programmers were inexperienced, you see, so the management felt that this was the best way. It did (of course) turn on us with a vengeance. VB's ease of use does not turn amateurs into professional programmers; it is no substitute for actual knowledge and experience.

The Java language definition is superb in spots, but it does have holes. One hole is the lack of destructors. Garbage collection is fine, but what about objects that encapsulate files, network connections, window handles, or other system resources? You're forced to create methods for explicit destruction, and miss the beauty of C++ stack unwinding. Another hole is the lack of a preprocessor. I know that this lack is a result of a conscious decision, and I even understand the rationale behind it; I merely happen to disagree. You don't deny grown men beef merely because it's unfit food for babies.

In spite of these and other holes (lack of `const`, for example), Java is a well-designed language with, I believe, a substantial role to play. Java still suffers — badly — from the immaturity of the tools and libraries surrounding it, and the marketing wars and quasi-political power struggles don't help any. Those are not unique to Java though.

In truth, there is no "best programming language," and you'd do well not to get religious on this issue. (That's *my* prerogative.) Choose the tool best suited to the job at hand.

I do believe that C++ is the best general-purpose programming language in widespread use available to the professional programmer. It is also the most difficult to learn and to use, which is why I emphasized "professional." Java may yet threaten it, at least in some areas. Java's design more or less eliminates several notorious classes of errors, including pointer arithmetic and memory management. This helps reduce the cost of software development, and, in most companies, it is difficult to argue with the bottom line.

Class Libraries

Why write a native Windows application? Given that I'm programming in C++, why not use a ready-made class library such as Microsoft Foundation Classes (MFC)? Again, a question with no "right" answer. I've written MFC applications in the past, and been reasonably satisfied with the process and the results. Here are some of the reasons I chose another route for this book:
- A book about native Windows programming holds interest for MFC programmers too, while a book about MFC programming is unlikely to interest those that write to the native Windows API.

- MFC is not a true black box; you cannot use it effectively unless you have extensive knowledge of the underlying API. If you're an MFC programmer, I hope you will take the time to read this book — to learn more about native Windows programming, to start thinking about how to design class libraries for Windows programming, and to start thinking "out of the MFC box."
- MFC is (among other things) an application framework that makes certain assumptions about how applications should look and behave. This certainly has benefits; it allows you to create a standard MFC application very quickly, for example. It can be a straightjacket, though; things that are not provided for in the application framework are often hard to do. You can, of course, write MFC applications without taking advantage of `CDocuments`, `CViews` and `CCmdTargets`. If so, you give up the major benefits of MFC anyway.

If you're building something that doesn't fit the MFC framework, you're better off devising your own framework. Cross-platform libraries blunt the sharp, platform-specific edge you need for true excellence.

Chapter 2

Designing for Users

From the UNIX world comes a text editor named vi. It's powerful and fast — provided you know how to use it. The problem with vi is that it is difficult to learn. A host of keyboard commands must be learned by heart — the user interface doesn't give you a clue as to what you can and can't do. The problem is compounded by vi's several *modes* — it has different modes for text insertion and text manipulation, for example. The modes are, in themselves, no disaster, but their invisibility is. Nothing indicates whether your keystrokes will be interpreted as text to be inserted or commands to be executed.

The vi editor violates the following principle of good user interface design:

"Program state should be visible in the user interface."

Curiously, by editing a configuration file (if you can find it), you can cause vi to display which mode it's in. This information is presented in a piece of screen real estate that's never used for anything else. Why this should require the editing of an obscure configuration file, or even be optional, is beyond me.

This doesn't bother expert vi users much, but it is truly galling for novices and occasional users. (I should know; I've been a member of all three categories.) One of our tasks as software designers is to ease the path from ignorance to enlightenment, and showing the user just what's going on is a big step in the right direction.

A traditional quandary for software design is the simultaneous accommodation of novices and experts. This is similar to learning to bicycle: once you know how, you'd like to get rid of the training wheels — they are just an impediment to efficient bicycling.

Catering to all user groups is difficult. Try it anyway; it can be done. Furthermore, the process of trying can help you refine or even totally rethink the application's conceptual model.

The following is a helpful guiding principle on the way:

"Provide more than one way of doing things."

The rationale behind this is that the novice, by definition ignorant of what can and cannot be done, must be able to browse his way to all the possibilities. This is what drop-down menus are for. The expert already knows what's in those menus and needs a faster access path. This is what keyboard shortcuts are for. As an essential part of this dualism, the keyboard shortcuts are displayed on the menus, giving the novice a chance of (a) realizing they exist and (b) learning them.

To design excellent software, you must put yourself in the user's shoes. Playing with your software is not the user's goal. The user's goal is to accomplish a task, such as changing the contents of a text file. Your job is to help the user reach this goal as painlessly as possible, not to show off your programming skills. (I know this sounds tautological, but it can really be difficult. In Chapter 20 I'll tell you about one part of TextEdit where I goofed; I'm sure there are others.) The best user interfaces are invisible — in the sense that they don't put up a barrier between the user and the task. Achieving this takes more design and programming skills than anything else I know; unfortunately, it's also less obvious than all the "cool" stuff, and less likely to bring you rave reviews.

User-centered design is a subject worthy of its own book; in this chapter, I confine myself to a few highlights. If you wish to pursue the subject further, Laura Arlov's *GUI Design for Dummies* or Alan Cooper's *About Face* are good places to begin (see Appendix B — Bibliography and Recommended Reading).

Polite Applications

Here is another guiding principle:

"Don't bother the user unnecessarily."

Alan Cooper uses the term *excise* to describe dialogs, message boxes, window movements, and other things that do not contribute to the user's goal (which, as I have already mentioned, is to accomplish a task, not to play with your software). Often enough, error messages are there for the programmer's convenience rather than the user's. Perhaps you should redesign the application to handle the error gracefully and invisibly, or perhaps you should redesign the conceptual model to make the "error" go away.

When you type commands in a console window, for example, there's always the possibility that you will mistype a file name. The resulting error must be handled somehow; I'm not suggesting that you pretend everything is fine when in fact it is not. If, on the other hand, you must select a file name from a list of available files, the possibility of mistyping goes away.

Some message boxes are just plain unnecessary. TextEdit uses the status bar to display messages; this makes for a more conversational and relaxed style of interaction. (If the user has chosen to hide the status bar, TextEdit may display a message box as a last resort.)

The status bar has one big problem in this role: most people don't pay it much attention. To remedy this problem, TextEdit's status bar displays highlighted text whenever it has something substantial to say (as shown in Figure 2.1).

In Chapter 15, I'll show you how to do away with message boxes in connection with search and replace.

Figure 2.1   Status bar with a message: Highlighting makes the user pay attention.

```
enum {
    MAX_STRINGS = 10,
    MAX_TEXT_LENGTH = 200,
```

Found **FindDlg** (passed the end of the file)   Ln 12

Robustness

No matter how well designed, a program that doesn't work the way it's supposed to work is unusable. In particular:

"Never lose the user's data!"

This is so obvious that I won't belabor the point. A large part of a program's robustness is a result of the imagination you bring to bear in imagining wild scenarios for what users might do.

Robustness is more than not losing data, though. If the application is unable to present a consistent world-view to the user, the user may rightly start to wonder whether the application really knows what's going on. The following scenario is obvious after the fact, but I was months into the TextEdit project before I thought of it: What happens if the user changes the file type during an editing session?

First, you need to know the following about TextEdit:

1. Although TextEdit doesn't have a Save As command, you can change the file name, including the extension, from the File menu or from the Properties dialog box.
2. TextEdit displays the icon that belongs with the file type, rather than an application-specific icon. This, I feel, is in a quite document-centric spirit.

If the user opens the properties dialog, changes the file extension from .txt to .cpp and clicks the Apply button, the icon on the dialog should change (see Figure 2.2). In addition, the textual type description should change, the dialog title should change, and the timestamp of last file access should change.

Figure 2.2   TextEdit displays different icons for different file types.

This may seem simple and obvious, perhaps, but that's just because "everything that's known is obvious." The average application — and the Windows desktop itself — has many, many such minor glitches. To minimize them, you must use your imagination.

Focused Design

Design your application before implementing it. If you don't, implementation issues will overshadow user requirements, and your application will lack focus. If you design as you go along, the result is likely to be a hodge-podge of bolted-together features rather than a unified whole. This is particularly true when a whole programming team is working on an application or a suite of applications. All team members won't think alike.

State the basic mission first. If somebody asks, "What does the program do?", how do you answer that in a single sentence?

The Windows Logo Program

The requirements for the Microsoft Windows Logo program contain many good ideas, and it is worth your while to check them out (http://msdn.microsoft.com/). I do not care one whit, however, about whether TextEdit qualifies for the Windows logo. The logo program is designed to promote Microsoft's agenda rather than yours or mine. If a logo requirement makes sense, fine. If not, disregard it — unless that Windows logo is important to your marketing department. The World According to Marketing catches up with us all occasionally.

User interface standards are good, insofar as they make it easier for users to move between different applications. Standards can also be bad, insofar as they help propagate questionable practices. Don't assume that a way of doing something is good merely because it is "standard." Use your judgement, and feel free to break standards when there is good reason to. Don't, however, break standards gratuitously.

Usability Testing

To design excellent software, you must put yourself in the user's shoes. Unfortunately, putting yourself in the user's shoes becomes nearly impossible after you've worked on a program for a while. This doesn't come about because all your compassion and empathy has suddenly left for places unknown, but because you get so used to your program that you can't see it the way a stranger would, no matter how hard you try.

You can alleviate this problem by doing *usability testing*. This has nothing to do with what programmer's usually think of as testing; usability testing is a design tool. You place someone (actually several someones, but one someone at a time please) in front of your program, give that someone a task to perform, then step back and observe what happens. Do not provide assistance! The temptation to do so is often overwhelming, and while doing so is certain to please your test subject, you won't learn anything that way. Success isn't interesting; failure is. It's when the user fails in his task, or takes too long succeeding, that you learn something useful.

Conceptual Models

A conceptual model is a mental map of the most important parts of a system and how they relate to each other. The term *mental model* is sometimes used as a synonym.

There is no "right" conceptual model of a given system. A street map of New York is useful for moving about on the surface, but unsuited for subway travel. A subway map presents a very different conceptual model of New York — useful for subway travel, but completely useless for moving about on the surface.

Whenever programmers design user interfaces, the conceptual model tends to grow out of the characteristics of the underlying system and the program's implementation. This may be appropriate if you're designing a tool for your fellow programmers, but less so if you're designing a self-service kiosk for the general public.

The conceptual model that underlies a user interface is critical to its usability. You can avoid many design blunders by following these simple precepts:

- Design the conceptual model from the user's point of view rather than the system's point of view.
- Establish and validate the conceptual model early in the project.

No matter what the relationship between the user interface and the underlying system, the following design principle always holds:

"The user interface should be as close as possible to the conceptual model."

Incidentally, you should put considerable care into the selection of tasks for usability testing or you may find that what you've learned has little value. What is the purpose of the program? What is the user's goal?

How does the user react to your program? Does he or she try to find a command in the wrong place? Perhaps you ought to move the command, or provide alternative access ways. Does the user have a totally wrong mental model of what's happening? If so, perhaps the conceptual model should be made more visible. Perhaps you should redesign your program around a different conceptual model.

Usability testing is best done with a crude prototype — on paper, even. If you invest much time and effort in a prototype, it becomes your baby. You lose face when people find fault with it; you get defensive about it. This is the wrong attitude for usability testing.

The right attitude for usability testing is to assume that your user interface is worthless, and pray that the users — who, no matter how wrong-headed, are always right — will show you just where you went wrong. If you find this attitude difficult, then at least try to simulate it by granting, for the sake of argument, the remote possibility that your software is not yet quite perfect.

After you've sucked this well dry, switch attitudes again. Users, no matter how good, are always wrong. They will tell you in specific detail how the software should behave and they will probably be wide of the mark. All car owners have opinions on cars, but would you want one to design yours? You improve your design not by letting the users tell you how to do your job, but by observing where and how users go wrong.

(The attitudes described in the previous two paragraphs are extremes. The trick is to balance them just so.)

Truly interesting findings may suggest a total redesign. This will never happen towards the end of a project. A pervasive change at a late stage is horrendously expensive, whereas a pervasive change in the early design phase is dirt-cheap. Start usability testing as early as possible; you can pin down the conceptual model and basic functionality from a paper prototype. Later, you can use a succession of electronic versions to hone details.

Whatever else you do, don't make a slip of the tongue and say "user testing" instead of "usability testing." You're testing the user interface, not the user and if you don't make this difference clear to your test subjects, before you know it, you won't have any.

The Unified File Model

In *Tog on Design*, Bruce Tognazzini says that the sole reason applications for the original Macintosh had an explicit Save command was the machine's lack of a hard drive. The machine's single drive couldn't hold both the program floppy and the data floppy at the same time, making automatic saving rather impractical. Even though the designers considered it conceptually wrong, explicit Save was forced upon them by this technological limitation.

The now standard conceptual model makes explicit the two copies of the document — the one on the disk and the working copy in memory. It forces aspects of the underlying implementation upon the user. Programmers and power users are used to this; their mental model correctly describes the true state of affairs.

For beginners, however, the concept of memory versus disk is a real hurdle. My father is a case in point. After he swapped his typewriter for a computer, he continued to use the computer as if it were a typewriter, limiting his editing to occasional use of the backspace key. He never saved his files; once he got his documents out of the printer, he was happy to let them evaporate. This was not because he's lacking in either intelligence or typing skills, but because this strange world of computer software was disconnected from anything in his experience. His mental model was of the computer as a time-delayed typewriter.

Eventually, he did learn how to save, and looked upon this newfound ability and found it good. With a program offering a different conceptual model, he would have had the ability to save from the start.

In *About Face*, Alan Cooper describes what he calls the *unified file model*. In the unified file model, there's just the one file — on disk. TextEdit uses this conceptual model, pretending that it is operating directly on the disk file rather than on a copy in memory (which, of course, is what's "really" happening). Because the unified file model is further removed from the underlying system than the standard model is, designers and programmers must do extra work to bridge the gap.

The standard model has two advantages. (a) You can discard all your changes with the click of a button — a sort of "master undo." Any replacement must implement some mechanism to do the same thing; TextEdit does this through the Abandon Changes command on the File menu. (b) Existing users are used to it and think it natural. It remains to be seen whether inertia can be overcome; I certainly got some static from my beta testers over it.

Chapter 3

Designing for Programmers

In the previous chapter, I discussed software usability from the user's point of view. Programmers are users, too, albeit with a different world view. Programmers, including yourself, are users of your source code.

Is your source code usable? How easily can I extend your program, how easy are your APIs to use — correctly? Do your APIs encourage robust programming, or do they actively court programming mistakes? Do you remember what you did two years ago? Two months ago? I know I don't.

This chapter examines a few issues that help make programmers' lives easier; more are scattered throughout the rest of the book.

Programming Guiding Principles

A *guiding principle* is a general rule to guide design decisions; it usually includes the rationale behind the rule. We already encountered a few guiding principles in the previous chapter and you'll find guiding principles for programming scattered throughout this book. They're all formatted like this one:

"Let the compiler catch the bugs."

This means compiling at the highest warning level available. It means defining STRICT before including any Windows header files. It means avoiding casts when you can (which is not all that often in Windows programming). It means using little tricks such as putting the constant first in all comparisons. Consider this code fragment:

```
if ( uiRetCode = IDOK ) {
    // ...
}
```

This example contains a bug. The controlling expression has one equal sign instead of two, so it is a (perfectly legal) assignment, rather than the intended comparison. Moreover, IDOK being non-zero, the expression is constant and always evaluates to true — the controlled clause is always executed.

If you code the statement like this instead, the compiler will catch the bug:

```
if ( IDOK = uiRetCode ) {
    // ...
}
```

Actually, most compilers will warn about "assignment in comparison" on the first example. This warning is one reason why many programmers fail to use all the help the compiler can give them — they *like* writing assignments in comparisons, and disable the warning to avoid complaints about constructs such as this:

```
if ( hdc = GetDC( hwnd ) ) {
    // ...
    ReleaseDC( hwnd, hdc );
}
```

Don't do it! The last time I was burned by an assignment in a comparison was in 1996. It cost me five hours of debugging, all of them unnecessary, and I vowed that it would never happen again.

If you absolutely must do the assignment on the fly, this formulation generates equivalent code on any decent compiler:

```
if ( 0 != (hdc = GetDC( hwnd )) ) {
    // ...
    ReleaseDC( hwnd, hdc );
}
```

Another reason to avoid assignments in comparisons is that it makes the code harder to read. Not unreadable, by any means, but harder. Furthermore, if you put each statement on a line by itself, the number of code lines gives a more accurate indication of the complexity of the code.

Obfuscated coding may be fun, but it has no place in production code. Program as clearly as possible; there is no such thing as being too clear.

This is better and easier to step through when debugging because it allows you to change the value of hdc before reaching the test:

```
hdc = GetDC( hwnd );
if ( 0 != hdc ) {
   // ...
   ReleaseDC( hwnd, hdc );
}
```

The one place where an assignment in a comparison is defensible is in the controlling expression of a `while` statement. Lifting the assignment may require its duplication — once before the statement, and once at the end of the controlled body. This cure is worse than the disease; code duplication fits firmly in the "Bad" category.

Getting Your Priorities Straight

What is most important in your current programming project? Should the program be as fast as possible? As small as possible? Does it have to be portable?

The answers to these and related questions vary from project to project, and, indeed, from module to module and from function to function. You will, however, do well to consider the questions up front, and come up with a prioritized list of what's important. Steve Maguire discusses this in his book *Writing Solid Code*. Experience shows that nobody can satisfy all requirements at the same time, which makes conscious prioritization all the more important.

Item	Definition
Correctness	The code works correctly. This item might seem superfluous, but experience tells me something else. Too often, I've seen programmers more concerned with speed than correctness.
Size	This does not refer to the number of source code lines, but to the total size of compiled code. It may also include run-time memory usage and overhead imposed by non-functional data such as strings used internally in the program.
Speed	This includes both execution speed (as measured by CPU usage) and perceived responsiveness from the user's point of view. These are not necessarily the same. A guideline is to make the code fast enough, but not to waste time making it faster than that. If you need to sort 5 records, choose bubble sort. If you are sorting a million records, choose Quicksort. Speed bottlenecks are rarely obvious. Before you decide that an operation or a subsystem needs optimization, try to get hard data on where the real bottleneck is.
Robustness	Tolerance towards erroneous input and other error conditions. This does not mean that a program or routine should accept garbage, but that it should handle it gracefully.

Chapter 3: Designing for Programmers

Item	Definition
Safety	Choose the implementation that you are most likely to develop without bugs. Bubble sort is safer than Quicksort, but Quicksort is faster than bubble sort. Tradeoffs between speed and safety are common.
Testability	A program should be easy to test.
Maintainability	Code that is easy to maintain typically has several characteristics: • It is easy to read and understand. • It is well encapsulated. This allows changes (updates or fixes) to be made with some confidence that it won't blow up something else. • Documentation, including comments in the code, is in agreement with the code.
Reusability	This can mean class or function reuse in the same project, or it can mean preparing for reuse in later projects. Designing for reuse typically has an overhead of around 50%, split among additional design time (particularly finding good generalizations), additional documentation requirements, and additional testing. A good compromise is often just to choose a design that does not preclude reuse. The best tool for this is known as *encapsulation*.
Portability	The code is reusable across platforms. Coding for portability may entail: • Using a cross-platform library • Using a subset of a language or library that is common and consistent across platforms • Isolating platform dependencies (see os.cpp)

To illustrate what I mean by testability, here's a code fragment from getPathFromIdListA in utils.cpp:

```
const BOOL bOK = SHGetPathFromIDListA( pidl, szAnsiPath );
if ( bOK ) {
    multiByteToWideChar( szAnsiPath, pwszPath, MAX_PATH );
}
```

I could have saved one line and one variable as follows:

```
if ( SHGetPathFromIDListA( pidl, szAnsiPath ) ) {
    MultiByteToWideChar( szAnsiPath, pwszPath, MAX_PATH );
}
```

These two versions are functionally equivalent, but the first is easier to debug. You can see the value of bOK, and when you're single stepping through the code, you can even change the value before the test. This provides you with an opportunity to cover both branches. (Actually, you may have to remove the const keyword to get the debugger's permission to change the value.)

Global Variables Considered Harmful

Global Variables Are Bad. We all learned that on our mothers' knees. TextEdit has no global variables, although it has several that are "global" to a single compilation unit.

A common strategy to avoid global variables is to create a structure containing all global data, create an instance of that structure at some point, and pass the structure to all functions requiring access to the globals.

This cure is worse than the disease; you still have fairly uncontrolled access to the variables, and additional parameters to boot. It helps to keep in mind *why* global variables are bad: because they break encapsulation, and because they make multithreading more difficult.

Assert Your Sanity

The `assert` macro evaluates its argument — if the expression evaluates to non-zero, it does nothing; if it evaluates to zero, it displays a diagnostic message and gives you a choice of whether to abort, debug, or continue. The `assert` macro is grossly underused.

The whole idea behind the `assert` macro is to identify logical errors during program development. An assertion is a sanity check on your assumptions. Here's an example from the `ArgumentList` class:

```
inline LPCTSTR ArgumentList::getArg( int nArg ) const {
   ...
   assert( 0 <= nArg && nArg < m_argc );
   return m_argv[ nArg ];
}
```

The `m_argc` member denotes the number of arguments present in the argument list; the assertion documents the assumption that we never call the `getArg` method with an argument that's out of range. If that happens, there's a bug in the program. With the assertion in place, you're much more likely to catch that bug during development and to do it in a way that lets you fix it cleanly and cheaply.

The `assert` macro is also a documentation tool. Consider the `isWindowsNT` function from `os.cpp`:

```
bool isWindowsNT( void ) {

   OSVERSIONINFO osvi = { sizeof osvi };
   assert( 0 == offsetof( OSVERSIONINFO, dwOSVersionInfoSize ) );

   return GetVersionEx( &osvi ) &&
      VER_PLATFORM_WIN32_NT == osvi.dwPlatformId;
}
```

The assertion serves to document what the initialization of the `osvi` variable is all about, namely initializing the size member, `dwOSVersionInfoSize`. It will also catch the problem whenever the size member turns out *not* to be the first member of the structure.

The `assert` macro is active only in debug code. Release builds define the `NDEBUG` preprocessor identifier, which causes `assert` to evaluate to nothing. In some cases, such as when creating a robust library, you may want to retain parameter validation code in release builds. You should still keep the assertions, though, because they alert you at run-time while debugging. It is much easier to catch and fix a live bug, when you can see the life-blood of data flowing through the veins of your code, than it is to do a post mortem on a dead program.

One common mistake is to put production code into the `assert` macro. For example:

```
assert( FindClose( hFind ) );
```

This documents that I expect `FindClose` to succeed, or that I see the likelihood of failure small enough that I won't bother with error handling, or that there is little to do in the way of recovery. If the function fails, it's probably because of a programming error (such as forgetting to call `FindFirstFile`), and the assertion will alert me to the problem.

Putting `FindClose` into the `assert` will work fine in a debug build. In a release build, however, `FindClose` won't be called. If you want to combine assertion with release-build execution, use the `verify` macro instead, which evaluates its argument even when `NDEBUG` is defined:

```
verify( FindClose( hFind ) );
```

The `assert` macro is defined in the standard header file `assert.h`; the `verify` macro is defined in the TextEdit include file `common.h`. I'll get back to this header file towards the end of Chapter 5.

Constantly on Guard

The `const` keyword is as underused as the `assert` macro. When the `const` keyword modifies a variable, it says that the value of that variable may not be changed:

```
const int i = 5;
i = 6; // Compilation error!
```

The benefits of `const` are many:
- It serves to document the programmer's intentions, i.e., "this variable is `const`, so it is not expected to change."
- It lets the compiler object whenever you do violate the `const`ness, either due to a programming mistake or due to faulty assumptions.
- When applied to parameters, `const` lets you pass references and pointers with full confidence that they will return unscathed.
- The `const` keyword is a hint to the compiler that the variable will not change. This hint can be used for optimization, or for placing variables in some form of read-only memory.
- The `const` keyword can be used instead of the preprocessor's #define statement for manifest constants. This allows typed constants under full control of the compiler proper, an improvement over the mindless textual substitution performed by the preprocessor.

All kinds of data may be declared `const`, including variables that are class instances. Classes may also have methods declared `const`. If an object is declared `const`, it is illegal to call non-`const` methods on that object. Methods that are callable on `const` objects must themselves be declared `const`.

The lack of `const` is a shortcoming of the Java programming language. Java does have the `final` keyword, which means the same as `const` when applied to simple types, but not when applied to object references. (A reference, in Java as in C++, is a controlled pointer.) It's the reference that's final, not the object — Java does not have `const` objects in the sense that C++ does.

There are really two types of `const`ness. There's the strict language-lawyer interpretation, and there's *conceptual* `const`ness. Consider an object that tries to be smart: A polygon object with a `getArea` method might, in the interest of optimization, cache the results from the area calculation, storing the result in the private instance variable `m_area`. Thus, `getArea` will immediately return the value of `m_area` when it believes this to be valid; otherwise, it will perform the calculation and update the cache variable for later use.

What happens if you call `getArea` on a `const` polygon object? A violation of strict `const`ness is what happens, and the compiler will object strongly to the updating of `m_area`. To get around this, declare `m_area` to be `mutable`. This lets you assign a value to it even from a method declared `const`.

The `const_cast` is another way of getting around this sort of thing. TextEdit uses this to get around parameters in the Windows API that should have been declared `const`, but aren't.

To see conceptual `const`ness from another angle, consider the TextEdit `EditWnd` class, which wraps a standard edit control. Its `setText` method does not change the C++ object, but it does change the wrapped `HWND`. Therefore, I've chosen to consider `setText` as non-`const`. Some programmers see this differently, and, again, there is no "right" answer.

Use Destruction Constructively

The destructor of a C++ object is called when the object goes out of scope (if it was allocated on the stack) or when it is deleted (if it was allocated on the heap). The constructor/destructor sandwich is one of the most elegant parts of the C++ language; it lets objects clean up after themselves without explicitly coding for it at the point of use.

Java does not have destructors, relying instead on automatic garbage collection. This is fine as long as the only resource you deal with is memory; it's less fine if an object allocates other resources, such as file handles, network connections, and GDI objects. The lack of destructors is one of my two main gripes with the Java language definition, the other being the lack of a preprocessor.

Destructors are intimately connected to C++ exception handling, a topic I'll return to in Chapter 6. When an exception propagates through the stack frames, each frame cleans up after itself by calling the destructors of all automatic (that is, stack-based) objects. This is known as "stack unwinding."

What if a destructor throws an exception? If this happens during stack unwinding, as well it might, the program dies horribly. Accordingly, the following design principle is really an ironclad rule that you should never break if you can possibly help it:

"Don't throw exceptions from destructors."

Automatic Pointers

Objects allocated on the stack are destroyed automatically. Not so with objects allocated on the heap; in their case you must invoke the `delete` operator, or in the case of arrays of objects, the `delete[]` operator.

Consider the `getWindowText` method from the `Window` class, which we'll look at in Chapter 4:

```
String Window::getWindowText( void ) const {

    const int nLength = GetWindowTextLength( *this );
    LPTSTR pszWindowText = new TCHAR[ nLength + 1 ];      //x1
    GetWindowText( *this, pszWindowText, nLength + 1 );
    const String strWindowText( pszWindowText );          //x2
    delete[] pszWindowText;
    return strWindowText;                                 //x3
}
```

If the program follows the nominal execution path, this code works correctly. Problems appear when things begin to fail though. The statements marked x1, x2, and x3 may throw exceptions:

- x1 will throw a memory exception if the allocation fails. This is not a problem because there is nothing to clean up.
- x3 invokes the `String` copy constructor, which, depending on the definition of the `String` class, may throw an exception for a variety of reasons. This is not a problem either because we've already cleaned up by deleting the memory that `pszWindowText` points to.
- x2 also invokes a String constructor, and this time we do have a problem. If the constructor throws an exception, we never get to delete the memory that `pszWindowText` points to.

In this example, the problem results in a "mere" memory leak. Sometimes it is much worse.

(The example assumes that an allocation failure in operator `new` throws an exception rather than returning a null pointer. Notwithstanding the C++ standard, we're getting into compiler-dependent territory here, and I'll return to the subject in Chapter 6.)

One way of handling such situations is to catch the exception, do whatever clean-up is necessary, and then rethrow the exception:

```
String Window::getWindowText( void ) const {

    const int nLength = GetWindowTextLength( *this );
    LPTSTR pszWindowText = new TCHAR[ nLength + 1 ];
    String strWindowText;
    try {
        GetWindowText( *this, pszWindowText, nLength + 1 );
        strWindowText.assign( pszWindowText );
```

```
    }
    catch ( ... ) {
        delete[] pszWindowText;
        throw; // pass exception to next handler in chain
    }
    delete[] pszWindowText;
    return strWindowText;
}
```

While this works correctly, it is verbose and difficult to read. Even worse, the clean-up code is duplicated — a guarantee for maintenance headaches. (Java has the edge on C++ when it comes to exception handling semantics; it allows a `finally` clause that is executed both during the normal flow of control and after an exception has been thrown.)

A better solution is to wrap the pointer to the heap-allocated memory in an object, making it a *smart pointer*. The essential part of a smart pointer class is its destructor, which (in simple cases) deletes the pointer that it wraps. (More complex cases may involve, say, reference counting.)

```
String Window::getWindowText( void ) const {

    const int nLength = GetWindowTextLength( *this );
    AutoString pszWindowText( nLength + 1 );
    GetWindowText( *this, pszWindowText, nLength + 1 );
    return pszWindowText;
}
```

The result is considerably more readable than either of the previous examples. We get rid of the delete statement; this saves us one line. As a fringe benefit, we also get rid of the temporary `String` object. The `return` statement invokes the `String(LPCTSTR)` constructor, and this happens before the `AutoString` object goes out of scope. The important part, though, is that the destructor is called even if an exception is thrown, as part of stack unwinding.

The C++ Standard Template Library (STL) defines a smart pointer, a template class named `auto_ptr`. I don't use this, relying instead on `AutoPtr` (in Listing 3.1, `AutoPtr.h`).

Why create a replacement for a perfectly good standard template? The reason is that `auto_ptr` is not perfectly good. In particular, it lacks a conversion operator to the pointer type it wraps, forcing the tedious use of the `get` method instead. I also added the `reset` method.

Both `auto_ptr` and `AutoPtr` have one little problem with respect to the `getWindowText` example above — their destructors invoke `delete` rather than the required `delete[]`. For this reason, I created a variant called `AutoArray`, defined in Listing 3.2, `AutoArray.h`. This class is not completely general; it has exactly the functionality I needed for TextEdit, no more.

(I'm being a bit of a purist here, as the difference between `delete` and `delete[]` only becomes important in the case of arrays of objects. Before freeing the memory, `delete[]` invokes the destructor of each object in the array. Plain `delete` does not. Because the elements of an `AutoString` array are of simple type, using `auto_ptr` or `AutoPtr` would actually work fine on any reasonable compiler.)

Listing 3.1 AutoPtr.h

```cpp
/*
 * $Header: /Book/AutoPtr.h 4      3.07.99 17:46 Petter $
 *
 * HINT: To see the object wrapped by AutoPtr during Visual C++
 * debugging, add the following line to the AUTOEXP.DAT file:
 * AutoPtr<*>=m_ptr=<m_ptr>
 */

#pragma once

template< class T >
class AutoPtr {
private:
    T *m_ptr;

public:
    explicit AutoPtr( T *ptr = 0 ) throw() : m_ptr( ptr ) {
    }
    ~AutoPtr() {
        delete m_ptr;          // NOTE: It's OK to delete a null pointer.
        reset_pointer( m_ptr );
    }
    void reset( T *ptr = 0 ) {
        T *pOldPtr = m_ptr;
        m_ptr = ptr;
        if ( ptr != pOldPtr ) {
            delete pOldPtr; // NOTE: It's OK to delete a null pointer.
        }
    }
    T *operator=( T *ptr ) throw() {
        m_ptr = ptr;
        return m_ptr;
    }
    operator T *() throw() {
        return m_ptr;
    }
    operator const T *() const throw() {
        return m_ptr;
```

```
    }
    operator void *() throw() {
        return m_ptr;
    }
    operator const void *() const throw() {
        return m_ptr;
    }
    T *operator->() throw() {
        return m_ptr;
    }
    const T *operator->() const throw() {
        return m_ptr;
    }
};
```

Listing 3.2 AutoArray.h

```
/*
 * $Header: /Book/AutoArray.h 4     3.07.99 17:46 Petter $
 *
 * HINT: To see the string wrapped by AutoString during Visual C++
 * debugging, add the following line to the AUTOEXP.DAT file:
 * AutoArray<*>=m_ptr=<m_ptr>
 */

#pragma once

template< class T >
class AutoArray {
private:
    T *m_ptr;

public:
    explicit AutoArray( int n ) throw() : m_ptr( new T[ n ] ) {
        assert( 0 != m_ptr );
    }
    explicit AutoArray( T *_ptr = 0 ) throw() : m_ptr( _ptr ) {
    }
    ~AutoArray() {
        delete[] m_ptr; // NOTE: It's OK to delete a null pointer.
        reset_pointer( m_ptr );
```

```
    }
    void alloc( int n ) {
        assert( 0 == m_ptr );
        m_ptr = new T[ n ];
    }
    T ** operator &() {
        return &m_ptr;
    }
    operator T *() throw() {
        return m_ptr;
    }
    operator const T *() const throw() {
        return m_ptr;
    }
    operator void *() throw() {
        return m_ptr;
    }
    operator const void *() const throw() {
        return m_ptr;
    }
};

typedef AutoArray< CHAR  > AutoStringA;
typedef AutoArray< WCHAR > AutoStringW;

#ifdef UNICODE
typedef AutoStringW AutoString;
#else
typedef AutoStringA AutoString;
#endif
```

The problem addressed by `AutoPtr` and `AutoArray` is not limited to memory; it applies to other resources as well — file handles, display contexts, network connections, et cetera ad nauseam. I include two examples here: The `AutoHandle` class wraps a Win32 `HANDLE`, while the `PaintStruct` class wraps — you guessed it — a `PAINTSTRUCT` (or rather, the sandwich-layer calls to `BeginPaint` and `EndPaint` that wrap the use of the `PAINTSTRUCT`). Such wrappers are usually trivial to implement.

To sum up:
- The wrappers are a programming convenience because you save the close/free/cleanup statement — the bottom layer of the sandwich.
- They help make the code more robust because you cannot forget to free the resource in question.

- Most importantly, they make the wrapped resource exception-safe.

Other examples of self-destructing wrapper classes are `FileMapping` (defined in `FileMapping.h`, described in Chapter 12), `TemporaryStatusIcon` (`Statusbar.h`), and `ClientDC` (`ClientDC.h`). In TextEdit, you will find many more.

Listing 3.3   AutoHandle.h

```
/*
 * $Header: /Book/AutoHandle.h 6      3.07.99 17:46 Petter $
 *
 * HINT: To see the handle wrapped by AutoHandle during Visual C++
 * debugging, add the following line to the AUTOEXP.DAT file:
 * AutoHandle<*>=<m_handle>
 */

#pragma once


class AutoHandle {
private:
    HANDLE m_handle;

public:
    explicit AutoHandle( HANDLE handle = 0 );
    ~AutoHandle();
    HANDLE operator=( HANDLE handle );
    operator HANDLE();
};


inline AutoHandle::AutoHandle( HANDLE handle ) : m_handle( handle ) {
}


inline AutoHandle::~AutoHandle() {
    if ( 0 != m_handle && INVALID_HANDLE_VALUE != m_handle ) {
        verify( CloseHandle( m_handle ) );
    }
}
```

```
inline HANDLE AutoHandle::operator=( HANDLE handle ) {
    m_handle = handle;
    return m_handle;
}



inline AutoHandle::operator HANDLE() {
    return m_handle;
}
```

Listing 3.4   PaintStruct.h

```
/*
 * $Header: /Book/PaintStruct.h 5      5.09.99 13:07 Petter $
 */

#pragma once


class PaintStruct : public tagPAINTSTRUCT {

private:
    HWND m_hwnd;

public:
    explicit PaintStruct ( HWND hwnd );
    ~PaintStruct ( void );
};


inline PaintStruct::PaintStruct ( HWND hwnd ) : m_hwnd( hwnd ) {

    assert( IsWindow( m_hwnd ) );
    BeginPaint( m_hwnd, this );
}



inline PaintStruct::~PaintStruct ( void ) {
```

```
    assert( IsWindow( m_hwnd ) );
    EndPaint( m_hwnd, this );
}
```

Programming Defensively

When you drive a car, you will have fewer accidents if you don't assume that other drivers always follow the rules of the road. When you program a computer, you will have fewer bugs if you don't assume that the functions you call are bug-free, or that code that calls your function is bug-free. When you're working on a particular function, assume that any code that calls it is buggy.

The File Properties dialog (in `PropertiesDlg.cpp`) demonstrates one of the principles of defensive programming. This dialog has an Apply button that, when invoked, applies any changes to file name or other file attributes. The button is initially disabled; it is automatically enabled whenever something changes. The dialog is notified of changes through `WM_COMMAND` messages from its controls.

If a file resides on a CD-ROM or a write-protected floppy, you can't change any of its attributes. For such files, all fields (except the Cancel button) are disabled, which means that the Apply button can never get enabled, right? Right. Nevertheless, I always check for "access denied" before I enable the Apply button and also before I invoke the code behind the button.

This suspenders-and-belt approach might seem like overkill. After all, the extra checks only come into play if there's a bug in the code. But who of us writes bug-free code consistently? I don't think the Properties dialog has any bugs at the moment, but that's beside the point. Defensive programming is more of an attitude than anything else.

How far to take this kind of double-checking is a judgement call. Its most valuable property is that it makes the program more robust in the face of changes. If you add a new check box to the dialog, for example, you might easily forget to disable it in case file access is denied.

Is Windows Object-Oriented?

Many years ago, an introductory text on Windows programming told me that Windows is object-oriented. The argument went like this: If you drag a window by its title bar, the rest of the window tags along. Therefore, a window is an object, and Windows is object-oriented.

This, of course, is rubbish. But the question remains, "Is Windows object-oriented?"

Object-oriented programming rests on three pillars: encapsulation, inheritance, and polymorphism. We should also add abstraction, which in this case means something quite concrete — the ability to create abstract data types such as C `struct`s. This abstraction business is sometimes misunderstood to mean "programming at a higher level of abstraction," i.e., that you operate on objects closer to the problem domain. While this tends to be true of object-oriented programming in general, it begs the point. This kind of abstraction emerges as a property of the system as a whole; it's not a building block that you plug in at the bottom.

The core object of Windows programming is the window. Externally, to you as an application programmer, a window manifests itself as an opaque `HWND` handle. It's a black box, the exact details of which are — or should be — of no interest. Internally, to the Windows system programmer, the HWND is a reference to a struct.

Some details of the internal HWND structure can be inferred, though, as they define the properties of the window. A particularly important member is the address of the window callback function. This window function determines the behavior of the window.

A window instance is created from a template called a *window class*. The "class" name is significant; it suggests that the original designers at least thought they were doing something object-oriented. Were they?

Encapsulation: You can store private data with a window in several ways. When you register a new window class, you can specify that additional bytes should be allocated for each window instance, tacked on to the end of the HWND structure. Because those extra bytes must be accessed by special API calls in 32-bit chunks, the facility is somewhat cumbersome to use and hardly what you would call an abstract data type. Its redeeming feature is that you can use these extra DWORDs to store pointers to heap-allocated structures.

In addition, you can store data as window properties; this is a more dynamic method that doesn't require you to reserve extra words in the HWND structure. This makes it especially suitable for use with windows of classes that you don't control.

Inheritance: One of the members of the HWND structure is the address of the callback function, the WNDPROC. To subclass a window, you replace this address with the address of your own function, while stashing away the original address. Your replacement window function handles any messages you care to override and sends the rest to the original function. You may also do pre- and post-processing relative to invocation of the original function.

Windows even has a primordial base object. As Java and Smalltalk have their respective Object classes, Windows has the DefWindowProc. The following program demonstrates this:

```
int WINAPI WinMain(
    HINSTANCE hinst, HINSTANCE, LPTSTR, int )
{
    WNDCLASS wndClass = {
        0, DefWindowProc, 0, 0, hinst,
        0, 0, 0, 0, "Object",
    };
    RegisterClass( &wndClass );
    HWND hwnd = CreateWindow( "Object", "Object",
        WS_OVERLAPPEDWINDOW | WS_VISIBLE,
        10, 10, 200, 100, HWND_DESKTOP, 0, hinst, 0 );

    MSG msg;
    while ( GetMessage( &msg, 0, 0, 0 ) ) {
        DispatchMessage( &msg );
    }
    return 0;
}
```

The resulting window lacks even the sense to paint its own client area, but it does have a title bar, and it responds correctly to resizing, maximizing, and minimizing (see Figure 3.1).

Figure 3.1 The `DefWindowProc` **window, with its client area full of garbage.**

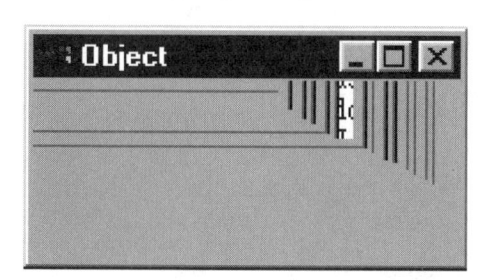

Only one thing is missing for this to be an almost perfectly well-behaved window. Even though `DefWindowProc` handles `WM_CLOSE` by calling `DestroyWindow`, neither the `WM_CLOSE` handler nor the `WM_DESTROY` handler calls `PostQuitMessage`. After the window has been destroyed, the application hangs forever on `GetMessage`. (It couldn't be otherwise, of course, or all applications would close shop every time one of its windows was destroyed.)

Polymorphism: This is really at the heart of windows programming because everything is message-based. Take `WM_GETTEXT` as an example. Many window types understand this message, but they handle it differently, according to their needs. A top-level window understands the message as referring to its title, while an edit control understands it as referring to its contents.

(If you like bizarre experiments, try to create a top-level edit window, and watch the ensuing confusion.)

So, Yes!

The answer to our question is a resounding "yes" — Windows programming is indeed object-oriented programming. The bad news is that the mechanics of Windows programming is totally out of whack with any object-oriented programming language. You need to do all the plumbing manually and this is so cumbersome as to obliterate many of the benefits of the object-orientation. In particular, all message parameters are stuffed into the `WPARAM` and `LPARAM` parameters to the window function, and the packing and unpacking of parameters is a nasty business that the word "type-safe" does not even begin to describe.

Programming Windows is easy,
Provided you do the right cast.
Of course, this technique is sleazy,
It's really a blast from the past.

In the next couple of chapters, we'll look at ways to deal with this.

Chapter 4

The Mechanics of Subclassing

In an ideal world, at least for C++ programmers, Windows would be C++ throughout. Subclassing a window would be a matter of subclassing a C++ class, creating a window would be a matter of invoking the window's constructor, message handling would be a matter of overriding virtual functions.

Unfortunately, Windows is not an ideal world for C++ programmers; the world turns out to be made of HWNDs rather than classes. There are two distinct paths to follow: Windows-type subclassing chains and polymorphic inheritance in the OO sense. We shall meet the challenge of creating a C++ wrapper for the HWND towards the end of this chapter. First, let's look at subclassing from a Windows (i.e., plain C) point of view because this forms the foundation for everything else.

Subclassing Defined

Window subclassing is subversion, pure and simple. When you subclass a window, you replace its window function with your own, and the original gets to see messages only at your whim. Usually you want to be good about this, and interfere no more than necessary. Otherwise, the whole exercise is pointless; if you greedily keep all messages to yourself, you would have been better off developing a new window class from scratch.

Chapter 4: The Mechanics of Subclassing

There are many reasons for subclassing. The most obvious reason is that you want to modify the behavior of existing windows, as I do in this chapter. Less obvious, perhaps, is subclassing in order to listen in on the message traffic. A toolbar might subclass its parent, for example, in order to listen for WM_SIZE messages. The TextEdit toolbar subclasses the main TextEdit window for this reason, and to let it catch its own notification messages. This makes it more of a self-contained widget.

The ToolTip control will subclass its parent if you ask it to, in order to spy on its mouse messages. This saves your window from having to forward all mouse messages to the ToolTip window.

Subclassing comes in several variants: Instance subclassing (a.k.a. local subclassing), global subclassing, and class cloning (a.k.a. superclassing).

Instance subclassing

Instance subclassing means to replace the window function of an existing window. A typical example is the subclassing of a specific edit control in a dialog box — to filter out illegal characters perhaps. This used to be a popular technique for creating numeric input fields before the advent of the ES_NUMBER window style.

When a dialog's WM_INITDIALOG message handler is invoked, all the edit controls exist already. The InstSub program is a complete example of instance subclassing an edit control to create a numeric input field. The resulting dialog is depicted in Figure 4.1.

Figure 4.1 **Instance subclassing in action. The upper edit field accepts only digits.**

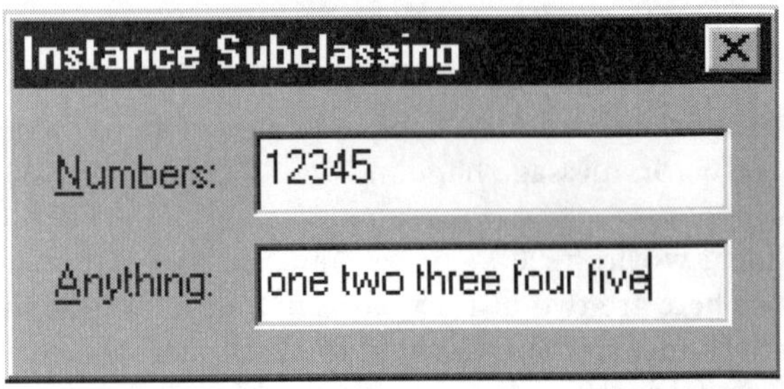

Building the InstSub example is a two-step process:

```
1. rc InstSub.rc
2. cl InstSub.cpp InstSub.res user32.lib
```

In spite of its overwhelming simplicity, InstSub illustrates several points:

- The actual subclassing is performed in the WM_INITDIALOG handler, by calling SetWindowLong with the GWL_WNDPROC parameter. (It is more convenient to use the SubclassWindow macro defined in windowsx.h, but in this example, I want to expose everything.)
- The address of the old window function is stored in the static variable s_savedEditWndProc. This works well enough in this simple example and will work as long as you subclass a single control, or a set of identical controls with identical subclassing histories. Real life is usually

less accommodating — perhaps the controls are of different classes, or perhaps one of them was already subclassed by somebody else.
- The invocation of the old window function is done through `CallWindowProc`. Don't call `s_savedEditWndProc` directly; it may not be a function address! This happens under Windows NT if you subclass a Unicode window with a non-Unicode window function or vice versa. In such cases, the system must translate the parameters of text-related messages, and the alleged window function is actually a pointer to some black-box data structure cooked up by `SetWindowLong`.
- This point has nothing to do with subclassing, but it is nevertheless worth noting: Even though the sample dialog has no buttons, the Enter and Escape keys still serve up `WM_COMMAND` messages with IDs `IDOK` and `IDCANCEL`, respectively. Starting in Chapter 13, I'll have more to say about dialog boxes and the dialog keyboard interface.
- Final point — `newEditWndProc` is simpleminded. It fulfills the goal of allowing only numeric input, but in so doing, it disables accelerators such as Ctrl-C and Ctrl-Z.

`InstSub` is the simplest working example I can think of; it is far from complete. Consider the clipboard accelerators: if you change the code to let them by without further ado, there's nothing to stop the user from pasting non-digits into the edit control. And, believe me, some users will. Me, for example.

Listing 4.1   InstSub.rc

```
// InstSub.rc — used for all three subclassing examples

#include <windows.h>

#define IDC_NUMBERS 1000

InstSubDlg DIALOG DISCARDABLE  0, 0, 139, 46
STYLE DS_MODALFRAME | DS_CENTER | WS_POPUP | WS_CAPTION | WS_SYSMENU
CAPTION "Instance Subclassing"
FONT 8, "MS Sans Serif"
{
    LTEXT     "&Numbers:",-1,7,9,31,8
    EDITTEXT  IDC_NUMBERS,44,7,88,14,ES_AUTOHSCROLL | WS_GROUP
    LTEXT     "&Anything:",-1,7,27,30,8
    EDITTEXT  -1,44,25,88,14,ES_AUTOHSCROLL | WS_GROUP
}

GlobSubDlg DIALOG DISCARDABLE  0, 0, 139, 46
STYLE DS_MODALFRAME | DS_CENTER | WS_POPUP | WS_CAPTION | WS_SYSMENU
CAPTION "Global Subclassing"
FONT 8, "MS Sans Serif"
```

```
{
    LTEXT     "&Numbers:",-1,7,9,31,8
    EDITTEXT  IDC_NUMBERS,44,7,88,14,ES_AUTOHSCROLL | WS_GROUP
    LTEXT     "&Anything:",-1,7,27,30,8
    EDITTEXT  -1,44,25,88,14,ES_AUTOHSCROLL | WS_GROUP
}

CloneDlg DIALOG DISCARDABLE  0, 0, 139, 46
STYLE DS_MODALFRAME | DS_CENTER | WS_POPUP | WS_CAPTION | WS_SYSMENU
CAPTION "Class Cloning"
FONT 8, "MS Sans Serif"
{
    LTEXT     "&Numbers:",-1,7,9,31,8
    CONTROL   "",IDC_NUMBERS,"NumericEdit",
              WS_BORDER | WS_TABSTOP | ES_AUTOHSCROLL | WS_GROUP,
              44,7,88,14
    LTEXT     "&Anything:",-1,7,27,30,8
    EDITTEXT  -1,44,25,88,14,ES_AUTOHSCROLL | WS_GROUP
}
```

Listing 4.2   InstSub.cpp

```cpp
#include <windows.h>

#define IDC_NUMBERS 1000

static WNDPROC s_savedEditWndProc;

static LRESULT CALLBACK newEditWndProc(
    HWND hwnd, UINT msg, WPARAM wParam, LPARAM lParam )
{
    switch ( msg ) {
    case WM_CHAR:
        if ( wParam < '0' || '9' < wParam ) {
            return 0; //*** EAT THE KEYSTROKE!
        }
        break;
```

```
      case WM_NCDESTROY:
         SetWindowLong( hwnd, GWL_WNDPROC, (LONG) s_savedEditWndProc );
         break;
      }

      return CallWindowProc(
         s_savedEditWndProc, hwnd, msg, wParam, lParam );
}

static BOOL CALLBACK dlgFunc(
   HWND hwnd, UINT msg, WPARAM wParam, LPARAM lParam )
{
   switch ( msg ) {
   case WM_INITDIALOG:
      s_savedEditWndProc = (WNDPROC) SetWindowLong(
         GetDlgItem( hwnd, IDC_NUMBERS ),
         GWL_WNDPROC, (LONG) newEditWndProc );
      break;
   case WM_COMMAND:
      if ( HIWORD( wParam ) == BN_CLICKED ) {
         EndDialog( hwnd, 0 );
      }
      break;
   }
   return FALSE;
}

int APIENTRY WinMain( HINSTANCE hinst, HINSTANCE, LPSTR, int ) {

   return DialogBox( hinst, "InstSubDlg" , HWND_DESKTOP, dlgFunc );
}
```

Global Subclassing

Global subclassing means changing elements of a window class structure using `SetClassLong`. In the `GlobSub` sample, we replace the window function. A new window's window function is initialized from the class structure when the window is created. Accordingly, existing windows are unaffected by global subclassing, but all new windows of that particular class are affected.

The `GlobSub` example in Listing 4.3 uses the same resource file as the `InstSub` example.

Chapter 4: The Mechanics of Subclassing

To set the class window function, we need an instance of the class. `WinMain` creates an edit control for that purpose, and discards it afterwards.

The dialog box function no longer handles `WM_INITDIALOG`. The numeric input edit control is nevertheless subclassed, and so is the other edit control. In fact, all edit controls are affected. The call to `GetOpenFileName` is a final demonstration of the power of global subclassing; it proves that our subversion of edit controls works fine even for dialogs we don't create ourselves.

Listing 4.3 GlobSub.cpp

```cpp
#include <windows.h>

#define IDC_NUMBERS 1000

static WNDPROC s_savedEditWndProc;

static LRESULT CALLBACK newEditWndProc(
    HWND hwnd, UINT msg, WPARAM wParam, LPARAM lParam )
{
    switch ( msg ) {
    case WM_CHAR:
        if ( wParam < '0' || '9' < wParam ) {
            return 0; //*** EAT THE KEYSTROKE!
        }
        break;
    }

    return CallWindowProc(
        s_savedEditWndProc, hwnd, msg, wParam, lParam );
}

static BOOL CALLBACK dlgFunc(
    HWND hwnd, UINT msg, WPARAM wParam, LPARAM lParam )
{
    if ( WM_COMMAND == msg && HIWORD( wParam ) == BN_CLICKED ) {
        EndDialog( hwnd, 0 );
    }
    return FALSE;
}

int APIENTRY WinMain( HINSTANCE hinst, HINSTANCE, LPSTR, int ) {
```

```
   HWND hwndEdit = CreateWindow( "edit", "",
      WS_POPUP, 0, 0, 0, 0, HWND_DESKTOP, (HMENU) 0, hinst, 0 );
   s_savedEditWndProc = (WNDPROC) SetClassLong(
      hwndEdit, GCL_WNDPROC, (LONG) newEditWndProc );
   DestroyWindow( hwndEdit );

   DialogBox( hinst, "GlobSubDlg" , HWND_DESKTOP, dlgFunc );

   OPENFILENAME openFileName = {
      sizeof( OPENFILENAME ), HWND_DESKTOP, hinst,
   };
   GetOpenFileName( &openFileName );

   hwndEdit = CreateWindow( "edit", "",
      WS_POPUP, 0, 0, 0, 0, HWND_DESKTOP, (HMENU) 0, hinst, 0 );
   SetClassLong( hwndEdit, GCL_WNDPROC, (LONG) s_savedEditWndProc );
   DestroyWindow( hwndEdit );

   return 0;
}
```

Class Cloning

Class cloning means to register a new window class based on an existing class. Functionally, it is a variant of global subclassing, but because you must register the cloned class under a new name, you have some control over which windows are subclassed. The Clone example clones the edit control to create a class named `NumericEdit`. In the resource file, I explicitly set the control class of the numeric entry field to `NumericEdit` rather than edit (see Listing 4.1).

If we fail to register a class named `NumericEdit` before instantiating the dialog box, said dialog box will fail to load, and the `DialogBox` function will return –1. (This is the default behavior, which can be overridden by applying the `DS_NOFAILCREATE` dialog style.)

It isn't mandatory to change the window function during class cloning. Sometimes you clone a class just to change the class style bits.

Listing 4.4 `Clone.cpp`

```
#include <windows.h>

#define IDC_NUMBERS 1000

static WNDPROC s_savedEditWndProc;
```

Chapter 4: The Mechanics of Subclassing

```c
static LRESULT CALLBACK newEditWndProc(
    HWND hwnd, UINT msg, WPARAM wParam, LPARAM lParam )
{
    switch ( msg ) {
    case WM_CHAR:
        if ( wParam < '0' || '9' < wParam ) {
            return 0; //*** EAT THE KEYSTROKE!
        }
        break;
    }

    return CallWindowProc(
        s_savedEditWndProc, hwnd, msg, wParam, lParam );
}

static BOOL CALLBACK dlgFunc(
    HWND hwnd, UINT msg, WPARAM wParam, LPARAM lParam )
{
    if ( WM_COMMAND == msg && HIWORD( wParam ) == BN_CLICKED ) {
        EndDialog( hwnd, 0 );
    }
    return FALSE;
}

int APIENTRY WinMain( HINSTANCE hinst, HINSTANCE, LPSTR, int ) {

    WNDCLASS wndClass = { 0 };
    GetClassInfo( hinst, "edit", &wndClass );
    s_savedEditWndProc = wndClass.lpfnWndProc;
    wndClass.lpfnWndProc = newEditWndProc;
    wndClass.lpszClassName = "NumericEdit";
    RegisterClass( &wndClass );

    DialogBox( hinst, "CloneDlg", HWND_DESKTOP, dlgFunc );
}
```

Thus endeth the subclassing tutorial. That's all there is to it, really, except for various esoteric techniques used to subclass windows in other processes, which I won't go into.

The next section presents the code that TextEdit uses to accomplish instance and global subclassing. The code uses other classes that I haven't described yet. For now, I'll just use the

String and Exception classes without further delay; I'll go into more detail about them in Chapters 5 and 6.

General Mechanism for Global Subclassing

It's in the nature of global subclassing that there is only one old window function to store, so the approach used in GlobSub is actually fine, except that it is bothersome to create a window of the usurped class merely in order to call SetClassLong. The main purpose of GlobalSubclasser is to hide the bother.

Curiously, SetClassLong and GetClassLong are both prototyped as returning DWORDs, even though the dwNewLong argument to SetClassLong is prototyped as LONG, i.e., a signed value.

Listing 4.5   GlobalSubclasser.h

```
/*
 * $Header: /Book/GlobalSubclasser.h 3     5.09.99 13:07 Petter $
 */

#pragma once


class GlobalSubclasser {
private:
   LPCTSTR m_pszWndClass;
   WNDPROC m_wndProc;
   WNDPROC m_wndProcSaved;

public:
   GlobalSubclasser( LPCTSTR pszWndClass, WNDPROC wndProcNew );
   virtual ~GlobalSubclasser() throw();
   LRESULT callOldProc(
      HWND hwnd, UINT uiMsg, WPARAM wParam, LPARAM lParam );
};

inline LRESULT GlobalSubclasser::callOldProc(
   HWND hwnd, UINT msg, WPARAM wParam, LPARAM lParam )
{
   assert( IsWindow( hwnd ) );
   assert( 0 != m_wndProcSaved );
   return CallWindowProc( m_wndProcSaved, hwnd, msg, wParam, lParam );
}
```

Listing 4.6   GlobalSubclasser.cpp

```cpp
/*
 * $Header: /Book/GlobalSubclasser.cpp 4      3.07.99 17:46 Petter $
 */

#include "precomp.h"
#include "GlobalSubclasser.h"
#include "Exception.h"
#include "addAtom.h"
#include "winUtils.h"
#include "utils.h"
#include "trace.h"


GlobalSubclasser::GlobalSubclasser(
   LPCTSTR pszWndClass, WNDPROC wndProcNew )

  : m_wndProc( wndProcNew )
  , m_wndProcSaved( 0 )
  , m_pszWndClass( pszWndClass )
{
   assert( isGoodStringPtrOrAtom( pszWndClass ) );
   assert( isGoodCodePtr( wndProcNew ) );

   trace( _T( "Creating global subclassing %s\n" ),
      stringFromAtom( pszWndClass ) );

   HWND hwnd = CreateWindow( pszWndClass, _T( "" ),
      WS_POPUP, 0, 0, 0, 0, HWND_DESKTOP, 0, getModuleHandle(), 0 );
   if ( IsWindow( hwnd ) ) {
      m_wndProcSaved = (WNDPROC) SetClassLong(
         hwnd, GCL_WNDPROC, reinterpret_cast< LONG >( wndProcNew ) );
      verify( DestroyWindow( hwnd ) );
   } else {
      const DWORD dwErr = GetLastError();
      trace( _T( "Global subclassing failure %s\nReason: %s\n" ),
         stringFromAtom( pszWndClass ),
         WinException( dwErr ).what() );
   }
```

General Mechanism for Global Subclassing

```cpp
      if ( 0 == m_wndProcSaved ) {
         FatalAppExit( 0, _T( "Global subclassing failed" ) );
      }
   }

GlobalSubclasser::~GlobalSubclasser() {

   trace( _T( "Destroying global subclasser %s\n" ),
      stringFromAtom( m_pszWndClass ) );

   try {
      assert( isGoodStringPtrOrAtom( m_pszWndClass ) );
      assert( 0 != m_wndProcSaved );
      if ( 0 != m_wndProcSaved ) {
         HWND hwnd = CreateWindow( m_pszWndClass, _T( "" ), WS_POPUP,
            0, 0, 0, 0, HWND_DESKTOP, 0, getModuleHandle(), 0 );
         if ( IsWindow( hwnd ) ) {
            assert( GetClassLong( hwnd, GCL_WNDPROC ) ==
               reinterpret_cast< DWORD >( m_wndProc ) );
            SetClassLong( hwnd, GCL_WNDPROC,
               reinterpret_cast< LONG >( m_wndProcSaved ) );
            verify( DestroyWindow( hwnd ) );
         }
      }

#if 0 // Test exception handling using div by zero:
      int y = 0;
      int x = 1 / y;
#endif
   }
   // No exceptions may leave the destructor!
   // This one's always called at exit time anyway.
   catch ( ... ) {
      trace( _T( "*** Exception in Subclasser dtor ignored\n" ) );
   }
}
```

General Mechanism for Instance Subclassing

The biggest problem with the `InstSub` example was the static storage of the old window function. A subclassing function that applies yellow backgrounds, for example, could conceivably be used both for edit controls and list boxes. Then you'd have to store two different pointers to two old window functions — rather difficult to do in a single static variable, and even if you used two, how would you know them apart? In a general solution, the pointer to the old window function must somehow be associated with the window handle itself.

In a general solution, other properties are desirable as well:

- It should be possible to apply multiple subclassings to a window.
- It should be possible to subclass and unsubclass in any order.
- The programming interface to a general mechanism must be easy to use, protect against programming mistakes, and be robust at run-time
- It is sometimes convenient to associate subclassing-specific data with a window; a general solution should offer this feature.

Another problem with `InstSub` is that it unsubclasses unconditionally. If somebody else had subclassed the window after `InstSub`, that somebody else would be hosed. A careful solution should check whether the current window function is the expected one and unhook only if it is.

Associating the Old Window Function with the Window Handle

Data can be associated with windows in two basic ways: (a) you can maintain a static list of associations (array, linked list, binary tree, hash table, post-it notes, engraved stone tablets) or (b) you can associate the data with the window itself (using either window properties or `SetWindowLong`).

If you were to use `SetWindowLong`, the `GWL_USERDATA` offset would be the only possible choice, given the requirement to subclass windows under somebody else's control. This might be OK within a single application, but hardly in a generally reusable library. True, you could reinstate the old value of `GWL_USERDATA` before calling window functions down the chain, but you would have no defense against subclasssings above you in the chain, or against application programmers ignorant of this little implementation detail using `GWL_USERDATA` for their own purposes.

According to conventional wisdom, window properties are less efficient than window words. Benchmarking

```
GetWindowLong( hwnd, GWL_USERDATA );
```

against

```
GetProp( hwnd, "test" );
```

verifies this. When I used an atom instead of the string for the property name, however, the tables were turned. Now `GetProp` was actually faster than `GetWindowLong`, at least on a Windows NT 4.0 window with a single property. In truth, though, this is a rather moot point — I've implemented subclassing using all these techniques and efficiency has never been a noticeable problem.

One solution to the problem of multiple subclassings is to store the old window function as a property, using a unique property name for each subclassing. With multiple subclassings, this suggests an image of saved window functions sticking out all over the window like pins from a pincushion. While I've used this "porcupine" technique successfully, it does have one disadvantage: the subclassings are isolated from one another and unhooking *must* be done in reverse order of subclassing. To remedy this, the `InstanceSubclasser` maintains a linked list of subclassing descriptors:

```
class Node {
public:
    WNDPROC m_wndProc;
    WNDPROC m_wndProcSaved;
    void    *m_pUserData;
    Node    *m_pNext;
    ...
};
```

This allows subclassing and unsubclassing with gay abandon, provided you stick to using `InstanceSubclasser`. You're still vulnerable to "foreign" subclassings, though, and no perfect solution exists to deal with this particular problem.

The head of the list can now be attached to the window using a single window property, or it can be maintained in a static table.

One advantage of using static storage is encapsulation — window properties are exposed to the rest of the world, and it is within the realm of possibility that some Bad Person will steal our property. Another advantage is that we won't leak window properties if something gets screwed up. One example of a screw-up is when somebody else subclasses after us, then fails to get out of the way before WM_DESTROY or WM_NCDESTROY.

In spite of the above, `InstanceSubclasser` uses a window property to store the head of the subclassing list. Perhaps this is only old habit on my part, but it feels more "right" in some sense.

Unhooking

The `InstanceSubclasser` class lets you unsubclass at any time, provided nobody else is in the way. A subclassing using `InstanceSubclasser` will unhook automatically on either WM_DESTROY or WM_NCDESTROY, again provided nobody else is in the way. Both of these messages are used for unhooking in common subclassing schemes; and by getting out of the way at WM_DESTROY time, we allow subclassings below us to unhook on WM_DESTROY if they so desire. If we have a subclassing above us that doesn't unhook until WM_NCDESTROY, our first attempt to unhook (on WM_DESTROY) will fail, but our second attempt (on WM_NCDESTROY) will succeed.

The tool tip doesn't unhook at all, as far as I can tell, and thus blocks every prior subclassing from unhooking. For that reason, the `Toolbar` class most carefully lets the tool tip subclass *before* subclassing its edit child.

Sadly, there is no way to create a subclassing scheme that's guaranteed to work under all circumstances. `InstanceSubclasser` covers 99% of what you'll ever need though.

(Discourse continues on page 54.)

Listing 4.7 InstanceSubclasser.h

```cpp
/*
 * $Header: /Book/InstanceSubclasser.h 5      5.09.99 13:07 Petter $
 */

#pragma once

class Node;
class InstanceSubclasser {
private:
   WNDPROC m_wndProc;
   static ATOM sm_atom;

   static Node *getHead( HWND hwnd );
   static bool setHead( HWND hwnd, const Node *pNewHead );
   Node *findNode( HWND hwnd ) const;

public:
   explicit InstanceSubclasser( WNDPROC wndProc );
   ~InstanceSubclasser() throw();
   bool subclass( HWND hwnd, void *pUserData = 0 );
   bool unSubclass( HWND hwnd );
   void *getUserData( HWND hwnd ) const;
   LRESULT callOldProc(
      HWND hwnd, UINT uiMsg, WPARAM wParam, LPARAM lParam );

   // Convenience for subclassings that use user data to store a HWND:
   HWND getUserDataAsHwnd( HWND hwnd );
};

inline HWND InstanceSubclasser::getUserDataAsHwnd( HWND hwnd ) {

   return reinterpret_cast< HWND >( getUserData( hwnd ) );
}
```

Listing 4.8   `InstanceSubclasser.cpp`

```cpp
/*
 * $Header: /Book/InstanceSubclasser.cpp 5    20.08.99 16:33 Petter $
 */

#include "precomp.h"
#include "InstanceSubclasser.h"
#include "Exception.h"
#include "addAtom.h"
#include "winUtils.h"
#include "trace.h"

#define getWndProc( hwnd ) \
    ( (WNDPROC) GetWindowLong( hwnd, GWL_WNDPROC ) )
#define PROP_NAME MAKEINTRESOURCE( sm_atom )
#define ATOM_NAME _T( "subclass_list_rootPtr" )


class Node {
public:
    WNDPROC m_wndProc;
    WNDPROC m_wndProcSaved;
    void    *m_pUserData;
    Node    *m_pNext;

    Node( HWND hwnd, WNDPROC wndProc, void *pUserData, Node *pNext );
};

ATOM InstanceSubclasser::sm_atom = 0;

Node::Node( HWND hwnd, WNDPROC wndProc, void *pUserData, Node *pNext )
    : m_wndProc      ( wndProc )
    , m_pUserData    ( pUserData )
    , m_pNext        ( pNext )
    , m_wndProcSaved( SubclassWindow( hwnd, wndProc ) )
{
    assert( 0 != m_wndProcSaved );
    trace( _T( "creating node for [%s]: %#x (saving %#x)\n" ),
        getWindowDescription( hwnd ), m_wndProc, m_wndProcSaved );
```

```
      if ( 0 == m_wndProcSaved ) {
         throw SubclassException();
      }
   }

InstanceSubclasser::InstanceSubclasser( WNDPROC wndProc )
      : m_wndProc( wndProc )
{
   assert( isGoodCodePtr( m_wndProc ) );
   trace( _T( "Creating instance subclasser %#x\n" ), wndProc );
   sm_atom = globalAddAtom( ATOM_NAME );
   assert( 0 != sm_atom );
   if ( 0 == sm_atom ) {
      throw SubclassException();
   }
}

InstanceSubclasser::~InstanceSubclasser() throw() {

   trace( _T( "Destroying instance subclasser %#x\n" ), m_wndProc );
   assert( 0 != sm_atom );
   verify( 0 == GlobalDeleteAtom( sm_atom ) );
}

inline Node *InstanceSubclasser::getHead( HWND hwnd ) {

   assert( IsWindow( hwnd ) );
   return reinterpret_cast< Node * >( GetProp( hwnd, PROP_NAME


bool InstanceSubclasser::setHead( HWND hwnd, const Node *pNewHead

   assert( IsWindow( hwnd ) );

   if( 0 != GetProp( hwnd, PROP_NAME ) ) {
      verify( RemoveProp( hwnd, PROP_NAME ) );
   }
   if ( 0 != pNewHead ) {
      verify( SetProp( hwnd, PROP_NAME, (HANDLE) pNewHead ) );
   }
```

```cpp
      return (HANDLE) pNewHead == GetProp( hwnd, PROP_NAME );
}

inline Node *InstanceSubclasser::findNode( HWND hwnd ) const {

   Node *pNode = getHead( hwnd );
   int iCounter = 1000;

   while ( 0 != pNode && m_wndProc != pNode->m_wndProc ) {
      if ( --iCounter < 0 ) {
         assert( false );
         return 0;
      }
      pNode = pNode->m_pNext;
   }
   return pNode;
}

bool InstanceSubclasser::subclass( HWND hwnd, void *pUserData ) {

   assert( IsWindow( hwnd ) );
   WNDPROC const curr = getWndProc( hwnd );
   trace( _T( "subclassing [%s] with %#x (saving %#x)\n" ),
      getWindowDescription( hwnd ), m_wndProc, curr );

   Node *pNode = findNode( hwnd );
   if ( 0 != pNode ) {
      trace( _T( "subclass: %s is already hooked with %#x. " )
         _T( "Replacing user data %#x with %#x\r\n" ),
         getWindowDescription( hwnd ), m_wndProc,
         pNode->m_pUserData, pUserData );
      pNode->m_pUserData = pUserData;
      return false; //*** METHOD EXIT POINT
   }

   if ( curr == m_wndProc ) {
      trace( _T( "subclass: %#x is already hooked\r\n" ), m_wndProc );
      return false; //*** METHOD EXIT POINT
   }
```

```cpp
   Node *pHead = getHead( hwnd );
   pNode = new Node( hwnd, m_wndProc, pUserData, pHead );
   assert( 0 != pNode );
   if ( !setHead( hwnd, pNode ) ) {
      trace( _T( "failed to set head node\n" ) );
      SubclassWindow( hwnd, pNode->m_wndProcSaved );
      delete pNode;
      throw SubclassException();
   }
   return true;
}

bool InstanceSubclasser::unSubclass( HWND hwnd ) {

   trace( _T( "unsubclass %s (%#x)\r\n" ),
      getWindowDescription( hwnd ), m_wndProc );
   assert( IsWindow( hwnd ) );

   Node *pNode = findNode( hwnd );
   if ( 0 == pNode ) {
      trace( _T( "subclassing %#x does not exist\r\n" ), m_wndProc );
      return FALSE;
   }

   Node *pHead = getHead( hwnd );
   if ( pHead == pNode ) {
      WNDPROC const curr = getWndProc( hwnd );
      if ( curr != m_wndProc ) {
         trace( _T( "unsubclass found unexpected " )
            _T( "wndproc %#x instead of %#x at top of stack\r\n" ),
            curr, pHead->m_wndProc );
         trace( _T( "unsubclass NOT unhooking %#x, leaving %#x\r\n" ),
            m_wndProc, curr );
         return FALSE; //*** METHOD EXIT POINT
      }
      SubclassWindow( hwnd, pNode->m_wndProcSaved );
      setHead( hwnd, pNode->m_pNext );
   } else {
```

```
      Node *pCurr = pHead;
      while ( pCurr->m_pNext != pNode ) {
         pCurr = pCurr->m_pNext;
      }
      assert( pCurr->m_pNext == pNode );
      if ( pCurr->m_wndProcSaved != m_wndProc ) {
         trace( _T( "unsubclass: %#x is between %#x and %#x\r\n" )
            _T( "NOT unhooking\r\n" ),
            pCurr->m_wndProcSaved, pCurr->m_wndProc, m_wndProc );
         return FALSE; //*** METHOD EXIT POINT
      }
      pCurr->m_pNext         = pNode->m_pNext;
      pCurr->m_wndProcSaved = pNode->m_wndProcSaved;
   }

   delete pNode;
   return TRUE;
}

void *InstanceSubclasser::getUserData( HWND hwnd ) const {

   const Node *pNode = findNode( hwnd );
   assert( IsWindow( hwnd ) );
   return 0 != pNode ? pNode->m_pUserData : 0;
}

LRESULT InstanceSubclasser::callOldProc(
   HWND hwnd, UINT uiMsg, WPARAM w, LPARAM l )
{
   assert( IsWindow( hwnd ) );

   const Node *pNode = findNode( hwnd );
   assert( 0 != pNode );
   if ( 0 == pNode ) {
      throw SubclassException();
   }
   WNDPROC const oldProc = pNode->m_wndProcSaved;
   assert( 0 != oldProc );
```

```
    if ( WM_DESTROY == uiMsg || WM_NCDESTROY == uiMsg ) {
        unSubclass( hwnd );
    }

    return CallWindowProc( oldProc, hwnd, uiMsg, w, l );
}
```

The Window Class: Wrapping the HWND

As I mentioned at the start of this chapter, creating a C++ wrapper for a HWND is a challenge. The ideal solution would hide the HWND completely — subclassing a window would be done by subclassing the C++ way and messages would be handled by overriding virtual functions. We do, however, face a number of obstacles. Here are a few things to consider:

- C++ member functions — methods — have an implicit "this" pointer, a pointer to the object instance. The Windows API, unfortunately, understands nothing of "this" pointers, so the callback function can't be a member function. It must be static.
- The WNDPROC actually does have an explicit "this" pointer — the HWND parameter. Any solution must have some way of mapping HWNDs to instances of C++ classes. Vice versa too, of course, but that's trivial.
- Windows has a huge number of predefined messages. Creating virtual functions for them all is expensive.
- Extending the base class — adding new virtual methods to deal with new Windows messages, for example — would require you to recompile the entire world. The Windows subclassing chain is much more dynamic and requires nothing of the kind.
- The process of creating a window is unrelated to the C++ constructor. You can ask Windows to create a HWND for you, but it will be more difficult to persuade Windows to instantiate your corresponding C++ object when a Window is created outside your control.
- The process of destroying a window is unrelated to the C++ destructor. You can ask Windows to destroy a HWND for you, but you can't, in general, invoke a C++ destructor from the WM_DESTROY handler. The C++ object must be able to exist without an attached HWND.
- You must deal with system-defined windows such as controls. If you don't use any of those, you can create your own little OO world, but you will also throw away many of the benefits of using Windows in the first place. In such a universe, there would be only one window function in the traditional Windows sense.

Mapping a C++ object to a HWND is trivial; all you have to do is include a HWND member variable in the class definition. Going in the opposite direction, from a HWND to a C++ object, you have the same options that we had with InstanceSubclasser: some kind of static storage, window words, or window properties.

(There is another option: you can dynamically generate a code stub that calls a member function, then install this code stub as the window function. Microsoft's Active Template Library (ATL) uses a mechanism based on this elegant principle. The solution's main drawback is that it is necessarily processor-dependent. As a curious side effect, all window instances have different window functions, even if they are of the same class.)

Microsoft Foundation Classes (MFC) maintains a mapping table between HWNDs and CWnds. Something like this is probably necessary, given that MFC attempts to hide the HWND completely. If you call CWnd::FromHandle, for example, you receive a pointer to a CWnd object. The function searches the mapping table, and if it finds the HWND, it returns the address of the corresponding CWnd object. If not, it creates a new CWnd object for you. Because you don't know whence it came, you (a) cannot delete it, and (b) cannot store it for later use. MFC itself keeps track of which CWnds are temporary and deletes them on idle cycles. This is either weird and wonderful, or it's just weird; take your pick.

The main problem with global mapping tables is something else though. If you maintain a single global table, you need to provide thread-safe access, with the overhead that entails. If you use Thread Local Storage (TLS) to maintain one table per thread, as MFC does, you run into problems if you share CWnd objects between threads.

The TextEdit Window class uses (you guessed it) the InstanceSubclasser to do the subclassing. Because InstanceSubclasser allows us to store arbitrary data per subclassing per window, it gives us not only subclassing, but a reference to the C++ object as well.

All windows wrapped by Window objects are subclassed using the same window function, Window::wndProc. Derived classes may override any of the virtual functions defined in the Window class, including dispatch, which in one sense is the "real" window function. The whole point of wndProc is that we need a static function as our ambassador from C++-land to Windows; all wndProc really does is to get hold of the attached Window object so that we can call methods on it.

The set of messages selected for the virtual function treatment is rather arbitrary. To handle a new message, you have the choice between adding a new virtual method and overriding the dispatch method. The quest for overall simplicity and convenience should guide your choice.

The Window class defines default handlers for all messages, either through the virtual methods or through the dispatch method. These invariably pass the messages on to the original window function.

Listing 4.9   Window.h

```
/*
 * $Header: /Book/Window.h 15    3.07.99 17:47 Petter $
 *
 * The Window class is a general C++ wrapper class for HWNDs.
 * The sendMessage method is a case in point of the strict vs.
 * conceptual const-ness dilemma -- the compiler does not object
 * to a const sendMessage, but SendMessage in general is decidedly
 * not const with regard to the actual HWND.
 *
 * A protected const variant of sendMessage is provided for the
 * benefit of const member functions of derived classes.
 */
```

Chapter 4: The Mechanics of Subclassing

```cpp
#pragma once

#include "String.h"
#include "InstanceSubclasser.h"

class Window {
private:
   static LRESULT CALLBACK wndProc(
      HWND hwnd, UINT msg, WPARAM wParam, LPARAM lParam );

protected:
   HWND m_hwnd;
   void attach( HWND hwnd );
   void detach( void );
   LRESULT sendMessage(
      UINT msg, WPARAM wParam = 0, LPARAM lParam = 0 ) const;

   static InstanceSubclasser sm_windowSubclasser;

   void assertValid( void );
   void assertValid( void ) const;

public:
   Window( HWND = 0 );
   virtual ~Window();

   operator HWND() const;

   LRESULT sendMessage(
      UINT msg, WPARAM wParam = 0, LPARAM lParam = 0 );
   virtual LRESULT dispatch(
      UINT msg, WPARAM wParam = 0, LPARAM lParam = 0 );

   virtual void onPaint( HDC hdc );
   virtual void onDestroy( void );
   virtual void onCommand( int id, HWND hwndCtl, UINT codeNotify );
   virtual LRESULT onNotify( const int id, const LPNMHDR pHdr );
   virtual void onLButtonDown(
      BOOL fDoubleClick, int x, int y, UINT keyFlags );
```

```cpp
    virtual void onSettingChange( LPCTSTR pszSection );
    virtual void onSysColorChange( void );

    String getWindowText( void ) const;
    void setWindowText( const String& strText );

    static Window *windowFromHWND( HWND hwnd );
};

// Inline Window functions:

inline Window::Window( HWND hwnd ) : m_hwnd( hwnd ) {

    if ( IsWindow( hwnd ) ) {
        attach( hwnd );
        assertValid();
    }
}

/**
 * Note that this operator is safe to call for null pointers.
 * We never expect to do so, hence the assertValid.
 */
inline Window::operator HWND() const {

    assertValid();
    return 0 != this ? m_hwnd : 0;
}

inline LRESULT Window::sendMessage(
    UINT msg, WPARAM wParam, LPARAM lParam )
{
    assertValid();
    return SNDMSG( m_hwnd, msg, wParam, lParam );
}

inline LRESULT Window::sendMessage(
    UINT msg, WPARAM wParam, LPARAM lParam ) const
```

```
{
    assertValid();
    return SNDMSG( m_hwnd, msg, wParam, lParam );
}

inline void Window::setWindowText( const String& strText ) {

    assertValid();
    SetWindowText( m_hwnd, strText.c_str() );
}

inline Window *Window::windowFromHWND( HWND hwnd ) {

    assert( IsWindow( hwnd ) );
    Window *pWindow = reinterpret_cast< Window * >(
        sm_windowSubclasser.getUserData( hwnd ) );
    assert( 0 == pWindow || hwnd == pWindow->m_hwnd );
    return pWindow;
}

inline void Window::assertValid( void ) {

    assert( isGoodPtr( this ) );
    assert( IsWindow( m_hwnd ) );
}

inline void Window::assertValid( void ) const {

    assert( isGoodConstPtr( this ) );
    assert( IsWindow( m_hwnd ) );
}
```

Listing 4.10 Window.cpp

```
/*
 * $Header: /Book/Window.cpp 16    5.09.99 13:07 Petter $
 */

#include "precomp.h"
#include "Window.h"
```

```cpp
#include "AutoArray.h"
#include "Exception.h"
#include "trace.h"

InstanceSubclasser Window::sm_windowSubclasser( Window::wndProc );

Window::~Window() {

   assert( isGoodPtr( this ) );
   if ( IsWindow( m_hwnd ) ) {
      verify( DestroyWindow( *this ) );
      assert( 0 == m_hwnd ); // See XXX comment below.
   }
}

void Window::attach( HWND hwnd ) {

   assert( isGoodPtr( this ) );
   assert( IsWindow( hwnd ) );
   m_hwnd = hwnd;
   sm_windowSubclasser.subclass( m_hwnd, this );
   assertValid();
}

void Window::detach( void ) {

   assertValid();
   sm_windowSubclasser.unSubclass( m_hwnd );
   m_hwnd = 0;
}

/**
 * May throw MemoryException.
 */
String Window::getWindowText( void ) const {

   assertValid();
   const int nLength = GetWindowTextLength( *this );
   AutoString pszWindowText( nLength + 1 );
```

```
    GetWindowText( *this, pszWindowText, nLength + 1 );
    return pszWindowText;
}

void Window::onPaint( HDC hdc ) {

    assertValid();
}

void Window::onDestroy( void ) {

    assertValid();
}

void Window::onCommand( int id, HWND hwndCtl, UINT codeNotify ) {

    assertValid();
}

LRESULT Window::onNotify( const int id, const LPNMHDR pHdr ) {

    assertValid();
    return sm_windowSubclasser.callOldProc(
        m_hwnd, WM_NOTIFY,
        static_cast< WPARAM >( id ),
        reinterpret_cast< LPARAM >( pHdr ) );
}

void Window::onLButtonDown(
    BOOL fDoubleClick, int x, int y, UINT keyFlags )
{
    assertValid();
}

void Window::onSettingChange( LPCTSTR pszSection ) {

    assertValid();
}
```

```cpp
void Window::onSysColorChange( void ) {

   assertValid();
}

/**
 * The dispatcher.
 */
LRESULT Window::dispatch( UINT msg, WPARAM wParam, LPARAM lParam ) {

   assertValid();

   switch ( msg ) {
   case WM_PAINT:
      onPaint( reinterpret_cast< HDC >( wParam ) );
      break;

   case WM_DESTROY:
      onDestroy();
      break;

   case WM_COMMAND:
      onCommand(
         GET_WM_COMMAND_ID   ( wParam, lParam ),
         GET_WM_COMMAND_HWND( wParam, lParam ),
         GET_WM_COMMAND_CMD  ( wParam, lParam ) );
      break;

   case WM_NOTIFY:
      return
         onNotify( wParam, reinterpret_cast< NMHDR * >( lParam ) );

   case WM_LBUTTONDOWN:
   case WM_LBUTTONDBLCLK:
      onLButtonDown( WM_LBUTTONDBLCLK == msg,
         (int)(short)LOWORD( lParam ),
         (int)(short)HIWORD( lParam ), (UINT) wParam );
      break;
```

Chapter 4: The Mechanics of Subclassing

```cpp
      case WM_SYSCOLORCHANGE:
         onSysColorChange();
         break;

      case WM_SETTINGCHANGE:
         onSettingChange( reinterpret_cast< LPCTSTR >( lParam ) );
         break;
   }

   const LRESULT lResult =
      sm_windowSubclasser.callOldProc( m_hwnd, msg, wParam, lParam );

#ifdef _DEBUG
   const Window *pWindow = windowFromHWND( m_hwnd );
   if ( this != pWindow ) { // Disconnected.
      assert( 0 == pWindow );
      m_hwnd = 0;            // See XXX comment above.
   }
#endif // _DEBUG

   return lResult;
}

LRESULT CALLBACK Window::wndProc(
   HWND hwnd, UINT msg, WPARAM wParam, LPARAM lParam )
{
   assert( IsWindow( hwnd ) );

   Window *pWindow = windowFromHWND( hwnd );
   assert( 0 != pWindow );
   if ( 0 == pWindow ) {
      FatalAppExit(
         0, _T( "Window not found in Window::wndProc\n" ) );
   }

   assert( hwnd == pWindow->m_hwnd );
   return pWindow->dispatch( msg, wParam, lParam );
}
```

Section II

Foreground

Chapter 5

The Bare Bones

This chapter gives you an overview of the TextEdit application architecture — the skeleton of the application, if you like. But first, this message from our sponsors:

"Encapsulate what is likely to change."

This is an important object-oriented design principle. (Word's grammar checker insist that a "design principle" ought to be a "design principal." This illustrates another principal: if you try to pass your software off as "intelligent," make sure it's really smart or it will appear to be really stupid.) (This, by the way, is nothing compared with what the spell checker of Word 2.0 did to me a few years ago: it insisted that "northwest" should be "northeast." I don't usually mind Word correcting my spelling, but I refuse to let it correct my geography!)

The temptation is great to encapsulate and generalize everything in sight, but this may be a bad idea. It takes longer to design and implement general, reusable classes than it does to create exactly what you need for your application. The interaction with a generalized class tends to be more complex, leading to more functional code, giving bugs more opportunity to creep in, making the code more difficult to follow and more complex to maintain. You do gain flexibility, but you may never use the bulk of it.

In TextEdit, the editing control is designed to be pluggable. Accordingly, it has a nice and clean interface, as defined by the abstract class `AbstractEditWindow`. Any interaction with the edit control should use that interface.

Such is theory. In practice, the abstract base class implements several of the operations, secure in the knowledge that the actual editing control is either an edit control or a rich edit control. This has the advantage of avoiding duplicate code in the `EditWnd` and `RichEditWnd` classes; it has the disadvantage that it may need changing the moment we introduce a control that doesn't use, say, `EN_CHANGE` notifications.

To get notifications from an `AbstractEditWindow`, you must implement the `EditListener` interface. Among other things, the `EditListener` wraps the `EN_*` notifications, so that the listener won't have to worry about such implementation details:

```
class EditListener {
public:
    virtual void onChange   ( void ) = 0;
    virtual void onMaxText  ( void ) = 0;
    virtual void onErrSpace ( void ) = 0;
    virtual void onPosChange( const Point& position ) = 0;
};
```

A truly general `EditListener` interface would have a reference to the `AbstractEditWindow` as a parameter in all the notifications. In TextEdit, the `EditListener` interface is implemented by the Editor object, which already knows about the only `AbstractEditWindow` in the application. This parameter is therefore unnecessary, and, being more concerned with overall simplicity than OO purity, I chose to skip it.

A truly general `AbstractEditWindow` class would allow registration of multiple `EditListeners`. If you are familiar with the Java Abstract Windowing Toolkit (AWT), this should ring a bell. At any rate, TextEdit doesn't need this, so `AbstractEditWindow` does not provide it.

The Toolbar class, which wraps the toolbar, is an example of a more pragmatic approach. Whenever I need to do something to the toolbar that the Toolbar class interface doesn't support, I either implement it directly in terms of the Windows API or I extend the class interface, depending on how much coffee I've had lately. If I need to do something several places in the program, I'm more likely to change the class interface, but I won't lose sleep over it either way. (The coffee is another matter.)

Furthermore, the `Toolbar` class contains TextEdit-specific code that makes it non-reusable as it stands. The "proper" thing to do would be to create a general `Toolbar` class and extend it with a `TextEditToolbar` class. That's useful the moment I have more than one application with a toolbar, but as long as I don't, it's dead weight. One more class to think about, two more source files, and additional cogitation to determine how these classes should share their responsibilities? No thanks; not unless I get something in return.

The Major Organs

The core of TextEdit consists of one window function and three C++ classes. There is a large supporting cast as well, but these are the stars:

- The main window function (`mainWndProc` in `mainwnd.cpp`), which is described in Chapter 9
- The `Editor` class, which lives in symbiosis with `MainWndProc` and is the nearest thing TextEdit has to a global application object

The Major Organs 67

- The `Document` class, which handles disk files
- The `AbstractEditWnd` class, which wraps the editing widget.

The relationships between these are shown in Figure 5.1.

The main entry point is defined in `WinMain.cpp`. The `WinMain` function does a small amount of initialization, then sets up the outermost `try`/`catch` block of the "exception handling onion" (a vegetable I shall get back to in the next chapter). Next, it calls the `init` function, whose job it is to interpret any arguments, possibly produce a `Document` object and an `Editor` object, and possibly to create the main window. (The `init` function is discussed in detail in Chapter 7.) Once the main window is up and running, control is transferred to TextEdit's main message loop, buried in the `Editor:run` method.

Figure 5.1   Application architecture overview.

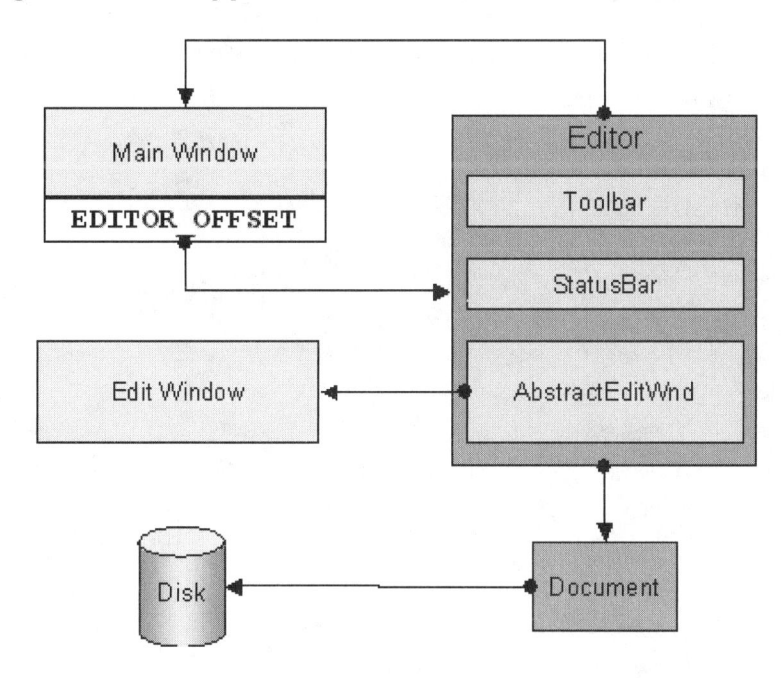

Listing 5.1   WinMain.cpp

```
/*
 * $Header: /Book/WinMain.cpp 17     20.08.99 16:33 Petter $
 */

#include "precomp.h"
#include "resource.h"
#include "init.h"
```

```
#include "handlers.h"
#include "Exception.h"
#include "language.h"
#include "mainwnd.h"
#include "winUtils.h"
#include "persistence.h"
#include "os.h"
#include "trace.h"

#ifdef UNICODE
#pragma comment( linker, "/entry:wWinMainCRTStartup" )
#else
#pragma comment( linker, "/entry:WinMainCRTStartup" )
#endif

int WINAPI _tWinMain(
   HINSTANCE hinst, HINSTANCE, LPTSTR pszCmdLine, int nShow )
{
   trace( _T( "TextEdit _tWinMain( \"%s\" )\n" ), pszCmdLine );

#if defined( _DEBUG ) && defined( _CRTDBG_REPORT_FLAG ) && 0
   {
      int nDebugFlags = _CrtSetDbgFlag( _CRTDBG_REPORT_FLAG );
      nDebugFlags |= _CRTDBG_LEAK_CHECK_DF;
      nDebugFlags |= _CRTDBG_CHECK_ALWAYS_DF;
      _CrtSetDbgFlag( nDebugFlags );
   }
#endif

   setNewLanguage( getLanguage() );

   int nRetCode = -1;
   HRESULT hres = coInitialize();
   if ( !SUCCEEDED( hres ) ) {
      messageBox( HWND_DESKTOP, MB_ICONERROR | MB_OK,
         IDS_COM_INIT_ERROR, ComException( hres ).what() );
      return false;
   }
```

```
    initThreadErrorHandling();

    try {
        AutoEditor pEditor;
        // In case of exception thrown during init.
        pEditor = init( pszCmdLine, nShow );
        assert( isGoodPtr( (Editor *) pEditor ) );
        nRetCode = pEditor->run();
    }
    catch ( const CancelException& ) {
        ; // OK, just terminate.
    }
    catch ( const AccessDeniedException& x ) {
        messageBox( HWND_DESKTOP, MB_ICONERROR | MB_OK,
            IDS_ACCESS_DENIED, x.what() );
    }
    catch ( const Exception& x ) {
        // We get here in case of accidents during init.
        messageBox( HWND_DESKTOP, MB_ICONERROR | MB_OK,
            IDS_INIT_ERROR, x.what() );
    }
    catch ( ... ) {
        // We get here in case of SEHs that we don't translate.
        assert( false );
        messageBox(
            HWND_DESKTOP, MB_ICONERROR | MB_OK, IDS_FATAL_ERROR );
    }

    exitThreadErrorHandling();
    CoUninitialize();

    return nRetCode; // Goodbye, and thanks for all the fish.
}
```

The Heart

The heart of TextEdit — indeed, of any Windows application — is the message pump. TextEdit's message pump resides in the Editor class — not for any deep philosophical reason, but because most of what might be termed "global application data" is contained within that class.

Here is a simplified version of `Editor::run`:

```
int Editor::run( HINSTANCE hinst ) {

    MSG msg = { 0, 0, static_cast< WPARAM >( -1 ) };

    BOOL bRun = true;
    while ( bRun ) {
        try {
            while ( bRun = GetMessage( &msg, 0, 0, 0 ) ) {
                if ( !TranslateAccelerator( m_hwnd, m_hacc, &msg ) &&
                    !isToolbarDialogMessage( &msg ) )
                {
                    TranslateMessage( &msg );
                    DispatchMessage ( &msg );
                }
            }
        }
        catch ( various exceptions ) {
            ...
        }
    }

    return msg.wParam;
}
```

Two things here are of particular interest. First, there is a double `while` loop, although one would be sufficient from a logical point of view. This is done to increase efficiency. Setting up a try block involves considerable overhead, so I want to avoid doing it for every message that's pumped through the system. With a double loop, the try block is set up once when we start, then once for every exception that makes it this far.

Second, `TranslateAccelerator` is called before `isToolbarDialogMessage` (which wraps `IsDialogMessage`). This is to ensure that the accelerators work even when the focus is in one of the controls on the toolbar. If I switch the order, accelerators such as Ctrl+O (File Open) and Ctrl+F (Edit Find) don't work whenever the focus is in the tab edit field or on the Read Only checkbox.

A side effect of this ordering is that the main window's clipboard accelerators (Ctrl+C, Ctrl+X, and Ctrl+V) take precedence over the tab edit field's accelerators. If this were an issue, the various command handlers would have to check which window had the keyboard focus before applying their corresponding commands. The whole issue illustrates something that is not a design principle, but merely a sad fact of life: it can be difficult to get smooth interaction if every box is black.

The Editor Class

Mapping all the parts of TextEdit to corresponding parts of the human body in a meaningful way is going to be difficult, so I'll quit while I'm ahead.

The `Editor` class lives in close symbiosis with the main window function and implements much of what the user perceives as commands in the TextEdit user interface. There's `openFile` and `printFile`, `save`, `restoreOriginal`, and `searchAndSelect`, and many more. The `searchAndSelect` function is a front-end to the actual searching machinery, implemented in `AbstractEditWnd` and its descendants. Searching is a surprisingly complex business; the `Editor::searchAndSelect` method, for example, is mainly concerned with the not-as-trivial-as-you-would-have-thought task of figuring out whether or not the file was wrapped while searching.

I'll get back to search and replace in Chapter 15.

The `Editor` class also implements the `EditListener` interface, mentioned at the start of this chapter. This means that it receives notifications from the edit control and is thus responsible for updating the line/column indicator on the status bar, for example.

You can find the declaration of the `Editor` class (as well as definitions of inline methods and functions) in Listing 5.2. The implementation is in `Editor.cpp` on the accompanying CD-ROM. (Discourse continues on page 76.)

Listing 5.2   `Editor.h`

```
/*
 * $Header: /Book/Editor.h 17    3.07.99 17:46 Petter $
 */

#pragma once

#include "AbstractEditWnd.h"
#include "String.h"
#include "Document.h"
#include "Toolbar.h"
#include "Statusbar.h"
#include "utils.h"

typedef AutoPtr< AbstractEditWnd > AutoEditWnd   ;
typedef AutoPtr< Document        > AutoDocument  ;
typedef AutoPtr< Toolbar         > AutoToolbar   ;
typedef AutoPtr< Statusbar       > AutoStatusbar ;
```

```cpp
class Editor : public EditListener {

private:
    HWND            m_hwndMain;
    HACCEL          m_haccel;
    AutoEditWnd     m_pEditWnd;
    AutoDocument    m_pDocument;
    AutoToolbar     m_pToolbar;
    AutoStatusbar   m_pStatusbar;

    HFONT m_hfontFixed;
    HFONT m_hfontProportional;

    LOGFONT m_logFontFixed;
    LOGFONT m_logFontProportional;

    bool m_hasFixedFont;
    bool m_isClean;
    bool m_isWhistleClean;

    LPTSTR getContents( void );
    void updateToolbar( void );

    static void CALLBACK autoSaveTimerProc( HWND, UINT, UINT, DWORD );

    void assertValid( void );
    void assertValid( void ) const;

public:
    Editor( HWND hwndParent, AutoDocument *ppDocument );
    ~Editor();

    HWND getMainWnd( void );
    void detach( HWND hwndMain );
    AbstractEditWnd *getEditWnd( void );
    Toolbar *getToolbar( void );
    Statusbar *getStatusbar( void );
    Document *getDocument( void );
    void setDocument( Document *pNewDocument );
```

```cpp
void setTitle( void );
void refreshToolbar( void );
void setSettings( void );
void setWordWrap( bool bOn );

void loadAcceleratorTable( HINSTANCE = getModuleHandle() );
int run();

void openFile( const String& strPath );
void copyFile( void );
void printFile( void );
bool save( void ) throw();
bool saveIfNecessary( void );
void restoreOriginal( void );
bool searchAndSelect(
   const String& strSearchPattern, bool *pbWrapped = 0 );
int getAutoSaveTime( void ) const;
void saveState( void );

HFONT getFont( void ) const;
HFONT getFont( bool bFixedFont ) const;
void setFont( bool isFixedFont );
bool hasFixedFont( void ) const;
const LOGFONT *getLogFont( void ) const;
const LOGFONT *getLogFont( bool bFixed ) const;
void setLogFont( const LOGFONT *pLogFont, bool bFixed );

String getMenuDescription( HMENU hmnuPopup ) const;
String getMenuItemDescription(
   int nItem, const String& strLast ) const;

bool isToolbarDialogMessage( MSG *pMsg );

void clean( void );
bool isClean( void ) const;
bool isWhistleClean( void ) const;
void setReadOnly( bool bReadOnly );
bool getReadOnly( void ) const;
```

```cpp
    friend Editor *getEditor( HWND hwnd );

protected: // implementation of EditListener
    virtual void onChange  ( void );
    virtual void onMaxText ( void );
    virtual void onErrSpace( void );
    virtual void onPosChange( const Point& position );
};

typedef AutoPtr< Editor > AutoEditor;

inline HWND Editor::getMainWnd( void ) {

    assert( isGoodPtr( this ) );
    assert( IsWindow( m_hwndMain ) );
    return m_hwndMain;
}

inline void Editor::detach( HWND hwndMain ) {

    assert( IsWindow( m_hwndMain ) );
    assert( m_hwndMain == hwndMain );
    m_hwndMain = 0;
}

inline AbstractEditWnd *Editor::getEditWnd( void ) {

    assert( isGoodPtr( this ) );
    assert( isGoodPtr( m_pEditWnd ) );
    return m_pEditWnd;
}

inline Toolbar *Editor::getToolbar( void ) {

    assert( isGoodPtr( this ) );
    assert( isGoodPtr( m_pToolbar ) );
    return m_pToolbar;
}
```

```cpp
inline Statusbar *Editor::getStatusbar( void ) {

   assert( isGoodPtr( this ) );
   assert( isGoodPtr( m_pStatusbar) );
   return m_pStatusbar;
}

inline Document *Editor::getDocument( void ) {

   assert( isGoodPtr( this ) );
   assert( isGoodPtr( m_pDocument ) );
   return m_pDocument;
}

inline bool Editor::hasFixedFont( void ) const {

   assert( isGoodConstPtr( this ) );
   return m_hasFixedFont;
}

inline const LOGFONT *Editor::getLogFont() const {

   assert( isGoodConstPtr( this ) );
   return getLogFont( hasFixedFont() );
}

inline const LOGFONT *Editor::getLogFont( bool bFixed ) const {

   assert( isGoodConstPtr( this ) );
   return bFixed ? &m_logFontFixed : & m_logFontProportional;
}

inline bool Editor::isToolbarDialogMessage( MSG *pMsg ) {

   assert( isGoodHeapPtr( this ) );
   assert( isGoodPtr( pMsg ) );
   const HWND hwndToolbar = *getToolbar();
   return 0 != IsDialogMessage( hwndToolbar, pMsg );
}
```

```
inline void Editor::clean( void ) {
   m_isClean = true;
}

inline bool Editor::isClean( void ) const {

   assert( isGoodConstPtr( this ) );
   return m_isClean && m_pDocument->isClean();
}

inline bool Editor::isWhistleClean( void ) const {

   assert( isGoodConstPtr( this ) );
   return m_isWhistleClean;
}

inline void Editor::assertValid( void ) {

   assert( isGoodPtr( this ) );
   static_cast< const Editor * >( this )->assertValid();
}

inline void Editor::assertValid( void ) const {

   assert( isGoodConstPtr( this ) );
   assert( 0 == m_hwndMain || IsWindow( m_hwndMain ) );
}
```

The Document Class

The Document class is in charge of disk files. It reads and writes files, it moves, copies and deletes files, it prints files (or parts of files), and it translates file contents to and from Unicode, and between MS-DOS-style and Unix-style line separators (CR-LF or just LF).

To facilitate the Abandon Changes command, we need to store the original contents of the file. This is also the responsibility of the Document class.

Chapter 10 explains how to create persistent variables using the registry. The Document class allows you to create persistent variables on a per-document basis.

I'll return to the implementation of the Document class in Chapter 12. (Discourse continues on page 82.)

Listing 5.3   Document.h

```
/*
 * $Header: /Book/Document.h 19    20.08.99 16:33 Petter $
 */

#pragma once

#include "String.h"
#include "AutoPtr.h"
#include "AutoHandle.h"
#include "Exception.h"

#define DEFINE_PERSISTENT_DOC_INT( name, def, type )         \
   inline int get ## name( int nDef ) const {                \
      return getPersistentInt( _T( #name ), nDef, type );    \
   };                                                        \
   inline int get ## name( void ) const {                    \
      return get ## name( def );                             \
   };                                                        \
   inline void set ## name( int nValue ) {                   \
      setPersistentInt( _T( #name ), nValue, type );         \
   }

#define DEFINE_PERSISTENT_DOC_STRING( name )                 \
   inline String get ## name( void ) const {                 \
      return getPersistentString( _T( #name ) );             \
   };                                                        \
   inline void set ## name( const String& strValue ) {       \
      setPersistentString( _T( #name ), strValue );          \
   }

class Document {
private:
   WIN32_FILE_ATTRIBUTE_DATA m_FileAttributes;

   String     m_strFileName;
   bool       m_isUnicode;
   bool       m_hasUnicodeTranslationError;
   bool       m_hasUnixLineFeeds;
```

```cpp
    UINT       m_uiDriveType;
    bool       m_isReadOnly;
    bool       m_bAccessDenied;
    bool       m_bBinary;
    bool       m_bDirty;

    enum { NULL_REPLACEMENT = _T( '?' ) };

    HANDLE openFile( HWND hwnd );
    void createOrgCopy( HANDLE hFile );
    void deleteOrgCopy( void );
    LPTSTR convert( const LPVOID pbRawFile, DWORD dwBytes );
    LPTSTR getContents( const String& strFile, int *pnBytes );
    HFONT createPrintFont( HDC hdc );

    String getRegistryPath( void ) const;
    String getRegistryFileTypePath( void ) const;
    int getPersistentInt(
       LPCTSTR pszName, int nDefault, bool bType ) const;
    void setPersistentInt(
       LPCTSTR pszName, int nValue, bool bType );
    String getPersistentString( LPCTSTR pszName ) const;
    void setPersistentString( LPCTSTR pszName, const String& str );
    bool modifyAttribs(
       const String& strFile, DWORD dwAdd, DWORD dwRemove = 0 );

    void assertValid( void );
    void assertValid( void ) const;

public:
    Document( HWND hwnd, LPCTSTR pszFile = 0 );
    ~Document();

    void save( HWND hwnd, const void *pRawContents, int nBytes );
    void update( HWND hwnd, LPTSTR pszNewContents, int nLength = -1 );
    void addCRs( LPTSTR *ppsz ) throw( MemoryException );
    void removeCRs( LPTSTR psz );
    void print( HDC hdc, LPCTSTR pszText, int nCopies = 1 );
    bool deleteFile( HWND hwnd );
    bool modifyAttribs( DWORD dwAdd, DWORD dwRemove = 0 );
```

```cpp
const String& getPath( void ) const;
bool setPath( HWND hwnd, const String& strNewPath );
String getFileTypeDescription( bool bDisplay = false ) const;
String getTitle( void ) const;
LPTSTR getContents( int *pnBytes = 0 );
LPTSTR getOrgContents( int *pnBytes = 0 );
bool isBinary( void ) const;
bool isFloppy( void ) const;
bool isReadOnly( void ) const;
bool isAccessDenied( void ) const;
bool isClean( void ) const;
void clean( void );
bool isUnicode( void ) const;
void setUnicode( bool bUnicode );
bool hasUnixLineFeeds( void ) const;
void setUnixLineFeeds( bool bUnixLineFeeds );

static String createRegistryPath( const String& strRealPath );
static bool s_bEndSession; // Set to true on WM_ENDSESSION.

// These persistent variables are saved for
// file types as well as individual files:
DEFINE_PERSISTENT_DOC_INT( FixedFont, 1, true );
DEFINE_PERSISTENT_DOC_INT( WordWrap , 1, true );
DEFINE_PERSISTENT_DOC_INT( Tabs     , 4, true );

// These persistent variables are saved only for individual files:
DEFINE_PERSISTENT_DOC_INT( Left        , CW_USEDEFAULT, false );
DEFINE_PERSISTENT_DOC_INT( Top         , CW_USEDEFAULT, false );
DEFINE_PERSISTENT_DOC_INT( Width       , CW_USEDEFAULT, false );
DEFINE_PERSISTENT_DOC_INT( Height      , CW_USEDEFAULT, false );
DEFINE_PERSISTENT_DOC_INT( WindowState , SW_SHOWNORMAL, false );
DEFINE_PERSISTENT_DOC_INT( Running     , 0            , false );
DEFINE_PERSISTENT_DOC_INT( SelStart    , 0            , false );
DEFINE_PERSISTENT_DOC_INT( SelEnd      , 0            , false );
DEFINE_PERSISTENT_DOC_INT( FirstLine   , 0            , false );

// Page setup (per document):
```

```
    DEFINE_PERSISTENT_DOC_INT( LeftMargin       , 0, false );
    DEFINE_PERSISTENT_DOC_INT( TopMargin        , 0, false );
    DEFINE_PERSISTENT_DOC_INT( RightMargin      , 0, false );
    DEFINE_PERSISTENT_DOC_INT( BottomMargin     , 0, false );
    DEFINE_PERSISTENT_DOC_INT( MarginsAreMetric, 0, false );

    DEFINE_PERSISTENT_DOC_STRING( OrgCopy );
};

#undef DEFINE_PERSISTENT_DOC_INT

inline const String& Document::getPath( void ) const {

    assertValid();
    return m_strFileName;
}

inline bool Document::isBinary( void ) const {

    assertValid();
    return m_bBinary;
}

inline bool Document::isFloppy( void ) const {

    assertValid();
    return DRIVE_REMOVABLE == m_uiDriveType;
}

inline bool Document::isReadOnly( void ) const {

    assertValid();
    if ( DRIVE_CDROM == m_uiDriveType ) {
       return true;
    }
    const DWORD dwAttribs =
       GetFileAttributes( m_strFileName.c_str() );
    return 0 != ( dwAttribs & FILE_ATTRIBUTE_READONLY );
}
```

The Document Class

```cpp
inline bool Document::isAccessDenied( void ) const {

   assertValid();
   return m_bAccessDenied; // LATER: Ask the file? May take time.
}

inline bool Document::isClean( void ) const {

   assertValid();
   return !m_bDirty;
}

inline void Document::clean( void ) {

   assertValid();
   m_bDirty = false;
}

inline bool Document::isUnicode( void ) const {

   assertValid();
   return m_isUnicode;
}

inline void Document::setUnicode( const bool bUnicode ) {

   assertValid();
   if ( bUnicode != m_isUnicode ) {
      m_isUnicode = bUnicode;
      m_bDirty = true;
   }
}

inline void Document::setUnixLineFeeds( const bool bUnixLineFeeds ) {

   assertValid();
   if ( bUnixLineFeeds != m_hasUnixLineFeeds ) {
      m_hasUnixLineFeeds = bUnixLineFeeds;
```

```
        m_bDirty = true;
    }
}

inline bool Document::hasUnixLineFeeds( void ) const {

    assertValid();
    return m_hasUnixLineFeeds;
}

inline bool Document::modifyAttribs( DWORD dwAdd, DWORD dwRemove ) {

    assertValid();
    return modifyAttribs( getPath(), dwAdd, dwRemove );
}

inline void Document::assertValid( void ) {

    assert( isGoodPtr( this ) );
    static_cast< const Document * >( this )->assertValid();
}

inline void Document::assertValid( void ) const {

    assert( isGoodConstPtr( this ) );
}
```

The AbstractEditWnd Class

The AbstractEditWnd class defines the interface that all concrete edit window classes must implement. It also implements some of the functionality directly; particularly operations that can be defined purely in terms of other AbstractEditWnd operations — getLineCount, for example, which no one bothers to override.

TextEdit includes two examples of concrete edit window classes: EditWnd, which uses the standard edit control, and RichEditWnd, which uses the rich edit control. The actual construction of one of these is done in the factory method AbstractEditWnd::create. It checks whether the module RICHED20.DLL can be loaded; if so, it creates a RichEditWnd. If not, its fallback strategy is to create an EditWnd. In a debug build, you can force TextEdit to create a standard edit control by using the /edit switch on the command line.

If you wish to use a different editing control, you must (a) wrap it in a class derived from AbstractEditWnd and (b) provide for its creation in AbstractEditWnd::create.

The rich edit control in 'plain text mode' is vastly superior to the standard edit control in most ways. It offers multi-level undo and redo, drag and drop editing, and overall better behavior. Its most serious problem is that there is no good way to set the number of spaces to display for each tab stop — it does not understand the EM_SETTABSTOPS message, and the EM_SETPARAFORMAT message is geared towards word processing rather than plain text editing. I've found no satisfactory solution to this; as a result, the rich edit version doesn't give you any control over how tabs are displayed. My only consolation is that Notepad doesn't do this either. (Discourse continues on page 86.)

Listing 5.4   AbstractEditWnd.h

```
/*
 * $Header: /Book/AbstractEditWnd.h 16    20.08.99 16:33 Petter $
 *
 * Defines AbstractEditWnd and the pure interface EditListener.
 */

#pragma once

#include "String.h"
#include "Window.h"
#include "AutoPtr.h"
#include "geometry.h"

class EditListener;

/**
 * This is an _almost_ pure interface to an actual edit window.
 */
class AbstractEditWnd : public Window {
private:
   int getVisibleLineCount( HFONT hfont ) const;
   int moveInsertionPoint( int nLine, int nColumn );

   EditListener *m_pEditListener;
   int          m_nCurLine     ;
   int          m_nCurColumn   ;
   int          m_nLastEnd     ;

protected:
   AbstractEditWnd( void );
```

```cpp
public:
   virtual LRESULT dispatch(
      UINT msg, WPARAM wParam = 0, LPARAM lParam = 0 );

   void resetPosition( void );

//#ifdef _DEBUG
   static bool bForceEdit;
//#endif

   virtual int getSearchText( LPTSTR psz, UINT cb ) const = 0;
   virtual void getText( LPTSTR psz, UINT cb ) const = 0;
   virtual void setText( LPCTSTR psz ) = 0; // WM_SETTEXT

   virtual int   getTextLength( void ) const;
   virtual int   getLineCount ( void ) const;
   virtual Point getCurPos    ( void ) const = 0;

   /**
    * getSel returns true if there actually is a selection,
    * i.e., start is less than end.
    */
   virtual bool getSel( int *pnStart = 0, int *pnEnd = 0 ) const = 0;
   virtual bool getSel( String *pstrSelection )            const = 0;
   virtual void setSel( int nStart = 0, int nEnd = -1 )          = 0;
   virtual void replaceSel( LPCTSTR psz )                        = 0;
   virtual bool getWord( String *pstrWord )                const = 0;

   virtual int lineFromChar( UINT ich )          const = 0;
   virtual int getFirstVisibleLine( void )       const = 0;
   virtual void setFirstVisibleLine( int nLine ) const = 0;

   virtual bool canUndo( void )         const = 0;
   virtual bool undo( void )                  = 0;
   virtual String getUndoName( void ) const = 0;

   virtual bool hasRedo( void )        const = 0;
   virtual bool canRedo( void )        const = 0;
```

```cpp
    virtual bool redo( void                        ) = 0;
    virtual String getRedoName( void ) const = 0;

    virtual bool canSetTabs( void ) const = 0;

    virtual bool isDirty( void ) const = 0;
    virtual void clean( bool bEmptyUndo = true ) = 0;

    virtual void cutSelection( void ) = 0;
    virtual void copySelection( void ) = 0;
    virtual void paste( void ) = 0;
    virtual void deleteSelection( void ) = 0;

    virtual void setReadOnly( bool bReadOnly ) = 0;
    virtual bool isReadOnly( void ) const = 0;

    virtual void setSpacesPerTab( int nSpaces ) = 0;
    virtual void setWordWrap( bool bWordWrap ) = 0;

    virtual bool searchAndSelect(
        const String& strSearchPattern,
        const bool bMatchWholeWord,
        const bool bMatchCase,
        const int  nDirection );
    virtual int replaceInSelection(
        const String& strSearchPattern,
        const String& strReplacePattern,
        const bool bMatchWholeWord,
        const bool bMatchCase );

    void scroll( UINT nWhat );
    void bringCaretToWindow( HFONT hfont );
    EditListener *getEditListener( void );

    // Factory method:
    static AbstractEditWnd *create( HWND hwndParent,
        LPCTSTR pszText, EditListener *pEditListener, bool bWordWrap );
};
```

```
/**
 * This is a pure interface.
 * Use it to listen to AbstractEditWnd events.
 */
class EditListener {
public:
    virtual void onChange   ( void ) = 0;
    virtual void onMaxText  ( void ) = 0;
    virtual void onErrSpace ( void ) = 0;
    virtual void onPosChange( const Point& position ) = 0;
};

inline AbstractEditWnd::AbstractEditWnd( void )
    : m_pEditListener( 0 )
    , m_nCurLine     ( -1 )
    , m_nCurColumn   ( -1 )
    , m_nLastEnd     ( -1 )
{
}

inline void AbstractEditWnd::resetPosition( void ) {
    m_nCurLine = m_nCurColumn = m_nLastEnd = -1;
}

inline EditListener *AbstractEditWnd::getEditListener( void ) {
    return m_pEditListener;
}
```

Of Strings and PATHNAMEs

Let's take a timeout here, to look at some common definitions and data types that are used throughout TextEdit. You need to know about these to follow the code that comes along presently. First, the String class, which has already been used without further explanation in previous examples.

String

The String type is just my name for the std::string type from the Standard C++ Template Library (STL). It equates to a string or a wstring, depending on whether _UNICODE is defined. The String type is defined in Listing 5.5, String.h.

Listing 5.5 String.h

```
/*
 * $Header: /Book/String.h 8     3.07.99 17:46 Petter $
 *
 * Wraps the string type from the standard C++ library.
 */

#pragma once

typedef std::wstring StringW;
typedef std::string  StringA;

#ifdef _UNICODE

typedef StringW String;

#else

typedef StringA String;

#endif
```

PATHNAME

A PATHNAME is a character array of length MAX_PATH. It is defined in Listing 5.6, common.h, as follows:

```
typedef WCHAR PATHNAMEW[ MAX_PATH + 1 ];
typedef CHAR  PATHNAMEA[ MAX_PATH + 1 ];

#ifdef UNICODE
    typedef PATHNAMEW PATHNAME;
#else
    typedef PATHNAMEA PATHNAME;
#endif
```

Whenever a PATHNAME (or any other string array) is declared, it is initialized thusly:

```
PATHNAME szTempPath = { 0 };
```

An alternative formulation would be this:

```
PATHNAME szTempPath = _T( "" );
```

The first formulation is preferable, as it is independent of Unicode and ANSI strings, and thus doesn't require use of the _T macro. Zero is an accommodating constant; it adapts to l- values of any size.

The PATHNAME type is an imperfect solution to the file name problem. If MAX_PATH changes, as well it might, we must recompile the application.

Beware of URLs, which are not subject to the MAX_PATH limit. The wininet.h header file defines the following (arbitrary) constants:

```
#define INTERNET_MAX_PATH_LENGTH    2048
#define INTERNET_MAX_SCHEME_LENGTH  32 // longest protocol name length
#define INTERNET_MAX_URL_LENGTH         (INTERNET_MAX_SCHEME_LENGTH \
                                        + sizeof("://") \
                                        + INTERNET_MAX_PATH_LENGTH)
```

dim

The dim macro is defined in Listing 5.6, common.h, as follows:

```
#define dim( x ) (sizeof( x ) / sizeof( ( x )[ 0 ] ))
```

It is handy for figuring out the number of elements in an array. TextEdit uses this macro a lot with strings, as this is crucial for Unicode builds. For an ANSI build, the dim of a character array is equal to its sizeof; for a Unicode build, dim is half of its sizeof.

PRIVATE

C and C++ use the static keyword for several different things. When a variable declaration is static at function or class scope, or a function declaration is static at class scope, it means that the variable is global (albeit with limited visibility), as opposed to being allocated on the stack or as part of a class instance. When a variable or function declaration is static at file scope, it means that the variable is private to the current compilation unit.

Because the semantics of these uses of static are unrelated, I've created the PRIVATE macro, which I use for the latter meaning. The PRIVATE macro is also defined in Listing 5.6, common.h.

Listing 5.6   common.h

```
/*
 * $Header: /Book/common.h 8      3.07.99 17:46 Petter $
 *
 * Common definitions.
 */

#pragma once

#ifndef SNDMSG
#define SNDMSG ::SendMessage
```

```cpp
#endif

#define FILE_SHARE_NONE 0

inline BOOL isGoodWritePtr( LPVOID addr, UINT ucb ) {
   return !IsBadWritePtr( addr, ucb );
}

inline BOOL isGoodReadPtr( LPCVOID addr, UINT ucb ) {
   return !IsBadReadPtr( addr, ucb );
}

inline BOOL isGoodStringPtr( LPCTSTR psz ) {
   return !IsBadStringPtr( psz, INT_MAX );
}

inline BOOL isGoodStringPtrOrAtom( LPCTSTR psz ) {
   return ( 0 == HIWORD( psz ) && 0 != LOWORD( psz ) ) ||
      isGoodStringPtr( psz );
}

// Use these with some care on arrays!
#define isGoodPtr( ptr ) \
   isGoodWritePtr( ( ptr ), sizeof( *(ptr) ) )
#define isGoodConstPtr( ptr ) \
   isGoodReadPtr ( ( ptr ), sizeof( *(ptr) ) )

#if defined( _DEBUG )
   #if defined( _CRTDBG_REPORT_FLAG )
      #define isGoodHeapPtr( p ) \
         ( _CrtIsValidHeapPointer( p ) && isGoodConstPtr( p ) )
   #else
      #define isGoodHeapPtr isGoodPtr
   #endif
#else
   #define isGoodHeapPtr( p ) true
#endif

#define isGoodCodePtr( func ) \
   !IsBadCodePtr( reinterpret_cast< FARPROC >( func ) )
```

```
#define dim( x ) (sizeof( x ) / sizeof( ( x )[ 0 ] ))

#ifdef _DEBUG
   #define verify( b )          assert( b )
   #define reset_pointer( p )   ((p) = 0)
   #undef  reset_pointer
   #define reset_pointer( p )  \
      ( memset( &( p ), 0xacACacAC, sizeof( p ) ), \
        assert( 4 == sizeof( p ) ) )
   #define unused( x ) ( x )
#else
   #define verify( b )          ( b )
   #define reset_pointer( p )
   #define unused( x )
#endif

#define PRIVATE static

#if 0
#if defined( _DEBUG ) && defined( _MSC_VER ) && (1200 <= _MSC_VER)
   #define _CRTDBG_MAP_ALLOC
   #define _MFC_OVERRIDES_NEW
   #include <crtdbg.h>
   _CRTIMP void * __cdecl operator new(
      unsigned int, int, const char *, int );
   inline void __cdecl operator delete(
      void * _P, int, const char *, int )
   {
      ::operator delete( _P );
   }
   #define new new( _NORMAL_BLOCK, __FILE__, __LINE__ )
#endif
#endif

typedef WCHAR PATHNAMEW[ MAX_PATH + 1 ];
typedef CHAR  PATHNAMEA[ MAX_PATH + 1 ];

#ifdef UNICODE
```

```
    typedef PATHNAMEW PATHNAME;
#else
    typedef PATHNAMEA PATHNAME;
#endif
```

Chapter 6

Exceptions

When your application calls a function, there's always a chance that the function fails to carry out its assigned duties. Possible causes are multifarious — a file was not found, a network file server crashed, the system could not allocate memory, a computation overflowed, the system is corrupt, your application is corrupt, the government is corrupt — the list is endless.

The occasional failure is unavoidable. Failing gracefully is, however, infinitely preferable to falling flat on your face.

Sometimes you don't care if a function failed. Perhaps it wasn't terribly important, perhaps the function has already reported the problem to the user, or perhaps no reasonable course of action exists. The `WaitCursor` class (see Chapter 11) is an example of no-fail software. Its methods don't need to communicate success or failure to the caller because the caller doesn't care one way or another.

Other times, you do care, if for no other reason that you must tell the user that you failed to print his file. Failure can be reported through two basic mechanisms: return codes and exceptions. From modern computer literature, one often gets the impression that exceptions are in some way "better" than return codes, but that distinction is meaningless. The goal is to reduce total complexity to a minimum. Often enough, exceptions support that goal best, but by no means always.

There is one truly bad way and it occurs all too often in real life. Programmers new to exceptions will often just treat them as a complicated form of return codes, enclosing each function call in a `try` block, with one or more `catch` blocks for each function call. This is a lot more wordy and unreadable than just using return codes — when used properly, exceptions separate functional code from error handling, making it much easier to follow the logic of the nominal path.

Your application lives in a hostile environment, and a certain amount of paranoia is fully justified. If you design error handling as an integral part of your application architecture, you stand a chance of protecting yourself. If you don't, you'll get yourself into trouble, sooner rather than later.

Return Codes

When you do use return codes, keep the following design principle in mind:

"Never mix return values with return codes."

Why not? The standard library function `getchar` is a good example. It reads a character from the standard input, returning a byte-sized value. Because all possible byte-sized values are permissible character codes, none are left over to signal conditions such as end-of-file. This problem has been "solved" by having the function return not a `char`, but an `int`, thus allowing the special return value `EOF`, equal to –1.

`EOF` falls outside the byte range. If you stuff the return value from `getchar` into a variable of type `char`, seemingly a reasonable thing to do, only the low byte is retained, and `EOF` becomes undistinguishable from `0xff`. The `char` variable never compares equal to `EOF`.

Consider `atoi`, which converts a string to an integer. The return value of this function is the desired integer. Unfortunately, because all the possible return values are permissible integers, none are left over to signal errors. This problem has been "solved" by designating zero as an error return. Thus, applying `atoi` to the string "garbage" returns zero. Applying it to the string "0" also returns zero.

If the conversion overflows, the result is "undefined." Why not return zero in this case, too? Because the implementation does not even know that the result has overflowed! I would imagine that the quest for the Holy Grail of Efficiency is more to blame than laziness. "Efficiency" is the root of, if not all, then at least the occasional evil: programmers' obsession with efficiency sometimes overshadows more important goals, such as correctness.

In one sense, `atoi` doesn't have "errors." It all depends on how you define its behavior and `atoi`'s behavior is defined in terms of its implementation. This is totally backwards; as a result, `atoi` is unusable without additional error checking. This kind of programming is shaky under the best of circumstances, but if you apply `atoi` directly to user input, you're really courting disaster.

Consider `malloc`. This function also uses a special value — zero, again — to signal failure. In contrast to `atoi`'s error value, `malloc`'s error value is outside the range of valid pointer values — the null pointer is a well-defined concept in C and C++ programming. But no attention is drawn to the possibility of failure and it is therefore less likely that error checking will actually be performed. I was once involved with a large UNIX application in which all calls to `malloc` were simply assumed to succeed. When I asked why, the programmer said, in essence, "if memory allocation fails, we're already in shit so deep that we've no chance of bailing out."

The standard C library is a notorious violator of the principle of separating return values from return codes and I shudder when I contemplate the debugging man-years that have been wasted on this. If you look at the evolution of the Windows API, you'll find a distinct trend towards better separation of return values and return codes. Once upon a time, for example, there was a function named `GetWindowOrg`, declared like this:

```
DWORD GetWindowOrg( HDC );
```

The return value stuffed two 16-bit coordinates into a `DWORD`. This left no good way to signal errors and created a tight coupling between the function and the size of GDI coordinates. Contrast this with its successor, `GetWindowOrgEx`:

```
BOOL GetWindowOrgEx( HDC, LPPOINT );
```

Here we have a clean separation between return code and return value, and changing the coordinate type from 16 to 32 to any number of bits becomes a simple matter of a recompile.

Exceptions

The C language doesn't have exception handling, except in the limited form provided by `setjmp` and `longjmp`, and in the form of language extensions to deal with Structured Exception Handling (SEH) under 32-bit Windows.

The C++ language does have exception handling. Aside from syntax, one major difference from `setjmp`/`longjmp` is the "unwinding of the stack." This means that the destructors of all stack-allocated objects are called before the exception handler is invoked, giving each stack frame a chance to clean up after itself. Another difference is that throwing a real exception invokes the first applicable handler it finds on the stack, rather than a specifically identified handler, as does `longjmp`.

Two-Stage Construction

C++ constructors lack return values. This is no accident. If they did, you'd have a problem with allocating arrays of objects — which element's constructor should be responsible for the return value?

The natural way to signal errors in a C++ constructor is by means of exceptions. This can be an inconvenience though — sometimes you actually want return codes.

A common solution to this conundrum is called *two-stage construction*. The constructor simply does nothing that might cause problems; instead, some method is called after construction to do the "real" initialization. Consider the MFC `CFile` class for example. `CFile` is designed to work both ways, depending on which constructor you use. One way is to use the default (i.e., parameterless) constructor, which does not open any files, followed by a call to the Open method, which returns an error code if it fails to open the specified file. The other way is to use a constructor that takes a file name; this constructor throws an exception if it fails to open the file.

There is no "right" or "wrong" here; the guiding principle to follow is this:

"Keep total program complexity to a minimum."

The `VersionInfo` class demonstrates yet another option. If the constructor fails, it sets an internal flag to indicate this and the application must call the auxiliary method `isValid` before actually using the instance.

Global Object Constructor Exceptions

What happens if you throw an exception from the construction of a global object — one at file scope? You can only catch it by getting compiler-dependent.

In the case of a Visual C++ program, your real entry point is not `WinMain`, but an `extern "C"` function called `WinMainCRTStartup` (or `wWinMainCRTStartup`, if you are a Unicode application). This function performs all the initialization required and then calls `WinMain` (or `wWinMain`, as the case may be). Among other things, it calls a function named `_initterm`, which walks a list of function pointers and calls them. The `_initterm` function is first called with a list of run-time library initializers, for example `_initstdio`, and then with a list of C++ constructors for global objects.

To catch an exception thrown during the construction of a global object, you must override `WinMainCRTStartup`, or its equivalent in other environments. If you don't need the C Runtime Library (CRT) and have no static instances of classes, this may actually be a good idea because it reduces the size of the executable and speeds up loading. Otherwise, it is a bad idea; you'd have to copy all the initialization code, and you'd have no guarantee that the next compiler release wouldn't break your code. As for porting to other compilers, that's out.

The TextEdit Exception Classes

(Discourse continues on page 106.)

Listing 6.1   `Exception.h`

```
/*
 * $Header: /Book/Exception.h 16    20.08.99 16:33 Petter $
 *
 * Declares the Exception class and its descendants.
 */

#pragma once

#include <winerror.h>
#include "String.h"
#include "trace.h"

#define INTERCEPT_SEH 1
```

The TextEdit Exception Classes

```cpp
/**
 * Functional code should not handle the generic Exception class,
 * only its descendants.
 */
class Exception {
public:

#ifdef _DEBUG
   Exception() { trace( _T( "Exception ctor\n" ) ); }
   virtual ~Exception() { trace( _T( "Exception dtor\n" ) ); }
#endif

   virtual String getDescr( void ) const = 0;
   //virtual LPCTSTR what( void ) const;
};

#if 1
#define what() getDescr().c_str()
#else
inline LPCTSTR Exception::what( void ) const {
   return getDescr().c_str();
}
#endif

class CancelException : public Exception {
public:
   virtual String getDescr( void ) const {
      return _T( "CancelException" );
   }
};

class NullPointerException : public Exception {
public:
   virtual String getDescr( void ) const {
      return _T( "NullPointerException" );
   }
};

#if INTERCEPT_SEH
```

```cpp
class sehException : public Exception {
public:
   virtual String getDescr( void ) const;
};

class InvalidHandleException : public sehException {
public:
   virtual String getDescr( void ) const;
};

class AccessViolationException : public sehException {
public:
   virtual String getDescr( void ) const;
};

class DivideByZeroException : public sehException {
public:
   virtual String getDescr( void ) const;
};

class StackOverflowException : public sehException {
public:
   virtual String getDescr( void ) const;
   static StackOverflowException& getStackOverflowException();
};

#endif // INTERCEPT_SEH

class MemoryException : public Exception {
public:
   virtual String getDescr( void ) const;
   static MemoryException& getMemoryException( void );
};

class WinException : public Exception {
protected:
   const DWORD m_dwErr; // Error code from winerror.h

protected:
   String m_strDescr;
```

```cpp
public:
   WinException(
      const String& strDescr, DWORD dwErr = GetLastError() );
   WinException( DWORD dwErr = GetLastError() );

   resetLastError( void ) const;

   virtual String getDescr( void ) const;
};

inline WinException::resetLastError( void ) const {

   SetLastError( m_dwErr );
}

String getError(
   const String& strDescr, DWORD dwErr = GetLastError() );

inline String getError( DWORD dwErr = GetLastError() ) {
   return getError( _T( "" ), dwErr );
}

class ComException : public WinException {
public:
   ComException( HRESULT hres );

   virtual String getDescr( void ) const;
};

inline ComException::ComException( HRESULT hres )
   : WinException( hres )
{
}

class SubclassException : public WinException {
public:
   virtual String getDescr( void ) const;
};
```

```cpp
#define DECLARE_SIMPLE( name, err ) \
   class name : public WinException {             \
   public:                                        \
      name( LPCTSTR pszDescr )                    \
         : WinException( pszDescr, err ) {};      \
      name( const String& strDescr )              \
         : WinException( strDescr, err ) {};      \
      virtual String getDescr( void ) const {     \
         return WinException::getDescr(); }       \
   };

DECLARE_SIMPLE( FileNotFoundException    , ERROR_FILE_NOT_FOUND    );
DECLARE_SIMPLE( PathNotFoundException    , ERROR_PATH_NOT_FOUND    );
DECLARE_SIMPLE( AccessDeniedException    , ERROR_ACCESS_DENIED     );
DECLARE_SIMPLE( SharingViolationException, ERROR_SHARING_VIOLATION );

class CommonDialogException : public WinException {
public:
   CommonDialogException( DWORD dwErr = CommDlgExtendedError() );
   virtual String getDescr( void ) const;
};

void throwException(
   const String& strDescr, DWORD dwErr = GetLastError() );

inline void throwException( DWORD dwErr = GetLastError() ) {
   throwException( _T( "" ), dwErr );
}

#define throwMemoryException() \
   throw MemoryException::getMemoryException()
```

Listing 6.2 Exception.cpp

```cpp
/*
 * $Header: /Book/Exception.cpp 16    20.08.99 16:33 Petter $
 */

#include "precomp.h"
#include "Exception.h"
```

```cpp
#include "trace.h"
#include "formatMessage.h"

#if INTERCEPT_SEH

String sehException::getDescr( void ) const {
   return _T( "Unknown System Exception" );
};

String DivideByZeroException::getDescr( void ) const {
   return _T( "Division by zero" );
};

String StackOverflowException::getDescr( void ) const {
   return _T( "Stack overflow" );
};

String InvalidHandleException::getDescr( void ) const {
   return _T( "Invalid handle" );
};

String AccessViolationException::getDescr( void ) const {
   return _T( "Access violation" );
};

static StackOverflowException theStackOverflowException;

StackOverflowException&
StackOverflowException::getStackOverflowException( void ) {
   return theStackOverflowException;
}

#endif // INTERCEPT_SEH

String getError( const String& strDescr, DWORD dwErr ) {

   String strError( strDescr );
   if ( !strDescr.empty() ) {
      strError += _T( "\n" );
   }
```

```cpp
      LPTSTR pszMsgBuf = 0;

#ifdef _DEBUG
   const DWORD dwLen =
#endif

      FormatMessage (
         FORMAT_MESSAGE_FROM_SYSTEM      |
         FORMAT_MESSAGE_ALLOCATE_BUFFER  |
         FORMAT_MESSAGE_IGNORE_INSERTS   ,
         0, dwErr,
         // LANGIDFROMLCID( GetThreadLocale() ),
         MAKELANGID( LANG_NEUTRAL, SUBLANG_DEFAULT ),
         reinterpret_cast< LPTSTR >( &pszMsgBuf ),
         0, 0 );

   if ( 0 == pszMsgBuf ) {
      pszMsgBuf = reinterpret_cast< LPTSTR >(
         LocalAlloc( LPTR, 50 * sizeof( TCHAR ) ) );
      assert( 0 != pszMsgBuf );
      wsprintf( pszMsgBuf, _T( "Unknown API error (%lu)" ), dwErr );
   }

   assert( 0 == dwLen || _tcsclen( pszMsgBuf ) == dwLen);
   strError += pszMsgBuf;
   LocalFree( pszMsgBuf );
   reset_pointer( pszMsgBuf );

#ifdef _DEBUG
   strError += formatMessage( _T( " [%1!u!]" ), dwErr );
#endif

   return strError;
}

WinException::WinException( const String& strDescr, DWORD dwErr )
   : m_dwErr( dwErr )
   , m_strDescr( strDescr )
```

```cpp
{
}

WinException::WinException( DWORD dwErr )
    : m_dwErr( dwErr )
    , m_strDescr( _T( "" ) )
{
}

String WinException::getDescr( void ) const {

    return getError( m_strDescr, m_dwErr );
}

String ComException::getDescr( void ) const {

    switch ( m_dwErr ) {
    case S_OK:
        return _T( "Success." );

    case S_FALSE:
        return _T( "The COM library is already initialized." );

    case REGDB_E_CLASSNOTREG:
        return
            _T( "A specified class is not registered in the " )
            _T( "registration database. Also can indicate that the " )
            _T( "type of server you requested in the CLSCTX " )
            _T( "enumeration is not registered or the values for " )
            _T( "the server types in the registry are corrupt." );

    case CLASS_E_NOAGGREGATION:
        return
            _T( "This class can't be created as part of an aggregate." );
    }

    return getError( _T( "Com Error" ), m_dwErr );
}
```

```cpp
String SubclassException::getDescr( void ) const {
    String strDescr(
       _T( "Internal error: Window subclassing failed\n\n" ) );
    strDescr += WinException::getDescr();
    return strDescr;
}

static MemoryException theMemoryException; // ERROR_OUTOFMEMORY

MemoryException& MemoryException::getMemoryException( void ) {
    return theMemoryException;
}

String MemoryException::getDescr( void ) const {
    return _T( "Out of memory" );
}

CommonDialogException::CommonDialogException( DWORD dwErr )
    : WinException( dwErr )
{
}

String CommonDialogException::getDescr( void ) const {

    static struct {
        DWORD    dwErr;
        LPCTSTR  pszErr;
    } const aErrorTable[] = {
        { CDERR_FINDRESFAILURE , _T( "Unable to find resource"    ) },
        { CDERR_NOHINSTANCE    , _T( "No HINSTANCE"               ) },
        { CDERR_INITIALIZATION , _T( "Initialization error"       ) },
        { CDERR_NOHOOK         , _T( "No hook"                    ) },
        { CDERR_LOCKRESFAILURE , _T( "Unable to lock resource"    ) },
        { CDERR_NOTEMPLATE     , _T( "No template"                ) },
        { CDERR_LOADRESFAILURE , _T( "Unable to load resource"    ) },
        { CDERR_STRUCTSIZE     , _T( "Wrong structure size"       ) },
        { CDERR_LOADSTRFAILURE , _T( "Unable to load string"      ) },
        { FNERR_BUFFERTOOSMALL , _T( "Buffer too small"           ) },
        { CDERR_MEMALLOCFAILURE, _T( "Memory allocation failure"  ) },
```

```
        { FNERR_INVALIDFILENAME,  _T( "Invalid file name"    ) },
        { CDERR_MEMLOCKFAILURE  , _T( "Unable to lock memory" ) },
        { FNERR_SUBCLASSFAILURE, _T( "Unable to subclass"    ) },
    };

    for ( int iErr = 0; iErr < dim( aErrorTable ); ++iErr ) {
        if ( aErrorTable[ iErr ].dwErr == m_dwErr ) {
            return aErrorTable[ iErr ].pszErr; //*** METHOD EXIT POINT
        }
    }

    return formatMessage(
        _T( "Unknown common dialog error %1!lu!" ), m_dwErr );
}

void throwException( const String& strDescr, DWORD dwErr ) {

    if ( ERROR_NOT_ENOUGH_MEMORY == dwErr ||
         ERROR_OUTOFMEMORY       == dwErr )
    {
        throw MemoryException::getMemoryException();
    }

    switch ( dwErr ) {
    case ERROR_FILE_NOT_FOUND: throw FileNotFoundException( strDescr );
    case ERROR_PATH_NOT_FOUND: throw PathNotFoundException( strDescr );
    case ERROR_ACCESS_DENIED : throw AccessDeniedException( strDescr );
#if 0
    case ERROR_SHARING_VIOLATION:
                        throw SharingViolationException( strDescr );
#endif
    }

    throw WinException( strDescr, dwErr );
}
```

Converting Allocation Failures to Exceptions

C++ programs usually call `operator new` rather than `malloc`. Behind the scenes, though, the typical `operator new` implementation calls `malloc` to actually allocate memory; `malloc`, in turn, may call on the operating system for help. At any rate, while the C++ standard mandates that an exception be thrown on failure, Microsoft's compiler returns a null pointer if the allocation request fails. As a result, much code is littered with checks such as this:

```
LPTSTR pszMyString = new TCHAR[ MAX_PATH ];
if ( 0 == pszMyString ) {
   // handle error
}
```

Luckily, you can make even Microsoft's `operator new` throw an exception on failure. The `_set_new_mode` function lets you decide whether an allocation failure should return zero or call an application-defined function; the `_set_new_handler` allows you to specify the function to call if an allocation fails. In this callback, you can do just about anything you like, such as throwing an exception. Just keep in mind that you may not have a lot of memory to play with!

Recovering from Errors

Some things you just can't do much about. If your stack is corrupted, for example, your chances of bailing out are slim indeed; this is the software equivalent of taking a sledgehammer to the computer. Most errors aren't that bad though, and your chances of a graceful recovery depend on your error-handling architecture.

Guiding principle in imperative form:

"Don't lose the user's data!"

If TextEdit has problems getting started, it doesn't matter too much. If we can inform the user of the cause before we call it quits, that's sufficient. If, however, we run into problems in the middle of saving the text file, we have to bend over backwards to recover.

The error handling architecture in TextEdit is somewhat akin to an onion. The outer skin of the onion is the `try/catch` block in `WinMain`. Exceptions that make it this far are fatal; the user is informed of the problem's cause via a message box and the application dies.

Going deeper into the onion, we find the main message loop, in the `Editor::run` method. Each message is dispatched in a `try/catch` block; everything caught here is recoverable. Whenever an exception makes it here, some operation has failed; perhaps the user should be informed.

As we approach the core of the onion, we come to the handling of individual messages and commands. Some messages are relatively unimportant; it doesn't really matter whether the `onMenuSelect` handler failed to set the text in the status bar. Others, such as the `onCommandSave` handler, are so critical that they handle all irregularities deep in their guts and only let exceptions float to the surface under the most unusual circumstances.

The onion has comparatively few layers. With exception-safe objects, it turns out that you don't need to catch exceptions all over the place; most are allowed to propagate through many levels.

Guiding principle for exception handling:

"Don't handle general exceptions in functional code."

That's the purview of architectural code. A corollary is that we need different exceptions for different problems; it's insufficient merely to use error codes. This is difficult in practice, because `winerror.h` defines thousands of error codes. Thus, in handling the `WinException`, functional code is allowed to catch it, check the code, and pass it on if the shoe didn't fit. Mostly, though, code that can actually recover from the problem is so close to it as to use `GetLastError` directly, and `WinException` is caught only to provide error reporting.

This rule has one exception: you may `catch` and re-`throw` an exception, provided you use it as you would a `finally` clause. The onion contains such emergency aid stations in various places — in the `Dialog` class, for example. It catches all exceptions, enables the parent window, and then re-`throw`s the exception. (An emergency aid station in an onion? I think my vegetable metaphor is breaking down...)

Microsoft PowerPoint got this right. My installation must be screwed up somehow; whenever I click on the font size combo box, PowerPoint cogitates for a while, then throws up a message box saying that an unexpected error has occurred and that I should save my work and restart PowerPoint. As soon as I acknowledge the message box, I can continue working as though nothing had happened. Annoying as this problem is, it beautifully demonstrates graceful recovery in the face of something Very Bad.

A down side of a completely integrated exception architecture is that it becomes hard to snatch a single class or function out of its context and reuse it somewhere else — you need to take all the exception baggage with you. Because of this, some general functions in TextEdit don't use all the facilities available. The `VersionInfo` class, for example, doesn't use TextEdit's `getModuleFileName` function, but relies instead on the underlying `GetModuleFileName`.

Structured Exception Handling and C++ Exceptions

Structured Exception Handling (SEH) is built into the Win32 operating systems. Windows throws system-level exceptions for a number of reasons, such as stack overflow, memory access violations, and divisions by zero. (TextEdit, by the way, automatically multiplies by zero to compensate for accidentally dividing by zero.) (Joke!)

To allow C and C++ programmers access to SEH, Microsoft defined language extensions in the form of __try, __catch and __finally keywords. Unfortunately, SEH is incompatible with C++ exception handling. It's OK to have both in the same program, but not in the same function.

Luckily, there's a solution: You can install a translator function to translate SEH exceptions into C++ exceptions. Windows calls the translator function with parameters describing the structured exception, enough to let you throw a C++ exception of your choice.

Listing 6.3   handlers.cpp

```cpp
/*
 * $Header: /Book/handlers.cpp  14     3.07.99 17:46 Petter $
 *
 * Defines translator for system-level exceptions
 * (SEH, Structured Exception Handling)
 * to C++ exceptions and the C++ allocation_failure handler.
 *
 * Exports: initThreadErrorHandling and exitThreadErrorHandling.
 * These functions set up and restore handlers on a per-thread basis.
 */

#include "precomp.h"
#include "handlers.h"
#include "os.h"
#include "Exception.h"
#include "trace.h"
#include <new.h>

// Parameters to _set_new_mode:
#define SNM_RETURN_NULL_ON_FAILURE  0
#define SNM_CALL_NEW_HANDLER        1

// This variable is allocated on a per thread basis,
// using TLS (Thread Local Storage):
PRIVATE __declspec( thread ) _se_translator_function
    s_tls_saved_se_translator = 0;

#if INTERCEPT_SEH

/**
 * This function translates SEH exceptions to C++ exceptions.
 * It is installed using _set_se_translator in
 * the initThreadErrorHandling function.
 */
void __cdecl se_translator(
    unsigned int uiCode, EXCEPTION_POINTERS *pE )
{
    trace( _T( "se_translator( %#x, %#x )\n" ),
```

```
            uiCode, pE->ExceptionRecord->ExceptionFlags );
      trace( _T( "                ( %#x, %#x )\n" ),
         pE->ExceptionRecord->ExceptionAddress,
         pE->ExceptionRecord->ExceptionCode );

      switch ( uiCode ) {
      case STATUS_INTEGER_DIVIDE_BY_ZERO:
         throw DivideByZeroException();

      case STATUS_STACK_OVERFLOW:
         throw StackOverflowException::getStackOverflowException();

      case STATUS_INVALID_HANDLE:
         throw InvalidHandleException();

      case STATUS_ACCESS_VIOLATION:
         throw AccessViolationException();

      case STATUS_NO_MEMORY:
         throwMemoryException();
      }

      throw sehException(); // Store uiCode, perhaps?
}

#endif // INTERCEPT_SEH

/**
 * This function gets called whenever malloc experiences a failure:
 */
PRIVATE void __cdecl allocation_failure( size_t size ) {

#ifdef _DEBUG
   // Calling trace here is not a good idea,
   // as we may be operating on limited resources.
   // Call OutputDebugString directly instead.
   static TCHAR szMsg[ 30 ] = { 0 };
   wsprintf( szMsg, _T( "allocation_failure: %d\n" ), size );
   OutputDebugString( szMsg );
#endif
```

```
        throwMemoryException();
        assert( false ); // Never gets here...
}

/**
 * Sets up memory allocation failure handling and
 * SEH translator for current thread.
 */
void initThreadErrorHandling( void ) {

#if INTERCEPT_SEH
    assert( 0 == s_tls_saved_se_translator );
    s_tls_saved_se_translator =
        _set_se_translator( se_translator );
#endif

    _set_new_handler( (_PNH) allocation_failure );
    _set_new_mode( SNM_CALL_NEW_HANDLER );
}

/**
 * Restores memory allocation failure handling and
 * original (if any) SEH translator for current thread.
 * This function may not crash!
 */
void exitThreadErrorHandling( void ) {

    __try {
        _set_new_mode( SNM_RETURN_NULL_ON_FAILURE );
        _set_new_handler( (_PNH) 0 );

#if INTERCEPT_SEH
        verify( se_translator ==
            _set_se_translator( s_tls_saved_se_translator ) );
#endif
    }
    __finally {
    }
}
```

Chapter 7

Off the Launch Pad

As with skinning a cat, there is more than one way to start a Win32 application. There are GUI ways and there are console ways; some of them have to do with *shell integration*, a concept that is also touched in Chapter 20.

The starting of an application has two sides — the outside and the inside. This chapter is mostly concerned with the inside, in particular, all the possible values of the `pszCmdLine` parameter to `WinMain`. This is not as trivial as it sounds.

Listing 7.1   Exploring the Command Line

The following simple program proved helpful for exploring the results of various actions:

```
int WinMain( HINSTANCE, HINSTANCE, LPSTR pszCmdLine, int ) {
    MessageBox( 0, pszCmdLine, "Arguments", MB_OK );
}
```

Click, Drag, and Drop

In the following, I assume that the GUI shell is the Windows Explorer. While other shells are certainly possible, they'd better deliver similar functionality if they want to survive in the market place.

TextEdit can be started directly in several ways. After selecting the TextEdit icon, you can double-click, right-click, and select Open from the context menu, or hit the Enter key. The result is in any case that the shell calls `CreateProcess`, and eventually TextEdit's `WinMain` is invoked.

The `pszCmdLine` parameter is now empty. In a situation like this, Notepad lets you edit an "untitled" file, one that exists in memory only. TextEdit, on the other hand, has a conceptual model that supposedly works directly on files — there is no concept of a separate memory image. Although this is an illusion, it means that untitled files are out — we must create a suitably named file in a suitable location. This is handled by the `createNewFile` function in `createNewFile.cpp`.

A user's default data directory can be retrieved using the `SHGetSpecialFolderLocation` function with the `CSIDL_PERSONAL` parameter. On my machine, this defaults to `C:\WinNT\Profiles\`*myUserName*`\Personal`. Being inside the system directory, this doesn't strike me as a particularly good place to store user data, so the TextEdit installation program allows users to select a different default directory. This location is maintained through the Options dialog. (Discourse continues on page 116.)

Listing 7.2 `createNewFile.cpp`

```cpp
/*
 * $Header: /Book/createNewFile.cpp 10    20.08.99 16:33 Petter $
 */

#include "precomp.h"
#include "createNewFile.h"
#include "Exception.h"
#include "AutoHandle.h"
#include "AutoShellObject.h"
#include "formatMessage.h"
#include "resource.h"
#include "persistence.h"
#include "utils.h"
#include "fileUtils.h"
#include "winUtils.h"

/**
 * Callback function for SHBrowseForFolder.
 * If this continues to be used several places, make it common!
 */
PRIVATE int CALLBACK bff_callback(
    HWND hwnd, UINT uMsg, LPARAM lParam, LPARAM lpData )
{
    switch ( uMsg ) {
    case BFFM_INITIALIZED:
```

```
         if ( 0 != lpData ) {
            SNDMSG( hwnd, BFFM_SETSELECTION, 1, lpData );
         }
         break;

      case BFFM_SELCHANGED:
         adjustDefaultButtonStyle( GetDlgItem( hwnd, IDOK ) );
         break;
      }

      return 0;
}

/**
 * If this function fails, there is no place whatsoever to put a file!
 */
String getDefaultPath( void ) {

   return getSpecialFolderLocation( CSIDL_PERSONAL );
}

PRIVATE String getNewDocumentPath( HWND hwndParent ) {

   const String strMessage = loadString( IDS_FIND_FOLDER );
   TCHAR szDisplayName[ MAX_PATH ] = { 0 };
   BROWSEINFO browseInfo = {
      hwndParent, 0, szDisplayName, strMessage.c_str(),
      BIF_RETURNONLYFSDIRS | BIF_STATUSTEXT,
      bff_callback,
   };

   String strNewDocumentPath;
   AutoShellObject< ITEMIDLIST > pidl(
      SHBrowseForFolder( &browseInfo ) );
   if ( (ITEMIDLIST *) 0 != pidl ) {
      strNewDocumentPath = getPathFromIDList( pidl );
   } else {
      trace( _T( "No default directory\n" ) );
      throw CancelException();
   }
```

```
      return strNewDocumentPath;
}

// TODO -- check for writability of directory/disk!
String createNewFile(
   HWND hwndParent,
   create_new_file_args what_kind,
   HANDLE hIn,
   LPCTSTR pszPath,
   LPCTSTR pszTitle )
{
   String strNewPath;
   if ( file_for_copy == what_kind ) {
      strNewPath = pszPath;
   } else {
      strNewPath = getDocumentPath( getDefaultPath().c_str() );
      if ( strNewPath.empty() ) {
         strNewPath = getNewDocumentPath( hwndParent );
      }
      assert( 0 < strNewPath.length() );

      if ( !CreateDirectory( strNewPath.c_str(), 0 ) ) {
         const DWORD dwErr = GetLastError();
         if ( NOERROR != dwErr && ERROR_ALREADY_EXISTS != dwErr ) {
            throwException(
               _T( "Unable to create directory" ), dwErr );
         }
      }
      setDocumentPath( strNewPath.c_str() );
   }
   addPathSeparator( &strNewPath );

   DWORD dwErr = NOERROR + 1; // Anything but NOERROR.
   for ( DWORD dwIndex = 1; NOERROR != dwErr; ++dwIndex ) {

      static int anStringID[ 3 ][ 2 ] = {
         { IDS_NEW_FILE_1, IDS_NEW_FILE_N },
         { IDS_STDIN_1   , IDS_STDIN_N    },
```

```
            { IDS_COPY_1   , IDS_COPY_N     },
    };

    const String strFmt =
        loadString( anStringID[ what_kind ][ 1 < dwIndex ] );
    String strNewFile( strNewPath );
    strNewFile += formatMessage( strFmt, dwIndex, pszTitle );
    if ( file_for_copy != what_kind ) {
        strNewFile += getDefaultExtension();
    }

    SetLastError( NOERROR );   // For the benefit of Windows 95
    AutoHandle hNewFile( CreateFile( strNewFile.c_str(),
        GENERIC_WRITE, FILE_SHARE_NONE, 0,
        CREATE_NEW, FILE_ATTRIBUTE_NORMAL, 0 ) );
    dwErr = GetLastError();
    if ( INVALID_HANDLE_VALUE != hNewFile ) {
        assert( NOERROR == dwErr );
#ifdef _DEBUG
        if ( NOERROR != dwErr ) {
            messageBox( hwndParent, MB_OK | MB_ICONERROR,
                _T( "Can't create %1 (%2!d!)\n'cause...: %3" ),
                strNewFile.c_str(),
                hNewFile,
                getError( dwErr ).c_str() );
        }
#endif
        if ( 0 != hIn ) {
            copyFile( hIn, hNewFile );
        }
        strNewPath = strNewFile;
        break; //*** LOOP EXIT POINT
    } else {
        switch ( dwErr ) {
        case ERROR_FILE_EXISTS:
        case ERROR_ALREADY_EXISTS:
            break;
        case ERROR_FILE_NOT_FOUND:
        case ERROR_PATH_NOT_FOUND:
```

```
                default:
                    throwException(
                        _T( "Unable to create new file" ), dwErr );
                }
            }
        }
        assert( NOERROR              == dwErr ||
                ERROR_ALREADY_EXISTS == dwErr ||
                ERROR_FILE_EXISTS    == dwErr );

        return strNewPath;
    }
```

If you wish to edit the file `sample.txt`, you can drag an icon representing the file onto the TextEdit icon. This time, `pszCmdLine` points to the full path of `sample.txt` and TextEdit opens the file. Most sample programs handle this straightforward case correctly.

You can also drag multiple files onto the TextEdit icon. This is where it starts getting moderately messy; the shell strings all the file names together with a space between them:

```
c:\sample1.txt c:\sample2.txt
```

Now what? Because TextEdit is an SDI application, we can only open one file per instance. Unless you want to get bizarre, the only answer is to start more TextEdit instances. The primary instance of TextEdit (the one invoked by the shell) parses the parameter list and takes the first file name for its own. Then it starts a new instance of itself, passing the remaining file name parameters to the new instance. This starts a cascade of recursive invocations that bottoms out when the final instance gets but one file name, poor thing.

Notepad treats the whole command line as a single file name, which may lead to the problem shown in Figure 7.1:

Figure 7.1 Notepad in action. Parsing two consecutive file names as one doesn't always work.

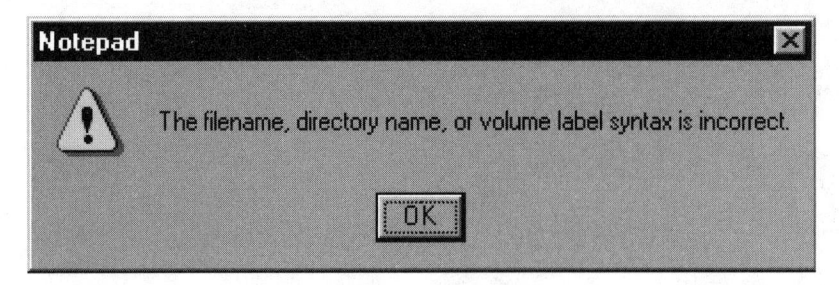

The problem here appears to be the second colon, which makes the file name syntactically invalid. Try it from the command line, omitting the offending syntax:

```
notepad sample1.txt sample2.txt
```

Figure 7.2 Notepad in action again. Two consecutive file names constitute a valid file name, but the file does not exist.

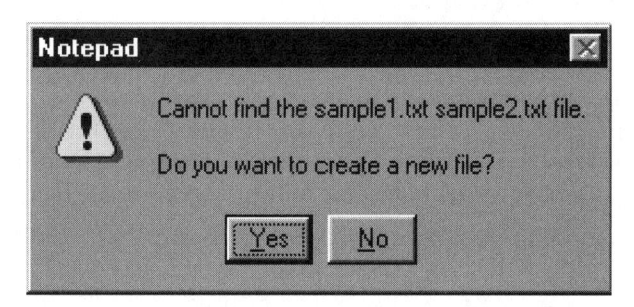

This message box may not look too bright, but Notepad's strategy actually turns out fine if you forget to quote a file name containing spaces. TextEdit also tries this approach before considering each argument as a separate file name.

Shell Integration

These are the direct ways you can start the app from a GUI shell; they work with all applications and all data files. If the shell knows that TextEdit is associated with a specific file type (such as .txt), other possibilities open up.

You can open a text file by double-clicking its icon. The shell looks up the application association with .txt files (and if that application is still Notepad, you and I are no longer on speaking terms) and starts the program, passing the file name in pszCmdLine.

You can do this with multiple files too. Select a bunch of files, and press Enter. From the user's point of view, this is much the same as dragging one or more files onto the TextEdit icon. What happens behind the scenes is quite different: instead of passing all the file names to a single TextEdit instance, the shell starts one instance of TextEdit for each file opened.

There's another difference: if you drag text files onto the TextEdit icon, the file names sent to TextEdit are converted to the short 8.3 form, if necessary. If it didn't, any file names with spaces would screw things up. The up side of this is that we don't have to worry about spaces in the file names when parsing the command string. The down side is that we need to convert all file names to their long forms before displaying them to the user.

If you Open a bunch of text files, the file names sent to TextEdit are in their long form. Because long file names may contain spaces, each file name *must* be enclosed in double quotes. If not, TextEdit will assume that there are multiple file names on the command line. The shell does not put on the quotes for you; you have to specify this in the registry entries, e.g.:

```
[HKEY_CLASSES_ROOT\txtfile\shell\open\command]
@="\"C:\\Program Files\\TextEdit\\TextEdit.exe\" \"%1\""
```

Notepad's registry entries neither have nor need the quotes, by the way, as Notepad interprets the command line as a single file name anyhow.

I shall describe the registry in more detail in later chapters.

The shell also supports printing. If the right entries are set in the registry, the shell displays a Print command on the context menu whenever you right-click sample.txt. The Print command starts TextEdit with the following pszCmdLine:

```
/p "c:\sample.txt"
```

It is our responsibility to recognize the /p switch and to act appropriately.

Alternatively, you can drag sample.txt to a printer icon. This results in a printto command, which is a little more complicated — it is taken as an order to use a specific printer, rather than the default printer. The printto command has the following general form

```
/pt <file_name> <printer_name> <driver_name> <port_name>
```

Here is a sample pszCmdLine:

```
/pt "c:\sample.txt" "HP DeskJet 600" "RASD.DLL" "LPT1:"
```

If you use Shell integration to Print multiple files, the shell starts a new TextEdit instance for each, so we need not worry about multiple /p or /pt switches.

Another shell integration concept is the SendTo folder. You don't need to mess with the registry to use it; just create a shortcut to TextEdit.exe in the SendTo folder. This adds a "TextEdit" entry to the "Send To" submenu of the Explorer's context menu. The result of using the Send To command is the same as when you drag tiles onto the TextEdit icon, i.e., a single application instance receives a string of one or more 8.3 file names separated by white space.

Windows NT maintains one SendTo folder per user.

GUI Summary

To sum up, the GUI shell can give us the following command lines:
- Empty
- One or more 8.3 file names separated by spaces
- A single long file name enclosed in double quotes
- The switch /p followed by a long file name enclosed in double quotes
- The switch /pt followed by a long file name enclosed in double quotes, a printer name, a printer driver name, and a port name. The port name, by the way, is a relic from Win16, no longer used.

The Console Connection

Let us leave the GUI shell for a while, and look instead at command line interpreters, or shells. The standard command shell for Windows 9x is command.com, while the one for Windows NT is cmd.exe. For our purposes, their behaviors are similar enough to ignore their differences.

You can start TextEdit by typing textedit at the command prompt. If you start a console program this way, the command shell waits patiently until the program has finished executing. A console program is marked /SUBSYSTEM:CONSOLE at link time. TextEdit, however, is marked /SUBSYSTEM:WINDOWS at link time, so the command shell returns to the prompt immediately after calling CreateProcess.

As with the GUI shell, you can pass one or more file names as parameters to TextEdit. Any file names that contain spaces should be enclosed in quotes, but aside from that, you're free to mix long and short, quoted and unquoted forms. The command line is total chaos compared with the GUI shell.

> This illustrates one of the great advantages of the GUI paradigm, namely the use of constraints. Rather than typing a command, you must select it from a menu; rather than typing a file name, you are forced to select it from a list. Typos are no longer possible, and one source of errors is eliminated. The GUI constraint paradigm also illustrates the best possible form of "error handling:" redesign the application so that the source of the error goes away.

What happens if you type something like "TextEdit *.txt"? That depends on the command processor you are using. UNIX command shells expand wildcards automatically, resulting in a command line of, say, "textedit sample1.txt sample2.txt." Unfortunately, neither command.com nor cmd.exe do wildcard expansion, so TextEdit must deal with this on its own.

On the face of it, this would seem to require special treatment of arguments with wildcards, but this isn't so. In the first place, if you treat sample.txt as a wildcard pattern and do a search using FindFileFirst and FindFileNext, you will find exactly one matching file, namely sample.txt. We can, in other words, treat all arguments as wildcard patterns without getting into trouble.

Even better, we can sidestep the whole issue by linking with setargv.obj, which gives us wildcard expansion for free. (Most compilers come with a similar relocatable object file, though it might have another name, such as wildargs.obj.)

If no files match, the program is passed the exact parameter string as typed, i.e., "*.txt".

If you try passing *.txt to Notepad, it complains that it "cannot open the '*.txt' file." This happens no matter how many files match the pattern. Notepad also tells you "to make sure that a disk is in the drive specified," and the user is left wondering whether the program has suffered brain damage. Oxygen deprivation, perhaps. The least we can do is to recognize the alleged file name as a wildcard pattern and report that no matching files were found.

What about long versus short file names? That doesn't require any special treatment either. The function GetLongPathName converts short names to long names, but if it is fed a long name, it will simply return that name. In other words: all file names — long and short — may safely be passed through GetLongPathName.

The one unfortunate thing about GetLongPathName is that it's only available on Windows 98 and Windows 2000. Consequently, TextEdit has its own function, called getLongPathName, defined in Listing 7.3, getLongPathName.cpp.

A different, and possibly better, approach to the implementation of getLongPathName would have been to apply FindFirstFile to each path element in turn.

Listing 7.3   getLongPathName.cpp

```cpp
/*
 * $Header: /Book/getLongPathName.cpp 10    20.08.99 16:33 Petter $
 */

#include "precomp.h"
#include "AutoComReference.h"
#include "AutoShellObject.h"
#include "utils.h"
#include "os.h"
#include <shlobj.h>

// LATER: Create a Filename class; handle named streams properly.
String getLongPathName( const String& strShort ) {

   String strLong;

   AutoComReference< IShellFolder > pShellFolder;
   HRESULT hres = SHGetDesktopFolder( &pShellFolder );
   if ( SUCCEEDED( hres ) ) {

#ifdef UNICODE
#define wszShort const_cast< LPWSTR >( strShort.c_str() )
#else
      PATHNAMEW wszShort = { 0 };
      multiByteToWideChar( strShort.c_str(), wszShort );
#endif

      ULONG ulEaten = 0;
      ULONG ulAttributes = 0;
      AutoShellObject< ITEMIDLIST > pidl;
      hres = pShellFolder->ParseDisplayName( HWND_DESKTOP, 0,
         wszShort, &ulEaten, &pidl, &ulAttributes );
      if ( SUCCEEDED( hres ) ) {
         strLong = getPathFromIDList( pidl );
      }
   }

   // In case of failure, keep the short name:
```

```
    if ( !SUCCEEDED( hres ) || strLong.empty() ) {
       strLong = strShort;
    }

    return strLong;
}
```

Wild cards require no special treatment, nor do long and short file names. This illustrates a design principle:

"If possible, avoid special cases."

Special cases require more code; in particular, they require branching. This makes testing that much harder and gives bugs additional opportunities to creep in. Bugs abound anyhow; why invite more?

Nevertheless, one particular kind of file does require special treatment: the shortcut. Win32 "shortcuts" are not real links, merely files with a .lnk extension. The file system does not resolve shortcuts; the Explorer does. If you double-click a shortcut, the Explorer resolves it before handing you the file, so no special handling is necessary. Not so the command-line shell; you're fed the .lnk file, and that's that.

This is all handled by the function resolveName (see Listing 7.4, resolveName.cpp); its job is to figure out if the file is a link, and if so, to figure out which file the link references. All files pass through resolveName; the special handling is hidden on the inside. The inside, by the way, uses the IShellLink COM interface to resolve the link.

Resolving links is an issue with the Open common dialog as well. This dialog is discussed in Chapter 14.

Listing 7.4 resolveName.cpp

```
/*
 * $Header: /Book/resolveName.cpp 10   3.07.99 17:46 Petter $
 */

#include "precomp.h"
#include "os.h"
#include "utils.h"
#include "trace.h"

#include "AutoComReference.h"

/**
 * If pszSrc refers to a link, pszDst will be the file that
 * the link refers to. If pszSrc does not refer to a link,
```

```
 * pszDst will be equal to pszSrc. It is OK if these point
 * to the same buffer. pszDst should have a length of at least
 * MAX_PATH + 1 characters.
 */
bool resolveName( LPTSTR pszDst, LPCTSTR pszSrc ) {

    assert( isGoodStringPtr( pszDst ) );
    assert( isGoodStringPtr( pszSrc ) );

    PATHNAME szFullPathName = { 0 };
    LPTSTR pszFilePart = 0;
    const DWORD dwChars = GetFullPathName(
        pszSrc, dim( szFullPathName ), szFullPathName, &pszFilePart );
    if ( 0 < dwChars ) {
        pszSrc = szFullPathName;
    }

    if ( pszDst != pszSrc ) {
        _tcscpy( pszDst, pszSrc ); // assume failure, use org file name
    }

    bool isShortcut = false;
    try {
        // Get a pointer to the IShellLink interface.
        AutoComReference< IShellLink >
            psl( CLSID_ShellLink, IID_IShellLink );
        AutoComReference< IPersistFile >
            ppf( IID_IPersistFile, psl );

        PATHNAMEW wsz = { 0 };

#ifdef UNICODE
        _tcscpy( wsz, pszSrc );
#else
        multiByteToWideChar( pszSrc, wsz );
#endif

        // Load the shortcut. Fails if non-existens or non-link.
        // Succeeds if empty file, so we check for this below.
```

```
            HRESULT hres = ppf->Load( wsz, STGM_READ );
            if ( !SUCCEEDED( hres ) ) {
               assert( E_FAIL == hres );
            } else {
               // Resolve the link.
               hres = psl->Resolve( HWND_DESKTOP, SLR_ANY_MATCH );
               if ( SUCCEEDED( hres ) ) {
                  // Get the path to the link target.
                  PATHNAME szGotPath = { 0 };
                  WIN32_FIND_DATA wfd = { 0 };
                  psl->GetPath( szGotPath, MAX_PATH, &wfd, SLGP_SHORTPATH );

                  // Happens if file not found.
                  if ( 0 != szGotPath[ 0 ] ) {
                     isShortcut = true;
                     _tcscpy( pszDst, szGotPath );
                  }
               }
            }
         }
         catch ( const ComException& x ) {
            trace( _T( "resolveName: ComException: %s\n" ), x.what() );
         }

         return isShortcut;
      }
```

Consider the following command line:

```
C> textedit sample1.txt sample2.txt /p sample3.txt sample4.txt
```

Should we print all the files, or only the one immediately following the /p switch, or all the files following the /p switch? Or should we disallow the whole command line on grounds of silliness?

Handling all possible variations in a reasonable way requires unreasonable contortions. TextEdit does allow the invocation, by printing all the files. Any other interpretation would be needlessly complex, both for the user and the programmer.

File Not Found

What if a file doesn't exist? There are several ways to handle this, and Notepad is quite sensible about it — Notepad asks the user if it should create a new file by the given name. TextEdit extends this a bit: it explains that the file does not exist and the user is presented with the following choices:

- Create the file as named.
- Browse for an existing file, or just to get a different name and location for a new file.
- Exit TextEdit.

Figure 7.3   **TextEdit can't find a file. You may create a new file or browse for an existing file.**

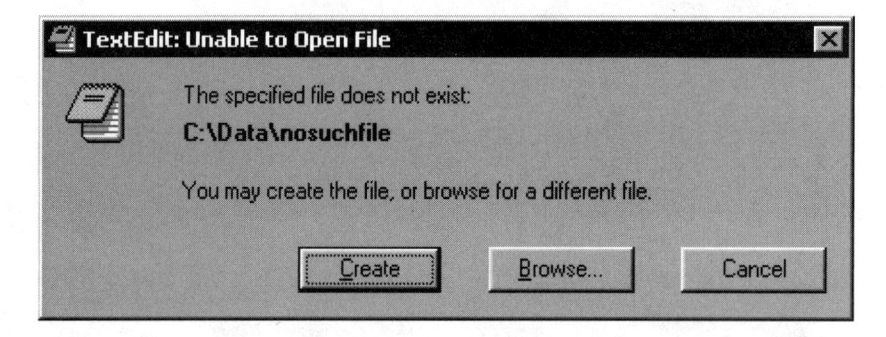

If the file name contains wildcard characters, the procedure is slightly different, as you can't create a file with wildcard characters in the file name. TextEdit explains that no matching files were found, and goes on to explain what a wildcard character actually is.

Figure 7.4   **No files match a wildcard pattern. Because some users will be unfamiliar with wildcards, the message box explains the concept. The explanation is not so intrusive as to bother power users.**

From there, the choices are as previously mentioned, except that creating the file as named is obviously out of the question.

Even if a file does exist, there are potential problems. The user may have limited access rights, or perhaps the file has been locked by a different application. Chapter 12 deals with this.

Read-Only

A file can be read-only in many ways, some more permanent than others:
- The read-only file attribute is set
- The file resides on a CD-ROM
- The file resides on a write-protected floppy disk
- The user has no access or read-only access. This can happen even on a Windows 9x system, if you're connected to a network, or if another application has locked the file.

In other words, the file might be read-only or the file's location might be read-only. Or not even read...

Other Anomalies

What happens if you double-click `sample.txt` while you are already editing the file with TextEdit? We have two possibilities — either we open the file in a second instance of TextEdit, or we bring the first instance to the top. Notepad takes the first route, which is a reasonable one for a traditional program. This paradigm has caused endless confusion and heartache among users that never realized they had five letters to grandma open at once. Besides, it fits badly (to put it mildly) with the unified file model, so TextEdit takes the second route. Before opening `sample.txt`, it checks whether the file is already open in a previous instance of TextEdit. If so, that instance is brought to the top, and the new instance quietly terminates. This is handled by `activateOldInstance` (see Listing 7.5, `activateOldInstance.cpp`).

Listing 7.5 `activateOldInstance.cpp`

```
/*
 * $Header: /Book/activateOldInstance.cpp 11 20.08.99 16:33 Petter $
 *
 * activateOldInstance has one weakness -- it will only catch
 * "real" instances, which have an editing window open. If a
 * previous instance was started with the /p switch, we won't
 * catch it here.
 */

#include "precomp.h"
#include "activateOldInstance.h"
#include "main_class.h"
#include "winUtils.h"
#include "addAtom.h"
#include "resource.h"
```

```
/**
 * This struct is used to pass information to the enumProc below.
 * We use an ATOM rather than a string to identify the document,
 * as strings can't be sent across Win32 process boundaries.
 * Discusion: WM_COPYDATA?
 */
struct EnumStruct {
    HWND hwnd;
    ATOM aDocName;
};

/**
 * Callback function for EnumWindows.
 */
PRIVATE BOOL CALLBACK enumProc( HWND hwnd, LPARAM lParam ) {

    if ( isClass( hwnd, MAIN_CLASS ) ) {
        EnumStruct *pEnumStruct =
            reinterpret_cast< EnumStruct * >( lParam );
        DWORD dwResult = 0;
        const LRESULT lResult = SendMessageTimeout(
            hwnd, WM_APP, 0, pEnumStruct->aDocName,
            SMTO_ABORTIFHUNG, 3000, &dwResult );
        if ( 0 != lResult && 0 != dwResult ) {
            pEnumStruct->hwnd = hwnd;
            return FALSE; // Stop enumerating windows.
        }
    }
    return TRUE;         // Continue enumerating windows.
}

/**
 * Loop over all existing TextEdit instances
 * and ask if they have this document:
 */
bool activateOldInstance( LPCTSTR pszPath, bool bPrinting ) {

    PATHNAME szPath = { 0 };
    const DWORD dwLength =
        GetShortPathName( pszPath, szPath, dim( szPath ) );
```

```
    if ( 0 == dwLength || dim( szPath ) < dwLength ) {
        return false;
    }
    assert( dwLength == _tcsclen( szPath ) );

    ATOM aDocName = globalAddAtom( szPath );
    if ( 0 != aDocName ) {
        EnumStruct enumStruct = { 0, aDocName };
        EnumWindows( enumProc,
            reinterpret_cast< LPARAM >( &enumStruct ) );
        verify( 0 == GlobalDeleteAtom( aDocName ) );
        if ( IsWindow( enumStruct.hwnd ) ) {
            HWND hwndToActivate = GetLastActivePopup( enumStruct.hwnd );
            verify( SetForegroundWindow( hwndToActivate ) );
            if ( bPrinting ) {
                FORWARD_WM_COMMAND(
                    enumStruct.hwnd, ID_FILE_PRINT, 0, 0, PostMessage );
            }
            return true;
        }
    }

    return false;
}
```

Conflicts and problems are still possible, of course — the file might be open in a different program, or the user may rename or delete the file while we're editing. The file may reside on a removable volume that is removed, or on a network server that just crashed.

Multiple instances of the same file on a command line don't cause problems; this is handled automatically.

Command-Line Piping

Consider the following command line:

```
C> dir | textedit
```

Wouldn't it be nice if the output from the `dir` command were to appear in TextEdit? This was not a viable proposition under Win16, but it's dead easy under Win32. The following call works even for GUI programs:

```
HANDLE hIn = GetStdHandle( STD_INPUT_HANDLE );
```

To stay in character, TextEdit must of course create a file in which to keep the standard input. This is handled analogously to creating a new file, by the same function, `createNewFile` (Listing 7.2, `createNewFile.cpp`).

Mixing file name parameters with piping works just fine; the following will edit both `sample.txt` and the output from the `dir` command, in two separate instances of TextEdit:

```
C> dir | textedit sample.txt
```

If you wish to print a file from the command line, this is one convoluted way of doing it:

```
C> type sample.txt | textedit /p
```

Command-line pipes are only for experts such as thee and me — a beginner won't even realize the capability is there. Power users will love it, though, and don't forget that beginners and intermediates rely on experts for advice on what software to buy. Cater to your power users!

Drag and Drop Revisited

So far, we've talked of dragging one or more text file icons onto the TextEdit icon. You can also drag a text file icon onto a running instance of TextEdit. TextEdit identifies itself as capable of handling the `WM_DROPFILES` message by calling `DragAcceptFiles` during main window creation, so the Explorer will happily send us a `WM_DROPFILES` message. In response, TextEdit will open the dropped file in place of the current file.

What should we do if somebody drops multiple files on us? That is actually a somewhat thorny problem. For an MDI application, it is perfectly natural to open multiple files, but for an SDI application, this would be a distinctly unnatural act.

Notepad ignores all the files but one, which is certainly a reasonable design decision. Another possibility would be to string all the files together into a composite. This is perhaps the most "natural" action possible for an SDI application, but really too bizarre for serious consideration.

What TextEdit actually does is open one of the files in the existing window, and start new instances for all the others. This is a conceptually imperfect solution, but it's the best I can think of.

Handling the `WM_DROPFILES` message involves two functions: `DragQueryFile` and `DragFinish`. The handler can be found in `mainwnd.cpp`, and it looks like this:

```
LOCAL void onDropFiles( HWND hwnd, HDROP hdrop ) {
    const UINT DRAGQUERY_NUMFILES = (UINT) -1;
    const int nFiles = DragQueryFile(
        hdrop, DRAGQUERY_NUMFILES, 0, 0 );
    for ( int iFile = nFiles - 1; 0 <= iFile; --iFile ) {
        PATHNAME szDragFile = { 0 };
        verify( 0 < DragQueryFile(
            hdrop, iFile, szDragFile, dim( szDragFile ) ) );
        if ( 0 == iFile ) {
```

```
            getEditor( hwnd )->openFile( szDragFile );
        } else {
            startInstance( szDragFile, SW_SHOW );
        }
    }
    DragFinish( hdrop );
}
```

If the `DragQueryFile` function is invoked with the second parameter equal to –1, the function just returns the number of files dropped; otherwise, the second parameter is an index.

Additional Switches

TextEdit understands several other switches. Some, such as `/min` and `/max`, are conveniences, while others, such as `/setup`, allow the single executable to function in several completely different ways. The complete list of command-line switches is summarized in Table 7.1.

Table 7.1 Command-line switches.

Option	Explanation
/boot	Checks the registry for files marked "running," and starts a TextEdit instance for each.
/edit	Forces use of the standard edit widget rather than the rich edit widget. This switch is only available in debug builds.
/last	Opens previous file (MRU 1).
/min	Start TextEdit minimized.
/max	Start TextEdit maximized.
/p /print	Print, showing the print dialog.
/pt /printto	Print to a specific printer, don't show the print dialog.
/setup	Start the TextEdit installation and maintenance subsystem. A TextEdit installation disk should include either `Setup.exe.lnk` (a shortcut to `TextEdit.exe /setup`) or a TextEdit executable renamed to `setup.exe` or `install.exe`.

Should we allow the hyphen to signal command-line switches? The hyphen, or minus sign, is the standard option signal on UNIX, and many DOS and Windows programs accept it in addition to the slash. There is only one hitch — it is perfectly legitimate to start a file name with a hyphen.

No conflict arises when TextEdit is started from the GUI shell. Any hyphens are certain to be somewhere inside the path name, and so won't be recognized as the start of a switch. From the command line, however, it is necessary to say something like `textedit .\-myFile.txt` rather than `textedit -myFile.txt`. Otherwise, TextEdit gets confused by the `myFile` switch, which it has never heard of.

To confuse things further, the slash is a perfectly good separator of path elements. It's only the internal commands in `COMMAND.COM` and `CMD.EXE` that think otherwise; the file system is happy with slashes going either way.

In TextEdit, both the slash and the hyphen signal a switch, but all unrecognized switches are assumed to be file names. In `init.cpp`, you will find some vestigial code that warns against unrecognized options. I removed that code after writing the above couple of paragraphs and TextEdit will now happily accept both `/myDirectory/-myFile` and `-myFile` as arguments.

All this confusion has two drawbacks. A misspelled switch is treated as a file name, and files with option names need some path decoration on the command line (e.g., the file `-max` must be specified as `.\-max` or `./-max`). Even more confusing, specifying `textedit *` in a directory that only contains the file `-max`, will result in the editing of a new file in a maximized window, hardly what was intended. (Specifying `textedit ./*` works, though.)

We live in an imperfect world and can only do the best we can. These drawbacks are not serious enough to lose sleep over.

Accessing the Command Line

I've talked a lot about `pszCmdLine` in this chapter, but we don't actually use it. We could, but we would then have to parse it, something the C Runtime Library (CRT) is perfectly capable of doing for us.

The `main` function of a console application gets its parameters in predigested form, with `argc` giving the number of arguments, and `argv` giving the arguments themselves. This parameter parsing does more than just find all the white space; it also handles quoted arguments correctly. It turns out that `argc` and `argv` are accessible from `/SUBSYSTEM:WINDOWS` programs, too, through the global CRT variables `__argc` and `__argv`.

The `ArgumentList` class is in charge of command lines. In addition to wrapping access to `__argc` and `__argv`, it handles the command line switches (options).

Listing 7.6 ArgumentList.h

```
/*
 * $Header: /Book/ArgumentList.h 12    5.09.99 13:06 Petter $
 *
 * Command-line parsing.
 *
 * The command line parameter to the ArgumentList constructor is
 * unused; it's left in for the benefit of implementations that
 * don't have access to argc/argv and need to do their own parsing.
 */

#pragma once
```

```cpp
#include "String.h"
#include "AutoArray.h"

class ArgumentList {
private:
   int       m_argc;
   AutoArray< LPCTSTR > m_argv;

#ifdef _DEBUG
   bool isValid( void ) const;
#endif // _DEBUG

public:
   ArgumentList( LPCTSTR /* pszCmdLine */ );

   int getNumArgs( void ) const;
   LPCTSTR getArg( int nArg ) const;
   LPCTSTR getArg( int nArg, bool bConsume = false );
   bool isOption( int nArg ) const; // ??
   bool hasOption( LPCTSTR pszOption );
   void consume( int nArg );
};

inline int ArgumentList::getNumArgs( void ) const {

   assert( isValid() );
   return m_argc;
}

inline LPCTSTR ArgumentList::getArg( int nArg ) const {

   assert( isValid() );
   assert( 0 <= nArg && nArg < m_argc );
   return m_argv[ nArg ];
}

inline LPCTSTR ArgumentList::getArg( int nArg, bool bConsume ) {
```

```
    assert( isValid() );
    assert( 0 <= nArg && nArg < m_argc );
    const LPCTSTR pszArgument = m_argv[ nArg ];
    if ( bConsume ) {
        consume( nArg );
    }
    return pszArgument;
}

/**
 * An argument is considered an option
 * if preceeded by a slash or a minus.
 * The point of call can choose to consider unrecognized
 * options to be file names. TextEdit does this.
 */
inline bool ArgumentList::isOption( int nArg ) const {

    assert( isValid() );
    assert( 0 <= nArg && nArg < m_argc );

    LPCTSTR const pszArg = getArg( nArg );
    return _T( '/' ) == *pszArg || _T( '-' ) == *pszArg;
}
```

Listing 7.7   ArgumentList.cpp

```
/*
 * $Header: /Book/ArgumentList.cpp 9      20.08.99 16:33 Petter $
 *
 * Implements command line handling.
 */

#include "precomp.h"
#include "ArgumentList.h"

ArgumentList::ArgumentList( LPCTSTR /* pszCmdLine */ ) {

    assert( isGoodPtr( this ) );
    assert( isGoodReadPtr( &__argc, sizeof __argc ) );
    assert( isGoodReadPtr( &__targv, sizeof __targv ) );
```

```
    assert(
        isGoodReadPtr( __targv, __argc * sizeof( __targv[ 0 ] ) ) );

    m_argc = __argc;

    // Using the system-supplied array appears to work OK,
    // but I am wary of messing with parameters that really
    // should have been const in the first place.
    // Hence the semi-deep copy. Since the strings themselves are
    // const, a deep copy is not necessary.

#if 0
    m_argv = __targv;
    assert( 0 == m_argv[ m_argc ] );
#else
    m_argv.alloc( m_argc + 1 );
    for ( int iArg = 0; iArg < m_argc; ++iArg ) {
        m_argv[ iArg ] = __targv[ iArg ];
    }
    assert( 0 == __targv[ m_argc ] );
    m_argv[ m_argc ] = 0;
#endif
}

bool ArgumentList::hasOption( LPCTSTR pszOption ) {

    assert( isValid() );

    bool bOption = false;
    for ( int iArg = 1; iArg < m_argc; ++iArg ) {
        if ( isOption( iArg ) &&
             0 == _tcsicmp( pszOption, getArg( iArg ) + 1 ) )
        {
            bOption = true;
            consume( iArg-- );
        }
    }
    return bOption;
}
```

```
void ArgumentList::consume( int nArg ) {

   assert( isValid() );
   assert( 0 <= nArg && nArg < m_argc );

   for ( int iArg = nArg; iArg < m_argc; ++iArg ) {
      m_argv[ iArg ] = m_argv[ iArg + 1 ];
   }

   --m_argc;
   assert( 0 == m_argv[ m_argc ] );
}

#ifdef _DEBUG

bool ArgumentList::isValid( void ) const {

   bool bValid = isGoodConstPtr( this ) && 0 < m_argc &&
      isGoodReadPtr( m_argv, (m_argc + 1) * sizeof( *m_argv ) );
   if ( bValid ) {
      for ( int iArg = 0; iArg < m_argc; ++iArg ) {
         if ( !isGoodStringPtr( m_argv[ iArg ] ) ) {
            bValid = false;
            break;
         }
      }
      assert( 0 == m_argv[ m_argc ] );
   }
   return bValid;
}

#endif // _DEBUG
```

Listing 7.8   init.cpp

```
/*
 * $Header: /Book/init.cpp 20    5.09.99 13:07 Petter $
 */
```

```cpp
#include "precomp.h"
#include "init.h"
#include "resource.h"
#include "main_class.h"
#include "ArgumentList.h"
#include "Document.h"
#include "WaitCursor.h"
#include "Exception.h"
#include "Editor.h"
#include "MRU.h"
#include "Registry.h"
#include "VersionInfo.h"
#include "mainwnd.h"
#include "resolveName.h"
#include "formatMessage.h"
#include "fileUtils.h"
#include "printFile.h"
#include "winUtils.h"
#include "utils.h"
#include "setup.h"
#include "reboot.h"
#include "activateOldInstance.h"
#include "startInstance.h"
#include "createNewFile.h"

#ifdef _DEBUG
#include "AbstractEditWnd.h"
#endif

// Mark this code segment as discardable; we won't need after startup:
#if defined( _MSC_VER ) && (1020 < _MSC_VER)
#pragma code_seg( "INIT" )
#pragma comment( linker, "/section:INIT,ERD" )
#endif

PRIVATE String makeCommandLine(
   bool bPrinting, const ArgumentList &argumentList )
{
   assert( 1 < argumentList.getNumArgs() );
```

```
   String strCommandLine;
   for ( int iArg = 1; iArg < argumentList.getNumArgs(); ++iArg ) {
      strCommandLine += formatMessage(
         _T( " \"%1\"" ), argumentList.getArg( iArg ) );
   }
   if ( bPrinting ) {
      strCommandLine += _T( " /p" );
   }
   return strCommandLine;
}

PRIVATE String makeCommandLine(
   bool bPrinting, const String &strFile )
{
   String strCommandLine =
      formatMessage( _T( " \"%1\"" ), strFile.c_str() );
   if ( bPrinting ) {
      strCommandLine += _T( " /p" );
   }
   return strCommandLine;
}

PRIVATE bool isValidHandle( HANDLE hfile )  {

   if ( hfile == INVALID_HANDLE_VALUE ) {
      return false;
   }
   const DWORD dwType = GetFileType( hfile ) & ~FILE_TYPE_REMOTE;
   return FILE_TYPE_PIPE == dwType || FILE_TYPE_DISK == dwType;
}

PRIVATE void initCommonControls( void ) {

   // This has been tested with 5.0 to throw exception.
   // This test caught one bug in WinException::getDescr,
   // and another one in formatMessageV, which goes to
   // show the value of testing all code paths.
   const WORD   wMinimumVersionHi = 4;
   const WORD   wMinimumVersionLo = 70; // 71;
```

```
      const DWORD dwMinimumVersion =
         MAKELONG( wMinimumVersionLo, wMinimumVersionHi );

      INITCOMMONCONTROLSEX init_cc_ex = {
         sizeof init_cc_ex, ICC_WIN95_CLASSES,
      };
      if ( !InitCommonControlsEx( &init_cc_ex ) ) {
         throwException( _T( "InitCommonControlsEx failed" ) );
      }

      // Verify version of common controls:
      VersionInfo versionInfo( _T( "COMCTL32.DLL" ) );
      if ( !versionInfo.isValid() ) {
         throwException( _T(
            "Unable to get version information for Common Controls" ) );
      }

      DWORD dwHigh = 0;
      if ( !versionInfo.getFileVersion( 0, &dwHigh ) ) {
         throwException( _T(
            "Unable to determine version of Common Controls" ) );
      }

      if ( dwHigh < dwMinimumVersion ) {
         const String strError = formatMessage(
            IDS_WRONG_COMCTL32_VERSION,
            (UINT) wMinimumVersionHi, (UINT) wMinimumVersionLo,
            (UINT) HIWORD( dwHigh  ), (UINT) LOWORD( dwHigh ) );
         throwException( strError, NOERROR );
      }
   }
}

PRIVATE void initReboot( void ) {

   const String strProgram = getModuleFileName();
   Registry::setString( HKEY_CURRENT_USER,
      RUNONCE_PATH, _T( "TextEdit Restart" ),
      _T( "%1 /boot" ), strProgram.c_str() );
}
```

```cpp
PRIVATE bool shouldUpgrade( const String& strInstalled ) {

   const VersionInfo viOld( strInstalled.c_str() );
   const VersionInfo viNew( getModuleHandle() );
   DWORD dwVersionLoOld = 0;
   DWORD dwVersionHiOld = 0;
   DWORD dwVersionLoNew = 0;
   DWORD dwVersionHiNew = 0;
   if ( viOld.isValid() && viNew.isValid() &&
      viOld.getFileVersion( &dwVersionLoOld, &dwVersionHiOld ) &&
      viNew.getFileVersion( &dwVersionLoNew, &dwVersionHiNew ) )
   {
      return
         dwVersionHiNew < dwVersionHiOld ? false :
         dwVersionHiOld < dwVersionHiNew ? true  :
         dwVersionLoOld < dwVersionLoNew ;
   }
   return false;
}

PRIVATE bool isSetup( ArgumentList *pArgumentList ) {

   assert( isGoodPtr( pArgumentList ) );

   if ( pArgumentList->hasOption( _T( "setup" ) ) ) {
      return true;
   }

   const String strProgram = getModuleFileName();
   PATHNAME szBaseName = { 0 };
   _tsplitpath( strProgram.c_str(), 0, 0, szBaseName, 0 );

   if ( 0 == _tcsicmp( szBaseName, _T( "setup" ) ) ||
        0 == _tcsicmp( szBaseName, _T( "install" ) ) )
   {
      return true;
   }
```

```cpp
      const String strInstalledProgram = getInstallPath();
      if ( strInstalledProgram.empty() ) {
         return true;
      }

      // If others are already running, never mind.
      if ( FindWindow( MAIN_CLASS, 0 ) ) {
         return false;
      }

      // So far, no setup. If we're running a different exe from the
      // installed one, check if the installed one would like to be
      // upgraded. Unless, of course, there were parameters, in which
      // case that would be an unwarranted intrusion.
      if ( 1 == pArgumentList->getNumArgs() &&
           shouldUpgrade( strInstalledProgram ) )
      {
         const UINT uiRet = messageBox( HWND_DESKTOP,
            MB_ICONQUESTION | MB_YESNOCANCEL, IDS_UPGRADE_WARNING,
            strProgram.c_str(), strInstalledProgram.c_str() );
         if ( IDCANCEL == uiRet ) {
            throw CancelException();
         }
         return IDYES == uiRet;
      }

      return false;
   }

Editor *init( LPCTSTR pszCmdLine, int nShow ) {

   const HINSTANCE hinst = getModuleHandle();

   initCommonControls();

   assert( isGoodStringPtr( pszCmdLine ) );
   ArgumentList argumentList( pszCmdLine );
```

```cpp
    if ( argumentList.hasOption( _T( "boot" ) ) ) {
        reboot();
        throw CancelException();
    }

    if ( argumentList.hasOption( _T( "clean" ) ) ) {
        clean();
        throw CancelException();
    }
    startInstance( _T( "-clean" ) );

    // Better not do this *before* calling reboot, or we'll loop:
    initReboot();

    if ( isSetup( &argumentList ) ) {
        const bool bSilent = argumentList.hasOption( _T( "silent" ) );
        setup( bSilent );
        throw CancelException();
    }

    const bool bMin      = argumentList.hasOption( _T( "min"     ) );
    const bool bMax      = argumentList.hasOption( _T( "max"     ) );
    const bool bOpenLast = argumentList.hasOption( _T( "last"    ) );
    const bool bPrintTo  = argumentList.hasOption( _T( "pt"      ) ) ||
                           argumentList.hasOption( _T( "printto" ) );
    const bool bPrint    = argumentList.hasOption( _T( "p"       ) ) ||
                           argumentList.hasOption( _T( "print"   ) );

#ifdef _DEBUG
    AbstractEditWnd::bForceEdit =
        argumentList.hasOption( _T( "edit" ) );
#endif

    if ( bMin ) {
        nShow = SW_SHOWMINIMIZED;
    }
    if ( bMax ) {
        nShow = SW_SHOWMAXIMIZED;
    }
```

```cpp
#if 0
    // Catch unrecognized options and complain.
    // We don't do this, but rather attempt to open them as files.
    for ( int iArg = 1; iArg < argumentList.getNumArgs(); ++iArg ) {
        if ( argumentList.isOption( iArg ) ) {
            LPCTSTR const pszArg = argumentList.getArg( iArg );
            messageBox( HWND_DESKTOP,
                MB_OK | MB_ICONERROR, IDS_UNKNOWN_OPTION, pszArg );
            throw CancelException();
        }
    }
#endif

    // Strip the first file name off the command line, if indicated:
    LPCTSTR pszDocName = 0;
    LPCTSTR pszPrinter = 0;
    LPCTSTR pszDriver  = 0;
    LPCTSTR pszPort    = 0;
    String strArgAll; // Must be at this scope!


    HANDLE hIn = GetStdHandle( STD_INPUT_HANDLE );
    trace( _T( "hIn = %d\n" ), hIn );

    if ( !isValidHandle( hIn ) ) {
        if ( bOpenLast ) {
            const MRU mru;
            if ( 0 < mru.getCount() ) {
                static PATHNAME szLastFile = { 0 };
                _tcscpy( szLastFile, mru.getFile( ID_MRU_1 ).c_str() );
                pszDocName = szLastFile;
            } else {
                ; // When there are no files in the MRU list, the
                  // -last option fails quietly by creating a new file.
            }
        }
        if ( bPrintTo ) {
            if ( 0 == pszDocName ) {
                pszDocName = argumentList.getArg( 1, true );
```

```
      }
      if ( argumentList.getNumArgs() < 4 ) {
         messageBox( HWND_DESKTOP,
            MB_OK | MB_ICONERROR, IDS_PRINT_ARG_ERROR );
         throw CancelException();
      }
      pszPrinter = argumentList.getArg( 1, true );
      pszDriver  = argumentList.getArg( 1, true );
      pszPort    = argumentList.getArg( 1, true );
   }
   if ( 0 == pszDocName && 1 < argumentList.getNumArgs() ) {
      strArgAll = argumentList.getArg( 1 );
      const int nArgs = argumentList.getNumArgs();
      for ( int iArg = 2; iArg < nArgs; ++iArg ) {
         strArgAll += _T( ' ' );
         strArgAll += argumentList.getArg( iArg );
      }

      bool bFound = fileExists( strArgAll.c_str() );
      if ( bFound ) {
         pszDocName = strArgAll.c_str();
      } else {
         strArgAll += getDefaultExtension();
         bFound = fileExists( strArgAll.c_str() );
         if ( bFound ) {
            pszDocName = strArgAll.c_str();
         } else {
            pszDocName = argumentList.getArg( 1 );
         }
      }
      do {
         argumentList.consume( 1 );
      } while ( bFound && 1 < argumentList.getNumArgs() );
   }
}

// Must we start another instance?
if ( 1 < argumentList.getNumArgs() ) {
   startInstance(
      makeCommandLine( bPrint, argumentList ), nShow );
```

```
         // No reasonable way to handle a failure, so don't.
      }

      // Load the docment, if we can:
      AutoDocument pDocument( 0 );
      if ( 0 != pszDocName ) {
         assert( isGoodStringPtr( pszDocName ) );

         PATHNAME szRealDocName = { 0 };
         resolveName( szRealDocName, pszDocName );

         if ( !bPrintTo && activateOldInstance( szRealDocName, bPrint ) )
         {
            throw CancelException();
         }
         pDocument = new Document( HWND_DESKTOP, szRealDocName );
      } else if ( isValidHandle( hIn ) ) {
         String strNewFile =
            createNewFile( HWND_DESKTOP, file_for_stdin, hIn ).c_str();
         verify( CloseHandle( hIn ) );
         startInstance( makeCommandLine( bPrint, strNewFile ), nShow );
         throw CancelException();
      } else {
         pDocument =
            new Document( HWND_DESKTOP, createNewFile().c_str() );
      }
      assert( isGoodPtr( pDocument ) );

      if ( bPrint || bPrintTo ) {
         printFile( pDocument, pszPrinter, pszDriver, pszPort );
         throw CancelException();
      }

      // No more obstacles; we really are going to edit a file.

      HICON hicon = LoadIcon( hinst, MAKEINTRESOURCE( IDI_TEXTEDIT1 ) );
      WNDCLASSEX wc = {
      /* cbSize;         */ sizeof( WNDCLASSEX ),
      /* style;          */ 0,
```

```
    /* lpfnWndProc;    */ mainWndProc,
    /* cbClsExtra;     */ 0,
    /* cbWndExtra;     */ MAINWND_EXTRABYTES,
    /* hInstance;      */ hinst,
    /* hIcon;          */ hicon,
    /* hCursor;        */ LoadCursor( 0, IDC_ARROW ),
    /* hbrBackground;  */ 0, // Don't need one; never visible.
    /* lpszMenuName;   */ MAKEINTRESOURCE( IDR_MENU ),
    /* lpszClassName;  */ MAIN_CLASS,
    /* hIconSm;        */ hicon,
};

if ( 0 == RegisterClassEx( &wc ) ) { // Give up!
    throwException( _T( "RegisterClassEx failed" ) );
}

// NOTE: Do this before creating the window, otherwise
// the maximized state will be reset during window creation.
if ( SW_MAXIMIZE == pDocument->getWindowState( nShow ) ) {
    nShow = SW_MAXIMIZE;
}
if ( bMin ) {
    nShow = SW_SHOWMINIMIZED;
}
if ( bMax ) {
    nShow = SW_SHOWMAXIMIZED;
}

// Get the window size (default is CW_USEDEFAULT):
const int x  = pDocument->getLeft  ();
const int y  = pDocument->getTop   ();
const int cx = pDocument->getWidth ();
const int cy = pDocument->getHeight();

// Possible improvement: Initial default size based on font,
// contents and other windows, modified by screen size.
// Possible improvement: Adjust pos and size to reasonableness,
// to protect from malicious messing with the registry.
```

```
    HWND hwndMain = CreateWindowEx(
    /* dwExStyle     */ WS_EX_ACCEPTFILES | WS_EX_CONTEXTHELP,
    /* lpClassName   */ MAIN_CLASS,
    /* lpWindowName  */ _T( "" ),
    /* dwStyle       */ WS_OVERLAPPEDWINDOW | WS_CLIPCHILDREN,
    /* pos/size      */ x, y, cx, cy,
    /* hWndParent    */ HWND_DESKTOP,
    /* hMenu         */ 0, // Using class menu
    /* hInstance     */ hinst,
    /* lpParam       */ &pDocument );

    // Reset when assigned to Editor, to avoid autodestruction:
    assert( (Document *) 0 == pDocument );

    if ( !IsWindow( hwndMain ) ) {
        // Error handling?
        throwException( _T( "CreateWindowEx failed" ) );
    }

    ShowWindow( hwndMain, nShow );
    UpdateWindow( hwndMain );

    // The one and only Editor object is created in the main
    // window's WM_CREATE handler (onCreate in mainwnd.cpp).
    Editor *pEditor = getEditor( hwndMain );
    assert( isGoodPtr( pEditor ) );

    return pEditor;
}
```

Chapter 8

Child Windows

The TextEdit main windows is a standard SDI (Single Document Interface) application window with optional tool — and status bars, and a big, fat text editing window in the middle.

Figure 8.1   TextEdit in Action, with eight of its nine windows visible.

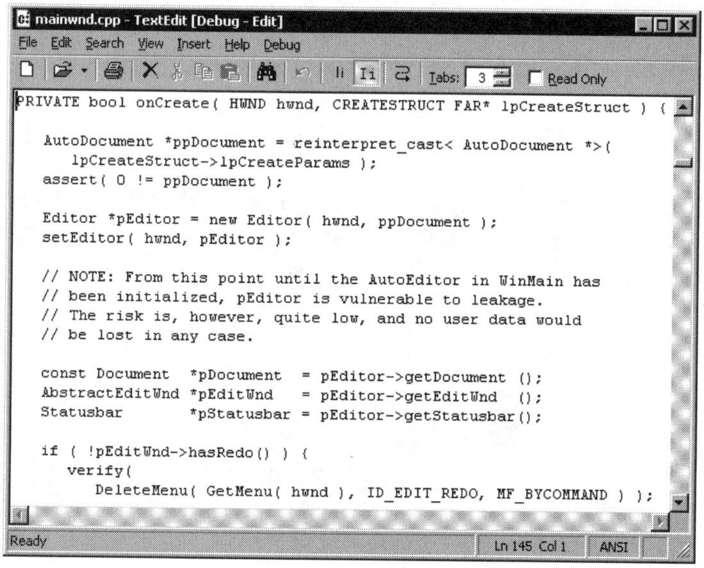

How many windows do you count in Figure 8.1? There are nine of them, eight of which are arranged in the following hierarchy:

```
The main application window
    The toolbar
        The "Tabs:" static label
        The editing field for number of spaces per tab
        The up/down control for the editing field
        The "Read Only" check box
    The editing window
    The status bar
```

The ninth window is the toolbar's ToolTip window, which was not present when the picture in Figure 8.1 was taken. The individual bitmaps on the toolbar are not windows; neither are the panes on the status bar. The scroll bars are part of the non-client area of the editing window. If this were OS/2 presentation manager, the scroll bars would be windows in their own right. Because this is Windows, they are not.

TextEdit has more windows than these though. Dialog boxes and their controls are windows too and I'll have more to say about them later, starting in Chapter 13.

Window Creation

The main window is created in the `init` function in `init.cpp`. The main window's `WM_CREATE` handler, `onCreate`, is responsible for creating the Editor object, which in turn creates the toolbar and the status bar. I shall have more to say about the main window in the next chapter, and I talked about the `AbstractEditWndProc` in the previous chapter. For now, let's concentrate on the toolbar and the status bar.

The Toolbar

The toolbar is a window of class `ToolbarWindow32`, implemented in `COMCTL32.DLL` and wrapped by the `Toolbar` class, a subclass of `Window`. The toolbar has four children if we're using an edit control, only one if we're using a rich edit control.

The toolbar is somewhat dynamic; it may change during a TextEdit session. This may happen if the user changes the desktop settings, or if the user changes the language (via the Options dialog box). Changing toolbar metrics on the fly turns out to be difficult, so the Editor class handles this by creating a new toolbar from scratch in its `refreshToolbar` method:

```
void Editor::refreshToolbar( void ) {

    assert( isGoodPtr( this ) );
    assert( isGoodPtr( m_pEditWnd ) );
    m_pToolbar.reset( new Toolbar( this, IDC_TOOLBAR,
        m_pEditWnd->hasRedo(), m_pEditWnd->canSetTabs() ) );
}
```

In other words, the old toolbar is deleted, and a new toolbar is created in its place.

The toolbar's tool tips come in two different flavors. We get tool tips for the buttons just by adding the `TBSTYLE_TOOLTIPS` style bit, but tool tips for the child controls must be added the hard way — control by control. The `Toolbar` constructor sends itself a `TB_GETTOOLTIPS` message to get hold of the tool tip window, then sends the tool tip a `TTM_ADDTOOL` message for each child:

```
HWND hwndToolTip =
   reinterpret_cast< HWND >( sendMessage( TB_GETTOOLTIPS ) );
if ( IsWindow( hwndToolTip ) ) {
   TOOLINFO toolInfo = {
      sizeof( TOOLINFO ),
      TTF_CENTERTIP | TTF_IDISHWND |
      TTF_SUBCLASS | TTF_TRANSPARENT,
      *this, reinterpret_cast< UINT >( hwndReadOnly ), { 0 },
      hinst, LPSTR_TEXTCALLBACK ,
   };
   SNDMSG( hwndToolTip,
      TTM_ADDTOOL, 0, reinterpret_cast< WPARAM >( &toolInfo ) );
   if ( canSetTabs ) {
      toolInfo.uId = reinterpret_cast< UINT >( hwndTabs );
      SNDMSG( hwndToolTip,
         TTM_ADDTOOL, 0, reinterpret_cast< WPARAM >( &toolInfo ) );
      toolInfo.uId = reinterpret_cast< UINT >( hwndUpDown );
      SNDMSG( hwndToolTip,
         TTM_ADDTOOL, 0, reinterpret_cast< WPARAM >( &toolInfo ) );
   }
}
```

The `onGetDispInfo` method handles the `TTN_GETDISPINFO` notification, which the tool tip sends to get the text to display. The child windows require a separate test for each, while the buttons are handled in a generic manner. The `loadToolTip` function (in `utils.cpp`) is a simple wrapper around `loadString` (also in `utils.cpp`). If the string contains a carriage return, everything up to and including the CR is deleted. (Everything in front of the CR is used to display the menu help text in the status bar.)

The Toolbar module defines two instance subclassings:

1. The edit control (containing the number of spaces per tab) is subclassed to pass page up and page down keys through to the edit window, to change the return value from the `WM_GETDLGCODE` message and to set and reset the status bar prompt in response to the `WM_SETFOCUS` and `WM_KILLFOCUS` messages.
2. The parent window is subclassed to intercept `WM_SIZE` and `WM_NOTIFY` messages. This could have been handled in the main window, of course, but by doing it this way, all code pertinent to the toolbar is kept in one class.

Chapter 8: Child Windows

The final item of interest is the `adjust` method, which calculates the position of the child windows. Like all such calculations, it is rather hairy, and also rather boring. Note that the final item in the toolbar's `TBBUTTON` array is a separator with the identifier `ID_TABPLACEHOLDER`; it exists only so that we can figure out where the buttons end. (Discourse continues on page 166.)

Listing 8.1 Toolbar.h

```
/*
 * $Header: /Book/Toolbar.h 15     20.08.99 16:33 Petter $
 */

#pragma once

#include "Window.h"
#include "AutoPtr.h"
#include "geometry.h"

enum {
    num_std_icons = STD_PRINT - STD_CUT + 1, // see commctrl.h
    fixed_icon    = num_std_icons + 0,
    prop_icon     = num_std_icons + 1,
    wordwrap_icon = num_std_icons + 2,
    find_icon     = num_std_icons + 3,
};

class Editor;
class Toolbar : public Window {
private: // TBSTYLE_WRAPABLE | CCS_NODIVIDER
    enum { WS_TOOLBAR = TBSTYLE_FLAT | TBSTYLE_TOOLTIPS | CCS_TOP };

    void adjust( bool bRepaint, bool hasRedo, bool canSetTabs );
    void setFonts( void );
    void setButtons( bool hasRedo );
    int  commandFromIndex( int nIndex );

    virtual void onCommand( int id, HWND hwndCtl, UINT codeNotify );
    virtual LRESULT onNotify( const int id, const LPNMHDR pHdr );
    virtual void onLButtonDown(
        BOOL fDoubleClick, int x, int y, UINT keyFlags );
```

```cpp
   virtual void onSettingChange( LPCTSTR pszSection );
   //virtual void onSysColorChange( void );

   void onDeltaPos   ( NMUPDOWN *pNmUpDown );
   bool onGetDispInfo( NMTTDISPINFO *pDispInfo );

   HWND getChild( UINT uiID ) const;

protected:
   void assertValid( void );
   void assertValid( void ) const;

public:
   Toolbar(
      Editor *pEditor, UINT uiID, bool hasRedo, bool canSetTabs );
   virtual ~Toolbar();

   bool isEnabled( UINT uiID ) const;
   void setEnabled( UINT uiID, bool bEnable );
   void check( UINT uiID, bool bCheck );

   // This retrieves a child window (*not* an image button):
   HWND getChild( UINT uiID );

   int getTabs( void );
   void setReadOnly( bool bReadOnly, bool bAccessDenied = false );
   bool getReadOnly( void ) const;
   void setSpacesPerTab( int nSpacesPerTab );
};

inline bool Toolbar::isEnabled( UINT uiID ) const {

   assertValid();
   return 0 != sendMessage( TB_ISBUTTONENABLED, uiID, 0 );
}

inline void Toolbar::setEnabled( UINT uiID, bool bEnable ) {
```

```cpp
    assertValid();
    sendMessage( TB_ENABLEBUTTON, uiID, bEnable );
}

inline void Toolbar::check( UINT uiID, bool bCheck ) {

    assertValid();
    sendMessage( TB_CHECKBUTTON, uiID, bCheck );
}

inline HWND Toolbar::getChild( UINT uiID ) const {

    assertValid();
    assert( (UINT) -1 != uiID && 0 != uiID );

    HWND hwndChild = GetDlgItem( m_hwnd, uiID );
    assert( IsWindow( hwndChild ) );
    return hwndChild;
}

inline HWND Toolbar::getChild( UINT uiID ) {

    return const_cast< const Toolbar * >( this )->getChild( uiID );
}

inline void Toolbar::assertValid( void ) {
    assert( isGoodPtr( this ) );
    Window::assertValid();
}

inline void Toolbar::assertValid( void ) const {
    assert( isGoodConstPtr( this ) );
    Window::assertValid();
}

#ifndef TBDDRET_DEFAULT
#define TBDDRET_DEFAULT 0
#endif
```

Listing 8.2 Toolbar.cpp

```cpp
/*
 * $Header: /Book/Toolbar.cpp 19    5.09.99 13:07 Petter $
 *
 * The toolbar automatically uses large icons when the user's
 * selected menu font gets above a suitable treshold. This treshold
 * is controlled by MenuFont::isLarge.
 */

#include "precomp.h"
#include "String.h"
#include "Exception.h"
#include "Editor.h"  // TODO: This is dirty. reorg!
#include "Toolbar.h"
#include "Registry.h"
#include "MenuFont.h"
#include "InstanceSubclasser.h"
#include "mainwnd.h"
#include "resource.h"
#include "trace.h"
#include "winUtils.h"
#include "utils.h"
#include "geometry.h"

PRIVATE LRESULT CALLBACK tabSubclassWndProc(
   HWND hwnd, UINT msg, WPARAM wParam, LPARAM lParam );
PRIVATE LRESULT CALLBACK toolbarParentSpy(
   HWND hwnd, UINT msg, WPARAM wParam, LPARAM lParam );

PRIVATE InstanceSubclasser s_tabSubclasser( tabSubclassWndProc );
PRIVATE InstanceSubclasser s_parentSubclasser( toolbarParentSpy );

void Toolbar::onCommand( int id, HWND hwndCtl, UINT codeNotify ) {

   switch ( id ) {
   case IDOK:
      FORWARD_WM_COMMAND(
         GetParent( *this ), ID_SET_TABS, 0, 0, PostMessage );
```

```
         //*** FALL THROUGH

      case IDCANCEL:
         if ( BN_CLICKED == codeNotify ) {
            SetFocus( GetParent( *this ) );
         }
         break;

      case IDC_READONLY:
         if ( BN_CLICKED == codeNotify ) {
            FORWARD_WM_COMMAND(
               GetParent( *this ), id, 0, 0, PostMessage );
         }
         break;
   }
}

// LATER: If the toolbar doesn't support drowdown, don't drop down!
bool onDropdown( HWND hwnd, NMTOOLBAR *pNmToolbar ) {

   assert( IsWindow( hwnd ) );
   assert( isGoodPtr( pNmToolbar ) );

   if ( ID_FILE_OPEN == pNmToolbar->iItem ) {
      HWND hwndToolbar = s_parentSubclasser.getUserDataAsHwnd( hwnd );
      assert( IsWindow( hwndToolbar ) );
      HMENU hmenu = CreatePopupMenu();
      if ( 0 != hmenu ) {
         RECT rc;
         SNDMSG( hwndToolbar, TB_GETRECT,
            pNmToolbar->iItem, reinterpret_cast< LPARAM >( &rc ) );

         POINT pt= { rc.left, rc.bottom };
         ClientToScreen( pNmToolbar->hdr.hwndFrom, &pt );

         // The main window's onInitMenu will add files.
         TrackPopupMenu( hmenu,
            TPM_LEFTALIGN | TPM_TOPALIGN | TPM_RIGHTBUTTON,
            pt.x, pt.y, 0, hwnd, 0 );
         DestroyMenu( hmenu );
```

```
      } else {
         trace( _T( "onDropdown.CreatePopupMenu failed: %s\n" ),
            WinException().what() );
      }
   }
   return TBDDRET_DEFAULT;
}

/**
 * This is called when the spin buttons attached to the
 * tab field are spun (or if the up/down arrows are used).
 */
void Toolbar::onDeltaPos( NMUPDOWN *pUpDown ) {

   assert( isGoodPtr( pUpDown ) );
   assert( IDC_TABUPDOWN == pUpDown->hdr.idFrom );

   if ( pUpDown->iPos + pUpDown->iDelta <= 4 ) {
      ;
   } else if ( pUpDown->iPos - (pUpDown->iDelta < 0 ) < 8 ) {
      if ( pUpDown->iDelta < 0 ) {
         pUpDown->iDelta = 4 - pUpDown->iPos;
      } else {
         pUpDown->iDelta = 8 - pUpDown->iPos;
      }
   } else if ( pUpDown->iPos - (pUpDown->iDelta < 0 ) < 16 ) {
      if ( pUpDown->iDelta < 0 ) {
         pUpDown->iDelta = 8 - pUpDown->iPos;
      } else {
         pUpDown->iDelta = 16 - pUpDown->iPos;
      }
   } else {
      pUpDown->iDelta = 16 - pUpDown->iPos;
   }
   PostMessage( GetDlgItem( *this, IDC_TABEDIT ), EM_SETSEL, 0, -1 );
}

/**
 * Get tooltip text.
 */
```

```cpp
bool Toolbar::onGetDispInfo( NMTTDISPINFO *pDispInfo ) {

   assertValid();
   assert( isGoodPtr( pDispInfo ) );

   // NOTE: The hwndFrom member refers to the tooltip control.
   const HWND hwndCtl =
      reinterpret_cast< HWND >( pDispInfo->hdr.idFrom );
   if ( GetDlgItem( *this, IDC_TABEDIT ) == hwndCtl ) {
     pDispInfo->lpszText = MAKEINTRESOURCE( IDS_TABS_TIP );
   } else if ( GetDlgItem( *this, IDC_TABUPDOWN ) == hwndCtl ) {
     pDispInfo->lpszText = MAKEINTRESOURCE( IDS_TABS_UPDOWN_TIP );
   } else if ( GetDlgItem( *this, IDC_READONLY ) == hwndCtl ) {
     pDispInfo->lpszText = MAKEINTRESOURCE( IDS_READ_ONLY_TIP );
   } else {
     String strToolTip = loadToolTip( pDispInfo->hdr.idFrom );
     pDispInfo->lpszText = pDispInfo->szText;
     _tcsncpy( pDispInfo->szText,
        strToolTip.c_str(), dim( pDispInfo->szText ) );
     pDispInfo->hinst = 0;
   }

   return true;
}

LRESULT Toolbar::onNotify( const int id, const LPNMHDR pHdr ) {

   assert( isGoodPtr( pHdr ) );

   switch ( pHdr->code ) {
   case UDN_DELTAPOS:
      onDeltaPos( reinterpret_cast< NMUPDOWN * >( pHdr ) );
      return 0;

   case TTN_GETDISPINFO:
      return onGetDispInfo(
         reinterpret_cast< NMTTDISPINFO * >( pHdr ) );
```

```
      case TBN_DROPDOWN:  // Never gets here; sent to parent,
         assert( false ); // intercepted in toolbarParentSpy.
      }

      return Window::onNotify( id, pHdr );
   }

   int Toolbar::commandFromIndex( int nIndex ) {

      assertValid();
      TBBUTTON button = { 0 };
      sendMessage(
         TB_GETBUTTON, nIndex, reinterpret_cast< LPARAM >( &button ) );
      return button.idCommand;
   }

   #ifndef TB_HITTEST
   #define TB_HITTEST (WM_USER + 69)
   #endif

   void Toolbar::onLButtonDown(
      BOOL fDoubleClick, int x, int y, UINT keyFlags )
   {
      assertValid();
      Window::onLButtonDown( fDoubleClick, x, y, keyFlags );

      if ( fDoubleClick ) {
         POINT pt = { x, y };
         const int nIndex = sendMessage(
            TB_HITTEST, 0, reinterpret_cast< LPARAM >( &pt ) );
         switch ( commandFromIndex( nIndex ) ) {
         case ID_VIEW_PROPORTIONALFONT:
            FORWARD_WM_COMMAND( GetParent( *this ),
               ID_VIEW_SETPROPORTIONALFONT, 0, 0, PostMessage );
            break;
         case ID_VIEW_FIXEDFONT:
            FORWARD_WM_COMMAND( GetParent( *this ),
               ID_VIEW_SETFIXEDFONT, 0, 0, PostMessage );
            break;
```

```
        }
    }
}

PRIVATE LRESULT CALLBACK tabSubclassWndProc(
    HWND hwnd, UINT msg, WPARAM wParam, LPARAM lParam )
{
    Editor *pEditor = reinterpret_cast< Editor * >(
        s_tabSubclasser.getUserData( hwnd ) );
    assert( isGoodPtr( pEditor ) );

    // TODO: Should reorg this as a filter, or subclass both controls!
    if ( WM_KEYDOWN == msg || WM_KEYUP == msg ) {
        if ( VK_NEXT == wParam || VK_PRIOR == wParam ) {
            pEditor->getEditWnd()->sendMessage( msg, wParam, lParam );
        }
    }

    LRESULT lResult =
        s_tabSubclasser.callOldProc( hwnd, msg, wParam, lParam );
    if ( WM_GETDLGCODE == msg ) {
        lResult &= ~(DLGC_WANTTAB | DLGC_WANTALLKEYS);
    } else if ( WM_SETFOCUS == msg ) {
        pEditor->getStatusbar()->setMessage( IDS_TAB_PROMPT );
    } else if ( WM_KILLFOCUS == msg ) {
        pEditor->getStatusbar()->update(
            pEditor->getEditWnd()->getCurPos() );
    }
    return lResult;
}
// TODO: On leaving the field, set contents to actual tab

PRIVATE LRESULT CALLBACK toolbarParentSpy(
    HWND hwnd, UINT msg, WPARAM wParam, LPARAM lParam )
{
    if ( WM_SIZE == msg ) {
        HWND hwndToolbar = s_parentSubclasser.getUserDataAsHwnd( hwnd );
        assert( IsWindow( hwndToolbar ) );
        SNDMSG( hwndToolbar, WM_SIZE, wParam, lParam );
```

```cpp
   } else if ( WM_NOTIFY == msg ) {
      NMHDR *pHdr = reinterpret_cast< NMHDR * >( lParam );
      if ( TBN_DROPDOWN == pHdr->code ) {
         return onDropdown( hwnd,
            reinterpret_cast< NMTOOLBAR * >( pHdr ) );
      }
   }
   return s_parentSubclasser.callOldProc( hwnd, msg, wParam, lParam );
}

Toolbar::Toolbar(
   Editor *pEditor, UINT uiID, bool hasRedo, bool canSetTabs )
{
   assert( isGoodPtr( this ) );

   const HINSTANCE hinst = getModuleHandle();

   attach( CreateWindowEx(
      0, TOOLBARCLASSNAME, 0, WS_CHILD | WS_VISIBLE | WS_TOOLBAR,
      0, 0, 0, 0, pEditor->getMainWnd(), (HMENU) uiID, hinst, 0 ) );
   assert( IsWindow( *this ) );
   if ( !IsWindow( *this ) ) {
      throwException( _T( "Failed to create toolbar" ) );
   }

   sendMessage( TB_BUTTONSTRUCTSIZE, sizeof( TBBUTTON ) );
   sendMessage( TB_SETINDENT, GetSystemMetrics( SM_CXEDGE ) );

#if ( 0x0400 <= _WIN32_IE ) && defined( TBSTYLE_EX_DRAWDDARROWS )
   sendMessage( TB_SETEXTENDEDSTYLE, 0, TBSTYLE_EX_DRAWDDARROWS );
#endif

   HWND hwndTabs    = 0;
   HWND hwndUpDown  = 0;
   if ( canSetTabs ) {
#ifdef _DEBUG
      HWND hwndTabsLabel =
#endif
         CreateWindowEx(
         0, _T( "STATIC" ), loadString( IDS_TABS_LABEL ).c_str(),
```

```
        WS_CHILD | WS_VISIBLE | SS_LEFT,
        0, 0, 0, 0, m_hwnd, (HMENU) IDC_TABLABEL, hinst, 0 );
    assert( IsWindow( hwndTabsLabel ) );

    hwndTabs = CreateWindowEx(
        WS_EX_CLIENTEDGE, _T( "EDIT" ), 0,
        WS_CHILD | WS_VISIBLE | WS_TABSTOP | WS_GROUP |
        ES_AUTOHSCROLL | ES_WANTRETURN | ES_MULTILINE |
        ES_RIGHT | ES_NUMBER,
        0, 0, 0, 0, m_hwnd, (HMENU) IDC_TABEDIT, hinst, 0 );
    assert( IsWindow( hwndTabs ) );

    hwndUpDown = CreateWindowEx(
        0, UPDOWN_CLASS, 0,
        WS_CHILD | WS_VISIBLE | WS_GROUP |
        UDS_AUTOBUDDY | UDS_SETBUDDYINT |
        UDS_ALIGNRIGHT | UDS_ARROWKEYS | UDS_HOTTRACK,
        0, 0, 0, 0, m_hwnd, (HMENU) IDC_TABUPDOWN, hinst, 0 );
    assert( IsWindow( hwndUpDown ) );

    SNDMSG( hwndUpDown,
        UDM_SETRANGE, 0, (LPARAM) MAKELONG( 16, 1 ) );
    SNDMSG( hwndUpDown,
        UDM_SETPOS  , 0, (LPARAM) MAKELONG(  4, 0 ) );
}

HWND hwndReadOnly = CreateWindowEx(
    0, _T( "BUTTON" ), loadString( IDS_READ_ONLY ).c_str(),
    WS_CHILD | WS_VISIBLE | WS_TABSTOP | WS_GROUP | BS_AUTOCHECKBOX,
    0, 0, 0, 0, m_hwnd, (HMENU) IDC_READONLY, hinst, 0 );
assert( IsWindow( hwndReadOnly ) );

// Add tool tips for the child controls:
HWND hwndToolTip =
    reinterpret_cast< HWND >( sendMessage( TB_GETTOOLTIPS ) );
if ( IsWindow( hwndToolTip ) ) {
    TOOLINFO toolInfo = {
        sizeof( TOOLINFO ),
        TTF_CENTERTIP | TTF_IDISHWND |
        TTF_SUBCLASS | TTF_TRANSPARENT,
```

```
                *this, reinterpret_cast< UINT >( hwndReadOnly ), { 0 },
                hinst, LPSTR_TEXTCALLBACK ,
            };
            SNDMSG( hwndToolTip,
                TTM_ADDTOOL, 0, reinterpret_cast< WPARAM >( &toolInfo ) );
            if ( canSetTabs ) {
                toolInfo.uId = reinterpret_cast< UINT >( hwndTabs );
                SNDMSG( hwndToolTip,
                    TTM_ADDTOOL, 0, reinterpret_cast< WPARAM >( &toolInfo ) );
                toolInfo.uId = reinterpret_cast< UINT >( hwndUpDown );
                SNDMSG( hwndToolTip,
                    TTM_ADDTOOL, 0, reinterpret_cast< WPARAM >( &toolInfo ) );
            }

#ifdef _DEBUG
            const LONG lToolTipWndProc =
                GetWindowLong( hwndReadOnly, GWL_WNDPROC );
            trace( _T( "lToolTipWndProc = %#x\n" ), lToolTipWndProc );
#endif
        }

        adjust( false, hasRedo, canSetTabs );

        if ( canSetTabs ) {
            // This should be done *after* we've created the tool
            // tips. The tool tip window subclasses hwndTabs, but
            // does not detach on window destruction. It's better
            // if we're on top of the food chain.
            verify( s_tabSubclasser.subclass( hwndTabs, pEditor ) );
        }

        // This may already be subclassed if we're recreating the toolbar,
        // which happens on WM_SETTINGCHANGE. Doesn't matter.
        s_parentSubclasser.subclass( pEditor->getMainWnd(), m_hwnd );
        assertValid();
    }

    void Toolbar::setButtons( bool hasRedo ) {

        assertValid();
```

```cpp
      TBADDBITMAP tbabmpStd = {
        HINST_COMMCTRL,
        MenuFont::isLarge() ? IDB_STD_LARGE_COLOR : IDB_STD_SMALL_COLOR,
      };
      TBADDBITMAP tbabmpCustom = {
        getModuleHandle(),
        MenuFont::isLarge() ? IDR_TOOLBAR_LARGE : IDR_TOOLBAR,
      };

   static const TBBUTTON tb[] = {
     { STD_FILENEW , ID_FILE_NEW   , TBSTATE_ENABLED, TBSTYLE_BUTTON   },
     { 0             , 0             , 0              , TBSTYLE_SEP      },
     { STD_FILEOPEN, ID_FILE_OPEN  , TBSTATE_ENABLED, TBSTYLE_DROPDOWN },
     { 0             , 0             , 0              , TBSTYLE_SEP      },
     { STD_PRINT   , ID_FILE_PRINT , TBSTATE_ENABLED                   },
     { 0             , 0             , 0              , TBSTYLE_SEP      },
     { STD_DELETE  , ID_EDIT_DELETE, TBSTATE_ENABLED                   },
     { STD_CUT     , ID_EDIT_CUT   , TBSTATE_ENABLED, TBSTYLE_BUTTON   },
     { STD_COPY    , ID_EDIT_COPY  , TBSTATE_ENABLED, TBSTYLE_BUTTON   },
     { STD_PASTE   , ID_EDIT_PASTE , TBSTATE_ENABLED, TBSTYLE_BUTTON   },
     { 0             , 0             , 0              , TBSTYLE_SEP      },
     { find_icon   , ID_EDIT_FIND  , TBSTATE_ENABLED                   },
     { 0             , 0             , 0              , TBSTYLE_SEP      },
     { STD_UNDO    , ID_EDIT_UNDO  , 0              , TBSTYLE_BUTTON   },
     { STD_REDOW   , ID_EDIT_REDO  , 0              , TBSTYLE_BUTTON   },
     { 0             , 0             , 0              , TBSTYLE_SEP      },

     { prop_icon, ID_VIEW_PROPORTIONALFONT,
                           TBSTATE_ENABLED, TBSTYLE_CHECKGROUP },
     { fixed_icon  , ID_VIEW_FIXEDFONT,
                           TBSTATE_ENABLED, TBSTYLE_CHECKGROUP },
     { 0             , 0             , 0              , TBSTYLE_SEP      },
     { wordwrap_icon,ID_VIEW_WORDWRAP, TBSTATE_ENABLED, TBSTYLE_CHECK   },

     { 0        , ID_TABPLACEHOLDER   , 0            , TBSTYLE_SEP      },
   };

   sendMessage(
     TB_ADDBITMAP, 15, reinterpret_cast< LPARAM >( &tbabmpStd ) );
```

```
    sendMessage(
        TB_ADDBITMAP, 4, reinterpret_cast< LPARAM >( &tbabmpCustom ) );
    sendMessage(
        TB_ADDBUTTONS, dim( tb ), reinterpret_cast< LPARAM >( tb ) );
    if ( !hasRedo ) {
        const int nIndex =
            sendMessage( TB_COMMANDTOINDEX, ID_EDIT_REDO );
        assert( 0 <= nIndex );
        verify( sendMessage( TB_DELETEBUTTON, nIndex ) );
    }
    sendMessage( TB_AUTOSIZE );
}

Toolbar::~Toolbar() {
}

SIZE measureDlgItem( HWND hwndCtl ) {

    assert( IsWindow( hwndCtl ) );
    TCHAR szText[ 100 ] = { 0 };
    GetWindowText( hwndCtl, szText, dim( szText ) );
    return measureString( szText );
}

SIZE getEditSize( HWND hwndEdit, LPCTSTR pszStipulatedContents ) {

    assert( IsWindow( hwndEdit ) );
    assert( isGoodStringPtr( pszStipulatedContents ) );
    SIZE size = measureString( pszStipulatedContents );

    const int nXEdge2 = 2 * GetSystemMetrics( SM_CXEDGE );
    const int nYEdge2 = 2 * GetSystemMetrics( SM_CYEDGE );

    size.cx += 2 + nXEdge2;
    size.cy += 2 + nYEdge2;

    return size;
}
```

```cpp
void Toolbar::adjust( bool bRepaint, bool hasRedo, bool canSetTabs ) {

    assertValid();
    setButtons( hasRedo );
    setFonts();

    const int nPad = GetSystemMetrics( SM_CXDLGFRAME );

    Rect rc = getWindowRect( *this );
    const int nHeight = rc.height();
    sendMessage( TB_GETRECT, ID_TABPLACEHOLDER, (LPARAM) &rc );
    OffsetRect( &rc, nPad, 0 );

    if ( canSetTabs ) {
        HWND hwndTabsLabel = GetDlgItem( *this, IDC_TABLABEL  );
        HWND hwndTabs      = GetDlgItem( *this, IDC_TABEDIT   );
        HWND hwndUpDown    = GetDlgItem( *this, IDC_TABUPDOWN );
        const SIZE sizeTabsLabel = measureDlgItem( hwndTabsLabel );
        const SIZE sizeTabs = getEditSize( hwndTabs, _T( "99999" ) );
        Rect rcUpDown = getWindowRect( hwndUpDown );
        const SIZE sizeUpDown = {
            rcUpDown.right  - rcUpDown.left,
            rcUpDown.bottom - rcUpDown.top };

        MoveWindow(
            hwndTabsLabel, rc.right, (nHeight - sizeTabsLabel.cy) / 2,
            sizeTabsLabel.cx, sizeTabsLabel.cy, bRepaint );
        rc.left = rc.right;
        OffsetRect( &rc, sizeTabsLabel.cx + nPad, 0 );

        const int nTabExtra = 4;
        MoveWindow( hwndTabs, rc.left, (nHeight - sizeTabs.cy) / 2,
            sizeTabs.cx + sizeUpDown.cx + nTabExtra, sizeTabs.cy,
            bRepaint );
        SNDMSG( hwndUpDown, UDM_SETBUDDY,
            reinterpret_cast< WPARAM >( hwndTabs ), 0 );
        OffsetRect( &rc, sizeTabs.cx + sizeUpDown.cx + 4 + nPad, 0 );

        rcUpDown = getWindowRect( hwndUpDown );
```

```cpp
         const RECT rcEditRect = {
            0, 0, sizeTabs.cx - rcUpDown.width(), sizeTabs.cy };
        SNDMSG( hwndTabs,
            EM_SETRECT, 0, reinterpret_cast< LPARAM >( &rcEditRect ) );
    }

    HWND hwndReadOnly = GetDlgItem( *this, IDC_READONLY );
    SIZE sizeReadOnly = measureDlgItem( hwndReadOnly );
    MoveWindow( hwndReadOnly,
        rc.left + 10, (nHeight - sizeReadOnly.cy) / 2,
        sizeReadOnly.cx + 50, sizeReadOnly.cy, bRepaint );
}

int Toolbar::getTabs( void ) {

    assertValid();
    BOOL bOK = false;
    int nTabs = GetDlgItemInt( *this, IDC_TABEDIT, &bOK, false );
    return nTabs;
}

void Toolbar::setSpacesPerTab( int nSpacesPerTab ) {
    HWND hwndTabsUpDown = getChild( IDC_TABUPDOWN );
    assert( IsWindow( hwndTabsUpDown ) );
    SNDMSG( hwndTabsUpDown,
        UDM_SETPOS, 0, (LPARAM) MAKELONG( nSpacesPerTab, 0 ) );
}

void Toolbar::setReadOnly( bool bReadOnly, bool bAccessDenied ) {

    HWND hwndReadOnly = getChild( IDC_READONLY );
    assert( IsWindow( hwndReadOnly ) );

    // If you really want to be paranoid, verify that it is,
    // indeed, a checkbox.

    Button_SetCheck( hwndReadOnly, bReadOnly ? 1 : 0 );
    Button_Enable( hwndReadOnly, !bAccessDenied );
}
```

```cpp
bool Toolbar::getReadOnly( void ) const {
   HWND hwndReadOnly = getChild( IDC_READONLY );
   return 0 != Button_GetCheck( hwndReadOnly );
}

void Toolbar::setFonts( void ) {

   assertValid();
   HFONT hfont = MenuFont::getFont();
   assert( 0 != hfont );
   for ( HWND hwndChild = GetTopWindow( *this );
      IsWindow( hwndChild );
      hwndChild = GetNextWindow( hwndChild, GW_HWNDNEXT ) )
   {
      SetWindowFont( hwndChild, hfont, true );
   }
}

void Toolbar::onSettingChange( LPCTSTR pszSection ) {

   assertValid();
   //FORWARD_WM_SETTINGCHANGE( hwndChild, pszSection, SNDMSG );
   if ( 0 == _tcsicmp( _T( "WindowMetrics" ), pszSection ) ) {
      //adjust( true );
   }
}
```

The Status Bar

The status bar is a window of class `msctls_statusbar32`, implemented in `COMCTL32.DLL` and wrapped by the `StatusBar` class, a subclass of the `Window` class. The status bar has no children; instead, it has four panes, identified by the enumeration `Statusbar::StatusBarParts`:

```cpp
enum StatusBarParts {
   message_part ,
   position_part,
   filetype_part,
   action_part  ,
};
```

(There are situations where status bars do have children; a typical example is the display of a progress bar during a lengthy operation.)

Most of the `Statusbar` class is devoted to providing convenient ways of setting texts and icons in the various panes.

Like the toolbar, the status bar subclasses the main window to intercept messages. The status bar is interested in `WM_SIZE` and `WM_DRAWITEM`. (Subclassing a window to listen in on the message traffic is different from MFC's message reflection mechanism, but the result is similar — improved encapsulation.)

The first pane is `SBT_OWNERDRAW`, because I want to display rich text in the pane and because I want to highlight some messages. The `paintHTML` function (in `HTML.cpp`) handles both; I'll get back to the details in Chapter 13.

The final item of interest is the `recalcParts` method, which (re-) calculates the sizes of the status bar panes in response to size changes in the main window. This is necessary because the first pane is the one that stretches.

Listing 8.3   Statusbar.h

```
/*
 * $Header: /Book/StatusBar.h 12    5.09.99 13:07 Petter $
 */

#pragma once

#include "Window.h"
#include "AutoPtr.h"
#include "geometry.h"

class Statusbar : public Window {
private:
   enum StatusBarParts {
      message_part ,
      position_part,
      filetype_part,
      action_part  ,
   };

   HICON m_hicon;
   int   m_nIndex;

   void __cdecl setMessageV( LPCTSTR pszFmt, va_list vl );
   void setText( int nIndex, LPCTSTR pszText );
```

```cpp
public:
    Statusbar( HWND hwndParent, UINT uiID );
    virtual ~Statusbar();

    void __cdecl setMessage( LPCTSTR pszFmt, ... );
    void __cdecl setMessage( UINT idFmt, ... );
    void __cdecl setHighlightMessage( UINT idFmt, ... );
    void __cdecl setErrorMessage( UINT idFlags, UINT idFmt, ... );
    void update( const Point& position );
    void setFileType( const bool isUnicode );
    void setIcon( int nIndex = 0 );
    void setIcon( HIMAGELIST hImageList, int nIndex );

    virtual void onSettingChange( LPCTSTR pszSection );
};

inline void Statusbar::setText( int nIndex, LPCTSTR pszText ) {

    sendMessage(
        SB_SETTEXT, nIndex, reinterpret_cast< LPARAM >( pszText ) );
}

class TemporaryStatusIcon {
private:
    Statusbar *m_pStatusbar;

public:
    TemporaryStatusIcon( Statusbar *, HIMAGELIST, int );
    TemporaryStatusIcon( Statusbar *, int );
    ~TemporaryStatusIcon();
};

inline TemporaryStatusIcon::TemporaryStatusIcon(
    Statusbar *pStatusbar, HIMAGELIST hImageList, int nIcon )
    : m_pStatusbar( pStatusbar )
{
    assert( isGoodPtr( m_pStatusbar ) );
    m_pStatusbar->setIcon( hImageList, nIcon );
}
```

```
inline TemporaryStatusIcon::TemporaryStatusIcon(
   Statusbar *pStatusbar, int nIcon )
   : m_pStatusbar( pStatusbar )
{
   assert( isGoodPtr( m_pStatusbar ) );
   m_pStatusbar->setIcon( nIcon );
}

inline TemporaryStatusIcon::~TemporaryStatusIcon() {
   assert( isGoodPtr( m_pStatusbar ) );
   m_pStatusbar->setIcon();
}

#if 0
class TemporaryStatusMessage {
private:
   Statusbar& m_Statusbar;

public:
   TemporaryStatusMessage( Statusbar& statusbar, int nIcon );
   ~TemporaryStatusMessage();
};

inline TemporaryStatusMessage::TemporaryStatusMessage(
   Statusbar& statusbar, int nIcon )
   : m_Statusbar( statusbar )
{
   m_Statusbar.setIcon( nIcon );
}

inline TemporaryStatusMessage::~TemporaryStatusMessage() {
   m_Statusbar.setIcon();
}
#endif
```

Listing 8.4 Statusbar.cpp

```cpp
/*
 * $Header: /Book/StatusBar.cpp   13      3.07.99 17:46 Petter $
 *
 * NOTE: Both Toolbar and Statusbar are tailored to TextEdit.
 * A more general approach would be to derive both from base classes.
 */

#include "precomp.h"
#include "Statusbar.h"
#include "MenuFont.h"
#include "HTML.h"
#include "InstanceSubclasser.h"
#include "formatMessage.h"
#include "formatNumber.h"
#include "graphics.h"
#include "utils.h"
#include "resource.h"

#ifndef SB_SETICON
#define SB_SETICON (WM_USER+15)
#endif

PRIVATE bool sm_bHighlight = false;

PRIVATE LRESULT CALLBACK statusbarParentSpy(
    HWND hwnd, UINT msg, WPARAM wParam, LPARAM lParam );

PRIVATE InstanceSubclasser s_parentSubclasser( statusbarParentSpy );

/**
 * Recalculates the sizes of the various status bar parts.
 */
PRIVATE void recalcParts( HWND hwndStatusbar, int nTotalWidth = -1 ) {

    assert( IsWindow( hwndStatusbar ) );

    if ( -1 == nTotalWidth ) {
        const Rect rc = getWindowRect( hwndStatusbar );
```

```
         nTotalWidth = rc.width();
      }

      const int nBorder = GetSystemMetrics( SM_CXEDGE );
      const int nWidth =
         nTotalWidth - GetSystemMetrics( SM_CXVSCROLL ) - nBorder - 1;
      const int nExtra = 4 * nBorder;

      const int nWidthUnicode =
         measureString( _T( "Unicode" ) ).cx + nExtra;
      const int nWidthPosition =
         measureString( _T( "Ln 99,999 Col 999" ) ).cx + nExtra;
      const int nWidthToolbarButton = GetSystemMetrics(
         MenuFont::isLarge() ? SM_CXICON : SM_CXSMICON );
      const int nWidthIcon = nWidthToolbarButton + nExtra;

      const int aParts[] = {
         nWidth - nWidthPosition - nWidthUnicode - nWidthIcon,
         nWidth - nWidthUnicode - nWidthIcon,
         nWidth - nWidthIcon,
         nWidth - 0, // If we use -1, we overflow into the sizing grip.
      };

      SNDMSG( hwndStatusbar, SB_SETPARTS,
         dim( aParts ), reinterpret_cast< LPARAM >( aParts ) );
}

PRIVATE void drawItem( DRAWITEMSTRUCT *pDIS ) {

      // This returns a pointer to the static
      // szMessageBuffer used in setMessageV:
      LPCTSTR pszText = reinterpret_cast< LPCTSTR >(
         SNDMSG( pDIS->hwndItem, SB_GETTEXT, 0, 0 ) );

      const int nSavedDC = SaveDC( pDIS->hDC );
      if ( sm_bHighlight ) {
         SetTextColor( pDIS->hDC, GetSysColor( COLOR_HIGHLIGHTTEXT ) );
         SetBkColor   ( pDIS->hDC, GetSysColor( COLOR_HIGHLIGHT     ) );
         fillSysColorSolidRect( pDIS->hDC,
            &pDIS->rcItem, COLOR_HIGHLIGHT );
```

```cpp
         pDIS->rcItem.left += GetSystemMetrics( SM_CXEDGE );
      } else {
         SetTextColor( pDIS->hDC, GetSysColor( COLOR_BTNTEXT ) );
         SetBkColor  ( pDIS->hDC, GetSysColor( COLOR_BTNFACE ) );
      }
      const int nHeight = Rect( pDIS->rcItem ).height();
      const int nExtra = nHeight - MenuFont::getHeight();
      pDIS->rcItem.top += nExtra / 2 - 1;
      pDIS->rcItem.left += GetSystemMetrics( SM_CXEDGE );
      paintHTML( pDIS->hDC, pszText, &pDIS->rcItem,
         GetWindowFont( pDIS->hwndItem ), PHTML_SINGLE_LINE );
      verify( RestoreDC( pDIS->hDC, nSavedDC ) );
   }

   PRIVATE LRESULT CALLBACK statusbarParentSpy(
      HWND hwnd, UINT msg, WPARAM wParam, LPARAM lParam )
   {
      const LRESULT lResult =
         s_parentSubclasser.callOldProc( hwnd, msg, wParam, lParam );
      if ( WM_SIZE == msg ) {
         HWND hwndStatusbar =
            s_parentSubclasser.getUserDataAsHwnd( hwnd );
         assert( IsWindow( hwndStatusbar ) );
         const int cx = LOWORD( lParam );
         recalcParts( hwndStatusbar, cx );
         SNDMSG( hwndStatusbar, WM_SIZE, wParam, lParam );
      } else if ( WM_DRAWITEM == msg ) {
         drawItem( reinterpret_cast< DRAWITEMSTRUCT * >( lParam ) );
      }
      return lResult;
   }

Statusbar::Statusbar( HWND hwndParent, UINT uiID )
   : m_hicon( 0 )
   , m_nIndex( 0 )
{

   assert( 0 != this );

   const HINSTANCE hinst = getModuleHandle();
```

```
   attach( CreateWindowEx(
      0, STATUSCLASSNAME, _T( "" ),
      SBARS_SIZEGRIP | WS_CHILD | WS_VISIBLE,
      0, 0, 0, 0,  hwndParent, (HMENU) uiID, hinst, 0 ) );
   assert( IsWindow( *this ) );
   if ( !IsWindow( *this ) ) {
      throwException( _T( "Unable to create status bar" ) );
   }

   onSettingChange( 0 ); // Sets the font and the parts.
   verify( s_parentSubclasser.subclass( hwndParent, m_hwnd ) );
   setMessage( IDS_READY );
}

Statusbar::~Statusbar() {

   if ( 0 != m_hicon ) {
      DestroyIcon( m_hicon );
   }
}

void __cdecl Statusbar::setMessageV( LPCTSTR pszFmt, va_list vl ) {

   // This *must* be a static buffer. Since the first pane is
   // SBT_OWNERDRAW, the status bar control doesn't know that
   // this is text; the lParam is merely 32 arbitrary bits of
   // application data, and the status bar doesn't retain the
   // text, just the pointer.
   static TCHAR szMessageBuffer[ 200 ];

   assert( isGoodStringPtr( pszFmt ) );
   if ( isGoodStringPtr( pszFmt ) ) {
      const String strMessage = formatMessageV( pszFmt, vl );
      _tcsncpy( szMessageBuffer,
         strMessage.c_str(), dim( szMessageBuffer ) );
   } else {
      _tcscpy( szMessageBuffer, _T( "Internal Error" ) );
   }
```

```
      int nPart = message_part | SBT_OWNERDRAW;
   if ( sm_bHighlight ) {
      nPart |= SBT_NOBORDERS; // SBT_POPOUT
      // This invalidation is necessary for SBT_NOBORDERS.
      // With SBT_POPOUT, it is not necessary.
      Rect rc;
      sendMessage( SB_GETRECT,
         message_part, reinterpret_cast< LPARAM >( &rc ) );
      InvalidateRect( *this, &rc, TRUE );
   }
   setText( nPart, szMessageBuffer );
}

void __cdecl Statusbar::setMessage( LPCTSTR pszFmt, ... ) {

   sm_bHighlight = false;

   va_list vl;
   va_start( vl, pszFmt );
   setMessageV( pszFmt, vl );
   va_end( vl );
}

void __cdecl Statusbar::setMessage( UINT idFmt, ... ) {

   sm_bHighlight = false;

   const String strFmt = loadString( idFmt );

   va_list vl;
   va_start( vl, idFmt );
   setMessageV( strFmt.c_str(), vl );
   va_end( vl );
}

void __cdecl Statusbar::setHighlightMessage( UINT idFmt, ... ) {

   sm_bHighlight = true;
```

```
   const String strFmt = loadString( idFmt );

   va_list vl;
   va_start( vl, idFmt );
   setMessageV( strFmt.c_str(), vl );
   va_end( vl );
}

void __cdecl Statusbar::setErrorMessage(
   UINT idFlags, UINT idFmt, ... )
{
   va_list vl;
   va_start( vl, idFmt );

   MessageBeep( idFlags );

   const String strFmt = loadString( idFmt );
   if ( IsWindowVisible( *this ) ) {
      sm_bHighlight = true;
      setMessageV( strFmt.c_str(), vl );
   } else {
      messageBoxV(
         GetParent( *this ), MB_OK | idFlags, strFmt.c_str(), vl );
   }

   va_end( vl );
}

void Statusbar::update( const Point& position ) {

#if 0 // Unit test of formatNumber
   trace( _T( "testing formatNumber: %d = %s\n" ),
      0, formatNumber( 0 ).c_str() );
   trace( _T( "testing formatNumber: %d = %s\n" ),
      123, formatNumber( 123 ).c_str() );
   trace( _T( "testing formatNumber: %d = %s\n" ),
      12345, formatNumber( 12345 ).c_str() );
   trace( _T( "testing formatNumber: %d = %s\n" ),
      1234567890, formatNumber( 1234567890 ).c_str() );
```

```
#endif

    const String strLine = formatNumber( position.y + 1 );
    const String strColumn = formatNumber( position.x + 1 );
    const String strPos = formatMessage(
        IDS_POSITION, strLine.c_str(), strColumn.c_str() );
    setText( position_part, strPos.c_str() );

    const HWND hwndEditWnd =
        GetDlgItem( GetParent( *this ), IDC_EDIT );
    if ( GetFocus() == hwndEditWnd ) {
        setMessage( IDS_READY );
    }
}

void Statusbar::setFileType( const bool isUnicode ) {

    setText( filetype_part,
        isUnicode ? _T( "\tUnicode\t" ) : _T( "\tANSI\t" ) );
}

void Statusbar::setIcon( int nIndex ) {

    const int nResource = MenuFont::isLarge() ? 121: 120;
    const HINSTANCE hinst = GetModuleHandle( _T( "COMCTL32" ) );
    const HIMAGELIST hImageList = ImageList_LoadImage( hinst,
        MAKEINTRESOURCE( nResource ),
         0, 0, CLR_DEFAULT, IMAGE_BITMAP,
        LR_DEFAULTSIZE | LR_LOADMAP3DCOLORS );
    setIcon( hImageList, nIndex );
    verify( ImageList_Destroy( hImageList ) );
}

void Statusbar::setIcon( HIMAGELIST hImageList, int nIndex ) {

    if ( 0 != m_hicon ) {
        DestroyIcon( m_hicon );
        m_hicon = 0;
    }
```

```
   m_nIndex = nIndex;
   if ( 0 != m_nIndex ) {
      m_hicon = ImageList_GetIcon( hImageList, m_nIndex, ILD_NORMAL );
   }

   sendMessage( SB_SETICON, action_part,
      reinterpret_cast< LPARAM >( m_hicon ) );
   UpdateWindow( *this );
}

void Statusbar::onSettingChange( LPCTSTR pszSection ) {

   const HFONT hfont = MenuFont::getFont();
   assert( 0 != hfont );
   SetWindowFont( *this, hfont, true );
   setIcon( m_nIndex );
   recalcParts( *this );
}
```

Chapter 9

The Main Window

The `mainWndProc` function (in Listing 9.4, `mainwnd.cpp`) implements the window function for TextEdit's main window and is the central switchboard of TextEdit. To do the switching, it employs the message cracker macros in `windowsx.h`. Even though `mainWndProc` contains the big switch statement of traditional window functions, the `HANDLE_MSG` macro delegates each message to an appropriate handler function in a (sort of) type-safe manner. At least the programmer doesn't need to worry about the parameter packing for the various messages. Furthermore, the macros are portable between Win16 and Win32. This is particularly important for messages such as `WM_COMMAND`, where the parameter packing changed.

Handling `WM_COMMAND` Messages

The `onCommand` handler function is a switchboard within a switchboard. In the same way that `mainWndProc` farms out message handling to individual functions, `onCommand` farms out command handling to individual functions. The only exception is the range of commands `ID_MRU_1` through `ID_MRU_9`, which is handled directly in `onCommand`. The command handlers could have been extended to handle ranges of commands, of course, but it hardly seems worth the bother.

One surprise is the existence of both `ID_EDIT_FINDNEXT`, which is on the menu, and `ID_ACCEL_FINDNEXT`, which is the command sent by the accelerator key F3. Yet both commands map to the `onEditFindNext` function. How come?

The reason is that the menu command "Find Next" is disabled when no previous search exists. If F3 mapped to `ID_EDIT_FINDNEXT`, this accelerator key would also be disabled. I do want it to do something, though: behave as though `ID_EDIT_FIND` had been selected. This is handled easily enough in `onEditFindNext`; the whole point of using two command IDs is to avoid disabling the accelerator merely because the menu item is disabled.

Some command handlers are pure debug scaffolding: `onDivideByZero`, `onAccessViolation`, `onOutOfMemory`, and `onStackOverflow`. Their only purpose is to exercise the exception handling; they are excluded from release builds.

`TestClass` is used to verify proper stack unwinding when an exception is thrown; all it does is trace its construction and its destruction:

```
class TestClass {
public:
    TestClass () { trace( _T( "TestClass ctor\n" ) ); }
    ~TestClass() { trace( _T( "TestClass dtor\n" ) ); }
};

PRIVATE void onAccessViolation( HWND ) {

    TestClass testClass;

    lstrcpy( 0, _T( "uh-oh!" ) ); // No exception
    _tcscpy( 0, _T( "uh-oh!" ) ); // Exception
}
```

My first implementation of `onAccessViolation` used `lstrcpy` to force an access violation. This failed though, in the sense that it didn't fail. The access violation is caught in the bowels of `lstrcpy`, which just fails quietly. This kind of "error handling" is an abomination; while it protects the program from crashing, it also protects the programmer from noticing what is certain to be a bug in the program. It certainly doesn't protect the program from working incorrectly.

The Clipboard User Interface

The implementation of the clipboard commands — cut, copy, and paste — is straightforward enough. Representing them properly in the user interface is a little trickier:
- Copy should be enabled iff text is selected.
- Cut should be enabled iff text is selected and the file is writeable.
- Paste should be enabled iff the clipboard contains text and the file is writeable.

(*Iff*, by the way, is shorthand for "if and only if.") The delete command is grouped with the clipboard commands on the Edit menu; it should be enabled iff the file is writeable and non-empty.

Enabling and disabling menu items is easy. We receive a `WM_INITMENU` message just before the menu opens and can enable and disable to our heart's content. The toolbar is another matter. Because it is always visible, we must enable and disable buttons synchronously in response to outside events.

Enabling and disabling of the cut and copy commands is done in `Editor::onPosChange`, which is called whenever something happens in the edit control, including when the selection changes.

To properly enable and disable the paste command, the TextEdit main window hooks itself into the clipboard viewer chain. Each member of the clipboard viewer chain is responsible for holding the next viewer in the chain; if any application fails to uphold this responsibility, the viewer chain collapses. This design stems from the early days of Windows and is not very robust. Today, this would probably (?) have been designed differently, as it is really asking for trouble.

At any rate, `mainwnd.cpp` has a static variable `s_hwndNextClipboardViewer` to do the job; it is initialized in `onCreate`:

```
s_hwndNextClipboardViewer = SetClipboardViewer( hwnd );
```

The window is unhooked from the chain again in `onDestroy`:

```
ChangeClipboardChain( hwnd, s_hwndNextClipboardViewer );
```

Once registered as a clipboard viewer, the window receives `WM_DRAWCLIPBOARD` messages whenever the clipboard contents change:

```
PRIVATE void onDrawClipboard( HWND hwnd ) {
   if ( IsWindow( s_hwndNextClipboardViewer ) ) {
      FORWARD_WM_DRAWCLIPBOARD( s_hwndNextClipboardViewer, SNDMSG );
   }
   enablePaste( hwnd );
}
```

The `enablePaste` function is responsible for actually enabling and disabling the paste command. Its implementation is trivial; the trick lies in calling it at the right time. The `onDrawClipboard` function takes care of this.

The hairiest part of clipboard viewerhood is handling someone else's unhooking from the chain. If the window just below us in the chain — `s_hwndNextClipboardViewer` — is bailing out, we must update the `s_hwndNextClipboardViewer` variable with the next window down the chain. If not, we just forward the `WM_CHANGECBCHAIN` message to `s_hwndNextClipboardViewer`:

```
PRIVATE void onChangeCBChain(
   HWND hwnd, HWND hwndRemove, HWND hwndNext )
{
   if ( s_hwndNextClipboardViewer == hwndRemove ) {
      s_hwndNextClipboardViewer = hwndNext;
   } else {
      FORWARD_WM_CHANGECBCHAIN( s_hwndNextClipboardViewer,
         hwndRemove, hwndNext, SNDMSG );
   }
}
```

An interesting experiment is to remove the forwarding of WM_DRAWCLIPBOARD, then start the clipboard viewer, then start TextEdit. The clipboard viewer is now essentially blind to changes of the clipboard contents! As I said, the design of the clipboard viewer chain is asking for trouble.

Persistence in the Main Window

TextEdit stores information about the position and size of the window used to edit a given file. That way, we can restore the window to the same position and size the next time that file is edited. The Editor::saveState method is responsible for — you guessed it — saving the state.

Many applications save state information of one kind or another, and a common approach is to save the state when the application exits. If the application (or the whole system) crashes, the state information is, unfortunately, lost.

TextEdit saves state information for the window whenever said state information has changed. When that happens, we get WM_SIZE, WM_MOVE, or WM_SYSCOMMAND messages. The natural thing to do would be to call saveState in response to these messages, but with full-window dragging, this can slow things down so much that the dragging gets noticeably more jerky. To avoid this problem, we start a half-second timer instead, and call saveState in response to the firing of the timer. The timer is reset on every new state-changing message, so state is only saved when the user stops dragging the window or pauses for more than half a second.

Why, I hear you ask, not use WM_EXITSIZEMOVE instead of this timer nonsense? This is due to an implementation oddity in Windows. Perhaps I'm even justified in calling it a bug, as I'm fairly sure it was unintentional: if you select one of the window tiling commands from the task bar context menu, WM_EXITSIZEMOVE is never sent. I know this to be true under Windows NT 4.0; it may not be true on all versions of Windows. That's irrelevant in any case; as long as one supported platform misbehaves, we need to handle the problem.

A final detail about full-window dragging: this can cause unsightly flashing of the caret in the edit window. To avoid this, the caret is hidden in response to WM_ENTERSIZEMOVE and shown again in response to WM_EXITSIZEMOVE. The problem noted above doesn't apply; when you move or size the window, both WM_ENTERSIZEMOVE and WM_EXITSIZEMOVE are sent.

Chapter 10 explains how to create persistent variables using the registry. The Document class allows you to create persistent variables on a per-document basis. Window position and window size, for example, are both stored per document.

Drag and Drop

To support file drag and drop, a window must do three things:

1. Call DragAcceptFiles(hwnd, TRUE) at startup time.
2. Call DragAcceptFiles(hwnd, FALSE) at destruction time.
3. Handle the WM_DROPFILES message.

Handling the message is a matter of calling DragQueryFile (perhaps several times), then calling DragFinish. Because TextEdit is an SDI application, we must settle the question of how to handle dropping of multiple files — we obviously can't open them all in the same application instance. TextEdit solves this in a manner similar to how it opens multiple files on the command line: it takes the first file for itself and sends the rest to `startInstance`:

```
PRIVATE void onDropFiles( HWND hwnd, HDROP hdrop ) {

   const UINT DRAGQUERY_NUMFILES = (UINT) -1;
   const int nFiles = DragQueryFile(
      hdrop, DRAGQUERY_NUMFILES, 0, 0 );
   for ( int iFile = nFiles - 1; 0 <= iFile; --iFile ) {
      PATHNAME szDragFile = { 0 };
      verify( 0 < DragQueryFile(
         hdrop, iFile, szDragFile, dim( szDragFile ) ) );
      if ( 0 == iFile ) {
         Editor *pEditor = getEditor( hwnd );
         pEditor->saveIfNecessary();
         pEditor->openFile( szDragFile );
      } else {
         const String strArg =
            formatMessage( _T( "\"%1\"" ), szDragFile );
         startInstance( strArg );
      }
   }
   DragFinish( hdrop );
}
```

Menu Management

TextEdit handles two messages that properly fall under the heading of menu management: `WM_INITMENU` and `WM_MENUSELECT`.

The `WM_INITMENU` message is sent just before a menu drops down and is intended to let you adjust menu items — enabling, disabling, checking and unchecking are typical chores. Because drop-down menus aren't visible all the time, it is sufficient to do this just before the menu opens, and usually easier, too. The toolbar is more of a problem. It is always visible, and demands immediate gratification.

In Listing 9.4, `mainwnd.cpp`, `WM_INITMENU` is handled by `onInitMenu`. Aside from enabling and disabling this and that, it also refreshes the MRU (Most Recently Used) file list. The `WM_INITMENU` message is sent for popup menus as well as for window menus, so the exact same function serves to append the MRU file list to the toolbar's File Open popup menu.

The `WM_MENUSELECT` message is sent when a menu or menu item is highlighted. Note that the `HANDLE_WM_MENUSELECT` macro in `windowsx.h` has a bug — it doesn't handle the `MENU_CLOSING` case correctly. For that reason, the macro is redefined in Listing 9.4, `mainwnd.cpp` (this time correctly).

In `mainwnd.cpp`, `WM_MENUSELECT` is handled by `onMenuSelect`. The message is handled to update the status bar with a description of the currently highlighted menu item. The Windows function `MenuHelp` can be used to take the drudgery out of this, but TextEdit doesn't use it. In the first place, `MenuHelp` can't display text for popup menus; in the second place, it doesn't give you much control over the string to display.

Popup menus don't, unfortunately, have useful IDs, so when a popup menu comes along, you must somehow figure out which menu it is. The most obvious and simple way to do this is to check the first menu item on the menu. If the first menu item is `ID_FILE_NEW`, for example, you have hold of the File menu. The problem with this approach is that it breaks if you insert a new item at the top of a menu, and it doesn't handle cascading menus without extra work.

TextEdit uses a different approach; it checks to see if the menu contains — anywhere — a given menu item. This approach is more robust than the first one. Both approaches can run into problems if a menu hierarchy has duplicate entries of the key IDs. One may hope that Microsoft adds IDs to popup menus some day; this feature has always been present in OS/2's Presentation Manager.

The `Editor` class has two helper functions that produce menu description strings. One is `getMenuDescription`, which handles submenus; the other is `getMenuItemDescription`, which handles menu items. The latter tries its best to be clever, and changes the description depending on whether an item is enabled or disabled, what the current file name is, or what the current selection is. This requires some hand coding, but the effect in the user interface is nice.

The `menuUtils` module, defines utility functions for use with menus and menu items. For the most part, these are simple wrappers for Windows functions. The only exception is `containsMenuItem`, which checks whether a menu or any of its submenus contains a command with a given ID. (Discourse continues on page 187.)

Listing 9.1   menuUtils.h

```
/*
 * $Header: /Book/menuUtils.h 7     3.07.99 17:46 Petter $
 */

#pragma once

#include "String.h"

inline void enableMenuItem( HMENU hmenu, UINT item, bool bEnable ) {
    assert( ::IsMenu( hmenu ) );
    EnableMenuItem( hmenu, item,
        MF_BYCOMMAND | ((bEnable) ? MF_ENABLED : MF_GRAYED) );
}

inline void checkMenuItem( HMENU hmenu, UINT item, bool bCheck ) {
```

```
   assert( ::IsMenu( hmenu ) );
   CheckMenuItem( hmenu, item, bCheck ? MF_CHECKED : MF_UNCHECKED );
}

inline void checkMenuRadioItem(
   HMENU hmenu, UINT itemFirst, UINT itemLast, UINT itemCheck )
{
   assert( ::IsMenu( hmenu ) );
   CheckMenuRadioItem(
      hmenu, itemFirst, itemLast, itemCheck, MF_BYCOMMAND );
}

bool containsItem( HMENU hmenu, UINT uiCmd, bool bRecursive = false );
void appendMenuItem(
   HMENU hmenu, UINT item, LPCTSTR pszText, bool bDefault = false );
void appendSeparator( HMENU hmenu );

String getMenuItemText( HMENU hmenu, UINT uiCmd );
void __cdecl setMenuItemText(
   HMENU hmenu, UINT uiCmd, LPCTSTR pszFmt, ... );
```

Listing 9.2   menuUtils.cpp

```
/*
 * $Header: /Book/menuUtils.cpp 10    3.07.99 17:46 Petter $
 */

#include "precomp.h"
#include "menuUtils.h"
#include "formatMessage.h"
#include "String.h"

/**
 * The recursive case is depth-first.
 */
bool containsItem( HMENU hmenu, UINT uiCmd, bool bRecursive ) {

   assert( IsMenu( hmenu ) );
   const int nItems = GetMenuItemCount( hmenu );
   for ( int iItem = 0; iItem < nItems; ++iItem ) {
```

```
        HMENU hmenuSub = GetSubMenu( hmenu, iItem );
        if ( IsMenu( hmenuSub ) ) {
            return bRecursive
                ? containsItem( hmenuSub, uiCmd, true ) : false;
        } else if ( GetMenuItemID( hmenu, iItem ) == uiCmd ) {
            return true;
        }
      }
    }
    return false;
}

String getMenuItemText( HMENU hmenu, UINT uiCmd ) {

    TCHAR szMenuItem[ 100 ] = { 0 };
    GetMenuString(
        hmenu, uiCmd, szMenuItem, dim( szMenuItem ), MF_BYCOMMAND );
    return szMenuItem;
}

/**
 * This avoids the error-prone ID repetition required by ModifyMenu.
 */
void __cdecl setMenuItemText(
    HMENU hmenu, UINT uiCmd, LPCTSTR pszFmt, ... )
{
    va_list vl;
    va_start( vl, pszFmt );
    String strMenuText( formatMessageV( pszFmt, vl ) );
    va_end( vl );

    ModifyMenu(
        hmenu, uiCmd, MF_BYCOMMAND, uiCmd, strMenuText.c_str() );
}

void appendMenuItem(
    HMENU hmenu, UINT item, LPCTSTR pszText, bool bDefault )
{
    assert( 0 == offsetof( MENUITEMINFO, cbSize ) );
    MENUITEMINFO menuItemInfo = {
```

```
      sizeof( MENUITEMINFO ), MIIM_ID | MIIM_TYPE | MIIM_STATE,
      MFT_STRING, MFS_ENABLED, item, 0, 0, 0, 0,
      const_cast< LPTSTR >( pszText ),
      sizeof( TCHAR ) * _tcsclen( pszText ),
   };
   if ( bDefault ) {
      menuItemInfo.fState |= MFS_DEFAULT;
   }
   verify( InsertMenuItem( hmenu, item, false, &menuItemInfo ) );
}

void appendSeparator( HMENU hmenu ) {

   assert( 0 == offsetof( MENUITEMINFO, cbSize ) );
   MENUITEMINFO menuItemInfo = {
      sizeof( MENUITEMINFO ), MIIM_TYPE,
         MFT_SEPARATOR, 0, 0, 0, 0, 0, 0, 0
   };
   verify( InsertMenuItem( hmenu, (UINT) -1, false, &menuItemInfo ) );
}
```

Messy Menus

The keyboard interface to the menu has its problems. Hold down the Alt key, press F, and the File menu pops up (or rolls down, whichever you prefer). Don't let go of that Alt key yet; look instead at the line that says "Properties... Alt+Enter."

Now imagine the neophyte with his Alt key down, looking at Figure 9.1 (either half) and trying to get to File Properties:

"OK, I have the Alt key down already, after doing Alt+F. All I have to do now is press Enter, lets see ... damn! What happened? Why did I get a new file?"

Or imagine him, the Alt key now released, still looking at Figure 9.1, pressing Ctrl+O for all he's worth, and still no Open dialog is forthcoming.

Microsoft, are you listening?

Accelerator Alignment

To align the accelerator descriptions in a column at the right-hand side of the menu, you include a tab character (\t) in the menu text. The left part of Figure 9.1 illustrates this. It also illustrates a problem with this approach; the accelerator descriptions are lined up beyond the widest item in the menu. The widest items are on the MRU list, which is visually disconnected from the rest of the menu. We could save a lot of real estate by ignoring the MRU list when determining the tab position.

An alternative is to replace \t with \a in the resource script. This aligns all the text that follows it flush right on the menu, as shown in the right-hand part of Figure 9.1. This menu is much more efficient in its use of pixels than the left-hand example, achieved at the cost of destroying the alignment of the accelerator descriptions.

I would dearly have loved to have the best of both worlds: the space efficiency of the right-hand variant with the alignment of the left-hand variant.

Microsoft, écoutez-vous?

Figure 9.1   The File menu is unnecessarily wide (left-hand menu), or the accelerators are not aligned (right-hand menu).

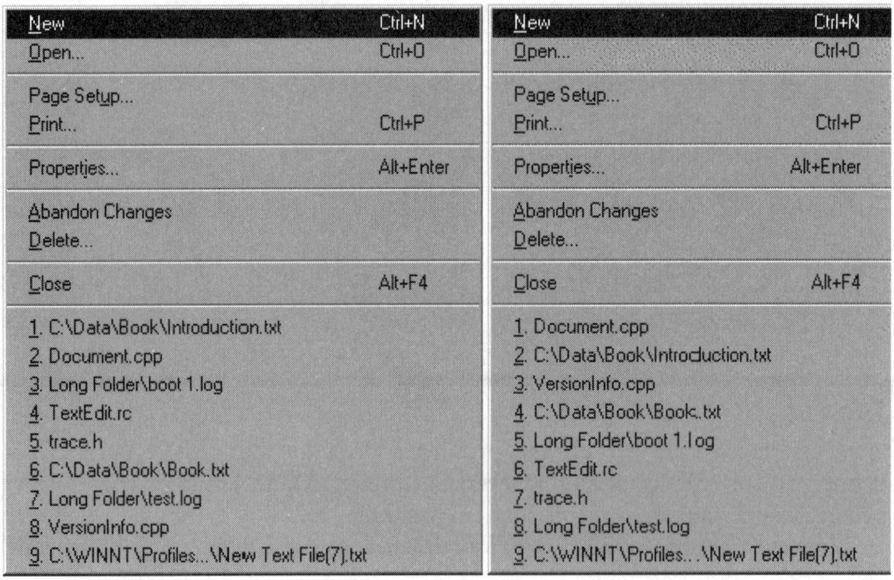

Hint: If you add menu items programmatically rather than from a resource script, replace \a with \b, or it won't work. I can't say whether this is a bug or a feature.

Communication Between TextEdit Instances

Different instances of TextEdit communicate using the WM_APP message. During startup, TextEdit checks to see if an already running instance has a given file loaded; it does this using WM_APP. (see the activateOldInstance module). The lParam is a global atom representing the file name. WM_APP returns 1 if the atom represents the currently loaded file, otherwise 0.

Changing User Settings

Windows broadcasts WM_SYSCOLORCHANGE or WM_SETTINGCHANGE messages whenever the user changes the customization of the Windows GUI. Handling WM_SYSCOLORCHANGE is straightforward; WM_SETTINGCHANGE is more complex. The language may have changed, so the menu bar must be redrawn. Font sizes may have changed; this may require recalculating the layout. The status bar uses the currently defined menu font (see the MenuFont class), and the toolbar uses large icons if the size of the menu font is above a certain threshold.

Many applications, such as the Windows Explorer, don't change the font in the status bar to reflect changes in the user's preferences. I find this rather strange.

Even TextEdit doesn't change the font in the dialogs, sad to say.

Notifications

The main window does not handle WM_NOTIFY. Yet, it does have a toolbar, complete with ToolTips and drop-down menu. Both these features are handled through WM_NOTIFY, so what's going on here?

The toolbar subclasses the main window, that's what's going on. It does this (a) in order to spy on WM_SIZE messages, and (b) in order to steal the WM_NOTIFY messages. That way, more functionality is encapsulated within the toolbar itself.

The Editor Connection

The main window's reference to the Editor object is stored as a window long. The registration of the main window class reserves MAINWND_EXTRABYTES extra bytes of storage for each instance.

Given the handle to the main window, the getEditor function retrieves the corresponding Editor object.

Listing 9.3   mainwnd.h

```
/*
 * $Header: /Book/mainwnd.h 9     3.07.99 17:46 Petter $
 */

#pragma once

#include "Exception.h"
#include "Editor.h"
#include "trace.h"

extern LRESULT CALLBACK mainWndProc(
    HWND hwnd, UINT msg, WPARAM wParam, LPARAM lParam );
```

```
#define EDITOR_OFFSET 0
#define MAINWND_EXTRABYTES sizeof( Editor * )

/**
 * This function returns a null pointer during startup.
 * When called after setup, the hwnd is null, too,
 * but GetWindowLong fails gracefully in that case.
 */
inline Editor *getEditor( HWND hwnd ) {
   Editor *pEditor = reinterpret_cast< Editor * >(
      GetWindowLong( hwnd, EDITOR_OFFSET ) );
   assert( 0 == pEditor || isGoodPtr( pEditor ) );
   if ( 0 == pEditor ) {
      trace( _T( "getEditor throws NullPointerException\n" ) );
      throw NullPointerException();
   }
   return pEditor;
}
```

Listing 9.4   mainwnd.cpp

```
/*
 * $Header: /Book/mainwnd.cpp 23    20.08.99 16:33 Petter $
 */

#include "precomp.h"
#include "mainwnd.h"
#include "Editor.h"
#include "Dialog.h"
#include "OptionsDlg.h"
#include "AboutDlg.h"
#include "FindDlg.h"
#include "DeleteDlg.h"
#include "FontDlg.h"
#include "PropertiesDlg.h"
#include "Toolbar.h"
#include "Registry.h"
#include "WaitCursor.h"
#include "Exception.h"
#include "AutoArray.h"
```

```cpp
#include "Statusbar.h"
#include "MenuFont.h"
#include "MRU.h"
#include "saveFile.h"
#include "openFile.h"
#include "printFile.h"
#include "setupPage.h"
#include "createNewFile.h"
#include "startInstance.h"
#include "formatMessage.h"
#include "fileUtils.h"
#include "menuUtils.h"
#include "winUtils.h"
#include "init.h"
#include "help.h"
#include "utils.h"
#include "os.h"
#include "persistence.h"
#include "timers.h"
#include "trace.h"
#include "resource.h"

#include "Help/map.hh"

#define HANDLE_WM_ENTERSIZEMOVE( \
    hwnd, wParam, lParam, fn ) ((fn)(hwnd), 0L)
#define HANDLE_WM_EXITSIZEMOVE( \
    hwnd, wParam, lParam, fn ) ((fn)(hwnd), 0L)
#define HANDLE_WM_POWERBROADCAST( hwnd, wParam, lParam, fn ) \
    (fn)((hwnd), (DWORD)(wParam), (DWORD)(wParam))
#define HANDLE_WM_HELP( hwnd, wParam, lParam, fn ) \
    (fn)((hwnd), reinterpret_cast< HELPINFO * >( lParam ))
#define HANDLE_WM_APP( hwnd, wParam, lParam, fn ) \
    (fn)((hwnd), static_cast< ATOM >( lParam ))

PRIVATE String s_strLast;
PRIVATE HWND s_hwndNextClipboardViewer;

PRIVATE void onSize( HWND hwnd, UINT state, int cx, int cy );
```

```
PRIVATE inline Toolbar *getToolbar( HWND hwnd ) {

   Editor *pEditor = getEditor( hwnd );
   assert( 0 != pEditor );
   Toolbar *pToolbar = pEditor->getToolbar();
   assert( 0 != pToolbar && IsWindow( *pToolbar ) );
   return pToolbar;
}

PRIVATE inline AbstractEditWnd *getEditWnd( HWND hwnd ) {

   Editor *pEditor = getEditor( hwnd );
   assert( 0 != pEditor );
   AbstractEditWnd *pEditWnd = pEditor->getEditWnd();
   assert( 0 != pEditWnd && IsWindow( *pEditWnd ) );
   return pEditWnd;
}

PRIVATE inline Document *getDocument( HWND hwnd ) {
   Editor *pEditor = getEditor( hwnd );
   assert( 0 != pEditor );
   return pEditor->getDocument();
}

PRIVATE Statusbar *getStatusbar( HWND hwnd ) {
   Editor *pEditor = getEditor( hwnd );
   assert( 0 != pEditor );
   return pEditor->getStatusbar();
}

PRIVATE void setFont( const HWND hwnd, bool bFixed ) {

   getEditor( hwnd )->setFont( bFixed );
}

PRIVATE void enablePaste( HWND hwnd ) {
   const bool bCanPaste =
      IsClipboardFormatAvailable( CF_TEXT ) &&
      !getEditWnd( hwnd )->isReadOnly();
```

```cpp
   getToolbar( hwnd )->setEnabled( ID_EDIT_PASTE, bCanPaste );
   enableMenuItem( GetMenu( hwnd ), ID_EDIT_PASTE, bCanPaste );
}


/**
 * Called when the size of the docked windows might
 * have changed (from onSettingChange) or when one
 * of them are shown or hidden (toggleDockedWindow).
 * (Docked windows, who dat? Toolbar and Statusbar, dat who.)
 */
PRIVATE void recalcLayout( const HWND hwnd ) {

   if ( !IsIconic( hwnd ) ) {
      const Rect rc = getClientRect( hwnd );
      onSize( hwnd, SIZE_RESTORED,
         rc.right - rc.left, rc.bottom - rc.top );
   }
   InvalidateRect( *getEditor( hwnd )->getToolbar(), 0, 0 );
}

PRIVATE inline void setEditor( HWND hwnd, Editor *pEditor ) {

   assert( 0 == pEditor || IsWindow( *pEditor->getEditWnd() ) );
   if ( 0 == pEditor ) {
      getEditor( hwnd )->detach( hwnd );
   }
   SetWindowLong( hwnd, EDITOR_OFFSET,
      reinterpret_cast< LONG >( pEditor ) );
}


/*
 * Message handlers:
 */

PRIVATE bool onCreate( HWND hwnd, CREATESTRUCT FAR* lpCreateStruct ) {

   AutoDocument *ppDocument = reinterpret_cast< AutoDocument *>(
      lpCreateStruct->lpCreateParams );
   assert( 0 != ppDocument );
```

```
   Editor *pEditor = new Editor( hwnd, ppDocument );
   setEditor( hwnd, pEditor );

   // NOTE: From this point until the AutoEditor in WinMain has
   // been initialized, pEditor is vulnerable to leakage.
   // The risk is, however, quite low, and no user data would
   // be lost in any case.

   const Document  *pDocument  = pEditor->getDocument ();
   AbstractEditWnd *pEditWnd   = pEditor->getEditWnd  ();
   Statusbar       *pStatusbar = pEditor->getStatusbar();

   if ( !pEditWnd->hasRedo() ) {
      verify(
         DeleteMenu( GetMenu( hwnd ), ID_EDIT_REDO, MF_BYCOMMAND ) );
   }

   pEditWnd->setFirstVisibleLine( pDocument->getFirstLine() );
   pEditWnd->setSel(
      pDocument->getSelStart(), pDocument->getSelEnd() );
   pEditor->setSettings();
   pStatusbar->update( pEditWnd->getCurPos() );
   if ( pDocument->isBinary() ) {
      pStatusbar->setHighlightMessage( IDS_BINARY );
   }
   enablePaste( hwnd );

   s_hwndNextClipboardViewer = SetClipboardViewer( hwnd );
   DragAcceptFiles( hwnd, true );

   return TRUE;
}

PRIVATE void onActivate(
   HWND hwnd, UINT state, HWND hwndActDeact, BOOL fMinimized )
{
   if ( WA_INACTIVE == state ) {
      getEditor( hwnd )->saveIfNecessary();
```

```cpp
      }
   }

   PRIVATE void onDestroy( const HWND hwnd ) {

      getEditor( hwnd )->saveState();
      assert( getEditor( hwnd )->isClean() );

      // SetMenu results in a number of messages, including
      // WM_SIZE. onSize throws a NullPointerException if
      // there is no Editor object, so the call to SetMenu
      // *must* come before we reset the Editor.
      verify( DestroyMenu( GetMenu( hwnd ) ) );
      SetMenu( hwnd, 0 );
      setEditor( hwnd, 0 );

      WinHelp( hwnd, getHelpFile(), HELP_QUIT, 0 );
      ChangeClipboardChain( hwnd, s_hwndNextClipboardViewer );
      DragAcceptFiles( hwnd, false );
      PostQuitMessage( 0 ); // Goodbye, and thanks for all the fish!
   }

   PRIVATE void onClose ( HWND hwnd ) {

      getEditor( hwnd )->saveIfNecessary();
      DestroyWindow( hwnd );
   }

   PRIVATE void openFile( HWND hwnd, const String& str ) {

      Editor *pEditor = getEditor( hwnd );
      if ( pEditor->saveIfNecessary() ) {
         pEditor->openFile( str );
      }
      enablePaste( hwnd );
   }

   class AutoDrop {
   private:
      HDROP m_hdrop;
```

```
public:
   AutoDrop( HDROP hdrop ) : m_hdrop( hdrop ) {
   }
   ~AutoDrop() {
      assert( 0 != m_hdrop );
      DragFinish( m_hdrop );
   }
};

PRIVATE void onDropFiles( HWND hwnd, HDROP hdrop ) {

   AutoDrop autoDrop( hdrop );

   const UINT DRAGQUERY_NUMFILES = (UINT) -1;
   const int nFiles = DragQueryFile(
      hdrop, DRAGQUERY_NUMFILES, 0, 0 );
   for ( int iFile = nFiles - 1; 0 <= iFile; --iFile ) {
      PATHNAME szDragFile = { 0 };
      verify( 0 < DragQueryFile(
         hdrop, iFile, szDragFile, dim( szDragFile ) ) );
      if ( 0 == iFile ) {
         openFile( hwnd, szDragFile );
      } else {
         const String strArg =
            formatMessage( _T( "\"%1\"" ), szDragFile );
         startInstance( strArg );
      }
   }
}

PRIVATE void onTimer( HWND hwnd, UINT id ) {

   switch ( id ) {
   case timer_save_state:
      KillTimer( hwnd, timer_save_state );
      getEditor( hwnd )->saveState();
      break;

   default:
```

```
            // This will cause any defined callback to be called.
            FORWARD_WM_TIMER( hwnd, id, DefWindowProc );
            break;
      }
}

PRIVATE void onSize( HWND hwnd, UINT state, int cx, int cy ) {

#if 0 // Both children subclass us, so no need to pass this on.
   FORWARD_WM_SIZE( *getStatusbar( hwnd ), state, cx, cy, SNDMSG );
   FORWARD_WM_SIZE(   *getToolbar( hwnd ), state, cx, cy, SNDMSG );
#endif

   if ( SIZE_MINIMIZED != state ) {
      if ( IsWindowVisible( *getStatusbar( hwnd ) ) ) {
         const Rect rc = getWindowRect( *getStatusbar( hwnd ) );
         cy -= rc.height();
      }

      int y = 0;
      if ( IsWindowVisible( *getToolbar( hwnd ) ) ) {
         const Rect rc = getWindowRect( *getToolbar( hwnd ) );
         y = rc.height();
         cy -= y;
      }

      AbstractEditWnd *pEditWnd = getEditWnd( hwnd );
      MoveWindow( *pEditWnd, 0, y, cx, cy, true );
   }

   // One might think that it would be more efficient to just
   // saveState for SIZE_MINIMIZED and SIZE_MAXIMIZED here, using
   // onExitSizeMove to save the state for SIZE_RESTORED.
   // Unfortunately, if you select a window tiling command from the
   // task bar context menu, WM_EXITSIZEMOVE is never sent.

   SetTimer( hwnd, timer_save_state, 500, 0 );
}
```

```c
PRIVATE void onMove( HWND hwnd, int x, int y ) {

   SetTimer( hwnd, timer_save_state, 500, 0 );
}

PRIVATE void onEnterSizeMove( const HWND hwnd ) {
   HideCaret( 0 );
}

PRIVATE void onExitSizeMove( const HWND hwnd ) {
   ShowCaret( 0 );
}

// Todo: Retain focus while deactivated?
PRIVATE void onSetFocus( const HWND hwnd, HWND /* hwndOldFocus */ ) {

   AbstractEditWnd *pEditWnd = getEditWnd( hwnd );
   if ( IsWindowVisible( *pEditWnd ) ) {
      SetFocus( *pEditWnd );
   }
}

PRIVATE void onDrawClipboard( HWND hwnd ) {

   if ( IsWindow( s_hwndNextClipboardViewer ) ) {
      FORWARD_WM_DRAWCLIPBOARD( s_hwndNextClipboardViewer, SNDMSG );
   }
   enablePaste( hwnd );
}

PRIVATE void onChangeCBChain(
   HWND hwnd, HWND hwndRemove, HWND hwndNext )
{
   if ( s_hwndNextClipboardViewer == hwndRemove ) {
      s_hwndNextClipboardViewer = hwndNext;
   } else {
      FORWARD_WM_CHANGECBCHAIN( s_hwndNextClipboardViewer,
         hwndRemove, hwndNext, SNDMSG );
   }
}
```

```
PRIVATE BOOL onQueryEndSession( HWND hwnd ) {

   Editor *pEditor = getEditor( hwnd );;
   pEditor->saveState();
   return pEditor->saveIfNecessary();
}

PRIVATE void onEndSession( HWND hwnd, BOOL fEnding ) {

   Document::s_bEndSession = 0 != fEnding;
}

PRIVATE LRESULT onPowerBroadcast(
   HWND hwnd, DWORD dwPowerEvent, DWORD dwData )
{
   // LATER: GetDevicePowerState( hfile );

#ifdef PBT_APMBATTERYLOW

   switch ( dwPowerEvent ) {
   case PBT_APMBATTERYLOW:
      break;
   case PBT_APMPOWERSTATUSCHANGE:
      break; // LATER: increase or decrease autosave interval
   case PBT_APMRESUMECRITICAL: // Sent only to drivers, not to apps.
      break; // Are we still in good shape?
   case PBT_APMRESUMESUSPEND:
      break; // Normal resumption.
   case PBT_APMQUERYSUSPEND:
      break; // Return BROADCAST_QUERY_DENY to deny
   case PBT_APMSUSPEND:
      break;// LATER: saveIfNecessary.
   }

#endif // PBT_APMBATTERYLOW

   return 0;
}
```

```cpp
PRIVATE inline void onSysColorChange( HWND hwnd ) {

   for ( HWND hwndChild = GetTopWindow( hwnd );
      IsWindow( hwndChild );
      hwndChild = GetNextWindow( hwndChild, GW_HWNDNEXT ) )
   {
      FORWARD_WM_SYSCOLORCHANGE( hwndChild, SNDMSG );
   }
}

PRIVATE void refreshMenu( HWND hwnd ) {

   if ( isWindowsNT() ) { // May have changed language.
      verify( DestroyMenu( GetMenu( hwnd ) ) );
      SetMenu( hwnd, LoadMenu( getModuleHandle(),
         MAKEINTRESOURCE( IDR_MENU ) ) );
      verify( DrawMenuBar( hwnd ) );
      getEditor( hwnd )->loadAcceleratorTable();
   }
   Editor *pEditor = getEditor( hwnd );
   pEditor->refreshToolbar();
   pEditor->setTitle();
}

PRIVATE inline void onSettingChange( HWND hwnd, LPCTSTR pszSection ) {

   refreshMenu( hwnd ); // May have changed language.
   MenuFont::refresh();
   for ( HWND hwndChild = GetTopWindow( hwnd );
      IsWindow( hwndChild );
      hwndChild = GetNextWindow( hwndChild, GW_HWNDNEXT ) )
   {
      FORWARD_WM_SETTINGCHANGE( hwndChild, pszSection, SNDMSG );
   }
   recalcLayout( hwnd );

   // In case the thousand separator has changed:
   getStatusbar( hwnd )->update( getEditWnd( hwnd )->getCurPos() );
```

```
}

PRIVATE inline BOOL onHelp( const HWND hwnd, HELPINFO *pHelpInfo ) {

   help( hwnd, pHelpInfo );
   return TRUE;
}

PRIVATE inline BOOL onApp( const HWND hwnd, ATOM atomDocName ) {

   PATHNAME szDocName = { 0 };
   GlobalGetAtomName( atomDocName, szDocName, dim( szDocName ) );
   const Document *pDocument = getDocument( hwnd );
   assert( isGoodConstPtr( pDocument ) );

#if 0 // Test code
   messageBox( hwnd, MB_OK,
      _T( "atom = %1!d! (%2!#x!)\nname = [%3]" ),
      atomDocName, atomDocName, szDocName );
#endif

   return 0 != pDocument &&
      areFileNamesEqual( pDocument->getPath(), szDocName );
}

/**
 * Note: This is called for *all* menus, including popups!
 */
PRIVATE void onInitMenu( HWND hwnd, HMENU hmenu ) {

   AbstractEditWnd *pEditWnd = getEditWnd( hwnd );

   String strTitle = getDocument( hwnd )->getTitle();
   fixAmpersands( &strTitle );
   const String strFmt = loadString( IDS_FILE_COPY );
   setMenuItemText(
      hmenu, ID_FILE_COPY, strFmt.c_str(),
      compactPath( strTitle.c_str(), 120 ).c_str() );
```

```cpp
const bool bHasText      = 0 < pEditWnd->getTextLength();
const bool bHasSelection = pEditWnd->getSel();
const bool bCanUndo      = pEditWnd->canUndo();
const bool bHasRedo      = pEditWnd->hasRedo();
const bool bCanRedo      = bHasRedo && pEditWnd->canRedo();

enableMenuItem( hmenu,
   ID_FILE_ABANDONCHANGES, !getEditor( hwnd )->isWhistleClean() );

String strDeleteFile = getMenuItemText(
   hmenu, ID_FILE_DELETE );
int iDotPos = strDeleteFile.find( _T( '.' ) );
if ( 0 <= iDotPos ) {
   strDeleteFile.erase( iDotPos );
}
if ( getShowDeleteDialog() ) {
   strDeleteFile.append( _T( "..." ) );
}
setMenuItemText( hmenu, ID_FILE_DELETE, _T( "%1" ),
   strDeleteFile.c_str() );

// TODO -- use Document instead, when fixed.
const bool bReadOnly = getEditWnd( hwnd )->isReadOnly();
enableMenuItem( hmenu, ID_FILE_DELETE, !bReadOnly );

enableMenuItem( hmenu, ID_EDIT_COPY         , bHasSelection );
enableMenuItem( hmenu, ID_EDIT_CUT          , bHasSelection );
enableMenuItem( hmenu, ID_EDIT_FINDSELECTION, bHasText      );
enableMenuItem( hmenu, ID_EDIT_DELETE, !bReadOnly && bHasText );
enableMenuItem( hmenu, ID_EDIT_SELECTALL    , bHasText );

setMenuItemText( hmenu, ID_EDIT_UNDO,
   loadString( IDS_UNDO ).c_str(),
   pEditWnd->getUndoName().c_str() );
enableMenuItem( hmenu, ID_EDIT_UNDO, bCanUndo );

if ( bHasRedo ) {
   setMenuItemText( hmenu, ID_EDIT_REDO,
      loadString( IDS_REDO ).c_str(),
      pEditWnd->getRedoName().c_str() );
```

```
      enableMenuItem( hmenu, ID_EDIT_REDO, bCanRedo );
   }

   enableMenuItem( hmenu, ID_EDIT_FIND, bHasText );
   enableMenuItem( hmenu, ID_EDIT_FINDNEXT,
      bHasText && 0 != s_strLast.size() );
   enableMenuItem( hmenu, ID_EDIT_FINDPREVIOUS,
      bHasText && 0 != s_strLast.size() );
   enableMenuItem( hmenu, ID_EDIT_REPLACE,
      bHasText && !pEditWnd->isReadOnly() );

   checkMenuItem( hmenu, ID_VIEW_TOOLBAR ,
      0 != IsWindowVisible(  *getToolbar( hwnd ) ) );
   checkMenuItem( hmenu, ID_VIEW_STATUSBAR,
      0 != IsWindowVisible( *getStatusbar( hwnd ) ) );

   // Append MRU items to the menu. If hmenu is a popup menu,
   // we're called after a toolbar drop-down, and we use hmenu
   // directly. If hmenu is the window's menu, get the file menu,
   // which is the first submenu:
   bool bShowAccelerators = false;
   HMENU hmenuFile = hmenu;
   if ( GetMenu( hwnd ) == hmenu ) {
      hmenuFile = GetSubMenu( hmenu, 0 );
      if ( containsItem( hmenuFile, ID_FILE_OPEN ) ) {
         bShowAccelerators = true;
      } else {
         hmenuFile = 0;
      }
   }

   if ( IsMenu( hmenuFile ) ) {
      for ( int id = ID_MRU_1; id <= ID_MRU_10; ++id ) {
         DeleteMenu( hmenuFile, id, MF_BYCOMMAND );
      }

      MRU().addFilesToMenu( hmenuFile, bShowAccelerators );
   }
}
```

```c
#define MENU_CLOSING 0xffff

// The macro defined in windowsx.h handles MENU_CLOSING incorrectly.
#undef HANDLE_WM_MENUSELECT
#define HANDLE_WM_MENUSELECT(hwnd, wParam, lParam, fn) \
   ((fn)((hwnd), (HMENU)(lParam), \
   (HIWORD(wParam) & MF_POPUP) ? 0L : (int)(LOWORD(wParam)), \
   (HIWORD(wParam) == MENU_CLOSING ? 0 : \
      HIWORD(wParam) & MF_POPUP ? \
      GetSubMenu((HMENU)lParam, LOWORD(wParam)) : 0L, \
   (UINT)(((short)HIWORD(wParam) == -1) ? \
      0xFFFFFFFF : HIWORD(wParam))), 0L)

PRIVATE void onMenuSelect( // WM_MENUSELECT
   HWND hwnd, HMENU hmenu, int nItem, HMENU hmnuPopup, UINT flags )
{
   const Editor *pEditor = getEditor( hwnd );
   assert( isGoodConstPtr( pEditor ) );

   Statusbar *pStatusbar = getStatusbar( hwnd );
   assert( isGoodPtr( pStatusbar ) );

   const AbstractEditWnd *pEditWnd = getEditWnd( hwnd );
   assert( isGoodConstPtr( pEditWnd ) );

   try {
      if ( MENU_CLOSING == LOWORD( flags ) ) {
         pStatusbar->update( pEditWnd->getCurPos() );
      } else {
         String strMessage;
         if ( IsMenu( hmnuPopup ) ) {
            strMessage = pEditor->getMenuDescription( hmnuPopup );
         } else {
            strMessage = pEditor->getMenuItemDescription(
               nItem, s_strLast );
         }
         pStatusbar->setMessage( strMessage.c_str() );
      }
```

```
   }
   catch ( ... ) {
      pStatusbar->update( pEditWnd->getCurPos() );
      throw;
   }
}


/**
 * Word Wrap function on View menu (toggle).
 */
PRIVATE void onViewWordWrap( HWND hwnd ) {

   assert( IsWindow( hwnd ) );
   HMENU hmenu = GetMenu( hwnd );
   assert( IsMenu( hmenu ) );
   UINT uiState = GetMenuState(
      hmenu, ID_VIEW_WORDWRAP, MF_BYCOMMAND );
   getEditor( hwnd )->setWordWrap( 0 == ( MF_CHECKED & uiState ) );
}


PRIVATE void toggleDockedWindow(
   const HWND hwndMain, const HWND hwndChild )
{
   assert( IsWindow( hwndMain ) );
   assert( IsWindow( hwndChild ) );

   const int nShow = IsWindowVisible( hwndChild ) ? SW_HIDE : SW_SHOW;
   ShowWindow( hwndChild, nShow );
   recalcLayout( hwndMain );
}


PRIVATE void onViewStatusbar( HWND hwnd ) {

   Statusbar *pStatusbar = getStatusbar( hwnd );
   toggleDockedWindow( hwnd, *pStatusbar );
   setStatusbarVisible( IsWindowVisible( *pStatusbar ) );
}


PRIVATE void onViewToolbar( HWND hwnd ) {
```

```
        Toolbar *pToolbar = getToolbar( hwnd );
        toggleDockedWindow( hwnd, *pToolbar );
        setToolbarVisible( IsWindowVisible( *pToolbar ) );
    }

PRIVATE void onEditCut( HWND hwnd ) {
    getEditWnd( hwnd )->cutSelection();
}

PRIVATE void onEditCopy( HWND hwnd ) {
    getEditWnd( hwnd )->copySelection();
}

PRIVATE void onEditPaste( HWND hwnd ) {
    getEditWnd( hwnd )->paste();
}

PRIVATE void onEditDelete( HWND hwnd ) {
    getEditWnd( hwnd )->deleteSelection();
}

PRIVATE void onEditUndo( HWND hwnd ) {
    getEditWnd( hwnd )->undo();
}

PRIVATE void onEditRedo( HWND hwnd ) {
    getEditWnd( hwnd )->redo();
}

PRIVATE void onEditSelectAll( HWND hwnd ) {
    getEditWnd( hwnd )->setSel( 0, -1 );
}

PRIVATE inline void search( HWND hwnd ) {

    if ( !getEditor( hwnd )->searchAndSelect( s_strLast ) ) {
        Statusbar *pStatusbar = getStatusbar( hwnd );
        if ( IsWindowVisible( *pStatusbar ) ) {
            pStatusbar->setErrorMessage( MB_ICONINFORMATION,
```

```
                IDS_STRING_NOT_FOUND, s_strLast.c_str() );
      } else {
         messageBox( hwnd, MB_ICONINFORMATION | MB_OK,
            IDS_STRING_NOT_FOUND, s_strLast.c_str() );
      }
   }
}

PRIVATE void onEditFind( HWND hwnd ) {

   AbstractEditWnd *pEditWnd = getEditWnd( hwnd );
   assert( 0 != pEditWnd );

   String strSelection;
   if ( !pEditWnd->getSel( &strSelection ) ) {
      if ( !pEditWnd->getWord( &strSelection ) ) {
         strSelection = s_strLast;
      }
   }

   // In case of msgs on status bar.
   getStatusbar( hwnd )->update( pEditWnd->getCurPos() );
   FindDlg findDlg( getEditor( hwnd ), strSelection );
   const UINT uiRetCode = findDlg.doModal( hwnd, IDD_EDITFIND );
   if ( IDOK == uiRetCode ) {
      s_strLast = findDlg.getSearchPattern();
   }
}

PRIVATE void onEditReplace( HWND hwnd ) {

   AbstractEditWnd *pEditWnd = getEditWnd( hwnd );
   assert( 0 != pEditWnd );

   String strSelection;
   if ( !pEditWnd->getSel( &strSelection ) ) {
      if ( !pEditWnd->getWord( &strSelection ) ) {
         strSelection = s_strLast;
      }
   }
```

```cpp
      // In case of msgs on status bar.
      getStatusbar( hwnd )->update( pEditWnd->getCurPos() );
      FindDlg findDlg( getEditor( hwnd ), strSelection, true );
      const UINT uiRetCode = findDlg.doModal( hwnd, IDD_EDITREPLACE );
      if ( IDOK == uiRetCode ) {
         s_strLast = findDlg.getSearchPattern();
      }
   }
}

PRIVATE void onEditFindNext( HWND hwnd ) {

   setBackwards( false );
   if ( s_strLast.empty() ) {
      onEditFind( hwnd );
   } else {
      search( hwnd );
   }
}

PRIVATE void onEditFindPrevious( HWND hwnd ) {

   setBackwards( true );
   if ( s_strLast.empty() ) {
      onEditFind( hwnd );
   } else {
      search( hwnd );
   }
}

PRIVATE void onFindSelection( HWND hwnd, bool bBackwards ) {

   setBackwards( bBackwards );
   AbstractEditWnd *pEditWnd = getEditWnd( hwnd );
   String str;
   if ( pEditWnd->getSel( &str ) || pEditWnd->getWord( &str ) ) {
      s_strLast = str;
   }
```

```cpp
      if ( s_strLast.empty() ) {
         MessageBeep( MB_ICONWARNING );
      } else {
         search( hwnd );
      }
   }
}

PRIVATE void onEditFindSelection( HWND hwnd ) {

   onFindSelection( hwnd, false );
}

PRIVATE void onFindPrevSelection( HWND hwnd ) {

   onFindSelection( hwnd, true );
}

PRIVATE void onFileNew( HWND hwnd ) {

   openFile( hwnd, createNewFile( hwnd ) );
}

PRIVATE void onFileNewEditor( HWND hwnd ) {

   startInstance( _T( "" ) );
}

PRIVATE void onFileOpen( HWND hwnd ) {

   assert( IsWindow( hwnd ) );
   assert( IsWindowEnabled( hwnd ) );

   try {
      PATHNAME szPath = { 0 };
      bool bNewFile = true;
      if ( openFile( hwnd, szPath, dim( szPath ), &bNewFile ) ) {
         if ( bNewFile ) {
            startInstance( szPath );
         } else {
            openFile( hwnd, szPath );
```

```
         }
      }
   }
   catch ( ... ) {
      trace( _T( "Exception in onFileOpen, enabling main wnd\n" ) );
      EnableWindow( hwnd, true );
      throw;
   }
}

PRIVATE void onFileCopy( HWND hwnd ) {

   getEditor( hwnd )->copyFile();
}



PRIVATE void onFilePrint( HWND hwnd ) {

   WaitCursor waitCursor;
   getEditor( hwnd )->printFile();
}

PRIVATE void onFilePageSetup( HWND hwnd ) {

   WaitCursor waitCursor;
   setupPage( hwnd, getDocument( hwnd ) );
}


/*
 * This makes the UI reflect changed file properties.
 * It is called after the PropertiesDlg exits, and it's
 * called in response to the Apply button in that dialog.
 */
PRIVATE void onFilePropsChanged( HWND hwnd ) {

   getEditor( hwnd )->setTitle();
   getStatusbar( hwnd )->setFileType(
      getDocument( hwnd )->isUnicode() );
   const bool bReadOnly = getDocument( hwnd )->isReadOnly();
```

```
      getEditor( hwnd )->setReadOnly( bReadOnly );
}

PRIVATE void onFileProperties( HWND hwnd ) {

   getEditor( hwnd )->saveIfNecessary();
   WaitCursor waitCursor;
   PropertiesDlg( hwnd, getDocument( hwnd ) );
   // The dialog itself takes care of invoking onFilePropsChanged.
}

PRIVATE void onFileRename( HWND hwnd ) {

   getEditor( hwnd )->saveIfNecessary();
   WaitCursor waitCursor;
   Document *pDocument = getDocument( hwnd );
   assert( isGoodPtr( pDocument ) );

   String strFullPath = pDocument->getPath();
   const bool bRetVal = saveFile(
      hwnd, &strFullPath, IDS_MOVE, IDD_MOVE_CHILD );
   if ( bRetVal ) {
      if ( pDocument->setPath( hwnd, strFullPath ) ) {
         onFilePropsChanged( hwnd );
      } else {
         getStatusbar( hwnd )->setHighlightMessage( IDS_FAILED_MOVE );
      }
   }
}

PRIVATE void onFileDelete( HWND hwnd ) {

   UINT uiRetCode = IDOK;
   if ( getShowDeleteDialog() ) {
      DeleteDlg deleteDlg( getDocument( hwnd )->getPath() );
      uiRetCode = deleteDlg.doModal( hwnd );
   }
```

```
      if ( IDOK == uiRetCode &&
         getDocument( hwnd )->deleteFile( hwnd ) )
      {
         getEditor( hwnd )->clean();
         PostMessage( hwnd, WM_CLOSE, 0, 0 );
      }
   }
}

PRIVATE void onFileAbandonChanges( HWND hwnd ) {

   WaitCursor waitCursor( _T( "load.ani" ) );
   getEditor( hwnd )->restoreOriginal();
}

PRIVATE void onFileClose( HWND hwnd ) {

   PostMessage( hwnd, WM_CLOSE, 0, 0 );
}

PRIVATE void onViewOptions( HWND hwnd ) {

   Editor *pEditor = getEditor( hwnd );
   assert( isGoodPtr( pEditor ) );

   OptionsDlg optionsDlg(
      pEditor->getLogFont( true  ),
      pEditor->getLogFont( false ) );
   if ( IDOK == optionsDlg.doModal( hwnd ) ) {
      pEditor->setLogFont( optionsDlg.getFixedFont       (), true  );
      pEditor->setLogFont( optionsDlg.getProportionalFont(), false );
      refreshMenu( hwnd ); // May have changed language.
   }
}

PRIVATE void onClickReadOnly( HWND hwnd ) {

   Editor *pEditor = getEditor( hwnd );
   const bool bReadOnly = pEditor->getReadOnly();
   pEditor->setReadOnly( bReadOnly );
```

```
      enablePaste( hwnd );
}

PRIVATE void onCommandReadOnly( HWND hwnd ) {

   Editor *pEditor = getEditor( hwnd );
   bool bReadOnly = pEditor->getReadOnly();
   bReadOnly = !bReadOnly;
   pEditor->setReadOnly( bReadOnly );
   enablePaste( hwnd );
}

PRIVATE void onCommandTabs( HWND hwnd ) {

   if ( getEditWnd( hwnd )->canSetTabs() ) {
      Toolbar *pToolbar = getToolbar( hwnd );
      assert( IsWindow( *pToolbar ) );

      HWND hwndTabs = pToolbar->getChild( IDC_TABEDIT );
      assert( IsWindow( hwndTabs ) );

      SetFocus( hwndTabs );
      Edit_SetSel( hwndTabs, 0, -1 );
   }
}

PRIVATE void onSetTabs( HWND hwnd ) {

   AbstractEditWnd *pEditWnd = getEditWnd( hwnd );
   if ( pEditWnd->canSetTabs() ) {
      Toolbar *pToolbar = getToolbar( hwnd );
      const int nSpacesPerTab = pToolbar->getTabs();
      pEditWnd->setSpacesPerTab( nSpacesPerTab );
      getDocument( hwnd )->setTabs( nSpacesPerTab );
   }
}

PRIVATE void onViewFixedFont( HWND hwnd ) {
```

```
   setFont( hwnd, true );
}

PRIVATE void onViewProportionalFont( HWND hwnd ) {

   setFont( hwnd, false );
}

PRIVATE void onViewSetFixedFont( HWND hwnd ) {

   LOGFONT logFont = *getEditor( hwnd )->getLogFont( true );
   if ( selectFont( hwnd, &logFont, 0, CF_FIXEDPITCHONLY ) ) {
      getEditor( hwnd )->setLogFont( &logFont, true );
   }
}

PRIVATE void onViewSetProportionalFont( HWND hwnd ) {

   LOGFONT logFont = *getEditor( hwnd )->getLogFont( false );
   if ( selectFont( hwnd, &logFont ) ) {
      getEditor( hwnd )->setLogFont( &logFont, false );
   }
}

PRIVATE void onViewSetFont( HWND hwnd ) {

   if ( getEditor( hwnd )->hasFixedFont() ) {
      onViewSetFixedFont( hwnd );
   } else {
      onViewSetProportionalFont( hwnd );
   }
}

PRIVATE void onViewToggleFont( HWND hwnd ) {

   if ( getEditor( hwnd )->hasFixedFont() ) {
      onViewProportionalFont( hwnd );
   } else {
      onViewFixedFont( hwnd );
```

```
      }
   }

   PRIVATE void onCommandScroll( HWND hwnd, UINT nWhat ) {
      AbstractEditWnd *pEditWnd = getEditWnd( hwnd );
      pEditWnd->scroll( nWhat );
      pEditWnd->bringCaretToWindow( getEditor( hwnd )->getFont() );
   }

   PRIVATE void onCommandScrollUp( HWND hwnd ) {
      onCommandScroll( hwnd, SB_LINEUP );
   }

   PRIVATE void onCommandScrollDown( HWND hwnd ) {
      onCommandScroll( hwnd, SB_LINEDOWN );
   }

   PRIVATE void onCommandDeleteLine( HWND hwnd ) {
      trace( _T( "onCommandDeleteLine" ) ); // LATER: Implement
   }

   PRIVATE void onCommandSave( HWND hwnd ) {

      WaitCursor waitCursor( _T( "save.ani" ) );

      const bool bSaved = getEditor( hwnd )->save();
      if ( bSaved ) {
         getStatusbar( hwnd )->setMessage(
            IDS_SAVED_FILE, getDocument( hwnd )->getPath().c_str() );
      } else {
         getStatusbar( hwnd )->setHighlightMessage( IDS_DIDNT_SAVE_FILE,
            getDocument( hwnd )->getPath().c_str() );
         MessageBeep( MB_ICONWARNING );
      }
   }

   PRIVATE void onHelpContents( HWND hwnd ) {

      WinHelp( hwnd, getHelpFile(), HELP_FINDER, 0 );
   }
```

```
PRIVATE void onHelpKeyboard( HWND hwnd ) {

   WinHelp(
      hwnd, getHelpFile(), HELP_CONTEXT, IDH_USING_THE_KEYBOARD );
}

PRIVATE void onHelpHomePage( HWND hwnd ) {

   // Note that plain ShellExecute has a bug when running under
   // Windows 9x. If it initiates a DDE conversation to open
   // a file, it does not close its end of the conversation.
   // This can lead to Bad Things when you try to close the
   // app (some web browser in our case).

   SHELLEXECUTEINFO shellExecuteInfo = {
      sizeof( SHELLEXECUTEINFO ),
      SEE_MASK_FLAG_DDEWAIT,
      hwnd,
      _T( "open" ),
      _T( "http://www.rdbooks.com" ),
      0, 0, SW_SHOWNORMAL,
   };

   verify( ShellExecuteEx( &shellExecuteInfo ) );
}

PRIVATE void onHelpAbout( HWND hwnd ) {

   AboutDlg aboutDlg( hwnd );
}

/**
 * Get rid of any messages on the status bar.
 */
PRIVATE void onResetStatusbar( HWND hwnd ) {

#if 1
   getStatusbar( hwnd )->update( getEditWnd( hwnd )->getCurPos() );
```

```
#else
   try {
      getStatusbar( hwnd )->update( getEditWnd( hwnd )->getCurPos() );
   }
   catch ( ... ) {
      trace( _T( "exception in onCommand\n" ) );
   }
#endif
}

#ifdef _DEBUG // Stuff to exercise SEH and other exception handling:

#pragma warning( disable: 4723 ) // potential divide by 0

PRIVATE void onDivideByZero( HWND ) {

   int x = 1;
   x = x / 0;
}

#pragma warning( default: 4723 ) // potential divide by 0

// TestClass is testing to see if we're unwinding properly.
class TestClass {
public:
   TestClass () { trace( _T( "TestClass ctor\n" ) ); }
   ~TestClass() { trace( _T( "TestClass dtor\n" ) ); }
};

PRIVATE void onAccessViolation( HWND ) {

   TestClass testClass;

   lstrcpy( 0, _T( "uh-oh!" ) ); // No exception
   _tcscpy( 0, _T( "uh-oh!" ) ); // Exception
   int *pNullPointer = 0;
   *pNullPointer = 0;              // Exception
}
```

```
PRIVATE void onOutOfMemory( HWND ) {

   new TCHAR[ INT_MAX - 100 ];
}

PRIVATE void onStackOverflow( HWND hwnd ) {

   onStackOverflow( hwnd );
}

#endif // _DEBUG

PRIVATE inline void onCommand(
   HWND hwnd, int id, HWND hwndCtl, UINT codeNotify )
{
   #define COMMAND( id, proc ) case id: proc( hwnd ); break

   switch ( id ) {

   COMMAND( ID_FILE_NEW              , onFileNew              );
   COMMAND( ID_FILE_NEW_EDITOR       , onFileNewEditor        );
   COMMAND( ID_FILE_OPEN             , onFileOpen             );
   COMMAND( ID_FILE_COPY             , onFileCopy             );
   COMMAND( ID_FILE_PRINT            , onFilePrint            );
   COMMAND( ID_FILE_PAGESETUP        , onFilePageSetup        );
   COMMAND( ID_COMMAND_PROPSCHANGED  , onFilePropsChanged     );
   COMMAND( ID_FILE_PROPERTIES       , onFileProperties       );
   COMMAND( ID_FILE_RENAME           , onFileRename           );
   COMMAND( ID_FILE_DELETE           , onFileDelete           );
   COMMAND( ID_FILE_ABANDONCHANGES   , onFileAbandonChanges   );
   COMMAND( ID_FILE_CLOSE            , onFileClose            );
   COMMAND( ID_VIEW_WORDWRAP         , onViewWordWrap         );
   COMMAND( ID_VIEW_STATUSBAR        , onViewStatusbar        );
   COMMAND( ID_VIEW_TOOLBAR          , onViewToolbar          );
   COMMAND( ID_EDIT_CUT              , onEditCut              );
   COMMAND( ID_EDIT_COPY             , onEditCopy             );
   COMMAND( ID_EDIT_PASTE            , onEditPaste            );
   COMMAND( ID_EDIT_DELETE           , onEditDelete           );
   COMMAND( ID_EDIT_UNDO             , onEditUndo             );
```

```cpp
    COMMAND( ID_EDIT_REDO                 , onEditRedo                 );
    COMMAND( ID_EDIT_SELECTALL            , onEditSelectAll            );
    COMMAND( ID_EDIT_FIND                 , onEditFind                 );
    COMMAND( ID_EDIT_FINDNEXT             , onEditFindNext             );
    COMMAND( ID_EDIT_FINDPREVIOUS         , onEditFindPrevious         );
    COMMAND( ID_ACCEL_FINDNEXT            , onEditFindNext             );
    COMMAND( ID_ACCEL_FINDPREVIOUS        , onEditFindPrevious         );
    COMMAND( ID_EDIT_FINDSELECTION        , onEditFindSelection        );
    COMMAND( ID_ACCEL_FINDPREVSELECTION   , onFindPrevSelection        );
    COMMAND( ID_EDIT_REPLACE              , onEditReplace              );
    COMMAND( ID_VIEW_FIXEDFONT            , onViewFixedFont            );
    COMMAND( ID_VIEW_PROPORTIONALFONT     , onViewProportionalFont     );
    COMMAND( ID_VIEW_SETFIXEDFONT         , onViewSetFixedFont         );
    COMMAND( ID_VIEW_SETPROPORTIONALFONT  , onViewSetProportionalFont  );
    COMMAND( ID_VIEW_SETFONT              , onViewSetFont              );
    COMMAND( ID_COMMAND_TOGGLEFONT        , onViewToggleFont           );
    COMMAND( ID_VIEW_OPTIONS              , onViewOptions              );
    COMMAND( ID_HELP_ABOUT                , onHelpAbout                );
    COMMAND( IDC_READONLY                 , onClickReadOnly            );
    COMMAND( ID_COMMAND_READONLY          , onCommandReadOnly          );
    COMMAND( ID_COMMAND_TABS              , onCommandTabs              );
    COMMAND( ID_COMMAND_SCROLLUP          , onCommandScrollUp          );
    COMMAND( ID_COMMAND_SCROLLDOWN        , onCommandScrollDown        );
    COMMAND( ID_COMMAND_DELETELINE        , onCommandDeleteLine        );
    COMMAND( ID_COMMAND_SAVE              , onCommandSave              );
    COMMAND( ID_SET_TABS                  , onSetTabs                  );
    COMMAND( ID_HELP_CONTENTS             , onHelpContents             );
    COMMAND( ID_HELP_KEYBOARD             , onHelpKeyboard             );
    COMMAND( ID_HELP_HOMEPAGE             , onHelpHomePage             );
    COMMAND( ID_COMMAND_RESETSTATUSBAR    , onResetStatusbar           );

#ifdef _DEBUG
    COMMAND( ID_DEBUG_DIVIDEBYZERO        , onDivideByZero             );
    COMMAND( ID_DEBUG_ACCESSVIOLATION     , onAccessViolation          );
    COMMAND( ID_DEBUG_OUTOFMEMORY         , onOutOfMemory              );
    COMMAND( ID_DEBUG_STACKOVERFLOW       , onStackOverflow            );
#endif
```

```
      case ID_MRU_1: case ID_MRU_2: case ID_MRU_3:
      case ID_MRU_4: case ID_MRU_5: case ID_MRU_6:
      case ID_MRU_7: case ID_MRU_8: case ID_MRU_9:
         {
            // Note: activateOldInstance will activate us,
            // too, if we're reloading the same file.
            const String strPath = MRU().getFile( id );
            openFile( hwnd, strPath );
         }
         break;
      }

      #undef COMMAND
}

PRIVATE inline void onSysCommand(
   HWND hwnd, UINT cmd, int x, int y )
{
   if ( SC_RESTORE == cmd ) {
      SetTimer( hwnd, timer_save_state, 500, 0 );
   }
   FORWARD_WM_SYSCOMMAND( hwnd, cmd, x, y, DefWindowProc );
}

/**
 * This is the window function of TextEdit's main window.
 * It's a central switching point for the whole application.
 */
LRESULT CALLBACK mainWndProc(
   HWND hwnd, UINT msg, WPARAM wParam, LPARAM lParam )
{
   switch ( msg ) {

   HANDLE_MSG( hwnd, WM_CREATE       , onCreate    );
   HANDLE_MSG( hwnd, WM_ACTIVATE     , onActivate  );
   HANDLE_MSG( hwnd, WM_DESTROY      , onDestroy   );
   HANDLE_MSG( hwnd, WM_CLOSE        , onClose     );
   HANDLE_MSG( hwnd, WM_DROPFILES    , onDropFiles );
   HANDLE_MSG( hwnd, WM_TIMER        , onTimer     );
```

```
        HANDLE_MSG( hwnd, WM_SIZE           , onSize           );
        HANDLE_MSG( hwnd, WM_MOVE           , onMove           );
        HANDLE_MSG( hwnd, WM_ENTERSIZEMOVE  , onEnterSizeMove  );
        HANDLE_MSG( hwnd, WM_EXITSIZEMOVE   , onExitSizeMove   );
        HANDLE_MSG( hwnd, WM_SETFOCUS       , onSetFocus       );
        HANDLE_MSG( hwnd, WM_INITMENU       , onInitMenu       );
        HANDLE_MSG( hwnd, WM_MENUSELECT     , onMenuSelect     );
        HANDLE_MSG( hwnd, WM_COMMAND        , onCommand        );
        HANDLE_MSG( hwnd, WM_SYSCOMMAND     , onSysCommand     );
        HANDLE_MSG( hwnd, WM_DRAWCLIPBOARD  , onDrawClipboard  );
        HANDLE_MSG( hwnd, WM_CHANGECBCHAIN  , onChangeCBChain  );
        HANDLE_MSG( hwnd, WM_QUERYENDSESSION, onQueryEndSession );
        HANDLE_MSG( hwnd, WM_ENDSESSION     , onEndSession     );
        HANDLE_MSG( hwnd, WM_POWERBROADCAST , onPowerBroadcast );
        HANDLE_MSG( hwnd, WM_SYSCOLORCHANGE , onSysColorChange );
        HANDLE_MSG( hwnd, WM_SETTINGCHANGE  , onSettingChange  );
        HANDLE_MSG( hwnd, WM_HELP           , onHelp           );
        HANDLE_MSG( hwnd, WM_APP            , onApp            );

    }

    return DefWindowProc( hwnd, msg, wParam, lParam );
}
```

Chapter 10

Customization and Persistence

Customization and persistence are closely linked. If J. Random Hacker's customization settings aren't preserved between sessions, she'll lose interest very quickly.

This chapter discusses TextEdit customization and how it uses the Windows registry to store persistent data.

Customizing Windows

Before we look at TextEdit-specific customization, let's look at some of the things the user can do to customize Windows itself, and what the consequences are for us. I won't go into things that don't affect us — we don't care if the user changes the desktop bitmap or the mouse pointer scheme, for example.

Color Schemes and Window Metrics

Figure 10.1 shows the Appearance tab of the Display Control Panel applet. This dialog allows you to change colors, fonts, and various metrics such as border widths.

Figure 10.1 **Customizing the appearance of windows. Check out `GetSystemMetrics` and `GetSysColor` before deciding on colors, fonts, and metrics for your application.**

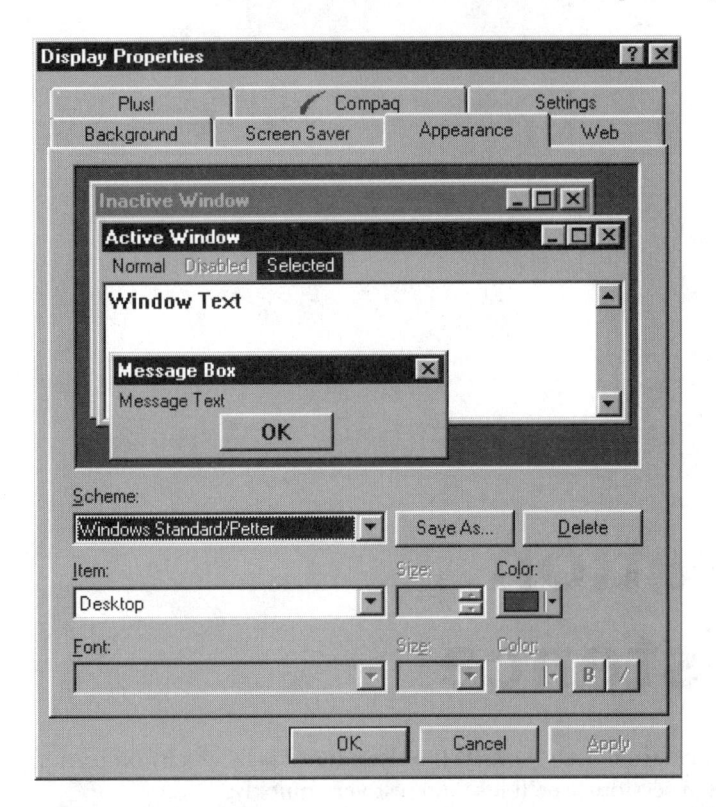

If the user changes the font for the active window title, we don't have to do anything; this is handled behind the scenes. If, however, the user changes the menu font, it does matter, because TextEdit uses the menu font for the status bar.

Why? Among the standard schemes in Figure 10.1 are some with high contrast and large fonts. When J. Random Hacker chooses such a scheme, it's for a reason — perhaps her eyesight is weak, or perhaps she needs to see the monitor from the back of the room. If the status bar font remained small in the face of such a change, it would be invisible. Many applications, and, indeed, parts of Windows itself, don't handle this well. The menu font may be 48 points, but everything else remains at eight points, unreadable to Jane. Even TextEdit is delinquent in this respect; the main window may be well behaved, but the dialogs don't change. This afflicts all applications I've seen, and it may have something to do with the lack of any global default dialog font. One possibility might be to use the message font, which *is* customizable.

Noticing the Changes

Clicking the OK button in Figure 10.1 may result in two different messages being broadcast: WM_SETTINGCHANGE and WM_SYSCOLORCHANGE. TextEdit has message handlers for these in mainwnd.cpp (as shown in Chapter 9).

The onSysColorChange function just passes the message on to all the child windows. They don't all need it, but all the common controls do, including toolbars and status bars. Passing it to everybody is the simplest way of ensuring that those that need it get it.

The onSettingChange function is more complex. The language may have changed, fonts may have changed, even the thousands separator may have changed — which impacts the row/column display in the status bar.

Retrieving the Font

The description of a UI font is stored in the registry as a blob. The menu font is stored under the following key:

```
HKEY_CURRENT_USER\Control Panel\Desktop\WindowMetrics\MenuFont
```

("Blob" is an acronym for a Binary Large OBject. Whether this blob deserves the adjective "large" is another matter.) This blob turns out to be a LOGFONT structure, and it can be used to instantiate a GDI object of the HFONT persuasion.

But, of course, there is no such thing as a LOGFONT structure. LOGFONT is a macro that evaluates to either LOGFONTA or LOGFONTW, depending on whether the preprocessor symbol UNICODE is defined. It turns out that the blob is a LOGFONTW under Windows NT. Under Windows 95, it's a LOGFONTA — almost. The first five members of the LOGFONTA structure are defined as LONG in wingdi.h; in the Windows 95 registry blob, they are shorts as defined in the LOGFONTWIN95REG structure in MenuFont.cpp.

Standard APIs to retrieve the various UI fonts would be appreciated. These could be implemented through new parameters to GetStockObject, for example. (Discourse continues on page 230.)

Listing 10.1 MenuFont.h

```
/*
 * $Header: /Book/MenuFont.h 6     3.07.99 17:46 Petter $
 *
 * Singleton class.
 */

#pragma once

class MenuFont {
private:
    HFONT m_hfontMenu;
    int   m_nCachedHeight;
```

```
    enum Limits { min_height = 6, max_height = 32 };

    static MenuFont theMenuFont;

public:
    MenuFont();
    ~MenuFont();

    static HFONT getFont( void );
    static void refresh( void );
    static int getHeight( void );
    static bool isLarge( void );
};

inline bool MenuFont::isLarge( void ) {
    return 16 <= getHeight();
}
```

Listing 10.2   MenuFont.cpp

```
/*
 * $Header: /Book/MenuFont.cpp 8     3.07.99 17:46 Petter $
 */

#include "precomp.h"
#include "MenuFont.h"
#include "Registry.h"
#include "os.h"
#include "trace.h"

MenuFont MenuFont::theMenuFont;

MenuFont::MenuFont() : m_hfontMenu( 0 ) {

    assert( this == &theMenuFont ); // One and only one!
    refresh();
}
```

```
MenuFont::~MenuFont() {
   trace( _T( "Menufont dtor" ) );
   if ( 0 != m_hfontMenu ) {
      DeleteFont( m_hfontMenu );
      m_hfontMenu = 0;
      trace( _T( " deletes font\n" ) );
   } else {
      trace( _T( " has no font!\n" ) );
   }
}

HFONT MenuFont::getFont( void ) {

   if ( 0 != theMenuFont.m_hfontMenu ) {
      return theMenuFont.m_hfontMenu;
   }
   return GetStockFont( DEFAULT_GUI_FONT );
}

int MenuFont::getHeight( void ) {

   return theMenuFont.m_nCachedHeight;
}

#pragma pack( 1 )

typedef struct LOGFONTWIN95REG {
   short lfHeight;
   short lfWidth;
   short lfEscapement;
   short lfOrientation;
   short lfWeight;
   BYTE  lfItalic;
   BYTE  lfUnderline;
   BYTE  lfStrikeOut;
   BYTE  lfCharSet;
   BYTE  lfOutPrecision;
   BYTE  lfClipPrecision;
   BYTE  lfQuality;
```

```
      BYTE  lfPitchAndFamily;
      CHAR  lfFaceName[ LF_FACESIZE ];
} LOGFONTWIN95REG;

#pragma pack()

void MenuFont::refresh( void ) {

   if ( 0 != theMenuFont.m_hfontMenu ) {
      DeleteFont( theMenuFont.m_hfontMenu );
      theMenuFont.m_hfontMenu = 0;
   }


   #define REG_PATH  _T( "Control Panel\\Desktop\\WindowMetrics" )
   #define REG_ENTRY _T( "MenuFont" )

   // Check for wild values:
   #define CHECKFONT( logfont )                                \
      if ( abs( logfont.lfHeight ) < min_height ) {            \
         logfont.lfHeight = min_height;                        \
      } else if ( max_height < abs( logfont.lfHeight ) ) {     \
         logfont.lfHeight = max_height;                        \
      }                                                        \
      logfont.lfEscapement = logfont.lfOrientation =           \
      logfont.lfUnderline = logfont.lfStrikeOut = 0

   bool isMenuFontOK = false;
   if ( isWindowsNT() ) {
      LOGFONTW logFontW = { 0 };
      isMenuFontOK = Registry::getBlob( HKEY_CURRENT_USER,
         REG_PATH, REG_ENTRY, &logFontW, sizeof logFontW );
      if ( isMenuFontOK ) {
         CHECKFONT( logFontW );
         theMenuFont.m_hfontMenu = CreateFontIndirectW( &logFontW );
         GetObject(
            theMenuFont.m_hfontMenu, sizeof logFontW, &logFontW );
         theMenuFont.m_nCachedHeight = abs( logFontW.lfHeight );
      }
   } else {
```

```cpp
        LOGFONTWIN95REG regFont = { 0 };
    isMenuFontOK = Registry::getBlob( HKEY_CURRENT_USER,
        REG_PATH, REG_ENTRY, &regFont, sizeof regFont );
    if ( isMenuFontOK ) {
        LOGFONTA logFontA = {
            regFont.lfHeight        ,
            regFont.lfWidth         ,
            regFont.lfEscapement    ,
            regFont.lfOrientation   ,
            regFont.lfWeight        ,
            regFont.lfItalic        ,
            regFont.lfUnderline     ,
            regFont.lfStrikeOut     ,
            regFont.lfCharSet       ,
            regFont.lfOutPrecision  ,
            regFont.lfClipPrecision ,
            regFont.lfQuality       ,
            regFont.lfPitchAndFamily,
        };
        strcpy( logFontA.lfFaceName, regFont.lfFaceName );
        CHECKFONT( logFontA );
        theMenuFont.m_hfontMenu = CreateFontIndirectA( &logFontA );
        GetObject(
            theMenuFont.m_hfontMenu, sizeof logFontA, &logFontA );
        theMenuFont.m_nCachedHeight = abs( logFontA.lfHeight );
    }
  }
  trace( _T( "Menufont::refresh: OK = %d\n" ), isMenuFontOK );


  #undef REG_PATH
  #undef REG_ENTRY
}
```

Windows Explorer

The Windows Explorer, too, allows itself to be customized, and some of these customizations afflict — er, affect — TextEdit.

Figure 10.2 **Customizing the Windows Explorer. Some of these settings are useful to applications; unfortunately, there aren't always documented ways to retrieve them.**

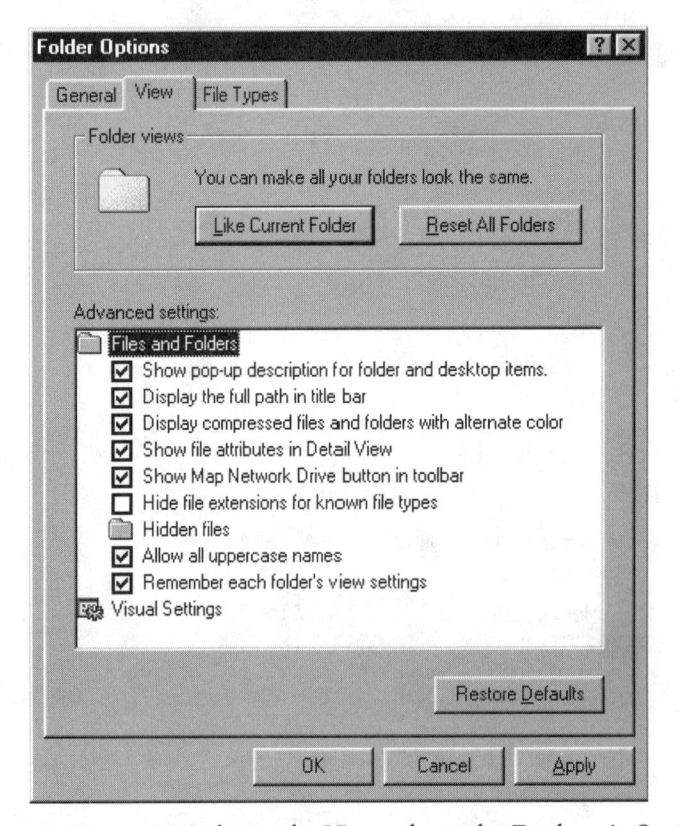

Figure 10.2 shows the View tab on the Explorer's Option dialog. The list has two entries that TextEdit uses:

1. Display the full path in the title bar.
2. Hide file extensions for known file types.

To get the file name to display in the title bar, TextEdit calls the `GetWindowTitle` function. This function takes care of the second point, but not the first. In fact, TextEdit never displays the full path in the title bar, as I've found no documented way of detecting this setting.

If you click the OK button in Figure 10.2, the Explorer broadcasts a `WM_SETTINGCHANGE` message The `onSettingChange` handler is simpleminded, and refreshes everything that might conceivably have changed.

Regional Settings

The ramifications of the Regional Settings Control Panel applet will be explored in more depth in Chapter 18; I'll just mention them here: TextEdit formats numbers and displays dates in the File Properties dialog, and measurements make an appearance in the Page Setup dialog.

Customizing TextEdit

TextEdit doesn't have a lot of explicit customization. You can hide or show the toolbar and status bars, and the View/Options dialog lets you change the proportional and fixed fonts. Then there's the behavior on File Delete; this function may or may not display a dialog box.

At this point, note one of the little conveniences that TextEdit offers: the Delete dialog can be turned off at the point where you are in the thick of things — in the Delete dialog itself. Note, also, that the Delete dialog tells you how to turn it back on, should you choose to turn it off. For obvious reasons, you can't do this in the Delete dialog.

That's all there is, on the application level. In addition, you can switch between the fixed and proportional fonts, you can toggle word wrapping, and you can change the number of spaces displayed per tab in the text. These settings are not purely global, though; they are handled per file type and, indeed, per individual file. I like to view my text files in a proportional font with word wrap on, while my program source files should display in a fixed font with word wrap off. No complex setuppery is required to achieve this; TextEdit simply remembers what I did last time and does it the same way next time.

Implicit Customization

For each individual file, TextEdit remember the position on the screen, and whether it was maximized. If you were editing the file when you closed Windows, TextEdit remembers this, too, and brings it back up when you restart Windows. If you had seven carefully aligned TextEdit windows on the screen when you closed Windows, you will have seven carefully aligned TextEdit windows on the screen when you restart Windows.

TextEdit remembers the position of dialog boxes. The first time you invoke a given dialog box, it will appear centered on the application (see the `centerDialog` function in `winUtils.cpp`). If you move the dialog, TextEdit remembers this, and will put it back where it was the next time you invoke it.

TextEdit remembers the content of dialog boxes. The Find dialog remembers previous search strings across invocations; the Delete dialog remembers whether it should send deleted files to the Recycle Bin.

Finally, there is the MRU (Most Recently Used) file list. This lets you open recently edited files at the click of a button; new files are added automatically.

In short, TextEdit has a memory. In the following, we'll look at how this is implemented.

Long-Term Memory

TextEdit uses the Windows registry for its long-term memory. The structure of TextEdit's registry entries is as follows:

```
HKEY_CURRENT_USER\Software\Andersen Consulting\TextEdit\
  Delete\
    SendToWasteBasket:    REG_DWORD (bool)
    ShowDeleteDialog:     REG_DWORD (bool)
  File Types\
    Text Document\
      FixedFont:          REG_DWORD (bool)
      WordWrap:           REG_DWORD (bool)
    <more file types>\
      FixedFont:          REG_DWORD (bool)
      Tabs:               REG_DWORD (bool)
      WordWrap:           REG_DWORD (bool)
  Files\
    C:|AUTOEXEC.BAT\
      FixedFont:          REG_DWORD (bool)
      Height:             REG_DWORD (number)
      Left:               REG_DWORD (number)
      Running:            REG_DWORD (bool)
      Tabs:               REG_DWORD (bool)
      Top:                REG_DWORD (number)
      Width:              REG_DWORD (number)
      WindowState:        REG_DWORD (number)
      WordWrap:           REG_DWORD (bool)
    <more files>\
      FixedFont:          REG_DWORD (bool)
      Height:             REG_DWORD (number)
      Left:               REG_DWORD (number)
      Running:            REG_DWORD (bool)
      Tabs:               REG_DWORD (bool)
      Top:                REG_DWORD (number)
      Width:              REG_DWORD (number)
      WindowState:        REG_DWORD (number)
      WordWrap:           REG_DWORD (bool)
  Fonts\
    FixedCharSet:         REG_DWORD (number)
    FixedFace:            REG_SZ    (string)
```

```
    FixedHeight:          REG_DWORD (number)
    FixedItalic:          REG_DWORD (bool)
    FixedWeight:          REG_DWORD (number)
    ProportionalCharSet:  REG_DWORD (number)
    ProportionalFace:     REG_SZ    (string)
    ProportionalHeight:   REG_DWORD (number)
    ProportionalItalic:   REG_DWORD (bool)
    ProportionalWeight:   REG_DWORD (number)
MRU\
    FileName0:            REG_SZ    (string)
    FileName1:            REG_SZ    (string)
    ...
    FileName19:           REG_SZ    (string)
Open\
    CustomFilter:         REG_SZ    (string)
    FilterIndex:          REG_DWORD (number)
Printer\
    BottomMargin:         REG_DWORD (number)
    Device:               REG_SZ    (string)
    Driver:               REG_SZ    (string)
    LeftMargin:           REG_DWORD (number)
    Orientation:          REG_DWORD (number)
    Paper:                REG_DWORD (number)
    Port:                 REG_SZ    (string)
    RightMargin:          REG_DWORD (number)
    TopMargin:            REG_DWORD (number)
Replace\
    Pattern0:             REG_SZ    (string)
    Pattern1:             REG_SZ    (string)
    ...
    Pattern9:             REG_SZ    (string)
Search\
    Backwards:            REG_DWORD (bool)
    MatchCase:            REG_DWORD (bool)
    MatchWholeWord:       REG_DWORD (bool)
    Pattern0:             REG_SZ    (string)
    Pattern1:             REG_SZ    (string)
    ...
    Pattern9:             REG_SZ    (string)
```

A vertical bar replaces each backslash in the file name keys. This is a simple textual substitution to avoid conflict with the use of the backslash in registry key names.

This may seem like a large amount of complex information to shuffle in and out of the registry. As we shall see, it is actually quite simple to use.

The Registry Interface

TextEdit's interface to the Windows registry is layered as follows:

1. At the bottom, we have the Windows registry API, which is quite low-level and cumbersome to use.
2. The `Registry` class encapsulates the registry API, and is a lot more convenient to use. The `Registry` class doesn't know the meaning of the data it shuffles around.
3. The file `persistence.h` defines a set of macros for defining "persistent variables." Instead of having a global variable named `FilterIndex`, you get a pair of functions, `getFilterIndex` and `setFilterIndex`. (Similar macros exist in the `Document` class, allowing document-local persistence, e.g., whether a specific file was maximized the last time it was open.)
4. Finally, we're getting to the functional layer, which has application-level meaning. Using the macros in `persistence.h`, we can define persistent variables galore.

Using this scheme has one great advantage over the more common method of saving all persistent information at the end of a session: if TextEdit crashes, changes to the settings are nevertheless retained.

Let's go back to level two for a moment, and look at the `Registry` class. This is a wrapper for a set of static functions; you can't instantiate a `Registry` object. In addition to being a high-level interface to the registry API, the `Registry` class performs one additional service: it decorates the key names so that we end up in the right sub-tree in the registry. Thus, "Search" becomes:

```
"Software\Andersen Consulting\TextEdit\Search"
```

Sometimes, though, we need to access information elsewhere in the registry. The following strings are recognized; if either is present, the key is retained as is:

```
#define WIN_SETTINGS _T( "Microsoft\\Windows\\CurrentVersion" )
#define CPL_SETTINGS _T( "Control Panel\\Desktop\\WindowMetrics" )
```

(Discourse continues on page 244.)

Listing 10.3 Registry.h

```
/*
 * $Header: /Book/Registry.h 12    3.07.99 17:46 Petter $
 */

#pragma once
```

```cpp
#ifndef _REGISTRY_H_
#define _REGISTRY_H_

#include "String.h"

class Registry {
private:
   static String formatKey( HKEY hkRoot, LPCTSTR pszKey );
   static HKEY createKey( HKEY hkRoot, LPCTSTR pszKey );
   static HKEY openFormattedKey(
      HKEY hkRoot, LPCTSTR pszKey, DWORD dwMode = KEY_READ );
   static HKEY openKey(
      HKEY hkRoot, LPCTSTR pszKey, DWORD dwMode = KEY_READ );

   Registry( void ) {
   };

   friend PRIVATE bool deleteRecursive( HKEY, LPCTSTR );

public:
   static int getInt( HKEY hkRoot,
      LPCTSTR pszKey, LPCTSTR pszName, int nDefault = 0 );
   static void setInt( HKEY hkRoot,
      LPCTSTR pszKey, LPCTSTR pszName, int nValue );

   static String getString(
      HKEY hkRoot, LPCTSTR pszKey,
      LPCTSTR pszName = _T( "" ), LPCTSTR pszDefault = 0 );
   static void __cdecl setString(
      HKEY hkRoot, LPCTSTR pszKey,
      LPCTSTR pszName = _T( "" ), LPCTSTR pszFmt = _T( "" ), ... );

   static bool getBlob(
      HKEY hkRoot, LPCTSTR pszKey,
      LPCTSTR pszName, LPVOID pBlob, UINT cb );

   static bool enumKeyNames(
      HKEY hkRoot, LPCTSTR pszKey, DWORD dwIndex, String *pstrName );
```

```
    static bool enumValues(
        HKEY hkRoot, LPCTSTR pszKey, DWORD dwIndex, String *pstrName );
                                    (
    static bool deleteEntry(
        HKEY hkRoot, LPCTSTR pszKey, LPCTSTR pszName = 0 );

    static String fileTypeDescriptionFromExtension(
        LPCTSTR pszExtension );
};

#endif // _REGISTRY_H_
```

Listing 10.4   Registry.cpp

```
/*
 * $Header: /Book/Registry.cpp 17    3.07.99 17:46 Petter $
 *
 * This is really a get/setProfile kind of thing.
 */

#include "precomp.h"
#include "registry.h"
#include "String.h"
#include "Exception.h"
#include "formatMessage.h"
#include "trace.h"

#define REGKEY_BASE   _T( "Software\\Andersen Consulting" )
#define APP_NAME      _T( "TextEdit" )

#define WIN_SETTINGS _T( "Microsoft\\Windows\\CurrentVersion" )
#define CPL_SETTINGS _T( "Control Panel\\Desktop\\WindowMetrics" )

String Registry::formatKey( HKEY hkRoot, LPCTSTR pszKey ) {

    assert( isGoodStringPtr( pszKey ) );

    String strKey;
    if ( HKEY_CURRENT_USER == hkRoot || HKEY_LOCAL_MACHINE == hkRoot )
    {
```

```
            if ( 0 == _tcsstr( pszKey, WIN_SETTINGS ) &&
                 0 == _tcsstr( pszKey, CPL_SETTINGS ) )
            {
                strKey = REGKEY_BASE _T( "\\" ) APP_NAME;
                if ( 0 != *pszKey ) {
                    strKey += _T( "\\" );
                }
            }
        }
    }

    if ( 0 != *pszKey ) {
        strKey += pszKey;
    }
    return strKey;
}

HKEY Registry::createKey( HKEY hkRoot, LPCTSTR pszKey ) {

    const String strKey = formatKey( hkRoot, pszKey );

    HKEY hk = openFormattedKey( hkRoot, strKey.c_str(), KEY_WRITE );
    if ( 0 != hk ) {
        return hk;
    }

    DWORD dwDisposition = 0;
    const long lResult = RegCreateKeyEx( hkRoot, strKey.c_str(), 0, 0,
        REG_OPTION_NON_VOLATILE, KEY_WRITE,
        reinterpret_cast< LPSECURITY_ATTRIBUTES >( 0 ),
        &hk, &dwDisposition );
    return NOERROR == lResult ? hk : 0;
}

/**
 * This functions exists merely to avoid calling formatKey
 * twice when the first openKey fails in createKey.
 */
HKEY Registry::openFormattedKey(
    HKEY hkRoot, LPCTSTR pszKey, DWORD dwMode )
```

```
{
   HKEY hk = 0;
   const long lResult =
      RegOpenKeyEx( hkRoot, pszKey, 0, dwMode, &hk );
   if ( NOERROR != lResult ) {
      trace( _T( "Unable to open registry key %s: %s\n" ),
         pszKey, WinException( lResult ).what() );
   }
   return NOERROR == lResult ? hk : 0;
}

HKEY Registry::openKey( HKEY hkRoot, LPCTSTR pszKey, DWORD dwMode ) {

   const String strKey = formatKey( hkRoot, pszKey );
   return openFormattedKey( hkRoot, strKey.c_str(), dwMode );
}

/**
 * @param hkRoot   HKEY_CURRENT_USER or HKEY_LOCAL_MACHINE
 * @param pszKey   Key name, e.g., "Settings\\RunMaximized"
 */
int Registry::getInt(
   HKEY hkRoot, LPCTSTR pszKey, LPCTSTR pszName, int nDefault )
{
   int nValue = nDefault;

   HKEY hk = openKey( hkRoot, pszKey );
   if ( 0 != hk ) {
      DWORD dwSize = sizeof nValue;
      DWORD dwType = 0;
#ifdef _DEBUG
      const long lResult =
#endif
      RegQueryValueEx( hk, pszName, 0, &dwType,
         reinterpret_cast< BYTE * >( &nValue ), &dwSize );
      // Check type and size for sanity:
      assert( 4 == dwSize );
      assert(
         REG_DWORD == dwType || ERROR_FILE_NOT_FOUND == lResult );
```

```
      verify( NOERROR == RegCloseKey( hk ) );
   }

   return nValue;
}

void Registry::setInt(
   HKEY hkRoot, LPCTSTR pszKey, LPCTSTR pszName, int nValue )
{
   assert( isGoodStringPtr( pszKey  ) );
   assert( isGoodStringPtr( pszName ) );

   HKEY hk = createKey( hkRoot, pszKey );
   if ( 0 != hk ) {
#ifdef _DEBUG
      const long lResult =
#endif
      RegSetValueEx( hk, pszName, 0, REG_DWORD,
         reinterpret_cast< CONST BYTE * >( &nValue ), sizeof nValue );
      assert( NOERROR == lResult );
      verify( NOERROR == RegCloseKey( hk ) );
   }
}

void __cdecl Registry::setString(
   HKEY hkRoot, LPCTSTR pszKey,
   LPCTSTR pszName, LPCTSTR pszFmt, ...   )
{
   assert( isGoodStringPtr( pszKey  ) );
   assert( isGoodStringPtr( pszName ) );
   assert( isGoodStringPtr( pszFmt  ) );

   va_list vl;
   va_start( vl, pszFmt );
   String str = formatMessageV( pszFmt, vl );
   va_end( vl );

   HKEY hk = createKey( hkRoot, pszKey );
   if ( 0 != hk ) {
```

```
#ifdef _DEBUG
      const long lResult =
#endif
      RegSetValueEx( hk, pszName, 0, REG_SZ,
         reinterpret_cast< CONST BYTE * >( str.c_str() ),
         (str.length() + 1) * sizeof( TCHAR ) );
      assert( NOERROR == lResult );
      verify( NOERROR == RegCloseKey( hk ) );
   }
}

String Registry::getString(
   HKEY hkRoot, LPCTSTR pszKey, LPCTSTR pszName, LPCTSTR pszDefault )
{
   PATHNAME sz = { 0 };
   if ( 0 != pszDefault ) {
      assert( isGoodStringPtr( pszDefault ) );
      assert( isGoodStringPtr( sz ) );
      assert( _tcsclen( pszDefault ) < dim( sz ) );
      verify( 0 != _tcsncpy( sz, pszDefault, dim( sz ) ) );
   }

   HKEY hk = openKey( hkRoot, pszKey );
   if ( 0 != hk ) {
      DWORD dwSize = sizeof sz; // Bytes, not characters.
      DWORD dwType = 0;
#ifdef _DEBUG
      const long lResult =
#endif
      RegQueryValueEx( hk, pszName, 0, &dwType,
         reinterpret_cast< BYTE * >( sz ), &dwSize );
      // Note that ERROR_MORE_DATA is one possible return value.
      // REG_EXPAND_SZ?
      assert( REG_EXPAND_SZ == dwType || REG_SZ == dwType ||
         ERROR_FILE_NOT_FOUND == lResult );
      verify( NOERROR == RegCloseKey( hk ) );
   }
   return sz;
}
```

```
bool Registry::getBlob(
   HKEY hkRoot, LPCTSTR pszKey,
   LPCTSTR pszName, LPVOID pBlob, UINT cb )
{
   HKEY hk = openKey( hkRoot, pszKey );
   if ( 0 != hk ) {
      DWORD dwSize = cb; // Bytes, not characters.
      DWORD dwType = 0;  // REG_BINARY expected
      const long lResult = RegQueryValueEx( hk, pszName, 0, &dwType,
         reinterpret_cast< BYTE * >( pBlob ), &dwSize );
      // Note that ERROR_MORE_DATA is one possible return value.
      verify( NOERROR == RegCloseKey( hk ) );
      assert( REG_BINARY == dwType );
      return NOERROR == lResult;
   }
   return false;
}

String Registry::fileTypeDescriptionFromExtension(
   LPCTSTR pszExtension )
{
   const String strClass =
      Registry::getString( HKEY_CLASSES_ROOT, pszExtension );
   const String strDescr =
      Registry::getString( HKEY_CLASSES_ROOT, strClass.c_str() );
   return strDescr;
}

bool enumOpenedKeyNames(
   HKEY hk, LPCTSTR pszKey, DWORD dwIndex, String *pstrName )
{
   assert( isGoodStringPtr( pszKey ) );
   assert( isGoodPtr( pstrName ) );

   PATHNAME szName  = { 0 };
   PATHNAME szClass = { 0 };
   DWORD dwNameSize = dim( szName );  // Characters, not bytes.
   DWORD dwClassSize = dim( szClass );
```

Chapter 10: Customization and Persistence

```cpp
      FILETIME ftLastWriteTime = { 0 };
      const long lResult = RegEnumKeyEx( hk, dwIndex, szName,
         &dwNameSize, 0, szClass, &dwClassSize, &ftLastWriteTime );
      if ( NOERROR == lResult ) {
         assert( 0 != pstrName );
         pstrName->assign( szName );
      } else if ( ERROR_NO_MORE_ITEMS != lResult ) {
         trace( _T( "RegEnumKeyEx %s: %s\n " ),
            pszKey, WinException( lResult ).what() );
      }
      return NOERROR == lResult;
   }

bool Registry::enumKeyNames(
   HKEY hkRoot, LPCTSTR pszKey, DWORD dwIndex, String *pstrName )
{
   bool bFound = false;
   HKEY hk = openKey( hkRoot, pszKey );
   if ( 0 != hk ) {
      bFound =
         enumOpenedKeyNames( hkRoot, pszKey, dwIndex, pstrName );
      verify( NOERROR == RegCloseKey( hk ) );
   }
   return bFound;
}

PRIVATE bool enumOpenedValues(
   HKEY hk, LPCTSTR pszKey, DWORD dwIndex, String *pstrName )
{
   PATHNAME szName  = { 0 };
   DWORD dwNameSize = dim( szName ); // Characters, not bytes.
   const long lResult = RegEnumValue(
      hk, dwIndex, szName, &dwNameSize, 0, 0, 0, 0 );
   if ( NOERROR == lResult ) {
      assert( 0 != pstrName );
      pstrName->assign( szName );
   } else if ( ERROR_NO_MORE_ITEMS != lResult ) {
      trace( _T( "RegEnumValue %s: %s\n " ),
         pszKey, WinException( lResult ).what() );
   }
```

```
      return NOERROR == lResult;
}

bool Registry::enumValues(
   HKEY hkRoot, LPCTSTR pszKey, DWORD dwIndex, String *pstrName )
{
   bool bFound = false;

   HKEY hk = openKey( hkRoot, pszKey );
   if ( 0 != hk ) {
      bFound = enumOpenedValues( hkRoot, pszKey, dwIndex, pstrName );
      verify( NOERROR == RegCloseKey( hk ) );
   }
   return bFound;
}

PRIVATE bool deleteRecursive( HKEY hkRoot, LPCTSTR pszKey ) {

   String strName;
   DWORD dwIndex = 0;
   HKEY hk = Registry::openFormattedKey( hkRoot, pszKey );
   if ( 0 == hk ) {
      return false;
   }
   while ( enumOpenedKeyNames( hk, pszKey, dwIndex, &strName ) ) {
      const String strKey(
         formatMessage( _T( "%1\\%2" ), pszKey, strName.c_str() ) );
      if ( !deleteRecursive( hkRoot, strKey.c_str() ) ) {
         ++dwIndex;
      }
   }
   verify( NOERROR == RegCloseKey( hk ) );
   const long lResult = RegDeleteKey( hkRoot, pszKey );
   if ( NOERROR != lResult ) {
      trace( _T( "Error deleting registry key %s: %s\n" ),
         pszKey, WinException( lResult ).what() );
   }
   return NOERROR == lResult;
}
```

```
bool Registry::deleteEntry(
   HKEY hkRoot, LPCTSTR pszKey, LPCTSTR pszName )
{
   if ( 0 == pszName ) {
      const String strKey = formatKey( hkRoot, pszKey );
      return deleteRecursive( hkRoot, strKey.c_str() ); //*** EXIT PT
   }

   HKEY hk = openKey( hkRoot, pszKey, KEY_ALL_ACCESS );
   bool bOK = 0 != hk;
   if ( bOK ) {
      const long lResult = RegDeleteValue( hk, pszName );
      if ( NOERROR != lResult ) {
         trace( _T( "Error deleting registry value %s in %s: %s\n" ),
            pszName, pszKey, WinException( lResult ).what() );
         bOK = false;
      }
      verify( NOERROR == RegCloseKey( hk ) );
   }

   return bOK;
}
```

Persistent Variables

Let's study one of the macros in persistence.h, DEFINE_PERSISTENT_BOOL, to see how it works:

```
#define DEFINE_PERSISTENT_BOOL( section, name )              \
   inline bool get ## name( void ) {                         \
      return 0 != Registry::getInt( HKEY_CURRENT_USER,       \
         _T( section ), _T( #name ), 0 );                    \
   };                                                        \
   inline void set ## name( bool bValue ) {                  \
      Registry::setInt( HKEY_CURRENT_USER,                   \
         _T( section ), _T( #name ), bValue );               \
   }
```

One use of the macro is this:

```
DEFINE_PERSISTENT_BOOL( "Search", MatchCase );
```

This expands to:

```
inline bool getMatchCase( void ) {
    return 0 != Registry::getInt( HKEY_CURRENT_USER,
        _T( "Search" ), _T( MatchCase ), 0 );
};
inline void setMatchCase( bool bValue ) {
    Registry::setInt( HKEY_CURRENT_USER,
        _T( "Search" ), _T( MatchCase ), bValue );
}
```

The macros for integers and strings are similar in structure. One deserves special mention: DEFINE_PERSISTENT_STRING_EX allows indexed persistent variables. After the declaration of

```
DEFINE_PERSISTENT_STRING_EX( "Search", Pattern );
```

I can write

```
setPattern( 1, _T( "someString" ) );
```

and end up with the following registry entry:

```
Software\Andersen Consulting\TextEdit\Search\Pattern1=someString
```

Most of the persistent variables are used across several modules, and therefore defined in persistence.h. Those that are used only by a single module are defined in that module, to reduce visibility.

Macros such as DEFINE_PERSISTENT_BOOL make it easy to define persistent variables — imagine coding all those getters and setters by hand! The down side is that the code is difficult to debug because multiple code lines are compressed into a single source line. You should always start with a hand-coded function, and only start using the code-generating macros when that function is fully debugged.

Listing 10.5 persistence.h

```
/*
 * $Header: /Book/persistence.h 8    3.07.99 17:46 Petter $
 */

#pragma once

#include "Registry.h"

#define DEFINE_PERSISTENT_BOOL( section, name )              \
    inline bool get ## name( void ) {                        \
        return 0 != Registry::getInt( HKEY_CURRENT_USER,     \
            _T( section ), _T( #name ), 0 );                 \
```

```
    };                                                      \
    inline void set ## name( bool bValue ) {                \
        Registry::setInt( HKEY_CURRENT_USER,                \
            _T( section ), _T( #name ), bValue );           \
    }

#define DEFINE_PERSISTENT_INT( section, name, def )         \
    inline int get ## name( void ) {                        \
        return Registry::getInt( HKEY_CURRENT_USER,         \
            _T( section ), _T( #name ), def );              \
    };                                                      \
    inline void set ## name( int nValue ) {                 \
        Registry::setInt( HKEY_CURRENT_USER,                \
            _T( section ), _T( #name ), nValue );           \
    }

#define DEFINE_PERSISTENT_STRING( section, name, def )      \
    inline String get ## name( LPCTSTR pszDefault ) {       \
        return Registry::getString( HKEY_CURRENT_USER,      \
            _T( section ), _T( #name ), pszDefault );       \
    };                                                      \
    inline String get ## name( void ) {                     \
        return get ## name( _T( def ) );                    \
    };                                                      \
    inline void set ## name( LPCTSTR pszValue ) {           \
        Registry::setString( HKEY_CURRENT_USER,             \
            _T( section ), _T( #name ), pszValue );         \
    }

#define DEFINE_PERSISTENT_STRING_EX( section, name )        \
    inline String get ## name( int nIndex ) {               \
        TCHAR szName[ 20 ];                                 \
        wsprintf( szName, _T( #name ) _T( "%d" ), nIndex ); \
        return Registry::getString( HKEY_CURRENT_USER,      \
            _T( section ), szName );                        \
    };                                                      \
    inline void set ## name( int nIndex, LPCTSTR pszValue ) { \
        TCHAR szName[ 20 ];                                 \
        wsprintf( szName, _T( #name ) _T( "%d" ), nIndex ); \
        Registry::setString( HKEY_CURRENT_USER,             \
```

```
            _T( section ), szName, pszValue );                    \
    }

DEFINE_PERSISTENT_INT(       "Fonts", FixedHeight , 10              );
DEFINE_PERSISTENT_INT(       "Fonts", FixedWeight , FW_NORMAL       );
DEFINE_PERSISTENT_INT(       "Fonts", FixedItalic , 0               );
DEFINE_PERSISTENT_STRING( "Fonts", FixedFace    , "Courier New" );
DEFINE_PERSISTENT_INT(       "Fonts", FixedCharSet, ANSI_CHARSET    );

DEFINE_PERSISTENT_INT(       "Fonts", ProportionalHeight , 10          );
DEFINE_PERSISTENT_INT(       "Fonts", ProportionalWeight , FW_NORMAL   );
DEFINE_PERSISTENT_INT(       "Fonts", ProportionalItalic , 0           );
DEFINE_PERSISTENT_STRING( "Fonts", ProportionalFace   , "Arial"      );
DEFINE_PERSISTENT_INT(       "Fonts", ProportionalCharSet,ANSI_CHARSET );

DEFINE_PERSISTENT_INT(          "Open" , FilterIndex, 1   );
DEFINE_PERSISTENT_STRING(       "Open" , CustomFilter, "" );

DEFINE_PERSISTENT_BOOL(         "Search", MatchWholeWord  );
DEFINE_PERSISTENT_BOOL(         "Search", MatchCase       );
DEFINE_PERSISTENT_BOOL(         "Search", Backwards       );
DEFINE_PERSISTENT_STRING_EX( "Search", Pattern            );
DEFINE_PERSISTENT_STRING_EX( "Search", Replacement        );

DEFINE_PERSISTENT_INT(          "View" , ToolbarVisible   , 1 );
DEFINE_PERSISTENT_INT(          "View" , StatusbarVisible , 1 );

DEFINE_PERSISTENT_INT(          "Delete", SendToWasteBasket, 1 );
DEFINE_PERSISTENT_INT(          "Delete", ShowDeleteDialog , 1 );

DEFINE_PERSISTENT_INT(    "", Language, -1 );
DEFINE_PERSISTENT_STRING( "", DocumentPath, "" );
```

Document Local Persistence

As an example of how document-local persistence works, consider how TextEdit initializes word wrapping when you load the file C:\Data\test.txt:

1. Start with the system default value, which for word wrapping is zero.
2. Check the file type of C:\Data\test.txt, and determine that this file is of type Text Document.

3. If the registry entry `Software\Andersen Consulting\TextEdit\File Types\Text Document\WordWrap` exists, use its value; otherwise keep the current one.
4. If the registry entry `Software\Andersen Consulting\TextEdit\Files\C:|Data|test.txt\WordWrap` exists, use its value; otherwise keep the current one.

If you change the word wrapping while editing `C:\Data\test.txt`, both these registry entries will be updated, and the new value will apply to new files of type `Text Document`, as well as any such file that doesn't have an explicit word wrap setting. It gets an explicit setting only if you change the setting while editing the file.

Document local persistence is implemented through macros defined in `Document.h`. Actually, there's only one such macro because all the values happen to be numbers:

```
#define DEFINE_PERSISTENT_DOC_INT( name, type )                     \
    inline int get ## name( int nDefault ) const {                  \
        return getPersistentInt( _T( #name ), nDefault, type );     \
    };                                                              \
    inline void set ## name( int nValue ) {                         \
        setPersistentInt( _T( #name ), nValue, type );              \
    }
```

This macro is similar to those defined in `persistence.h`, except that, instead of calling the getter and setter functions in the `Registry` class, they call a couple of `Document` methods that wrap those defined in the `Registry` class. These wrapper methods do two things: (a) they add the file name to the key (converting backslashes to vertical bars in the process), and (b) they handle everything to do with the file type settings. If the `type` parameter is true, information is saved for file types as well as for individual files. If the `type` parameter is false, information is only saved for individual files. Examples: fixed or proportional font is saved for both file types and individual files, while window position is only saved for individual files.

Because the macro generates code to call `Document` methods, it follows that the macro must be used inside the declaration of the `Document` class. A corollary is that the generated functions are themselves `Document` methods.

MRU

MRU means Most Recently Used. The MRU file list is implemented by the `MRU` class. In addition to managing a persistent file list in the registry, the `MRU` class also interfaces to the system-wide MRU file list, the one found under Documents in the Start Menu. You add files to this list by calling the `SHAddToRecentDocs` function. (Discourse continues on page 255.)

Listing 10.6   MRU.h

```
/*
 * $Header: /Book/MRU.h 11    3.07.99 17:46 Petter $
 */

#pragma once
```

```cpp
#include "String.h"
#include "resource.h" // Needs ID_MRU_*

class MRU {
private:
   enum {
      FILES_TO_SHOW      =   9, // Tested with 19.
      FILES_TO_REMEMBER  =  30,
      STRING_WIDTH       = 200, // Tested with 50.
   };

   bool m_bDirty;
   int  m_nCount;
   String m_astrEntries[ FILES_TO_REMEMBER ];

   bool findFile( const String& strFile, int *pnIndex ) const;

#ifdef _DEBUG
   static int s_nRefCount;
#endif

public:
   MRU();
   ~MRU();

   int getCount( void ) const;

   void addFile( const String& strFile );
   void addFilesToMenu( HMENU hmenu, bool bShowAccelerators );
   void removeFile( const String& strFile );
   void renameFile( const String& strOld, const String& strNew );

   String getFile( int iCmdID ) const;
   String getFileTitle( int iCmdID ) const;
};

inline String MRU::getFile( int iCmdID ) const {
```

Chapter 10: Customization and Persistence

```cpp
        assert( ID_MRU_1 <= iCmdID &&
                        iCmdID <= ID_MRU_1 + FILES_TO_REMEMBER );
    const int iFile = iCmdID - ID_MRU_1;
    assert( iFile < m_nCount );
    assert( !m_astrEntries[ iFile ].empty() );
    return m_astrEntries[ iFile ];
}

inline int MRU::getCount( void ) const {
    return m_nCount;
}
```

Listing 10.7   MRU.cpp

```cpp
/*
 * $Header: /Book/MRU.cpp 13     3.07.99 17:46 Petter $
 */

#include "precomp.h"
#include "Registry.h"
#include "menuUtils.h"
#include "fileUtils.h"
#include "MenuFont.h"
#include "resource.h"
#include "MRU.h"
#include "persistence.h"
#include "utils.h"
#include "trace.h"

DEFINE_PERSISTENT_STRING_EX( "MRU", FileName );

#ifdef _DEBUG
int MRU::s_nRefCount = 0;
#endif

MRU::MRU() : m_bDirty( false ), m_nCount( 0 ) {

    // Sanity check -- these *must* be consecutive:
    assert( ID_MRU_2 == ID_MRU_1 + 1 );
    assert( ID_MRU_3 == ID_MRU_2 + 1 );
```

```
   assert( ID_MRU_4  == ID_MRU_3 + 1 );
   assert( ID_MRU_5  == ID_MRU_4 + 1 );
   assert( ID_MRU_6  == ID_MRU_5 + 1 );
   assert( ID_MRU_7  == ID_MRU_6 + 1 );
   assert( ID_MRU_8  == ID_MRU_7 + 1 );
   assert( ID_MRU_9  == ID_MRU_8 + 1 );
   assert( ID_MRU_10 == ID_MRU_9 + 1 );

   m_nCount = 0;
   while ( m_nCount < FILES_TO_REMEMBER ) {
      m_astrEntries[ m_nCount ] = getFileName( m_nCount );
      if ( m_astrEntries[ m_nCount ].empty() ) {
         break; //*** LOOP EXIT POINT
      }
      ++m_nCount;
   }

   assert( 1 == ++s_nRefCount );
}

MRU::~MRU() {

   assert( m_nCount <= FILES_TO_REMEMBER );
   if ( m_bDirty ) {
      for ( int iFile = 0; iFile < FILES_TO_REMEMBER; ++iFile ) {
         const LPCTSTR pszEntry = iFile < m_nCount
            ? m_astrEntries[ iFile ].c_str() : _T( "" );
         setFileName( iFile, pszEntry );
      }
   }
   assert( 0 == --s_nRefCount );
}

bool MRU::findFile( const String& strFile, int *pnIndex ) const {

   assert( isGoodPtr( pnIndex ) );

   const LPCTSTR pszFile = strFile.c_str();
   for ( *pnIndex = 0; *pnIndex < m_nCount; ++*pnIndex ) {
      const LPCTSTR pszEntry = m_astrEntries[ *pnIndex ].c_str();
```

```cpp
            if ( 0 == _tcsicmp( pszFile, pszEntry ) ) {
                return true; //*** FUNCTION EXIT POINT
            }
        }

    return false; // Not found.
}

void MRU::addFile( const String& strFile ) {

    m_bDirty = true;

    // If the file is already in the list, move it to the top:
    int nFile = 0;
    if ( findFile( strFile, &nFile ) ) {
        // Move preceding items one step down:
        for ( int iFile = nFile; 0 < iFile; --iFile ) {
            m_astrEntries[ iFile ] = m_astrEntries[ iFile - 1 ];
        }
    } else { // It was not in the list, so append it.
        assert( m_nCount <= FILES_TO_REMEMBER );
        for ( int iFile = m_nCount; 0 < iFile; --iFile ) {

            // Move all items one step down, letting the last  item
            // fall off the bottom if the list was already full:
            if ( iFile < FILES_TO_REMEMBER - 1 ) {
                m_astrEntries[ iFile ] = m_astrEntries[ iFile - 1 ];
            }
        }

        if ( m_nCount < FILES_TO_REMEMBER ) {
            ++m_nCount;
        }
    }

    m_astrEntries[ 0 ] = strFile;
    SHAddToRecentDocs( SHARD_PATH, strFile.c_str() );
}
```

```cpp
void MRU::removeFile( const String& strFile ) {

   int nFile = 0;
   if ( findFile( strFile, &nFile ) ) {
      m_bDirty = true;
      assert( 0 < m_nCount );
      assert( m_nCount <= FILES_TO_REMEMBER );
      for ( int iFile = nFile; iFile < m_nCount - 1; ++iFile ) {
         assert( iFile + 1 < FILES_TO_REMEMBER );
         m_astrEntries[ iFile ] = m_astrEntries[ iFile + 1 ];
      }
      --m_nCount;
   }
}

void MRU::renameFile( const String& strOld, const String& strNew ) {

   int nFile = 0;
   if ( findFile( strOld, &nFile ) ) {
      m_bDirty = true;
      assert( nFile < m_nCount );
      assert( nFile < FILES_TO_REMEMBER );
      m_astrEntries[ nFile ] = strNew;
   }
}

PRIVATE inline LPCTSTR getFormatString(
   int iFile, bool bShowAccelerators )
{
   assert( 0 <= iFile && iFile < 19 );
   return
      1 == iFile && bShowAccelerators ? _T( "&&d. %s\tCtrl+F6" ) :
      9 <= iFile ? _T( "1&&d. %s" ) : _T( "&&d. %s" );
}

PRIVATE inline bool startsWith(
   LPCTSTR pszString, LPCTSTR pszTarget )
{
   assert( isGoodConstPtr( pszString ) );
```

```
      assert( isGoodConstPtr( pszTarget ) );
      return
         0 == _tcsncmp( pszString, pszTarget, _tcsclen( pszTarget ) );
}


PRIVATE bool pathRelativeToCurrent(
   LPTSTR pszRelativePath, LPCTSTR pszPath )
{
   PATHNAME szCurrPath = { 0 };
   verify( 0 != _tgetdcwd( 0, szCurrPath, sizeof szCurrPath ) );

   return 0 != PathRelativePathTo( pszRelativePath, szCurrPath,
      FILE_ATTRIBUTE_DIRECTORY, pszPath, 0 );
}

String MRU::getFileTitle( int iCmdID ) const {

   String strFile = getFile( iCmdID );

   PATHNAME szRelativePath = { 0 };
   pathRelativeToCurrent( szRelativePath, strFile.c_str() );
   if ( 0 == szRelativePath[ 0 ] ) {
      _tcscpy( szRelativePath, strFile.c_str() );
   } else if ( startsWith( szRelativePath, _T( ".\\" ) ) ) {
      // Remove current directory from path
      const int nLength = _tcslen( szRelativePath + 2 );
      memmove( szRelativePath, szRelativePath + 2,
         sizeof( TCHAR ) * ( nLength + 1 ) );
   } else if ( startsWith( szRelativePath, _T( "..\\" ) ) ) {
      // If path is above current dir, display complete path
      _tcscpy( szRelativePath, strFile.c_str() );
   }

   return szRelativePath;
}

void MRU::addFilesToMenu( HMENU hmenu, bool bShowAccelerators ) {

   const int nCount = __min( m_nCount, FILES_TO_SHOW );
```

```
    for ( int iFile = 0; iFile < nCount; ++iFile ) {

        String strFileTitle = getFileTitle( iFile + ID_MRU_1 );
        fixAmpersands( &strFileTitle );
        const String strCompactedFileTitle =
            compactPath( strFileTitle.c_str(), STRING_WIDTH );
        assert( strCompactedFileTitle.length() < MAX_PATH );

        TCHAR szMenuItem[ MAX_PATH + 6 ];
        wsprintf( szMenuItem,
            getFormatString( iFile, bShowAccelerators ),
            (iFile + 1) % 10,
            strCompactedFileTitle.c_str() );
        appendMenuItem( hmenu, ID_MRU_1 + iFile, szMenuItem );
    }
}
```

Data Sharing Across Instances

The registry is global and its contents are shared across all running instances of TextEdit. It follows that they all have the same MRU file list at all times, and that the contents of the Find dialog drop-down are shared, and that printer settings made in one instance are immediately reflected in other instances. (The only exception is if the dialog in question is active in the other TextEdit instance.)

Font changes are not reflected in concurrently running TextEdit instances. Again we see the difference between things that are initialized at specific times, such as when a menu drops down or a dialog box pops up, and things that are always visible in the user interface, such as toolbar icons and the current font. With a few well-chosen inter-instance notification messages, it would be relatively easy to reflect font changes immediately, and even to update the contents of active dialog boxes. If we were to take such a policy to its logical conclusion, we should replace the "one option dialog per instance" paradigm with something like the Windows Control Panel — one common dialog for all running instances.

To share or not to share, that is the question. Perhaps it would've been better to let each file store its own printer settings, for example. On the other hand, it is reassuring for the user to think of the printer as one object that behaves the same for all instances; if you change it, it stays changed. I just want to point out that such questions bear thinking about; I'm sorry to say that I seem to have mislaid the right answer.

RunOnce

So far, we've discussed TextEdit's use of the registry for persistent storage of user information. TextEdit also uses the registry to store setup information; this is discussed in Chapter 20. In this section, we'll look at how TextEdit instances are persistent across logoff and shutdown.

Windows knows about this registry key:

```
HKEY_CURRENT_USER\Software\Microsoft\Windows\CurrentVersion\RunOnce
```

Whenever Windows starts, it enumerates all key-value pairs under this key, and executes all the values as commands. The Windows Explorer uses this feature to restore all the Explorer windows.

A naïve (and all too common) use of this facility is to insert a `RunOnce` command in response to the `WM_ENDSESSION` message, e.g.:

```
HKEY_CURRENT_USER\Software\Microsoft\Windows\CurrentVersion\RunOnce\
    TextEdit="C:\Program Files\TextEdit\TextEdit.exe C:\Data\test.txt"
```

This approach has at least two problems:

1. If the system goes down catastrophically, we never see the `WM_ENDSESSION` message, and restart doesn't take place.
2. If multiple instances of TextEdit were running, they would have to ensure that each had a unique name. This is possible, of course, but it is certainly extra work.

What TextEdit actually does is the following: when TextEdit starts, it inserts the following under the `RunOnce` key:

```
TextEdit Restart="C:\Program Files\TextEdit\TextEdit.exe /boot"
```

It is not a problem if this overwrites an existing entry, as all entries are equal. The code to do this is located in `init.cpp`, and looks like this:

```
LOCAL void initReboot( void ) {

    const String strProgram = getModuleFileName();
    Registry::setString( HKEY_CURRENT_USER,
        RUNONCE_PATH, _T( "TextEdit Restart" ),
        _T( "%1 /boot" ), strProgram.c_str() );
}
```

The constant `RUNONCE_PATH` is defined in `setup.h`, as follows:

```
#define WIN_PATH _T( "Software\\Microsoft\\Windows\\CurrentVersion" )
#define RUNONCE_PATH WIN_PATH _T( "\\RunOnce" )
```

Next, the document local persistent variable `Running` is set to one. If TextEdit exits in response to `WM_ENDSESSION`, it remains one; otherwise, it's reset to zero. If Windows crashes, the value of `Running` remains 1, and restart will take place.

When TextEdit is started with the `/boot` option, it does the following:

1. It iterates over all the TextEdit files in the registry and invokes TextEdit anew for any files with Running = 1.
2. It purges the registry file list of any files that are no longer in the MRU list. If we didn't do this occasionally, the registry would fill up. Note, though, that the MRU list contains more

files than are shown in the File menu, so settings for an individual file last for a while after the file falls off the edge of the MRU menu.

Then it exits. Windows removes all RunOnce entries after executing them. If you don't start any new TextEdit instances this Windows session, no new reboot entry will be added, and there will be no restart.

The WM_QUERYENDSESSION/WM_ENDSESSION message pair have different behaviors under Windows 9x and Windows NT. Under Windows 9x, after each application responds with TRUE to the WM_QUERYENDSESSION message, they receive the WM_ENDSESSION message and are terminated. Under Windows NT, if you reply TRUE to WM_QUERYENDSESSION, you immediately receive WM_ENDSESSION and are terminated, even though other applications may still respond with FALSE to WM_QUERYENDSESSION.

I've tried to come up with good adjectives to describe this state of affairs (e.g., "weird," "ridiculous"), but they all strike me as understatements. I'll leave it as an exercise for the adjectivally-inclined reader.

Listing 10.8   reboot.cpp

```cpp
/*
 * $Header: /Book/reboot.cpp 10    3.07.99 17:46 Petter $
 */

#include "precomp.h"
#include "reboot.h"
#include "utils.h"
#include "trace.h"
#include "formatMessage.h"
#include "startInstance.h"
#include "fileUtils.h"
#include "winUtils.h"
#include "MRU.h"
#include "Registry.h"
#include "Document.h"
#include "Exception.h"

typedef std::map< int, String > StringMap;

inline bool enumKeyNames( DWORD dwIndex, String *pstrKey ) {
    return Registry::enumKeyNames(
        HKEY_CURRENT_USER, _T( "Files" ), dwIndex, pstrKey );
}
```

```
/**
 * Starts a TextEdit instance for any files marked as Running.
 */
PRIVATE void startInstances( void ) {

   const MRU mru;
   const int nFiles = mru.getCount();
   for ( int iFile = 0; iFile < nFiles; ++iFile ) {
      const String strFile = mru.getFile( iFile + ID_MRU_1 );
      const LPCTSTR pszFile = strFile.c_str();
      const String strEntry = Document::createRegistryPath( strFile );
      const String strFileKey = formatMessage(
         _T( "Files\\%1" ), strEntry.c_str() );
      const bool bRestart = 0 != Registry::getInt(
         HKEY_CURRENT_USER, strFileKey.c_str(), _T( "Running" ), 0 );
      if ( bRestart ) {
         if ( fileExists( pszFile ) ) {
            startInstance( formatMessage( _T( "\"%1\"" ), pszFile ) );
         }
         // No reasonable way to handle a startInstance failure;
         // we're running silently now, and would prefer not to
         // bother the user over a minor matter such as not
         // being able to restart TextEdit.
      }
   }
}

PRIVATE void checkExistence( void ) {

   MRU mru;

   int nFile = 0;
   while ( nFile < mru.getCount() ) {
      const String strFile = mru.getFile( nFile + ID_MRU_1 );
      if ( fileExists( strFile.c_str() ) ) {
         ++nFile;
      } else {
         mru.removeFile( strFile );
      }
```

```
        }
    }

    PRIVATE void deleteUnusedEntries( void ) {

        const MRU mru;
        const int nFiles = mru.getCount();

        // Delete entries in the Files registry subtree
        // if they're missing from the MRU list:
        int nFilesToDelete = 0;
        StringMap mapOfFilesToDelete;
        String strFileEntry;
        for ( DWORD dwIndex = 0;
            enumKeyNames( dwIndex, &strFileEntry );
            ++dwIndex )
        {
            bool bExistsInMRU = false;
            for ( int iFile = 0; iFile < nFiles; ++iFile ) {
                const String strFile = mru.getFile( iFile + ID_MRU_1 );
                const String strMruEntry =
                    Document::createRegistryPath( strFile );
                if ( 0 ==
                    _tcsicmp( strFileEntry.c_str(), strMruEntry.c_str() ) )
                {
                    bExistsInMRU = true;
                    break; //*** LOOP EXIT POINT
                }
            }
            if ( !bExistsInMRU ) {
                mapOfFilesToDelete[ nFilesToDelete++ ] = strFileEntry;
            }
        }

        for ( int iFile = 0; iFile < nFilesToDelete; ++iFile ) {
            StringMap::iterator iter = mapOfFilesToDelete.find( iFile );
            assert( mapOfFilesToDelete.end() != iter );
            if ( mapOfFilesToDelete.end() != iter ) {
                const String strKey = formatMessage(
```

```
                    _T( "Files\\%1" ), iter->second.c_str() );
                Registry::deleteEntry( HKEY_CURRENT_USER, strKey.c_str() );
            }
        }

        mapOfFilesToDelete.clear();
    }

    /**
     * Cleans nonexistent files from the MRU list and cleans the
     * registry of files no longer in the MRU list.
     */
    void clean( void ) {
        checkExistence();
        deleteUnusedEntries();
    }

    /**
     * Starts a TextEdit instance for any files marked as Running,
     * then cleans up.
     */
    void reboot( void ) {

        startInstances();
        clean();
    }
```

Food for Persistent Thought

Persistence as such is a Good Thing. Whether the TextEdit approach to persistence is correct in all cases is another matter. Issues to consider include:

- What should you store?
- Where should you store it?
- Which information should you store per user?
- Which information should you store per file?
- Does the information ever expire?

If you control the file format yourself, per-file information belongs in the file itself. The Microsoft Office products do this, and for any file format based on OLE structured storage, inserting additional streams would seem a reasonable option. Some standardized file formats also allows for this kind of thing — the Tagged Image File Format (TIFF), for example, is extensible, and allows you to store anything you like in the same file as the image(s). Other

TIFF readers will simply ignore your private tags; unfortunately, other TIFF editors will most likely obliterate them.

TextEdit deals with plain text files. This is the most general file format imaginable, with no internal structure at all except line breaks. Storing per-file information as part of the text stream is out of the question. There is another possibility, though, in file systems that support extended attributes or contents of some sort. The NTFS file system, for example, supports named streams in addition to the unnamed default stream (what you'd normally think of as the file's contents). It's an attractive option to use named streams to store window positions, older versions, change log, and so forth. Care must be taken to preserve such information when saving files; this is discussed briefly in "Saving" on page 277 of Chapter 12.

TextEdit must work even with the FAT file system, which means that per-file information must be stored outside the document file. Again, the possibilities are many — flat files, INI files, databases — anything you like, really. The major advantage of using the registry is that we can easily store both common and per-user information. The major disadvantage is that we cannot store anything we like in the registry. Storing backup copies of a file's contents would be a bad idea, for example; TextEdit handles files up to 2GB, and stuffing megabyte upon megabyte into the registry wouldn't do it any good. The registry is not a database, and best suited to relatively small, controlled amounts of information.

Per-file information can be stored in another file, alongside the document file. This is more visible to the end user than I like, and, if the per-file information includes older versions, creates problems on floppies. If you save both the file and its backup on the same disk, the useful capacity is halved. If you do supply versioning support, it is probably wise to give the user some control over it, as the impact on disk space may be significant.

If you're going to store per-application information on disk, create an application-specific directory under the directory that `getSpecialFolderLocation( CSIDL_APPDATA )` would retrieve. If TextEdit used this approach, application data might be stored in this location:

```
C:\WINNT\Profiles\<username>\Application Data\TextEdit
```

TextEdit stores information about individual files for as long as they remain in the extended MRU list. Other possibilities include setting a time limit on that kind of meta-information or using a combination of the two.

These few paragraphs just scratch the surface of the persistence question. They don't provide a full answer, but I hope they encourage you to think carefully about persistence.

Chapter 11

Wait a Moment...

Before I get into potentially time-consuming operations such as File I/O and printing, I'll digress into the subject of the wait cursor. I'll describe a problem with the typical implementation and discuss enhancements to the standard hourglass.

Most Windows applications display an hourglass cursor during lengthy operations. The implementation usually looks something like this:

```
// Set hourglass cursor, saving the current one:
const HCURSOR hcurSave = SetCursor( LoadCursor( 0, IDC_WAIT ) );
// ...perform lengthy operation here...
// Restore old cursor:
SetCursor( hcurSave );
```

SetCursor returns a handle to the previous cursor; this suggests such usage. Most Windows books I've seen do the above and the MFC class CWaitCursor encapsulates the same functionality.

What's wrong with this picture? Consider the following sequence of events:

1. When the lengthy operation starts, the cursor is an IDC_ARROW, a fact remembered by hcurSave.
2. During the operation, the user moves the mouse and the hourglass cursor comes to rest on a split bar.
3. The operation ends, and the cursor is changed back to an arrow.

The problem is that the cursor isn't *supposed* to be an arrow when it's on the split bar. As soon as the mouse pointer is moved, things will be dandy again, but in the meantime, there's this tiny crack in the smooth surface of illusion we strive to create for our users.

This particular crack is easily mended and the result is actually simpler to use than the standard example above. What we need is a function analogous to `InvalidateRect` that operates on the cursor. We no longer need to save the existing cursor, and the above example becomes:

```
// Set hourglass cursor:
SetCursor( LoadCursor( 0, IDC_WAIT ) );
// ...perform lengthy operation here...
// Restore normal cursor:
InvalidateCursor();
```

The implementation of `InvalidateCursor` is simple:

```
void InvalidateCursor ( void ) {
    POINT pt; // Screen coordinates!
    GetCursorPos( &pt );
    SetCursorPos( pt.x, pt.y );
}
```

This moves the cursor to its current location (i.e., the cursor does not actually move anywhere), forcing a `WM_SETCURSOR` message in the process. Doing it this way is a lot simpler than synthesizing and dispatching a `WM_SETCURSOR` message.

`GetCursorPos` and `SetCursorPos` changed somewhat during the migration from Win16 to Win32. In Win16, these were `void` functions; in Win32, they each return `TRUE` for success and `FALSE` for failure. As is its wont, however, Microsoft's documentation is vague about possible causes of failure.

An improved implementation of MFC's `CWaitCursor` class might have the following declaration:

```
class WaitCursor {
public:
    WaitCursor();
    ~WaitCursor();
    void restore();
};
```

The constructor and the `restore` method are both trivial; the interesting part is the destructor:

```
WaitCursor::WaitCursor() {
    SetCursor( LoadCursor( 0, IDC_WAIT ) ); // or call restore...
}
```

```
void WaitCursor::restore() {
   SetCursor( LoadCursor( 0, IDC_WAIT ) );
}

/**
 * Forces a WM_SETCURSOR message.
 */
WaitCursor::~WaitCursor() {
   POINT pt; // Screen coordinates!

#ifdef _WIN32
   if ( !GetCursorPos( &pt ) ) {
      trace( _T( "GetCursorPos Failed\n" ) );
   } else if ( !SetCursorPos( pt.x, pt.y ) ) {
      trace( _T( "SetCursorPos(%d,%d) Failed\n" ), pt.x, pt.y ) );
   }
#else // Win16
   GetCursorPos( &pt );
   SetCursorPos( pt.x, pt.y );
#endif
}
```

Changing the Cursor Image

The Microsoft Office suite comes with a nifty set of animated wait cursors that indicate just what kind of lengthy operation is going on — opening, saving or printing a file, for example. This is more than just a gimmick; it gives useful feedback that it would be nice to provide for TextEdit.

It obviously wouldn't do to steal Microsoft's cursors and ship them with TextEdit, but what about users that already have these cursors installed — surely it is OK for them to use the cursors?

Listing 11.1   WaitCursor.cpp

```
/*
 * $Header: /Book/WaitCursor.cpp 11    5.09.99 13:07 Petter $
 */

#include "precomp.h"
#include "trace.h"
#include "String.h"
#include "WaitCursor.h"
```

```
#define CURSOR_PATH _T( "Cursors\\" )

PRIVATE inline HCURSOR loadCursor( LPCTSTR pszName ) {
    return static_cast< HCURSOR >( LoadImage( 0, pszName,
        IMAGE_CURSOR, 0, 0,
        LR_DEFAULTSIZE | LR_DEFAULTCOLOR | LR_LOADFROMFILE ) );
}

/**
 * The constructor attempts to load the named cursor.
 * The pszName parameter should be relative to the Windows directory.
 */
WaitCursor::WaitCursor( LPCTSTR pszName )
    : m_hcur( 0 )
    , m_isFromFile( false )
{
    if ( 0 != pszName ) {
        String strCursor( CURSOR_PATH );
        strCursor += pszName;

        PATHNAME szWindowsDirectory = { 0 };
        const nChars = GetWindowsDirectory(
            szWindowsDirectory, dim( szWindowsDirectory ) );
        if ( 0 < nChars && nChars < dim( szWindowsDirectory ) ) {
            // We now have something like C:\\WINNT or C:\\WINDOWS.
            // There's a terminating \\ if it is a root directory.
            PATHNAME szCursorPath = { 0 };
            _tmakepath( szCursorPath, 0, szWindowsDirectory,
                strCursor.c_str() , 0 );

            // Sample szCursorPath = "C:\\WINNT\\Cursors\\load.ani"
            m_hcur = loadCursor( szCursorPath );
        }
    }
```

```
   m_isFromFile = (0 != m_hcur);
   if ( !m_isFromFile ) {
      m_hcur = LoadCursor( 0, IDC_WAIT ); // NOTE: LR_SHARED is undoc!
   }
   restore();
}

WaitCursor::~WaitCursor() {

   assert( 0 != m_hcur );
   if ( m_isFromFile ) {
      //verify( DestroyCursor( m_hcur ) ); // NOTE: This fails.
      DestroyCursor( m_hcur );
   }
   reset_pointer( m_hcur );

   POINT pt; // Screen coordinates.

   // SetCursorPos forces a WM_SETCURSOR message.
   if ( !GetCursorPos( &pt ) ) {
      trace( _T( "GetCursorPos failed!" ) );
      assert( false );
   } else if ( !SetCursorPos( pt.x, pt.y ) ) {
      trace( _T( "SetCursorPos( %d, %d ) failed!" ), pt.x, pt.y );
      assert( false );
   }
}

void WaitCursor::restore( void ) const {
   // Actually, 0 is an acceptable value for SetCursor,
   // but m_hcur is nevertheless not *supposed* to be 0 here:
   assert( 0 != m_hcur );
   SetCursor( m_hcur );
}
```

Chapter 12

File I/O

Figure 12.1 gives the highlights of how TextEdit handles files. On opening the file `sample.txt`, TextEdit immediately creates a copy of the file. In the figure, this copy is labeled "`original copy of sample.txt`," but in fact, the name is a pseudo-garbage string generated by `GetTempFileName`, for example "`te0123.tmp`."

270 Chapter 12: File I/O

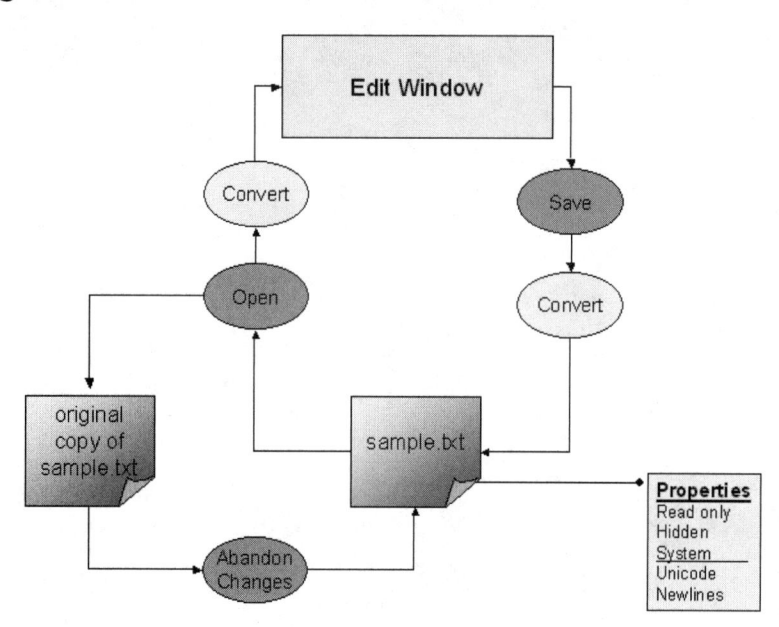

Figure 12.1 File I/O in TextEdit. The Document **class is in charge of this.**

The Document class handles all file I/O. The interface to the Document class was introduced in Chapter 5; it's time we took a look at the implementation.

Drive Type

To begin with, all the Document constructor knows is the file name. The file is passed through getLongFileName before it is assigned to the m_strFileName member. Next, getDriveType figures out what kind of drive the file resides on. Actually, all we care about is whether the file resides on a CD-ROM or a floppy. If it's on a CD-ROM, it's obviously a read-only file; if it's on a floppy, the floppy may be write-protected. In addition, the auto-save interval is much larger for floppies because it needs to be spun up before we can access the disk (see Editor::getAutoSaveTime).

The getDriveType function is a wrapper for the Windows function GetDriveType. If fed a UNC file name, this function returns DRIVE_NO_ROOT_DIR, for some curious reason.

Figuring out whether a floppy is write-protected is less straightforward than you might think. The only way I know is to attempt to create a file. If this fails with an error code of ERROR_WRITE_PROTECT, the floppy is write-protected. Merely opening a file for writing is insufficient, as this succeeds even on a write-protected floppy. You don't get an error until you actually try to write to the file.

Here is the isWriteProtectedDisk function from fileUtils.cpp:

```
bool isWriteProtectedDisk( LPCTSTR pszPath ) {

    assert( isGoodStringPtr( pszPath ) );
```

```
   PATHNAME szDir = { 0 };
   _tsplitpath( pszPath, szDir, 0, 0, 0 );

   PATHNAME szTest = { 0 };

   SilentErrorMode sem;
   if ( !GetTempFileName( szDir, _T( "te" ), 0, szTest ) ) {
      if ( ERROR_WRITE_PROTECT == GetLastError() ) {
         return true;
      }
   }
   verify( DeleteFile( szTest ) );
   return false;
}
```

SilentErrorMode

The `SetErrorMode` function controls who handles certain types of serious errors — you or Windows. In some cases, such as in the `isWriteProtectedDisk` function, I don't want Windows to display a dialog box if a critical error occurs, so I must call `SetErrorMode`. Because I also want to restore the normal state of affairs afterwards, I have, as usual, created an exception-safe wrapper class, so that a simple variable declaration is sufficient. This class is named `SilentErrorMode`.

Listing 12.1   SilentErrorMode.h

```
/*
 * $Header: /Book/SilentErrorMode.h 3     3.07.99 17:46 Petter $
 */

#pragma once

class SilentErrorMode {
private:
   UINT m_uiPrevMode;

public:
   SilentErrorMode( void );
   ~SilentErrorMode();
};
```

```
inline SilentErrorMode::SilentErrorMode( void ) {
    m_uiPrevMode = SetErrorMode(
        SEM_FAILCRITICALERRORS | SEM_NOOPENFILEERRORBOX );
};

inline SilentErrorMode::~SilentErrorMode() {
    SetErrorMode( m_uiPrevMode );
}
```

Opening Files

The `Document::openFile` method takes care of actually opening the file. To begin with, it tries to open the file in read/write mode. If that doesn't give us a valid file handle, it's time to listen to what `GetLastError` has to tell us.

If the error code is `ERROR_INVALID_NAME`, the likely explanation is that the file name contains wild cards. If a wild card pattern makes it this far, it's because no files matched the pattern. The `openFile` method displays a message box to that effect, then uses the `openFile` function (not the `Document` method of the same name) to let the user select a different file (or create a new one). If the user clicks OK, it tries to open the new file, otherwise it throws a `CancelException`.

That message box, by the way, could be dispensed with, because the explanation could just as well have been presented as part of the Open File dialog. Next version, for sure.

If we still don't have a valid file handle, and the error code is `ERROR_FILE_NOT_FOUND`, we try to append the default extension and open the file again. If the new error code is different from `ERROR_FILE_NOT_FOUND`, the file name with extension replaces the old file name. (A more advanced approach would be to try different extensions in turn, e.g., first `.txt`, then `.cpp`, and so on.)

If we still don't have a valid file handle, and the error code is `ERROR_ACCESS_DENIED` or `ERROR_SHARING_VIOLATION`, we try to open the file in read-only mode.

If we still don't have a valid file handle, and the error code is `ERROR_FILE_NOT_FOUND`, we call the `getNewFile` function to invoke `FileNotFoundDlg`, depicted in Figure 7.3.

If we still don't have a valid file handle, we give up, and throw a `WinException`.

We never have to think about closing files explicitly; the `AutoHandle` wrapper class (shown in Chapter 3) takes care of this.

Reading and Writing Files

TextEdit uses two different methods for reading and writing files. The `copyFile` function (`fileUtils.cpp`) uses the `ReadFile` and `WriteFile` functions, while everybody else use memory-mapped files. Memory-mapped files are handled by the `FileMapping` class, which takes care of all the tedious details.

Listing 12.2 FileMapping.h

```cpp
/*
 * $Header: /Book/FileMapping.h 6      3.07.99 17:46 Petter $
 */

#pragma once

/**
 * Mainly to get auto cleanup:
 */
class FileMapping {
private:
   HANDLE m_hMapping;
   void *m_pContents;

   void createMapping( HANDLE hFile, DWORD dwBytes, DWORD dwMode );

public:
   explicit FileMapping( HANDLE hFile );                    // Read
   explicit FileMapping( HANDLE hFile, DWORD dwBytes ); // Write
   ~FileMapping();
   operator const LPVOID() const;
   operator LPVOID();
};

inline FileMapping::FileMapping( HANDLE hFile )
   : m_hMapping ( 0 )
   , m_pContents( 0 )
{
   createMapping( hFile, 0, PAGE_READONLY );
}

inline FileMapping::FileMapping( HANDLE hFile, DWORD dwBytes )
   : m_hMapping ( 0 )
   , m_pContents( 0 )
{
   createMapping( hFile, dwBytes, PAGE_READWRITE );
}
```

```cpp
inline FileMapping::operator const LPVOID() const {
   return m_pContents;
}

inline FileMapping::operator LPVOID() {
   return m_pContents;
}
```

Listing 12.3   FileMapping.cpp

```cpp
/*
 * $Header: /Book/FileMapping.cpp 11    2.09.99 16:53 Petter $
 */

#include "precomp.h"
#include "Exception.h"
#include "FileMapping.h"

void FileMapping::createMapping(
   HANDLE hFile, DWORD dwBytes, DWORD dwMode )
{
   assert( PAGE_READONLY == dwMode || PAGE_READWRITE == dwMode );
   m_hMapping = CreateFileMapping(
      hFile, 0, dwMode, 0, dwBytes, 0 );
   if ( 0 == m_hMapping ) {
      throwException( _T( "CreateFileMapping failed" ) );
   }

   const DWORD dwAccess =
      PAGE_READONLY == dwMode ? FILE_MAP_READ : FILE_MAP_WRITE;
   m_pContents = MapViewOfFile(
      m_hMapping, dwAccess, 0, 0, dwBytes );
   if ( 0 == m_pContents ) {
      const DWORD dwErr = GetLastError();
      verify( CloseHandle( m_hMapping ) );
      m_hMapping = 0;
      throwException( _T( "MapViewOfFile failed" ), dwErr );
   }
}
```

```
/**
 * This destructor is the main reason for creating
 * this class in the first place.
 */
FileMapping::~FileMapping() {

    verify( UnmapViewOfFile( m_pContents ) );
    reset_pointer( m_pContents );

    verify( CloseHandle( m_hMapping ) );
    reset_pointer( m_hMapping );
}
```

Copying the Original

To get back on track: we're still in the Document constructor, having just opened the file. Next, we use GetFileInformationByHandle to retrieve information about the file, then call the createOrgCopy method to create a copy of the original contents. This method uses getTempFileName to — you guessed it — get a temporary file name, then uses copyFile to actually copy the bytes. The file containing the original copy is then made read-only and also hidden, so as not to confuse innocent users.

The last thing the Document constructor does is to call setRunning(1). Unless we call setRunning(0) at some point, this ensures that TextEdit will start editing the same document again after a reboot.

At this point, the Document object is initialized and ready to go, and its users can start calling the interesting methods, such as getContents, getOrgContents, save, and update.

What happens to the Document object when the user opens a new file? One possibility is to re-initialize the existing object; another possibility is to delete the existing object and create a new Document from scratch. TextEdit creates a new Document object, but sometimes it might be more convenient to re-initialize the old one.

Conversion

Figure 12.1 (on page 270) has two operations labeled "convert." The inbound conversion does two things — it translates, if necessary, Unicode to ANSI (or vice versa), and it converts, if necessary, UNIX-style line separators (a single new-line character) into MS-DOS line separators (a carriage return followed by a new-line character). The outbound conversion does the opposite, again, if necessary.

There is a design principle that says,

> *"Don't optimize before you've measured if it's worth it."*

The obvious reason is that there may be no noticeable (or even measurable) difference, in which case all your work will be for nothing. A less obvious (but more important) reason is that optimized implementations tend to be more complex than straightforward ones, so they are harder to get right and harder to debug. Consider sorting: if I only need to sort a few items, I invariably implement a bubble sort. It's small, I am confident that I can get it right the first time, and I don't have to crack a book to do it. A Quicksort, on the other hand, is considerably more complex, and I would never tangle with it without getting out a book or a previous implementation. Furthermore, I would test the a lot more carefully than I would the bubble sort, including all limit cases I could think of because it would be less obvious that I'd gotten all the details right.

The conversions in Figure 12.1 are good examples of functions that really need optimization. It took me a while to notice this, as early versions worked like a charm on my test files, none of which exceeded a few tens of kilobytes. Once I started testing with larger files, the execution times shot through the ceiling.

Here is some early code from the outbound converter to remove carriage returns from a string:

```
if ( m_hasUnixLineFeeds ) {
    for ( int iChar = 0; 0 != pszNewContents[ iChar ]; ++iChar ) {
        if ( _T( '\r' ) == pszNewContents[ iChar ] ) {
            if ( _T( '\n' ) == pszNewContents[ iChar + 1 ] ) {
                _tcscpy( pszNewContents + iChar,
                    pszNewContents + iChar + 1 );
            }
        }
    }
}
```

This snippet is obviously doing a lot of extra work, as it moves characters all the way to the end of the string each time a line separator is encountered. Still, the code is simple, and therefore difficult to get wrong. If the performance is good enough, as indeed, it seemed to be, why jump through hoops when the only noticeable result will be an increased likelihood of bugs?

This code turned out to have a huge performance problem. I replaced the code above with the code below. On a 2.2 MB test file with 56,000 lines of text, the execution time of the loop fell from a good-sized coffee break (over 16 minutes) to 0.071 seconds. I had expected things to improve, but speeding things up by four orders of magnitude is definitely above average.

```
const int nBytesPerChar =
    m_isUnicode ? sizeof( WCHAR ) : sizeof( char );
if ( m_hasUnixLineFeeds ) {
    LPCTSTR pszSrc = pszNewContents;
    LPTSTR  pszDst = pszNewContents;
    for ( ;; ) {
        const LPCTSTR pszCR = _tcschr( pszSrc, _T( '\r' ) );
        if ( 0 == pszCR ) {
            const int nLength = _tcslen( pszSrc ) + 1;
```

```
            memmove( pszDst, pszSrc, nLength * nBytesPerChar );
            break;                      //*** LOOP EXIT POINT
        }

        const int nLineLength = pszCR - pszDst + 1;
        memmove( pszDst, pszSrc, nLineLength * nBytesPerChar );
        pszDst += nLineLength;
        pszSrc += nLineLength;
        if ( _T( '\n') == pszSrc[ 0 ] ) {
            pszDst[ -1 ] = _T( '\n' );
            ++pszSrc;
        }
    }
}
```

As you can see, the code is considerably more complex. I wrote the first version practically without thinking; the second version required more care. Write trivial code whenever you can get away with it. It is faster to write, it is quicker to test, it is easier to understand, and it is smaller.

"Keep things as simple as possible, but not simpler than that."

There was a similar problem in the inbound converter — my first implementation used the String::insert operator to insert carriage returns, as this made for simple and obvious code. Unfortunately, the performance penalty I had to pay for this convenience was too high.

The inbound converter does one more thing — it detects and changes null characters. If any such are found (and changed), the m_bBinary member of Document is set, allowing us to warn the user (in onCreate in mainwnd.cpp).

Saving

A common approach to saving user files is to write the new contents to a new file. Once this new file is verified, the old file is deleted, and the new file is renamed. This approach, while careful of the contents, has a problem, especially on NTFS file systems: you may inadvertently change aspects of the original file, such as file attributes, original timestamps, owner, contents of named streams or security attributes. Even if you write the (non-trivial) code needed to save and restore this information, you're still vulnerable to new features in new file systems.

For this reason, TextEdit simply overwrites the existing file. Not so simply, really; the Document's save method is quite careful. Still, additional safety could have been bought by creating a backup copy of the existing file before saving.

The Document class actually has two methods that pertain to saving file contents: (a) the update method, which takes an LPTSTR and a character count as parameters, and (b) the save method, which takes a raw byte array and a byte count as parameters. The update method uses the save method to actually save the contents; the save method is also used for Abandon Changes, which does a raw copy of the contents.

Conflict of Interest

There are two classes of read-only files: those that have the read-only attribute set, and those that deny write access for a different reason. The file may reside on a CD-ROM, or (if the file system supports this) you might lack the requisite permissions. It may reside on a read-only floppy or it may be opened by another process. The difference between these two classes is that, in the first case, you have the option to change the file's status to writeable at any time.

In either case, though, a different process may pull the rug out from under us at any time, or, if the file resides on a floppy, the user might eject it without first consulting with TextEdit. TextEdit uses the KISS principle to deal with this: if someone has deleted the file behind our backs, we simply recreate it. If a different process has locked it down so that we can't write to it, or if a floppy has been ejected, we ask the user for a new file name. This solution is not perfectly smooth, but seems to work well enough in practice — the important thing is to ensure that we don't lose user data. Alternative approaches include file locking and monitoring the disk for changes; a solution based on this kind of thing would be considerably more complex.

Listing 12.4   Document.cpp

```
/*
 * $Header: /Book/Document.cpp 20    5.09.99 13:07 Petter $
 */

#include "precomp.h"
#include "Document.h"
#include "Exception.h"
#include "AutoArray.h"
#include "AutoHandle.h"
#include "MRU.h"
#include "FileMapping.h"
#include "Registry.h"
#include "SilentErrorMode.h"
#include "FileNotFoundDlg.h"
#include "formatMessage.h"
#include "fileUtils.h"
#include "winUtils.h"
#include "openFile.h"
#include "saveFile.h"
#include "persistence.h"
#include "utils.h"
#include "os.h"
```

```
#include "resource.h"
#include "trace.h"
#include <aclapi.h>
#include <time.h>

bool Document::s_bEndSession = false; // Set to true on WM_ENDSESSION.

#define FILE_TYPE _T( "File Types" )

PRIVATE String getTempFileName( void ) {

   PATHNAME szTempPath = { 0 };
   if ( 0 == GetTempPath( dim( szTempPath ), szTempPath ) ) {
      trace( _T( "Unable to get temp path: %s\n" ),
         getError().c_str() );
      _tcscpy( szTempPath, _T( "." ) );
   }

   PATHNAME szOrgCopy = { 0 };
   const UINT uiUniqueNumber =
      GetTempFileName( szTempPath, _T( "te" ), 0, szOrgCopy );
   if ( 0 == uiUniqueNumber ) {
      throwException( _T( "Unable to create temporary file" ) );
   }

   return szOrgCopy;
}

bool Document::modifyAttribs(
   const String& strFile, DWORD dwAdd, DWORD dwRemove )
{
   assertValid();
   return ::modifyAttribs( strFile, dwAdd, dwRemove );
}

void Document::createOrgCopy( HANDLE hIn ) {

   assertValid();
   assert( 0 != hIn );
```

```
    String strOrgCopy = getOrgCopy();
    if ( !strOrgCopy.empty() && fileExists( strOrgCopy.c_str() ) ) {
        return;
    }

    strOrgCopy = getTempFileName();
    setOrgCopy( strOrgCopy );
    verify( modifyAttribs( strOrgCopy, FILE_ATTRIBUTE_HIDDEN ) );

    // This block provides a scope for the AutoHandle, so that
    // it closes before we modify the file attributes.
    {
        AutoHandle hOrgCopy(
            CreateFile( strOrgCopy.c_str(), GENERIC_WRITE,
                FILE_SHARE_NONE, 0, OPEN_EXISTING, 0, 0 ) );
        if ( INVALID_HANDLE_VALUE == hOrgCopy ) {
            throwException( String(
                _T( "Can't open temp file for original copy " ) ) +
                strOrgCopy );
        }

        m_FileAttributes.nFileSizeHigh = 0;
        copyFile( hIn, hOrgCopy, &m_FileAttributes.nFileSizeLow );
    }
    verify( modifyAttribs( strOrgCopy, FILE_ATTRIBUTE_READONLY ) );

    // NOTE: The alleged documentation says nothing about what kind
    // of string is expected -- ANSI or Unicode! If you look at the
    // definition of SHCNF_PATH, though, you will find the answer.
    SHChangeNotify( SHCNE_CREATE | SHCNE_FREESPACE,
        SHCNF_PATH, strOrgCopy.c_str(), 0 );
}

HANDLE Document::openFile( HWND hwnd ) {

    assertValid();
    DWORD dwErr = 0;
    HANDLE hIn = ::openFile( m_strFileName.c_str(),
        GENERIC_READ_WRITE, FILE_SHARE_READ );
    if ( INVALID_HANDLE_VALUE == hIn ) {
```

```
      dwErr = GetLastError();
      if ( ERROR_INVALID_NAME == dwErr ) {
         messageBox( hwnd, MB_OK | MB_ICONINFORMATION,
            IDS_WILDCARDS, m_strFileName.c_str() );
         PATHNAME szNewPath = { 0 };
         const bool bOpenOK =
            ::openFile( hwnd, szNewPath, dim( szNewPath ), 0, false );
         if ( bOpenOK ) {
            m_strFileName = szNewPath;
            hIn = ::openFile( m_strFileName.c_str(),
               GENERIC_READ_WRITE, FILE_SHARE_READ );
         } else {
            throw CancelException();
         }
      } else if ( ERROR_FILE_NOT_FOUND == dwErr ) {
         String strFileNameWithExtension = formatMessage(
            _T( "%1.txt" ), m_strFileName.c_str() );
         hIn = ::openFile( strFileNameWithExtension.c_str(),
            GENERIC_READ_WRITE, FILE_SHARE_READ );
         dwErr = GetLastError();
         if ( ERROR_FILE_NOT_FOUND != dwErr ) {
            m_strFileName = strFileNameWithExtension;
         }
      }
   }

   if ( INVALID_HANDLE_VALUE == hIn ) {
      // Try to open as read-only.
      // What other errors could reasonably be handled here?
      if ( ERROR_ACCESS_DENIED == dwErr ||
           ERROR_SHARING_VIOLATION == dwErr )
      {
         hIn = ::openFile( m_strFileName.c_str(),
            GENERIC_READ, FILE_SHARE_READ );
         if ( INVALID_HANDLE_VALUE == hIn ) {
            dwErr = GetLastError();
         } else {
            m_isReadOnly = true;
            const DWORD dwAttribs =
               GetFileAttributes( m_strFileName.c_str() );
```

```cpp
              if ( 0 == ( dwAttribs & FILE_ATTRIBUTE_READONLY ) ) {
                m_bAccessDenied = true;
              }
            }
          }
        }

        if ( INVALID_HANDLE_VALUE == hIn ) {
          if ( ERROR_FILE_NOT_FOUND == dwErr ) {
            hIn = getNewFile( hwnd, &m_strFileName );
          }
        }

        if ( INVALID_HANDLE_VALUE == hIn ) {
          throwException( m_strFileName.c_str(), dwErr );
        }

        return hIn;
}

Document::Document( HWND hwnd, LPCTSTR pszFile )
    : m_strFileName( _T( "" ) )
    , m_isReadOnly( false )
    , m_hasUnixLineFeeds( false )
    , m_bAccessDenied( false )
    , m_bDirty( false )
{
    assertValid();
    assert( isGoodStringPtr( pszFile ) );

    m_strFileName = getLongPathName( pszFile );
    m_uiDriveType = getDriveType( m_strFileName );
    // Returns DRIVE_NO_ROOT_DIR for UNC paths...?!?

    if ( DRIVE_CDROM == m_uiDriveType ) {
      m_isReadOnly = true;
      m_bAccessDenied = true;
    } else if ( DRIVE_REMOVABLE == m_uiDriveType ) {
      if ( isWriteProtectedDisk( m_strFileName.c_str() ) ) {
        m_isReadOnly = true;
```

```
         m_bAccessDenied = true;
      }
   }

   AutoHandle hIn( openFile( hwnd ) );
   assert( INVALID_HANDLE_VALUE != hIn );

   BY_HANDLE_FILE_INFORMATION fileInfo = { 0 };
   const BOOL bOK = GetFileInformationByHandle( hIn, &fileInfo );
   if ( !bOK && !m_strFileName.empty() ) {
      throwException( _T( "GetFileInformationByHandle failed" ) );
   }

   m_FileAttributes.dwFileAttributes = fileInfo.dwFileAttributes;
   m_FileAttributes.ftCreationTime   = fileInfo.ftCreationTime;
   m_FileAttributes.ftLastAccessTime = fileInfo.ftLastAccessTime;
   m_FileAttributes.ftLastWriteTime  = fileInfo.ftLastWriteTime;
   m_FileAttributes.ftLastWriteTime  = fileInfo.ftLastWriteTime;
   m_FileAttributes.nFileSizeHigh    = 0;
   m_FileAttributes.nFileSizeLow     = fileInfo.nFileSizeLow;

   createOrgCopy( hIn );
   setRunning( 1 );
}

PRIVATE HANDLE openExistingFileOrCreateNew( const String& strFile ) {

   HANDLE hIn = CreateFile( strFile.c_str(),
      GENERIC_READ_WRITE, FILE_SHARE_READ, 0,
      TRUNCATE_EXISTING, 0, 0 );
   if ( INVALID_HANDLE_VALUE == hIn ) {
      const DWORD dwErr = GetLastError();
      if ( ERROR_FILE_NOT_FOUND == dwErr ) {
         hIn = CreateFile( strFile.c_str(),
            GENERIC_READ_WRITE, FILE_SHARE_READ, 0,
            CREATE_NEW, 0, 0 );
      }
   }
   return hIn;
}
```

```
int countNewLinesLackingCRs( LPCTSTR psz ) {

    assert( isGoodStringPtr( psz ) );

#ifdef _DEBUG
    const DWORD dwStartTime = GetTickCount();
#endif

    int nCount = 0;
    LPCTSTR pszSrc = psz;
    while ( 0 != (pszSrc = _tcschr( pszSrc, _T( '\n' ) ) ) ) {
        const LPTSTR pszPrev = charPrev( psz, pszSrc );
        if ( psz == pszSrc || _T( '\r' ) != *pszPrev ) {
            ++nCount;
        }
        pszSrc = charNext( pszSrc );
    }

#ifdef _DEBUG
    const DWORD dwSearchTime = GetTickCount() - dwStartTime;
    trace( _T( "countNewLinesLackingCRs: %u.%03u seconds (%s) \n" ),
        dwSearchTime / 1000, dwSearchTime % 1000, _T( "MS_DOS" ) );
#endif

    return nCount;
}

/**
 * Translate line feeds and remember what they were.
 * Unix-style (single \n) or DOS-style (\r\n).
 * This is not really necessary for the Rich Edit control.
 */
void Document::addCRs( LPTSTR *ppsz ) throw( MemoryException ) {

#if 0
    bool bHadNewLine  = false;
    bool bHadReturn   = false;
    bool bMaybeUnix   = false;
```

```
      bool bMaybeNotUnix = false;
#endif

   assertValid();
   assert( 0 != ppsz );
   assert( 0 != *ppsz );
   assert( isGoodStringPtr( *ppsz ) );

   int nOldLength = _tcslen( *ppsz );
   int nFixes = countNewLinesLackingCRs( *ppsz );
   m_hasUnixLineFeeds = 0 < nFixes;
   if ( 0 == nFixes ) {
      return;
   }

   const int nNewLength = nOldLength + nFixes;
   LPTSTR pszNew = new TCHAR[ nNewLength + 1 ];
   LPTSTR pszDst = pszNew + nNewLength;
   *pszDst = 0;

   LPCTSTR pszStart = *ppsz + nOldLength;
   LPCTSTR pszSrc = pszStart;

#ifdef _DEBUG
   const DWORD dwStartTime = GetTickCount();
#endif

   for ( ;; ) {
      // This invariant may not hold for multi-byte character sets.
      assert( pszDst - pszNew == pszSrc - *ppsz + nFixes );
      do {
         pszSrc = charPrev( *ppsz, pszSrc );
         pszDst = charPrev( pszNew, pszDst );
         if ( pszSrc < *ppsz ) {
            assert( false );
            break;
         }
      } while ( _T( '\n' ) != *pszSrc );
```

```
            const LPTSTR pszPrev = charPrev( *ppsz, pszSrc );
         if ( *ppsz == pszSrc || _T( '\r' ) != *pszPrev ) {
            const int nLength = pszStart - pszSrc;
            //pszDst -= nLength;
            memcpy( pszDst, pszSrc, nLength * sizeof( TCHAR ) );
            pszDst = charPrev( pszNew, pszDst );
            *pszDst = _T( '\r' );
            --nFixes;
            pszStart = pszSrc;
            if ( nFixes <= 0 ) {
               assert( 0 == nFixes );
               break; //*** LOOP EXIT POINT
            }
         }
      }
   }

   if ( *ppsz < pszSrc ) {
      const int nLength = pszStart - *ppsz;
      assert( pszNew + nLength == pszDst );
      memcpy( pszNew, *ppsz, nLength * sizeof( TCHAR ) );
   }

   // This invariant may not hold for multi-byte character sets.
   assert( pszDst - pszNew == pszSrc - *ppsz );

   delete[] *ppsz;
   *ppsz = pszNew;

#ifdef _DEBUG
   const DWORD dwReplaceTime = GetTickCount() - dwStartTime;
   trace( _T( "addCRs timing: %u.%03u seconds (%s) \n" ),
      dwReplaceTime / 1000, dwReplaceTime % 1000, _T( "UNIX" ) );
#endif
}

/**
 * The size of the buffer remains the same, so if n CRs are removed,
 * there will be n unused characters at the end of the string.
 */
void Document::removeCRs( LPTSTR psz ) {
```

```
    assertValid();

#ifdef _DEBUG
    DWORD dwTime = GetTickCount();
#endif

    LPCTSTR pszSrc = psz;
    LPTSTR  pszDst = psz;
    LPCTSTR pszCR;
    while ( 0 != (pszCR = _tcschr( pszSrc, _T( '\r' ) ) ) ) {
        const int nLineLength = pszCR - pszSrc + 1;
        memmove( pszDst, pszSrc, nLineLength * sizeof( TCHAR ) );
        pszDst += nLineLength;
        pszSrc += nLineLength;
        if ( _T( '\n' ) == *pszSrc ) {
            assert( _T( '\r' ) == *charPrev( psz, pszSrc ) );
            LPTSTR pszPrev = charPrev( psz, pszDst );
            assert( pszPrev < pszDst );
            assert( _T( '\r' ) == *pszPrev );
            *pszPrev = _T( '\n' );
            pszSrc = charNext( pszSrc );
        }
    }

    const int nLength = _tcslen( pszSrc ) + 1;
    assert( 1 <= nLength ); // Includes terminator.
    memmove( pszDst, pszSrc, nLength * sizeof( TCHAR ) );

#ifdef _DEBUG
    dwTime = GetTickCount() - dwTime;
    trace( _T( "removeCRs: %u.%03u seconds\n" ),
           dwTime / 1000, dwTime % 1000 );
#endif
}

/**
 * Saves text to disk, and is therefore critical.
 */
```

```
void Document::save(
    HWND hwnd, const void *pRawContents, int nBytes ) throw()
{
    assertValid();
    assert( isGoodReadPtr( pRawContents, nBytes ) );

    SilentErrorMode sem;

    AutoHandle hIn(
        openExistingFileOrCreateNew( m_strFileName ) );

LABEL_Retry:
    if ( INVALID_HANDLE_VALUE == hIn ) {
        String strFileName( m_strFileName );
        while ( saveFile( hwnd, &strFileName,
                        IDS_SAVEFILE, IDD_SAVE_CHILD ) )
        {
            hIn = openExistingFileOrCreateNew( strFileName );
            if ( INVALID_HANDLE_VALUE != hIn ) {
                setPath( hwnd, strFileName );
                break;
            }
        }
        if ( INVALID_HANDLE_VALUE == hIn ) {
            throwException( _T( "Unable to save file." ) );
        }
    }

    if ( 0 < nBytes ) {
        try {
            FileMapping fileMapping( hIn, nBytes );
            memcpy( fileMapping, pRawContents, nBytes );
        }
        catch ( const WinException& x ) {
            verify( CloseHandle( hIn ) );
            hIn = INVALID_HANDLE_VALUE;
            x.resetLastError();
            goto LABEL_Retry;
        }
```

```
        catch ( ... ) {
            verify( CloseHandle( hIn ) );
            hIn = INVALID_HANDLE_VALUE;
            messageBox(
                hwnd, MB_ICONERROR | MB_OK, IDS_SAVE_EXCEPTION );
            goto LABEL_Retry;
        }
    }
}

/**
 * NOTE: nLength may be larger than the string length.
 * Optimizations are possible; if no conversions are required,
 * we could even getText directly to the memory-mapped file.
 * NOTE: Buffer sizes etc. have not been tested with multi-byte
 * character sets.
 * NOTE: Abandon changes can be simplified
 * if no changes were saved to disk.
 */
void Document::update(
    HWND hwnd, LPTSTR pszNewContents, int nLength )
{
    assertValid();
    assert( isGoodStringPtr( pszNewContents ) );
    assert( (int) _tcsclen( pszNewContents ) <= nLength );

    trace( _T( "saving [%s]...\n" ), getPath().c_str() );
    if ( hasUnixLineFeeds() ) {
        removeCRs( pszNewContents );
    }

    const int nChars = _tcsclen( pszNewContents );
    const int nBytesPerChar =
        isUnicode() ? sizeof( WCHAR ) : sizeof( char );
    const int nBytes = nChars * nBytesPerChar;

    if ( m_isUnicode ) {

#ifdef UNICODE
        save( hwnd, pszNewContents, nBytes );
```

```
#else
      AutoStringW pwszBuffer( nChars + 1 );
      multiByteToWideChar( pszNewContents, pwszBuffer, nChars );
      save( hwnd, pwszBuffer, nBytes );
#endif

   } else {

#ifdef UNICODE
      AutoStringA pszBuffer( nChars + 1 );
      wideCharToMultiByte( pszNewContents, pszBuffer, nChars );
      save( hwnd, pszBuffer, nBytes );
#else
      save( hwnd, pszNewContents, nBytes );
#endif

   }
}

String Document::getTitle( void ) const {

   assertValid();
   PATHNAME szTitle = { 0 };
   const LPCTSTR pszPath = getPath().c_str();
   verify( 0 == GetFileTitle( pszPath, szTitle, dim( szTitle ) ) );
   return szTitle;
}

bool Document::setPath( HWND hwnd, const String& strNewPath ) {

   assertValid();
   bool bSuccess = true;
   if ( !areFileNamesEqual( getPath(), strNewPath ) ) {

      // The string arrays are needed for SHFILEOPSTRUCT.
      // The pFrom and pTo members are actually lists of
      // null-terminated file names; the list itself must be
      // doubly null-terminated.
```

```
      TCHAR szOldPath[ MAX_PATH + 2 ] = { 0 };
      _tcscpy( szOldPath, getPath().c_str() );

      TCHAR szNewPath[ MAX_PATH + 2 ] = { 0 };
      _tcscpy( szNewPath, strNewPath.c_str() );

      SHFILEOPSTRUCT shFileOpStruct = {
         hwnd, FO_MOVE, szOldPath, szNewPath,
         FOF_SIMPLEPROGRESS,
      };
      const int nErr = SHFileOperation( &shFileOpStruct );
      if ( 0 == nErr ) {
         MRU mru;
         mru.renameFile( m_strFileName, strNewPath );
         m_strFileName = strNewPath;
      } else {
         bSuccess = false;
      }
   }
   return bSuccess;
}

/**
 * Sets the original copy to 'readable' and delete it.
 * If modifyAttribs fails, there's not a lot we can do
 * about it, so we just try to delete the file anyway.
 */
void Document::deleteOrgCopy( void ) {

   assertValid();
   const String strOrgCopy = getOrgCopy();
   modifyAttribs( strOrgCopy, 0, FILE_ATTRIBUTE_READONLY );

   if ( DeleteFile( strOrgCopy.c_str() ) ) {
      SHChangeNotify( SHCNE_DELETE | SHCNE_FREESPACE,
         SHCNF_PATH, strOrgCopy.c_str(), 0 );
   } else {
      trace( _T( "deleteOrgCopy( %s ) failed: %s\n" ),
         strOrgCopy.c_str(), getError().c_str() );
   }
```

```
      setOrgCopy( _T( "" ) );
}

Document::~Document() {

   assertValid();
   setRunning( s_bEndSession );
   if ( !s_bEndSession ) {
      deleteOrgCopy();
   }
}

/**
 * The dwBytes count does *not* include the terminating 0.
 */
LPTSTR Document::convert( const LPVOID pbRawFile, DWORD dwBytes ) {

   assertValid();
   int nFlags = IS_TEXT_UNICODE_UNICODE_MASK;
   m_isUnicode = 0 != isTextUnicode( pbRawFile, dwBytes, &nFlags );

   trace( _T( "file is %s on %s\n" ),
      m_isUnicode ? _T( "UNICODE" ) : _T( "ANSI" ),
#ifdef UNICODE
      _T( "UNICODE" )
#else
      _T( "ANSI" )
#endif
      );

   m_hasUnicodeTranslationError = false;

   DWORD dwChars = dwBytes;
   if ( m_isUnicode ) {
      assert( 0 == dwBytes % 2 );
      dwChars = dwBytes / 2;
   }
   LPTSTR pszConvertedContents = new TCHAR[ dwChars + 1 ];
   assert( 0 != pszConvertedContents );
```

```cpp
        pszConvertedContents[ dwChars ] = 0;

    if ( m_isUnicode ) {

#ifdef UNICODE
        memcpy( pszConvertedContents, pbRawFile, dwBytes );
#else
        m_hasUnicodeTranslationError = wideCharToMultiByte(
            (LPCWSTR) pbRawFile, pszConvertedContents, dwChars );
#endif

    } else {

#ifdef UNICODE
        multiByteToWideChar(
            reinterpret_cast< LPCSTR >( pbRawFile ),
            pszConvertedContents, dwChars );
#else
        memcpy( pszConvertedContents, pbRawFile, dwBytes );
#endif

    }

    m_bBinary = false;
    for ( int iChar = 0; iChar < (int) dwChars; ++iChar ) {
        if ( 0 == pszConvertedContents[ iChar ] ) {
            m_bBinary = true;
            pszConvertedContents[ iChar ] = NULL_REPLACEMENT;
        }
    }

    assert( 0 == pszConvertedContents[ dwChars ] );
    pszConvertedContents[ dwChars ] = 0;
    return pszConvertedContents;
}

/**
 * This function allocates memory that the caller must release.
 * The AutoString template can be used to automate this.
 * This function never returns 0, but throws an exception on failure.
 */
```

```cpp
LPTSTR Document::getContents(
   const String& strFile, int *pnBytes = 0 )
{
   assertValid();
   assert( 0 == pnBytes || isGoodPtr( pnBytes ) );

   AutoHandle hFile( CreateFile( strFile.c_str(), GENERIC_READ,
      FILE_SHARE_READ, 0, OPEN_EXISTING, 0, 0 ) );
   if ( INVALID_HANDLE_VALUE == hFile ) {
      throwException( _T( "Unable to open " ) + strFile );
   }

   DWORD dwHiBytes = 0;
   const DWORD dwLoBytes = GetFileSize( hFile, &dwHiBytes );
   const dwErr = GetLastError();
   if ( 0xFFffFFff == dwLoBytes && NO_ERROR != dwErr ) {
      throwException( _T( "Unable to get file size" ), dwErr );
   }
   if ( 0 < dwHiBytes || INT_MAX < dwLoBytes ) {
      throwException(
         _T( "Cannot edit files larger than 2GB" ), dwErr );
   }

   assert( 0 == m_FileAttributes.nFileSizeHigh );
   assert( dwLoBytes == m_FileAttributes.nFileSizeLow );

   LPTSTR pszContents = 0;
   if ( 0 == dwLoBytes ) {
      pszContents = convert(
         _T( "" ), m_FileAttributes.nFileSizeLow );
   } else {
      const FileMapping fileMapping( hFile );
      pszContents = convert(
         fileMapping, m_FileAttributes.nFileSizeLow );
   }

   if ( 0 != pnBytes ) {
      *pnBytes = dwLoBytes;
   }
```

```
   assert( isGoodStringPtr( pszContents ) );
   return pszContents;
}

LPTSTR Document::getContents( int *pnBytes ) {

   assertValid();
   assert( 0 == pnBytes || isGoodPtr( pnBytes ) );

   return getContents( getPath(), pnBytes );
}

LPTSTR Document::getOrgContents( int *pnBytes ) {

   assertValid();
   assert( 0 == pnBytes || isGoodPtr( pnBytes ) );

   return getContents( getOrgCopy(), pnBytes );
}

/**
 * Create a unique registry path for a document.
 * To avoid confusion with the registry's
 * backslash usage, all path delimiters are replaced by bars.
 * The bar (|) is not a valid file name character,
 * but it is OK in a registry key.
 */
String Document::createRegistryPath( const String& strRealPath ) {

   assert( isGoodConstPtr( &strRealPath ) );
   String strPath( strRealPath );
   int iPos = -1;
   for ( ;; ) {
      iPos = strPath.find_first_of( _T( "\\/" ), iPos + 1 );
      if ( iPos < 0 ) {
         break; // ** LOOP EXIT POINT
      }
      strPath.replace( iPos, 1, 1, _T( '|' ) );
   }
```

```
      return strPath;
}


/**
 * Private function to create a unique registry path for
 * this document. See the static getRegistryPath above.
 */
String Document::getRegistryPath( void ) const {

   assertValid();
   const String strRegistryPath = createRegistryPath( getPath() );
   return formatMessage( _T( "Files\\%1" ), strRegistryPath.c_str() );
}

String Document::getFileTypeDescription( bool bDisplay ) const {

   assertValid();
   TCHAR szExt[ _MAX_EXT ] = { 0 };
   _tsplitpath( getPath().c_str(), 0, 0, 0, szExt );
   String strFileTypeDescription =
      Registry::fileTypeDescriptionFromExtension( szExt );
   if ( !bDisplay && strFileTypeDescription.empty() ) {
      strFileTypeDescription.assign(
         0 == szExt[ 0 ] ? _T( "empty" ) : szExt );
   }
   return strFileTypeDescription;
}

String Document::getRegistryFileTypePath( void ) const {

   assertValid();
   return formatMessage(
      FILE_TYPE _T( "\\%1" ), getFileTypeDescription().c_str() );
}


int Document::getPersistentInt(
   LPCTSTR pszName, int nDefault, bool bType ) const
{
```

```
    assertValid();
    if ( bType ) {
        const String strTypeKey( getRegistryFileTypePath() );
        nDefault = Registry::getInt(
            HKEY_CURRENT_USER, strTypeKey.c_str(), pszName, nDefault );
    }
    const String strFileKey( getRegistryPath() );
    return Registry::getInt(
        HKEY_CURRENT_USER, strFileKey.c_str(), pszName, nDefault );
}

void Document::setPersistentInt(
    LPCTSTR pszName, int nValue, bool bType )
{
    assertValid();
    const String strFileKey( getRegistryPath() );
    Registry::setInt(
        HKEY_CURRENT_USER, strFileKey.c_str(), pszName, nValue );
    if ( bType ) {
        const String strTypeKey( getRegistryFileTypePath() );
        Registry::setInt(
            HKEY_CURRENT_USER, strTypeKey.c_str(), pszName, nValue );
    }
}


String Document::getPersistentString( LPCTSTR pszName ) const {

    assertValid();
    const String strFileKey( getRegistryPath() );
    return Registry::getString(
        HKEY_CURRENT_USER, strFileKey.c_str(), pszName );
}

void Document::setPersistentString(
    LPCTSTR pszName, const String& str )
{
    assertValid();
    const String strFileKey( getRegistryPath() );
```

```
      Registry::setString(
         HKEY_CURRENT_USER, strFileKey.c_str(), pszName, str.c_str() );
}

bool Document::deleteFile( HWND hwnd ) {

   assertValid();
   FILEOP_FLAGS fileOpFlags = FOF_SIMPLEPROGRESS;
   if ( getSendToWasteBasket() ) {
      fileOpFlags |= FOF_ALLOWUNDO;
   }

   // The pFrom member of SHFILEOPSTRUCT is actually a list
   // of null-terminated file names; the list itself must be
   // doubly null-terminated. This is the reason for using the
   // szFileName buffer rather than getPath().c_str.
   TCHAR szFileName[ MAX_PATH + 2 ] = { 0 };
   _tcscpy( szFileName, getPath().c_str() );
   SHFILEOPSTRUCT shFileOpStruct = {
      hwnd, FO_DELETE, szFileName, _T( "\0" ), fileOpFlags,
   };
   const int nErr = SHFileOperation( &shFileOpStruct );
   if ( NOERROR != nErr ) {
      throw WinException( _T( "Unable to delete file" ), nErr );
   }
   if ( shFileOpStruct.fAnyOperationsAborted ) {
      trace( _T( "Didn't delete file %s\n" ), getPath().c_str() );
      return false;
   }

   m_bDirty = false;
   MRU mru;
   mru.removeFile( getPath() );

   trace( _T( "Deleted file %s, and removed from MRU list\n" ),
      getPath().c_str() );

   return true;
}
```

Chapter 13

About Dialogs

The logical continuation of the TextEdit story is really Chapter 14 — File Management. That subject, however, involves dialog boxes. Let's ease into the subject of dialog boxes through some easy ones, such as the About dialog and the Options dialog.

What is a Dialog Box, Anyway?

Everybody knows what a dialog box is, sort of. But what is it, really? Exactly what is it that makes a dialog box differ from other windows?

Dialog template resources are closely linked with Windows dialog box functions. Note, though, that the template may be constructed in memory — there's no rule that says it must come from a file. You can even sidestep the whole template by using `CreateWindow` or `CreateWindowEx` to add controls programmatically. Once a dialog is constructed, there's no way to get a reference to the original template. If there ever was one.

The key attributes of dialog boxes are supplied by the `DefDlgProc` and `IsDialogMessage` functions, in conjunction with the controls themselves. `DefDlgProc` is the window function for the predefined dialog box window class. If you supply your own class, you should pass unhandled messages to `DefDlgProc` rather than `DefWindowProc`. You must also ensure that the class defines at least `DLGWINDOWEXTRA` window bytes. The `IsDialogMessage` function supplies the keyboard interface. For modeless dialog boxes, you must call this function in your own message pump. Modal dialog boxes have their own message pump hidden in the murky depths of the `DialogBox` function, so you don't have to worry about it.

Chapter 13: About Dialogs

The dialog box keyboard interface carries out special processing for several keys. It allows you to navigate the input focus between the controls in the dialog, and to generate messages corresponding to certain buttons. The following table is copied from Microsoft's online documentation; it merits careful study:

Key	Action
Alt+*mnemonic*	Moves the input focus to the first control (having the WS_TABSTOP style) after the static control containing the given mnemonic.
Down	Moves the input focus to the next control in the group.
Enter	Sends a WM_COMMAND message to the dialog box function. The wParam parameter is set to IDOK or control identifier of the default push button.
Esc	Sends a WM_COMMAND message to the dialog box function. The wParam parameter is set to IDCANCEL.
Left	Moves the input focus to the previous control in the group.
Mnemonic	Moves the input focus to the first control (having the WS_TABSTOP style) after the static control containing the given mnemonic.
Right	Moves the input focus to the next control in the group.
Shift+tab	Moves the input focus to the previous control that has the WS_TABSTOP style.
Tab	Moves the input focus to the next control that has the WS_TABSTOP style.
Up	Moves the input focus to the previous control in the group.

Note in particular what this table says about the Enter and Escape keys: they send IDOK and IDCANCEL commands, respectively, *but there is no requirement that controls with IDOK or IDCANCEL IDs exist.*

Controls — windows that are meant to be children of dialog windows — must fulfill certain criteria to be good dialog citizens. They should understand window styles such as WS_TABSTOP and they should respond intelligently to messages such as WM_GETDLGCODE. If they have a keyboard interface, they should provide a visible indication of keyboard focus.

The Dialog Class

The Dialog class is a dialog-wrapping subclass of the Window class described in Chapter 4. But a dialog function is *not* the same as a window function. DefDlgProc is the default *window* function for dialogs; DefDlgProc, in turn, calls the user-defined *dialog* function (if and when it feels like it). The dialog function returns a BOOL rather than an LRESULT; the DlgProc and dispatchDlgMsg virtual methods are in charge of this.

To handle dialog commands, you should override onDlgCommand rather than onCommand. The first is called from the dialog function, while the latter is called from the window function. Given that the Dialog class subclasses DefDlgProc by virtue of being a Window, you can override anything you like, of course, but do keep this difference in mind.

The doModal method wraps the call to DialogBoxParam. A pointer to the Dialog object is passed as the lParam; this is used in DlgProc to attach the HWND to the Dialog object.

If a dialog box blows up, the parent window may remain disabled even though the dialog is gone, with no way to re-enable it. To avoid this, the `doModal` method has an "emergency aid station" that catches all exceptions and enables the parent.

Positioning the Dialog

The positioning of a dialog is a somewhat tortuous process. When `dispatchDlgMsg` handles the `WM_INITDIALOG` message, it starts by centering the dialog in relation to the TextEdit window. (The `DS_CENTER` window style, by the way, would center the dialog in the screen's working area, which is not what I want.) This is the default position for any TextEdit dialog. But consider — if our old friend Jane ever moves a dialog, it's because she thinks it looks better in the new spot. Wouldn't it be nice if TextEdit could remember this, and, the next time the dialog is invoked, place it in the same spot?

TextEdit dialog positions are persistent, although only within a single session. Positioning is handled by a pair of functions defined in `winUtils.cpp`, along with the static variable `thePointMap`:

```
typedef std::map< int, Point > PointMap;
PRIVATE PointMap thePointMap;

void savePosition( HWND hwnd, int id ) {

   Rect rc = getWindowRectInParent( hwnd );
   thePointMap[ id ] = Point( rc.left, rc.top );
}

void restorePosition( HWND hwnd, int id ) {

   centerDialog( hwnd );
   PointMap::iterator iter = thePointMap.find( id );
   if ( thePointMap.end() != iter) {
      MapWindowPoints(
         GetParent( hwnd ), HWND_DESKTOP, &iter->second, 1 );
      moveWindow( hwnd, iter->second.x, iter->second.y );
   }
   adjustToScreen( hwnd );
}
```

Note the call to `MapWindowPoints` — which ensures that the position of the dialog is remembered in relation to the application window rather than in relation to the screen.

If the `id` parameter doesn't appear in the map, the user is invoking the dialog for the first time and no repositioning is done. (Remember that the dialog has already been centered on the application window.) If the `id` parameter does appear in the map, the dialog is moved to the remembered position. Finally, the position is adjusted (if necessary) so that the dialog is inside the work area of the screen.

Where, then, does this `id` parameter come from? The dialog certainly can't tell you whence it came. Although most dialogs are created from dialog resources, and thus have IDs, you can't get this information from the dialog's `hwnd`. The purpose of `getResourceID()` virtual method is to retrieve the ID, which is hard-coded into the class definition. It is impossible to retain the position of dialogs not wrapped by the `Dialog` class. (Discourse continues on page 309.)

Listing 13.1   Dialog.h

```
/*
 * $Header: /Book/Dialog.h 13    3.07.99 17:46 Petter $
 */

#pragma once

#include "String.h"
#include "Window.h"

class Dialog : public Window {
protected:
    Dialog();
    virtual ~Dialog();

    virtual void onDestroy( void );

    virtual UINT getResourceID( void ) const = 0;
    virtual BOOL DlgProc( UINT msg, WPARAM wParam, LPARAM lParam );
    virtual BOOL onInitDialog( HWND hwndFocus, LPARAM lParam );
    virtual void onDlgCommand( int id, HWND hwndCtl, UINT codeNotify );

    void setDlgItemText( UINT id, const String& str );
    void setDlgItemText( UINT id, UINT idString );
    String getDlgItemText( const UINT id );
    void enableDlgItem( const UINT id, const bool bEnable );
    void showDlgItem( const UINT id );
    void hideDlgItem( const UINT id );
    void gotoDlgItem( const UINT id );
    void gotoNextDlgItem( void );
    void toggleIcon( UINT idOn, UINT idOff, bool bChecked );
    HWND getDlgItem( UINT id ) const;
```

```cpp
private:
   BOOL dispatchDlgMsg( UINT msg, WPARAM wParam, LPARAM lParam );
   static BOOL CALLBACK DlgProc(
      HWND hwnd, UINT msg, WPARAM wParam, LPARAM lParam );

public:
   UINT doModal( HWND hwndParent, UINT uiResource = 0 );
   UINT doModal( UINT uiResource = 0 );
};

inline void Dialog::enableDlgItem( UINT id, bool bEnable ) {
   assert( IsWindow( *this ) );
   HWND hwndCtl = getDlgItem( id );
   assert( IsWindow( hwndCtl ) );
   EnableWindow( hwndCtl, bEnable );
}

inline void Dialog::showDlgItem( const UINT id ) {
   assert( IsWindow( *this ) );
   HWND hwndCtl = getDlgItem( id );
   assert( IsWindow( hwndCtl ) );
   ShowWindow( hwndCtl, SW_SHOW );
}

inline void Dialog::hideDlgItem( const UINT id ) {
   assert( IsWindow( *this ) );
   HWND hwndCtl = getDlgItem( id );
   assert( IsWindow( hwndCtl ) );
   ShowWindow( hwndCtl, SW_HIDE );
}

inline void Dialog::gotoNextDlgItem( void ) {
   FORWARD_WM_NEXTDLGCTL( *this, 0, FALSE, SNDMSG );
}

inline void Dialog::gotoDlgItem( const UINT id ) {
   FORWARD_WM_NEXTDLGCTL( *this, getDlgItem( id ), TRUE, SNDMSG );
}
```

Chapter 13: About Dialogs

```cpp
inline HWND Dialog::getDlgItem( UINT id ) const {
    return GetDlgItem( *this, id );
}

inline UINT Dialog::doModal( UINT uiResource ) {

    return doModal( HWND_DESKTOP, uiResource );
}
```

Listing 13.2 `Dialog.cpp`

```cpp
/*
 * $Header: /Book/Dialog.cpp 19     20.08.99 16:33 Petter $
 */

#include "precomp.h"
#include "InstanceSubclasser.h"
#include "Dialog.h"
#include "Exception.h"
#include "AutoArray.h"
#include "MenuFont.h"
#include "winUtils.h"
#include "resource.h"
#include "geometry.h"
#include "help.h"
#include "utils.h"
#include "trace.h"

Dialog::Dialog() {
}

Dialog::~Dialog() {
    setHelpID( 0 );
}

/**
 * This should never be called!
 */
UINT Dialog::getResourceID( void ) const {
```

```cpp
      trace( _T( "pure virtual func Dialog::getResourceID called\n" ) );
      DebugBreak(); // This method should never be called!
      return 0;
}


/**
 * NOTE: Neither WM_DESTROY nor WM_NCDESTROY
 * get here under normal circumstances.
 */
BOOL Dialog::dispatchDlgMsg(
   UINT msg, WPARAM wParam, LPARAM lParam )
{
   switch ( msg ) {
   case WM_INITDIALOG:
      restorePosition( *this, getResourceID() );
      return onInitDialog( (HWND) wParam, lParam );

   case WM_COMMAND:
      return onDlgCommand(
         GET_WM_COMMAND_ID   ( wParam, lParam ) ,
         GET_WM_COMMAND_HWND ( wParam, lParam ) ,
         GET_WM_COMMAND_CMD  ( wParam, lParam ) ), TRUE;
   }

   return DlgProc( msg, wParam, lParam );
}

BOOL Dialog::DlgProc( UINT, WPARAM, LPARAM ) {
   return FALSE;
}


/**
 * NOTE: WM_NCDESTROY normally never gets here, and
 * when WM_DESTROY arrives, weÊre normally unhooked already.
 */
BOOL CALLBACK Dialog::DlgProc(
   HWND hwnd, UINT msg, WPARAM wParam, LPARAM lParam )
{
   assert( ::IsWindow( hwnd ) );
```

```cpp
   if ( WM_INITDIALOG == msg ) {
      Dialog *pDlg = reinterpret_cast< Dialog * >( lParam );
      assert( isGoodPtr( pDlg ) );
      pDlg->attach( hwnd );
   }

   Dialog *pDlg = static_cast< Dialog * >( windowFromHWND( hwnd ) );
   if ( 0 != pDlg ) {
      assert( isGoodPtr( pDlg ) );
      return pDlg->dispatchDlgMsg( msg, wParam, lParam );
   }
   // If pDlg is 0, we've been unhooked,
   // and are probably processing WM_DESTROY.

   return FALSE;
}

void Dialog::onDestroy( void ) {
   savePosition( *this, getResourceID() );
}

BOOL Dialog::onInitDialog( HWND hwndFocus, LPARAM lParam ) {
   return TRUE;
}

/**
 * This is not named onCommand, since that would override
 * the Window method rather than the Dialog method, and,
 * among other things, screw up the drop-down handling
 * (in dlgSubClasser.cpp).
 */
void Dialog::onDlgCommand( int id, HWND hwndCtl, UINT codeNotify ) {

   switch ( id ) {
   case IDOK:
   case IDCANCEL:
      verify( EndDialog( *this, id ) );
      break;
```

```cpp
      }
   }

   UINT Dialog::doModal( HWND hwndParent, UINT uiResource ) {

      assert(
         HWND_DESKTOP == hwndParent || IsWindowEnabled( hwndParent ) );
      if ( HWND_DESKTOP != hwndParent ) {
         FORWARD_WM_COMMAND(
            hwndParent, ID_COMMAND_RESETSTATUSBAR, 0, 0, SNDMSG );
      }

      const HINSTANCE hinst = getModuleHandle();

      try {
         if ( 0 == uiResource ) {
            uiResource = getResourceID();
         }
         setHelpID( uiResource );

         assert( 0 != uiResource );
         assert( 0 != hinst );
         assert( HWND_DESKTOP == hwndParent || IsWindow( hwndParent ) );

         const UINT uiRetCode = DialogBoxParam( hinst,
            MAKEINTRESOURCE( uiResource ), hwndParent, DlgProc,
            reinterpret_cast< LPARAM >( this ) );
         return uiRetCode;
      }
      catch ( ... ) {
         trace( _T( "Exception in Dialog::doModal %d (%#x)\n" ),
            uiResource, uiResource );
#if 1
         if ( IsWindow( *this ) ) {
            HWND hwndThis = *this;
            detach();
            EndDialog( hwndThis, -1 );
            //DestroyWindow( *this );
         }
```

```
#endif
        // To avoid, say, an access violation freezing the parent:
        if ( HWND_DESKTOP != hwndParent ) {
            EnableWindow( hwndParent, true );
        }
        throw;
    }
}

void Dialog::toggleIcon( UINT idOn, UINT idOff, bool bChecked ) {

    if ( bChecked ) {
        hideDlgItem( idOff );
        showDlgItem( idOn  );
    } else {
        hideDlgItem( idOn  );
        showDlgItem( idOff );
    }
}

void Dialog::setDlgItemText( UINT id, const String& str ) {

    HWND hwndCtl = getDlgItem( id );
    assert( IsWindow( hwndCtl ) );
    LockWindowUpdate( hwndCtl );
    SetWindowText( hwndCtl, str.c_str() );
    LockWindowUpdate( 0 );
}

void Dialog::setDlgItemText( UINT id, UINT idString ) {

    setDlgItemText( id, loadString( idString ) );
}

/**
 * Throws a MemoryException if the allocation fails.
 */
String Dialog::getDlgItemText( const UINT id ) {
```

```
    const int nLength =
        SendDlgItemMessage( *this, id, WM_GETTEXTLENGTH, 0, 0 );
    AutoString pszText( nLength + 1 );
    GetDlgItemText( *this, id, pszText, nLength + 1 );
    return pszText;
}
```

The About Box

The "About TextEdit" dialog box is about as simple as they come. The only complications are hidden in the `setFonts` and `setInfo` methods of the `AboutDlg` class; both are called from the `onInitDialog` method. In `setFonts`, note that the size of the new fonts is always relative to the original size, and that you must take the size change into account when constructing the dialog template by making sure the affected controls have enough room. The `setInfo` method uses the `VersionInfo` class to retrieve version information from the program. This class is independent of the TextEdit architecture, making it easy to reuse in other projects.

The only possible interaction is to dismiss the dialog, which is why I call it simple in spite of the rather extensive initialization.

Figure 13.1   The About dialog. Some `STATIC` widgets have been subjected to a `WM_SETFONT` message, while others have been subclassed.

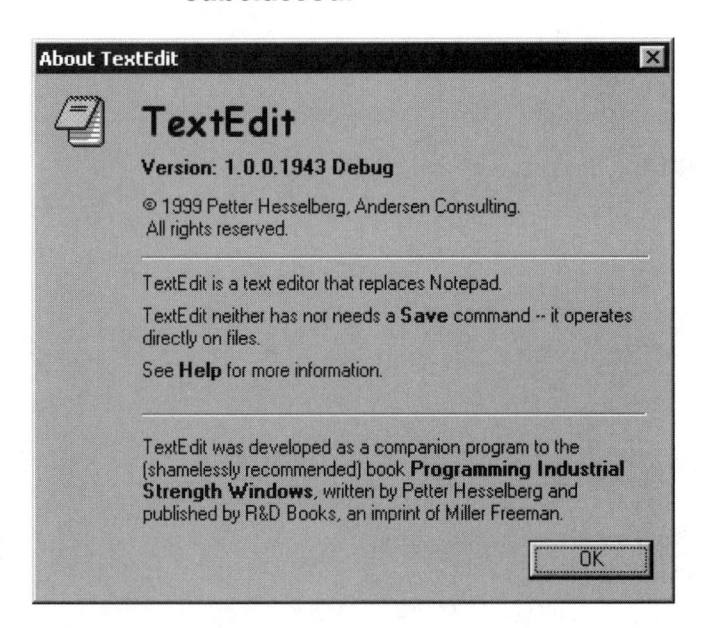

If you look at the dialog box in Figure 13.1, you'll note several different fonts. In the case of the program title and version, this is a simple matter of creating the desired font, then sending a `WM_SETFONT` message to the control. This is done using the `SetWindowFont` macro defined in `windowsx.h`.

More interesting is the boldfacing of individual words in the `IDC_COMMENTS` and `IDC_COMMERCIAL` controls. This is done by subclassing normal static controls. In `onInitDialog`, you'll find a pair of calls to `subclassHTML`, which is all it takes to accomplish this. Except, of course, for writing the `subclassHTML` function itself and accompanying paraphernalia. This is described in the sidebar "The HTML Static Control" on page 313.

Listing 13.3   `AboutDlg.cpp`

```
/*
 * $Header: /Book/AboutDlg.cpp 16    20.08.99 16:33 Petter $
 *
 * Handles the About dialog box. This is general enough for reuse.
 */

#include "precomp.h"
#include "resource.h"
#include "trace.h"
#include "formatMessage.h"
#include "AboutDlg.h"
#include "VersionInfo.h"
#include "HTML.h"
#include "utils.h"

void AboutDlg::setFonts( void ) {

   m_hfontBig = GetWindowFont( getDlgItem( IDC_TITLE ) );
   m_hfontBold = m_hfontBig;
   if ( 0 != m_hfontBig ) {
      LOGFONT logFont = { 0 };
      if ( GetObject( m_hfontBig, sizeof logFont, &logFont ) ) {
         logFont.lfWeight = FW_HEAVY;
         logFont.lfWidth  *= 2;
         logFont.lfHeight *= 2;
         const String strSavedFaceName( logFont.lfFaceName );
         _tcscpy( logFont.lfFaceName, _T( "Comic Sans MS" ) );
         m_hfontBig = CreateFontIndirect( &logFont );
         if ( 0 == m_hfontBig ) {
            _tcscpy( logFont.lfFaceName, _T( "Arial" ) );
            m_hfontBig = CreateFontIndirect( &logFont );
         }
```

```
            if ( 0 == m_hfontBig ) {
                _tcscpy( logFont.lfFaceName, strSavedFaceName.c_str() );
                m_hfontBig = CreateFontIndirect( &logFont );
            }
        }
        assert( 0 != m_hfontBold );
        if ( GetObject( m_hfontBold, sizeof logFont, &logFont ) ) {
            logFont.lfWeight = FW_BOLD;
            m_hfontBold = CreateFontIndirect( &logFont );
        }
    }
    if ( 0 != m_hfontBig ) {
        SetWindowFont( getDlgItem( IDC_TITLE ), m_hfontBig, false );
    }
    if ( 0 != m_hfontBold ) {
        SetWindowFont( getDlgItem( IDC_VERSION ), m_hfontBold, false );
    }
}

void AboutDlg::setInfo( void ) {

    const VersionInfo vi( getModuleHandle() );
    if ( !vi.isValid() ) {
        trace( _T( "Unable to retrieve version info\n" ) );
        return;
    }

    // Program name:
    LPCTSTR pszTitle = vi.getStringFileInfo( _T( "FileDescription" ) );
    assert( 0 != pszTitle );
    setDlgItemText( IDC_TITLE, pszTitle );
    String strFmt = getWindowText();
    setWindowText( formatMessage( strFmt, pszTitle ).c_str() );

    // Program version:
    const LPCTSTR pszVersion =
        vi.getStringFileInfo( _T( "FileVersion" ) );
    assert( 0 != pszVersion );
    strFmt = getDlgItemText( IDC_VERSION );
```

```
#ifdef _DEBUG
   strFmt += _T( " Debug" );
#endif

#ifdef UNICODE
   strFmt += L" (Unicode build)";
#endif

   setDlgItemText( IDC_VERSION,
      formatMessage( strFmt, pszVersion ).c_str() );

   // Copyright:
   const LPCTSTR pszCopyRight =
      vi.getStringFileInfo( _T( "LegalCopyright" ) );
   assert( 0 != pszCopyRight );
   setDlgItemText( IDC_COPYRIGHT,
      formatMessage( pszCopyRight ).c_str() );

   // Comments:
   const LPCTSTR psz = vi.getStringFileInfo( _T( "Comments" ) );
   assert( 0 != psz );
   setDlgItemText( IDC_COMMENTS, formatMessage( psz ).c_str() );
}

BOOL AboutDlg::onInitDialog( HWND hwndFocus, LPARAM lParam ) {

   setFonts();
   setInfo();

   subclassHTML( getDlgItem( IDC_COMMENTS   ) );
   subclassHTML( getDlgItem( IDC_COMMERCIAL ) );

   return true; // Let dialog manager set the focus.
}

UINT AboutDlg::getResourceID( void ) const {
   return IDD_ABOUT;
}
```

```
AboutDlg::AboutDlg( HWND hwndParent )
   : m_hfontBig ( 0 )
   , m_hfontBold( 0 )
{
#ifdef _DEBUG
   const UINT uiRetCode =
#endif

   doModal( hwndParent );
   assert( IDOK == uiRetCode || IDCANCEL == uiRetCode );
}

AboutDlg::~AboutDlg() {

   if ( 0 != m_hfontBold && m_hfontBig != m_hfontBold ) {
      verify( DeleteFont( m_hfontBold ) );
      m_hfontBold = 0;
   }
   if ( 0 != m_hfontBig ) {
      verify( DeleteFont( m_hfontBig ) );
      m_hfontBig = 0;
   }
}
```

The HTML Static Control

The resource script for the About TextEdit dialog box includes this line:

```
LTEXT  "TextEdit was developed as a companion program to the (shamelessly rec-
ommended) book <b>Programming Industrial Strength Windows</b>, written by Pet-
ter Hesselberg and published by R&D Books, an imprint of Miller Freeman.",
IDC_COMMERCIAL,42,130,205,37,SS_NOPREFIX
```

As you can see, the text of the static control is HTML (HyperText Markup Language). (Actually, it isn't, quite, but it does use HTML formatting codes.) If I didn't subclass the thing, the text would appear verbatim, including the formatting codes <b> and </b>.

The two main tasks involved in this are HTML parsing, handled by getToken, and HTML rendering, handled by paintHTML. These functions are implemented in HTML.cpp; the interface to the module is in HTML.h.

HTML Parsing

To keep the parsing engine small and simple, I implemented only the three HTML tags `<b>`, `</b>`, and `<p>`. These are all hard-coded into the parser; should you ever want to support additional tags, consider using a more flexible parser framework. In addition to the HTML tags, the parser understands about white space and text, making five token types in all.

To pick the HTML source string apart, I give it to `getToken`, which strips the first token off the source string. I call `getToken` repeatedly until the source string is empty, or until the client area of the control has been filled up, whichever comes first.

First, I must decide what kind of token it is. If the first character is any kind of white space, I've found a white space token. If the string starts with one of the supported tags, I have a tag token, and if it's neither a tag nor a white space, I have a text token on my hands.

Second, I strip the token off the source string. If the token is a white space token, I trim all leading white space off the string, as multiple white space characters should be merged into a single white space token. If it's a tag token, I strip off the tag, then set or clear the corresponding flag, as appropriate. If it's a text token, I figure out where the next token starts, and store the offset in the `iNext` variable. When I'm parsing the last token, `iNext` equals the length of the remaining string.

`getToken` returns false when the source string is empty.

HTML Rendering

The `WM_PAINT` message is handled by `onPaint`, which does housekeeping chores such as selecting appropriate colors into the device context. It defers the actual rendering to `paintHTML`, a useful function in its own right. Using `paintHTML`, you can render HTML in any display context; look at the TextEdit status bar for an example of this.

In truth, `paintHTML` doesn't do much but housekeeping chores itself, deferring the rendering to `doPaint`. This has no deep significance, but came about because `paintHTML` was becoming a bit unwieldy.

In `doPaint`, I call `getToken` to get the next token. If it's a paragraph token, I move the current position to the left margin, one and a half lines down. Otherwise, if the token string is empty, I ignore it. An empty token string means that `getToken` found the `<b>` or the `</b>` tag; this fact has already been recorded in the state of the `bBold` flag.

If it's a text token, I display it with `TextOut`. First, I select either the normal font or the bold font into the display context, depending on the value of `bBold`. Next, I measure the extent of the string. If the word is too wide to fit on the current line, I move to the start of the next line — unless I'm currently at the left-hand border. In that case, starting a new line won't help, as the word won't fit in any case. If I find that I've dropped below the bottom of the control's client area, I quit the loop.

A space is handled exactly like a word, except that I don't display it if it's the first thing on a line. Displaying a space with `TextOut` makes no visible marks on the display context, of course, but it does update the current position.

Actually, the above account doesn't tell the whole story. I claimed that, when a word is too long to fit, I just wrap to the next line. I also said that `paintHTML` is used by the status bar, which has but a single line of text. Wrapping to the next line is a useless strategy when only one line is available.

To handle this situation, pass the `PHTML_SINGLE_LINE` flag to `paintHTML`. If this flag is specified, `doPaint` doesn't wrap to the next line, but truncates the string as best it can — using compactPath. This function, defined in fileUtils.cpp, replaces part of the string with an ellipsis, so that it fits in the available space.

The window function for the Pocket HTML control is Simple_HTML_WndProc. In addition to painting in response to WM_PAINT, the window function uses fillSysColorSolidRect to clear the background in response to the WM_ERASE message.

Because I sometimes want to set the control's text dynamically, the WM_SETTEXT message must also be handled. Why? When the static control receives the WM_SETTEXT message, it repaints itself directly, rather than invalidating itself and waiting for WM_PAINT to arrive. This kind of (regrettably common) misbehavior is done to improve efficiency, but it does complicate subclassing. The subclassed WM_SETTEXT handler calls the original window function first, then invalidates the client area.

A final note about the Pocket HTML control: Both FindDlg and StatusBar like to highlight the text, as shown in Figure 15.6 on page 373. HTML.h defines a pair of functions — setHighlight and removeHighlight — that set or remove a window property called — you guessed it — "Highlight." If this property is set, a different set of colors is used to paint the background and the text. To avoid leakage, the highlight property is removed on WM_DESTROY. (Discourse continues on page 324.)

Listing 13.4   HTML.h

```
/*
 * $Header: /Book/HTML.h 9      3.07.99 17:46 Petter $
 *
 */

#pragma once

#include "winUtils.h"
#include "Exception.h"

void subclassHTML( HWND hwnd ) throw( SubclassException );

#define PHTML_MULTI_LINE  0x0
#define PHTML_SINGLE_LINE 0x1

void paintHTML( HDC hdc, LPCTSTR pszString, RECT *pRect, HFONT hfont,
    DWORD dwFlags = PHTML_MULTI_LINE, bool bDisabled = false );

#define HIGHLIGHT_PROP _T( "Highlight" )

inline void setHighlight( HWND hwnd ) {
```

```
   assert( IsWindow( hwnd ) );
   SetProp( hwnd, HIGHLIGHT_PROP, (HANDLE) 1 );
   InvalidateRect( hwnd, 0, TRUE );
}

inline void removeHighlight( HWND hwnd ) {

   assert( IsWindow( hwnd ) );
   assert( isClass( hwnd, _T( "static" ) ) );
   RemoveProp( hwnd, HIGHLIGHT_PROP );
   InvalidateRect( hwnd, 0, TRUE );
}

inline bool hasHighlight( HWND hwnd ) {

   assert( IsWindow( hwnd ) );
   assert( isClass( hwnd, _T( "static" ) ) );
   return 0 != GetProp( hwnd, HIGHLIGHT_PROP );
}

#undef HIGHLIGHT_PROP
```

Listing 13.5   HTML.cpp

```
/*
 * $Header: /Book/HTML.cpp 17    5.09.99 13:07 Petter $
 *
 * Subclassing of class "static" to display simple rich text.
 */

#include "precomp.h"
#include "Window.h"
#include "AutoArray.h"
#include "PaintStruct.h"
#include "HTML.h"
#include "InstanceSubclasser.h"
#include "fileUtils.h"
#include "graphics.h"
```

```
PRIVATE LRESULT CALLBACK Simple_HTML_WndProc(
   HWND hwnd, UINT msg, WPARAM wParam, LPARAM lParam );


PRIVATE InstanceSubclasser s_HTML_Subclasser( Simple_HTML_WndProc );

PRIVATE void trim( String &str ) {

   while ( _istspace( str[ 0 ] ) ) {
      str.erase( 0, 1 );
   }
}

PRIVATE bool getToken(
   String &str, bool &bPara, bool &bBold, String &strWord )
{
   if ( str.empty() ) {
      return false; //*** FUNCTION EXIT POINT
   }

   strWord = _T( "" );

   const int iSpace   = str.find_first_of( _T( " \t\r\n" ) );
   const int iPara    = str.find( _T( "<p>" ) );
   const int iBold    = str.find( _T( "<b>" ) );
   const int iEndBold = str.find( _T( "</b>" ) );

   bPara = ( 0 == iPara );
   if ( 0 == iSpace ) {
      strWord = _T( " " );
      trim( str );
      bPara = 0 == str.find( _T( "<p>" ) );
      if ( bPara ) {
         str = str.substr( 3 );
         trim( str );
      }
      return true;
   }
```

```
   if ( bPara ) {
      str = str.substr( 3 );
      trim( str );
   } else if ( 0 == iBold ) {
      bBold = true;
      str = str.substr( 3 );
      //trim( str );
   } else if ( 0 == iEndBold ) {
      bBold = false;
      str = str.substr( 4 );
      //trim( str );
   } else {
      int iNext = str.length();
      if ( 0 < iSpace && iSpace < iNext ) {
         iNext = iSpace;
      }
      if ( 0 < iPara && iPara < iNext ) {
         iNext = iPara;
      }
      if ( 0 < iBold && iBold < iNext ) {
         iNext = iBold;
      }
      if ( 0 < iEndBold && iEndBold < iNext ) {
         iNext = iEndBold;
      }

      if ( iNext < 0 ) {
         strWord = str;
         str.erase();
         trim( strWord );
      } else {
         strWord = str.substr( 0, iNext );
         str = str.substr( iNext );
      }
   }

   //trim( str );

   return true;
}
```

```
PRIVATE inline void textOut( HDC hdc, int x, int y, LPCTSTR psz ) {

   verify( TextOut( hdc, x, y, psz, _tcslen( psz ) ) );
}

PRIVATE void textOut( HDC hdc, LPCTSTR psz, bool bDisabled ) {

   if ( bDisabled ) {
      const COLORREF crText = GetSysColor( COLOR_3DHIGHLIGHT );
      const COLORREF crSaved = SetTextColor( hdc, crText );
      POINT ptCurrPos;
      verify( GetCurrentPositionEx( hdc, &ptCurrPos ) );
      const int nTextAlign = GetTextAlign( hdc );
      verify( GDI_ERROR !=
         SetTextAlign( hdc, nTextAlign & ~TA_UPDATECP ) );
      textOut( hdc, ptCurrPos.x + 1, ptCurrPos.y + 1, psz );
      verify( MoveToEx( hdc, ptCurrPos.x, ptCurrPos.y, 0 ) );
      verify( GDI_ERROR != SetTextAlign( hdc, nTextAlign ) );
      SetTextColor( hdc, crSaved );
   }
   textOut( hdc, 0, 0, psz );
}

PRIVATE void doPaint( HDC hdc, LPCTSTR pszString, const RECT &rc,
   HFONT hfontNormal, HFONT hfontBold, DWORD dwFlags, bool bDisabled )
{
   if ( bDisabled ) {
      SetBkMode( hdc, TRANSPARENT );
   }

   verify( MoveToEx( hdc, rc.left, rc.top, 0 ) );

   SIZE sizeText;
   verify(
      GetTextExtentPoint32( hdc, _T( "_y" ), 2, &sizeText ) );
   const int nLineHeight = sizeText.cy;

   bool bPara = false;
   bool bBold = false;
```

```
String str( pszString );
while ( !str.empty() ) {
   POINT ptCurrPos;
   verify( GetCurrentPositionEx( hdc, &ptCurrPos ) );

   String strWord;
   if ( !getToken( str, bPara, bBold, strWord ) ) {
      assert( str.empty() );
      break; //*** LOOP EXIT POINT
   }

   if ( bPara ) {
      if ( PHTML_SINGLE_LINE & dwFlags ) {
         textOut( hdc, _T( " " ), bDisabled );
      } else {
         MoveToEx(
            hdc, rc.left, ptCurrPos.y + 3 * nLineHeight / 2, 0 );
      }
   } else if ( !strWord.empty() ) {
      const HFONT hfont = bBold ? hfontBold : hfontNormal;
      SelectFont( hdc, hfont );

      verify( GetTextExtentPoint32( hdc,
         strWord.c_str(), strWord.length(), &sizeText ) );
      if ( rc.right < ptCurrPos.x + sizeText.cx ) {
         if ( PHTML_SINGLE_LINE & dwFlags ) {
            const int nWidth = rc.right - ptCurrPos.x;
            strWord = compactPath(
               strWord.c_str(), nWidth, hfont );
            textOut( hdc, strWord.c_str(), bDisabled );

            break; //*** LOOP EXIT POINT

         } else if ( rc.left < ptCurrPos.x ) {
            verify( MoveToEx(
               hdc, rc.left, ptCurrPos.y + nLineHeight, 0 ) );
         }
      }
   }
   verify( GetCurrentPositionEx( hdc, &ptCurrPos ) );
```

```
            if ( rc.bottom < ptCurrPos.y + sizeText.cy ) {
               break;
            }
            if ( rc.left < ptCurrPos.x || !_istspace( strWord[ 0 ] ) ) {
               textOut( hdc, strWord.c_str(), bDisabled );
            }
         }
      }
   }
}

/**
 * This is reused elsewhere; in the status bar, for example.
 * This function does *not* change the DC colors.
 */
void paintHTML(
   HDC hdc, LPCTSTR pszString,
   RECT *pRect, HFONT hfontNormal, DWORD dwFlags, bool bDisabled )
{
   HFONT hfontBold = 0;
   LOGFONT logFont = { 0 };
   if ( GetObject( hfontNormal, sizeof logFont, &logFont ) ) {
      logFont.lfWeight = FW_BOLD;
      hfontBold = CreateFontIndirect( &logFont );
   }
   if ( 0 == hfontBold ) {
      hfontBold = hfontNormal;
   }

   HRGN hrgnClip = CreateRectRgnIndirect( pRect );
   assert( 0 != hrgnClip );

   const int nSavedDC = SaveDC( hdc );

   const int nTextAlign = GetTextAlign( hdc );
   verify(
      GDI_ERROR != SetTextAlign( hdc, nTextAlign | TA_UPDATECP ) );
   verify( ERROR != SelectClipRgn( hdc, hrgnClip ) );
   SelectFont( hdc, hfontNormal );
```

```
      doPaint( hdc, pszString, *pRect,
         hfontNormal, hfontBold, dwFlags, bDisabled );

      verify( RestoreDC( hdc, nSavedDC ) );

      DeleteRgn( hrgnClip );
      if ( hfontNormal != hfontBold ) {
         DeleteFont( hfontBold );
      }
   }

PRIVATE void onPaint( HWND hwnd ) {

   const int nLength = GetWindowTextLength( hwnd );
   AutoString pszText( nLength + 1 );
   GetWindowText( hwnd, pszText, nLength + 1 );

   Rect rc = getClientRect( hwnd );

   PaintStruct ps( hwnd );
   const int nSavedDC = SaveDC( ps.hdc );

   const bool bHighlight = hasHighlight( hwnd );
   const COLORREF crText = GetSysColor(
      bHighlight ? COLOR_HIGHLIGHTTEXT :
      IsWindowEnabled( hwnd ) ? COLOR_BTNTEXT : COLOR_GRAYTEXT );
   const COLORREF crBk = GetSysColor(
      bHighlight ? COLOR_HIGHLIGHT : COLOR_3DFACE );

   SetTextColor( ps.hdc, crText );
   SetBkColor  ( ps.hdc, crBk   );

   if ( bHighlight ) {
      rc.left += 3; // Looks best with some extra offset
   }
   paintHTML( ps.hdc, pszText, &rc, GetWindowFont( hwnd ),
      PHTML_MULTI_LINE, !IsWindowEnabled( hwnd ) );

   verify( RestoreDC( ps.hdc, nSavedDC ) );
}
```

The About Box

```cpp
PRIVATE LRESULT CALLBACK Simple_HTML_WndProc(
   HWND hwnd, UINT msg, WPARAM wParam, LPARAM lParam )
{
   LRESULT lResult = 0;
   if ( WM_PAINT == msg ) {
      onPaint( hwnd );
   } else if ( WM_ERASEBKGND == msg ) {
      const Rect rc = getClientRect( hwnd );
      const bool bHighLight = hasHighlight( hwnd );
      fillSysColorSolidRect( reinterpret_cast< HDC >( wParam ), &rc,
         bHighLight ? COLOR_HIGHLIGHT : COLOR_BTNFACE );
   } else if ( WM_SETTEXT == msg ) {
      // The nasty static paints in response to WM_SETTEXT!
      SetWindowRedraw( hwnd, FALSE );
      lResult =
         s_HTML_Subclasser.callOldProc( hwnd, msg, wParam, lParam );
      SetWindowRedraw( hwnd, TRUE );
      InvalidateRect( hwnd, 0, TRUE );
   } else {
      if ( WM_NCDESTROY == msg ) {
         removeHighlight( hwnd );
      }
      lResult =
         s_HTML_Subclasser.callOldProc( hwnd, msg, wParam, lParam );
   }

   return lResult;
}

void subclassHTML( HWND hwnd ) throw( SubclassException ) {

   assert( IsWindow( hwnd ) );
   verify( s_HTML_Subclasser.subclass( hwnd ) );
}
```

The Options Dialog

The Options dialog box looks like this:

Figure 13.2 **The Options dialog. The icons on the left are illustrative only; they do not reflect state in any way.**

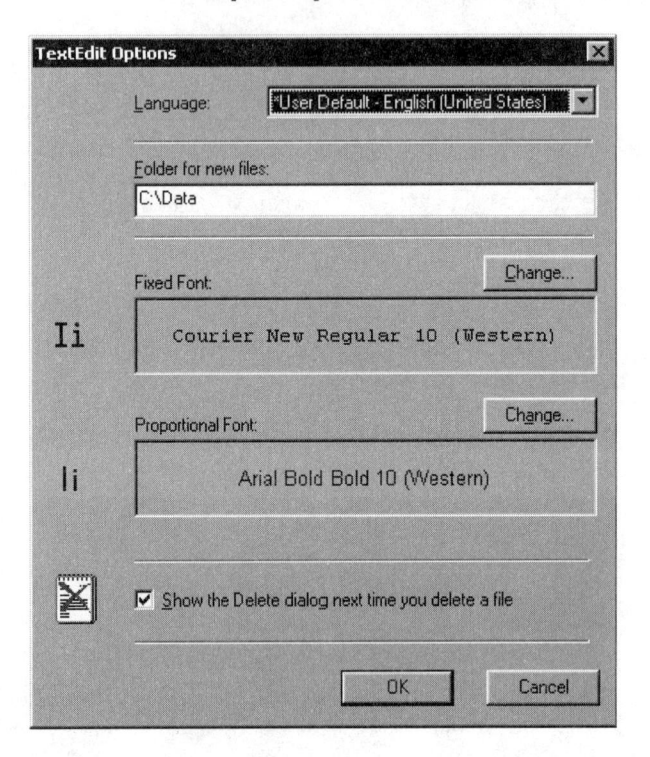

It is a little bit more complex, interaction-wise, than the About dialog. `AboutDlg` can get along with just the default `onDlgCommand` method defined in the Dialog base class, whereas `OptionsDlg` needs its own:

```
void OptionsDlg::onDlgCommand(
   int id, HWND hwndCtl, UINT codeNotify )
{
   switch ( id ) {
   case IDC_CHANGE_FIXED_FONT:
      if ( BN_CLICKED == codeNotify ) {
         changeFont( getDlgItem( IDC_FIXED_FONT_SAMPLE ),
            &m_logFontFixed, &m_hfontFixed, CF_FIXEDPITCHONLY );
      }
      break;
```

```
      case IDC_CHANGE_PROPORTIONAL_FONT:
        if ( BN_CLICKED == codeNotify ) {
          changeFont( getDlgItem( IDC_PROPORTIONAL_FONT_SAMPLE ),
             &m_logFontProportional, &m_hfontProportional );
        }
        break;

    case IDOK:
    case IDCANCEL:
      exitLanguageComboBox( *this );
      setShowDeleteDialog(
          0 != Button_GetCheck( getDlgItem( IDC_SHOWDELETEDIALOG ) ) );
      setDocumentPath( getDlgItemText( IDC_DOC_PATH ).c_str() );
      verify( EndDialog( *this, id ) );
      break;
    }
}
```

Enter with Care

The BUTTON window class supports a style bit named BS_DEFPUSHBUTTON. This draws the button with a heavy black border, indicating that it is the default button, and that you can activate it by pressing the Enter key.

The black border is just a visual clue; the functional aspects of the default button come from the dialog window class and the IsDialogMessage function. The dialog box has its own concept of a default button, which you can set using the DM_SETDEFID message. When a dialog receives this message, it may send WM_GETDLGCODE and BM_SETSTYLE to the indicated button as well as to the current default button.

This is less straightforward than it sounds. In particular, problems abound whenever you dynamically enable and disable buttons, or when you change the default button. Consider this code fragment from the onDlgCommand method of PropertiesDlg (described in Chapter 14):

```
switch ( id ) {
...
case IDC_APPLY:
  if ( BN_CLICKED == codeNotify ) {
    ...
    if ( applyChanges() ) {
      setDlgItemText( IDCANCEL, loadString( IDS_CLOSE ) );
      if ( GetFocus() == getDlgItem( IDC_APPLY ) ) {
        assert( IsWindowEnabled( getDlgItem( IDOK ) ) );
```

```
            gotoDlgItem( IDOK );
        }
        enableDlgItem( IDC_APPLY, false );
    }
  }
  break;
}
```

What happens if we disable the `IDC_APPLY` button, but omit the `gotoDlgItem( IDOK )` line? We lose the keyboard interface, that's what, and all keys simply go beep in the night. Furthermore, the Property dialog's Apply button retains its default border, even when disabled.

One of the possible flag parameters to the `MessageBox` function is `MB_NOFOCUS`, which ensures that no button has the initial focus. This is useful if you want to protect the `MessageBox` against accidental dismissal. To create a really obnoxious dialog box, let it respond to all `WM_COMMAND` messages with `SetFocus( 0 )`.

The most complex examples of dialog interaction TextEdit has to offer are the Find and Replace dialogs, described in Chapter 15.

Default Buttons and Multi-line Edit

I'd like to draw your attention to a user interface bug that runs rampant through the world of Windows applications. It involves the interaction of multi-line edit controls and default push buttons.

In the beginning was the multi-line edit control. Entering multiple lines was cumbersome in those days, as you were required to press Ctrl+Enter instead of just Enter. This was especially unfortunate whenever a default pushbutton was around; users would hit Enter to start a new line and promptly lose the whole dialog box (along with their peace of mind).

This whole Ctrl+Enter business was so obscure that many applications added extra text to educate users in proper procedure, i.e., "Hit Ctrl+Enter for new line." Mistakes were nevertheless common, even among experienced users.

Along came Windows 3.1 and the `ES_WANTRETURN` style, and all was well with the world. Or was it? The problem was now turned on its head; users would type some text and then hit Enter to invoke the default push button. What they got was a new line (along with a fresh set of aggravations).

The old style of interaction was merely bad. The new style was, when used in the wrong context, an actual bug in the user interface. That bug has been with us ever since.

There are three approaches to fixing the problem:

1. Read the user's mind to decide which action is appropriate — a new line or a button push.
2. Resurrect the Ctrl+Enter kludge.
3. Remove the fat border from the default button whenever a multi-line edit control with the `ES_WANTRETURN` style has the keyboard focus.

The first solution is beyond the current state of the art. By the time we get around to it, this little problem is most likely irrelevant anyway.

The second solution is easy; just remove the ES_WANTRETURN style from the edit control. Unfortunately, this results in a bad user interface.

The third solution is the only sensible way to handle the problem. Some applications use it, others don't. Still others are inconsistent; this last group even includes luminaries such as Word for Windows.

This WM_COMMAND handler code fragment implements this in the simplest possible way:

```
if ( IDC_MY_MULTILINE_EDIT == id ) {
   if ( EN_SETFOCUS == codeNotify ) {
      SendMessage( DM_SETDEFID, 0, 0 );
   } else if ( EN_KILLFOCUS == codeNotify ) {
      SendMessage( DM_SETDEFID, IDC_OK, 0 );
   }
   return TRUE;
}
```

If your dialog contains a button with the ID IDOK, the call

```
SendMessage( DM_SETDEFID, 0, 0 );
```

will give the OK button the default property. This is why the code fragment above uses IDC_OK, a value presumably different from 1.

Chapter 14

File Management

File management in the context of TextEdit is the management of a single file. It includes the ability to change file attributes such as the read-only flag, it includes renaming and repositioning of the file, and it includes deleting the file (and, incidentally, closing TextEdit).

Some file management functionality — toggling the read-only attribute — is exposed in the main window. For the rest, the Properties and Delete dialogs (`PropertiesDlg.cpp` and `DeleteDlg.cpp`) do the job, together with the `openFile` function and the `saveFile` function (which is accessible from the File menu as well as from the Properties dialog's Move button).

TextEdit also manages properties such as "Unicode." TextEdit detects whether a file is Unicode when it loads the file; changing this property determines how the file will be saved. The same holds true for the different ways of dividing the text file into lines: CR-LF or just LF.

File Properties

The Properties dialog displays information about the currently loaded file: file name, location, file type, file size, time stamps, file attributes, Unicode, and line separators. The layout of this dialog is similar to the Windows Explorer's Properties dialog (see Figure 14.1).

Figure 14.1 The Properties dialog is similar to the Exlorer's corresponding dialog.

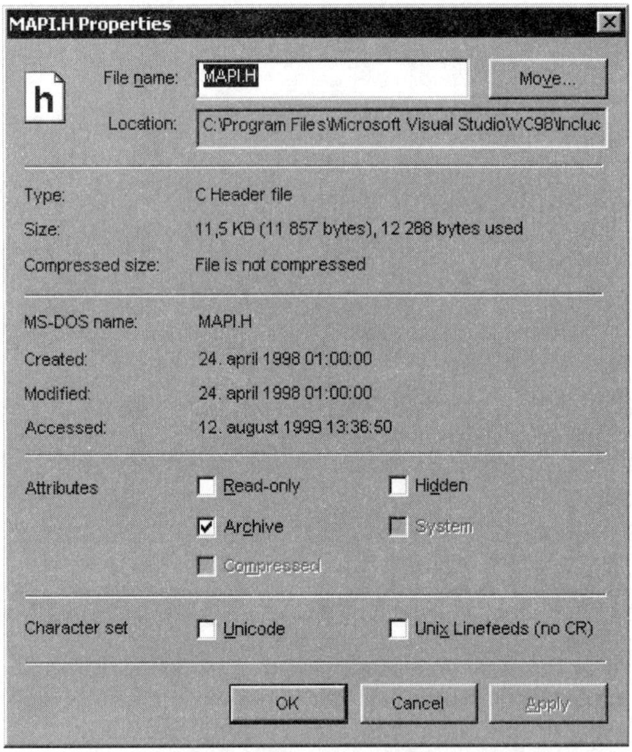

The dialog lets you change some of the attributes displayed in the dialog. You can change the file name on the fly, by typing a different name in the File Name field. To move the file to a different location, you must press the Move buttons to invoke a second dialog box (Figure 14.2); the Location field is read-only. This offloads everything to do with directories onto a common dialog designed for the purpose and avoids issues of how to handle non-existent directories, invalid path names and so forth. A better solution would be one that allowed both approaches.

The Move/Rename dialog allows you to change the file name as well as the file location — it's a "Save As..." dialog. The same dialog is available directly from the File menu (for improved visibility), and a variation is used in Document::save — if TextEdit is unable to write to the original file, it uses this dialog to get a new name and location (see Chapter 12).

You can change the file attributes Read Only, Hidden, Archive and Compressed; the System attribute is read-only. I followed Windows Explorer's lead in this; presumably, Microsoft's designers felt that the average user shouldn't mess with such things. Maybe so.

The Compressed attribute is different from the others: a "traditional" file attribute is just a flag in the file's directory entry, to be set or cleared using SetFileAttributes (see modifyAttribs in fileUtils.cpp). Compression, on the other hand, actually mangles the file's contents. To compress or uncompress a file, you must use the DeviceIoControl function (see compressFile in fileUtils.cpp).

Figure 14.2 Move or Rename File dialog. This is really a Save As dialog, with extra information on the top.

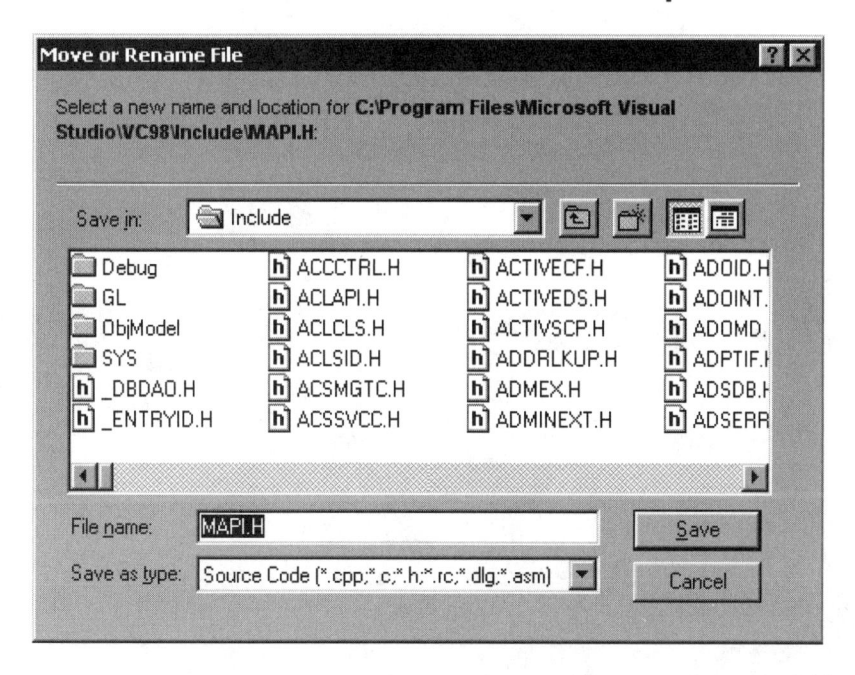

Compression of individual files is not supported on all file systems. In particular, it is not supported on FAT volumes. The Compressed check box should be enabled only if the underlying file system supports compression; this can be determined by the `GetVolumeInformation` function (see `supportsCompression` in `fileUtils.cpp`).

The Unicode and CR/LF "attributes" are even more different from the others, as they aren't properties of the file system at all, but functions of the file's contents. Changing these quasi-properties set or clear appropriate flags in the `Document` class; these flags determine how the file is saved.

The Properties dialog does not apply any changes until you click the Apply button or the OK button. Both of these invoke the `applyChanges` method in `PropertiesDlg`. In addition to applying changes, this method forwards an `ID_COMMAND_PROPSCHANGED` command to the parent window, which allows the main window to change whatever UI elements need changing — the file name displayed in the window title, read-only status, and so forth.

If you can't change a file's properties — if it's on a CD-ROM or a write-protected floppy, or if you don't have write access — everything except the Cancel button is disabled by the `onInitDialog` method. (Discourse continues on page 342.)

Chapter 14: File Management

Listing 14.1 PropertiesDlg.h

```
/*
 * $Header: /Book/PropertiesDlg.h 10    3.07.99 17:46 Petter $
 */

#pragma once

#include "Dialog.h"
#include "Document.h"

class PropertiesDlg : public Dialog {
private:
   Document *m_pDocument;
   String   m_strFormat;

   String formatBytes( DWORD dwBytes, bool bAddUsed );
   void setInfo( const WIN32_FIND_DATA& fd );
   bool applyChanges( void );
   bool onBrowse( void );
   void setFileName( const String& strPath );
   String getFileName( void );

protected:
   virtual BOOL onInitDialog( HWND hwndFocus, LPARAM lParam );
   virtual void onDlgCommand( int id, HWND hwndCtl, UINT codeNotify );

   virtual UINT getResourceID( void ) const;

public:
   PropertiesDlg( HWND hwndParent, Document *pDocument );
};
```

Listing 14.2 PropertiesDlg.cpp

```
/*
 * $Header: /Book/PropertiesDlg.cpp 17    5.09.99 13:07 Petter $
 *
 * LATER: Warning if data lost converting from Unicode!
 */
```

```cpp
#include "precomp.h"
#include "String.h"
#include "Registry.h"
#include "Exception.h"
#include "SilentErrorMode.h"
#include "Dialog.h"
#include "PropertiesDlg.h"
#include "HTML.h"
#include "WaitCursor.h"
#include "formatMessage.h"
#include "formatNumber.h"
#include "saveFile.h"
#include "fileUtils.h"
#include "resource.h"
#include "utils.h"
#include "os.h"

UINT PropertiesDlg::getResourceID( void ) const {
    return IDD_PROPERTIES;
}

PropertiesDlg::PropertiesDlg( HWND hwndParent, Document *pDocument )
    : m_pDocument( pDocument )
{
#ifdef _DEBUG
    const UINT uiRetCode =
#endif

    doModal( hwndParent, getResourceID() );
    assert( IDOK == uiRetCode || IDCANCEL == uiRetCode );
}

PRIVATE String formatFileTime( const FILETIME& ft ) {

    FILETIME local = ft;
    verify( FileTimeToLocalFileTime( &ft, &local ) );

    SYSTEMTIME st;
    verify( FileTimeToSystemTime( &local, &st ) );
```

```
   TCHAR szTime[ 100 ] = { 0 };
   GetTimeFormat(
      LOCALE_USER_DEFAULT, 0, &st, 0, szTime, dim( szTime ) );

   TCHAR szDate[ 100 ] = { 0 };
   GetDateFormat( LOCALE_USER_DEFAULT,
      DATE_LONGDATE, &st, 0, szDate, dim( szDate ) );

   return formatMessage( _T( "%1 %2" ), szDate, szTime );
}


String PropertiesDlg::formatBytes( DWORD dwBytes, bool bAddUsed ) {

   TCHAR szFileSize[ 100 ] = { 0 };
   StrFormatByteSize( dwBytes, szFileSize, dim( szFileSize ) );

   const String strByteSizeAll = formatNumber( dwBytes );
   wsprintf( szFileSize + _tcsclen( szFileSize ),
      loadString( IDS_BYTES ).c_str(), strByteSizeAll.c_str() );

   if ( bAddUsed ) {
      const DWORD dwClusterSize =
         getClusterSize( m_pDocument->getPath() );
      // We may not always get a cluster size --
      // can happen on network volumes, for example...
      if ( 0 != dwClusterSize ) {
         const DWORD dwClustersUsed =
            ( (dwBytes + dwClusterSize - 1) / dwClusterSize );
         const DWORD dwBytesUsed = dwClustersUsed * dwClusterSize;
         const String strBytesUsed = formatNumber( dwBytesUsed );
         wsprintf( szFileSize + _tcsclen( szFileSize ),
            loadString( IDS_BYTES_USED ).c_str(),
            strBytesUsed.c_str() );
      }
   }

   return szFileSize;
}
```

```
void PropertiesDlg::setInfo( const WIN32_FIND_DATA& fd ) {

   const String strTitle = m_pDocument->getTitle();
   const String strDialogTitle =
      formatMessage( m_strFormat, strTitle.c_str() );
   setWindowText( strDialogTitle );

   setFileName( m_pDocument->getPath() );
   setDlgItemText(
      IDC_FILETYPE, m_pDocument->getFileTypeDescription( true ) );

   LPCTSTR pszMsDosName = fd.cAlternateFileName;
   if ( 0 == pszMsDosName[ 0 ] ) {
      pszMsDosName = fd.cFileName;
   }
   setDlgItemText( IDC_MSDOS_NAME, pszMsDosName );

   // We don't handle files that big :-)
   assert( 0 == fd.nFileSizeHigh );
   const String strFileSize = formatBytes( fd.nFileSizeLow, true );
   setDlgItemText( IDC_FILESIZE, strFileSize );

   DWORD dwCompressedSize = 0;
   const bool isCompressed =
      (FILE_ATTRIBUTE_COMPRESSED & fd.dwFileAttributes) &&
      getCompressedFileSize( m_pDocument->getPath().c_str(),
      &dwCompressedSize );
   if ( isCompressed ) {
      const String strCompressedSize =
         formatBytes( dwCompressedSize, false );
      setDlgItemText( IDC_COMPRESSEDFILESIZE, strCompressedSize );
   } else {
      setDlgItemText( IDC_COMPRESSEDFILESIZE,
         loadString( IDS_FILE_NOT_COMPRESSED ) );
   }

   setDlgItemText(
      IDC_CREATED , formatFileTime( fd.ftCreationTime   ).c_str() );
```

```cpp
    setDlgItemText(
        IDC_MODIFIED, formatFileTime( fd.ftLastWriteTime ).c_str() );
    setDlgItemText(
        IDC_ACCESSED, formatFileTime( fd.ftLastAccessTime ).c_str() );

    SHFILEINFO fileInfo = { 0 };
    UINT uiFlags = SHGFI_ICON | SHGFI_TYPENAME;
    SHGetFileInfo( m_pDocument->getPath().c_str(), 0,
        &fileInfo, sizeof fileInfo, uiFlags );
    //setDlgItemText( IDC_FILETYPE, fileInfo.szTypeName );
    HWND hwndIcon = getDlgItem( IDC_FILEICON );
    Static_SetIcon( hwndIcon, fileInfo.hIcon );

    #define CHK_ATTR( id, attr) Button_SetCheck( \
        getDlgItem( id ), 0 != (attr & fd.dwFileAttributes) )
    #define CHK_BOOL( id, val) Button_SetCheck( \
        getDlgItem( id ), val )

    CHK_ATTR( IDC_ARCHIVE    , FILE_ATTRIBUTE_ARCHIVE    );
    CHK_ATTR( IDC_COMPRESSED , FILE_ATTRIBUTE_COMPRESSED );
    CHK_ATTR( IDC_READ_ONLY  , FILE_ATTRIBUTE_READONLY   );
    CHK_ATTR( IDC_HIDDEN     , FILE_ATTRIBUTE_HIDDEN     );
    CHK_ATTR( IDC_SYSTEM     , FILE_ATTRIBUTE_SYSTEM     );

    CHK_BOOL( IDC_UNICODE       , m_pDocument->isUnicode()       );
    CHK_BOOL( IDC_UNIXLINEFEEDS, m_pDocument->hasUnixLineFeeds() );

    #undef CHK_ATTR
    #undef CHK_BOOL

    const bool bReadOnly =
        0 != (FILE_ATTRIBUTE_READONLY & fd.dwFileAttributes);
    if ( !m_pDocument->isAccessDenied() ) {
        enableDlgItem( IDC_UNICODE      , !bReadOnly );
        enableDlgItem( IDC_UNIXLINEFEEDS, !bReadOnly );
    }
}

BOOL PropertiesDlg::onInitDialog( HWND hwndFocus, LPARAM lParam ) {
```

```
   SilentErrorMode sem;

   m_strFormat = getWindowText();

   WIN32_FIND_DATA fd = { 0 };
   HANDLE hFind =
      FindFirstFile( m_pDocument->getPath().c_str(), &fd );
   if ( INVALID_HANDLE_VALUE == hFind ) {
      messageBox( GetParent( *this ), MB_OK | MB_ICONERROR,
         IDS_PROPERTIES_ERROR,
         m_pDocument->getPath().c_str(), getError().c_str() );
      EndDialog( *this, IDCANCEL );
   } else {
      verify( FindClose( hFind ) );
      setInfo( fd );
      if ( m_pDocument->isAccessDenied() ) {
         enableDlgItem( IDC_FILENAME     , false );
         enableDlgItem( IDC_BROWSEPATH   , false );
         enableDlgItem( IDC_READ_ONLY    , false );
         enableDlgItem( IDC_HIDDEN       , false );
         enableDlgItem( IDC_ARCHIVE      , false );
         enableDlgItem( IDC_SYSTEM       , false );
         enableDlgItem( IDC_COMPRESSED   , false );
         enableDlgItem( IDC_UNICODE      , false );
         enableDlgItem( IDC_UNIXLINEFEEDS, false );
         enableDlgItem( IDOK             , false );
         sendMessage( DM_SETDEFID, IDCANCEL );
         gotoDlgItem( IDCANCEL );
      } else {
         gotoDlgItem( IDC_FILENAME );
      }
      if ( !supportsCompression( m_pDocument->getPath() ) ) {
         enableDlgItem( IDC_COMPRESSED, false );
      }
      // LATER: Disable unix/unicode if read-only
   }

   return FALSE; // We DID set the focus.
}
```

```cpp
// Is this sufficiently rigorous?
void PropertiesDlg::setFileName( const String& strPathName ) {

   PATHNAME szTitle = { 0 };
   verify( 0 == GetFileTitle(
      strPathName.c_str(), szTitle, dim( szTitle ) ) );

   int nPathLength = strPathName.length() - _tcslen( szTitle );
   const String strFile = strPathName.substr( nPathLength );

   // We want to display the terminating backslash
   // iff we're at the root directory:
   if ( 3 == nPathLength && _T( ':' ) == strPathName[ 1 ] ) {
      ;
   } else if ( 3 < nPathLength &&
            _T( '\\' ) == strPathName[ nPathLength - 1 ] )
   {
      --nPathLength;
   }
   const String strPath = strPathName.substr( 0, nPathLength );

   setDlgItemText( IDC_FILENAME, strFile );
   setDlgItemText( IDC_PATH    , strPath );
}

String PropertiesDlg::getFileName( void ) {

   const String strFile = getDlgItemText( IDC_FILENAME );
   const String strPath = getDlgItemText( IDC_PATH );
   PATHNAME szFullPath = { 0 };
   _tmakepath( szFullPath, 0, strPath.c_str(), strFile.c_str(), 0 );
   return szFullPath;
}

bool PropertiesDlg::onBrowse( void ) {

   String strFullPath = getFileName();
   const bool bRetVal = saveFile(
      *this, &strFullPath, IDS_MOVE, IDD_MOVE_CHILD );
```

```cpp
   if ( bRetVal ) {
      setFileName( strFullPath );
   }

   return bRetVal;
}

// TODO: Editor as parm rather than document?
bool PropertiesDlg::applyChanges( void ) {

   WaitCursor waitCursor( _T( "save.ani" ) );

   bool bSuccess = true;

   assert( isGoodPtr( this ) );
   assert( isGoodPtr( m_pDocument ) );

   m_pDocument->setUnicode     (
      0 != Button_GetCheck( getDlgItem( IDC_UNICODE      ) ) );
   m_pDocument->setUnixLineFeeds(
      0 != Button_GetCheck( getDlgItem( IDC_UNIXLINEFEEDS ) ) );

   DWORD dwAdd = 0;
   DWORD dwRemove = 0;

#define SET_ATTRIB( item, attrib ) \
   if ( Button_GetCheck( getDlgItem( item ) ) ) { \
      dwAdd |= attrib; \
   } else { \
      dwRemove |= attrib; \
   }

   SET_ATTRIB( IDC_ARCHIVE   , FILE_ATTRIBUTE_ARCHIVE    );
// SET_ATTRIB( IDC_COMPRESSED, FILE_ATTRIBUTE_COMPRESSED );
   SET_ATTRIB( IDC_READ_ONLY , FILE_ATTRIBUTE_READONLY   );
   SET_ATTRIB( IDC_HIDDEN    , FILE_ATTRIBUTE_HIDDEN     );
   SET_ATTRIB( IDC_SYSTEM    , FILE_ATTRIBUTE_SYSTEM     );
```

```
   if ( !m_pDocument->setPath( *this, getFileName() ) ) {
      bSuccess = false;
   }

   if ( supportsCompression( m_pDocument->getPath() ) ) {
      const bool bCompress =
         0 != Button_GetCheck( getDlgItem( IDC_COMPRESSED ) );
      if ( !compressFile( m_pDocument->getPath(), bCompress ) ) {
         bSuccess = false;
      }
   }

   // TODO: Method in Document, or rather Editor, to do this;
   // clear whistleclean flag!
   // Move whistleclean to Document, perhaps?
   if ( !m_pDocument->modifyAttribs( dwAdd, dwRemove ) ) {
      bSuccess = false;
   }

   HWND hwndParent = GetParent( *this );
   assert( IsWindow( hwndParent ) );
   FORWARD_WM_COMMAND(
      hwndParent, ID_COMMAND_PROPSCHANGED, 0, 0, SNDMSG );

   WIN32_FIND_DATA fd = { 0 };
   HANDLE hFind =
      FindFirstFile( m_pDocument->getPath().c_str(), &fd );
   if ( INVALID_HANDLE_VALUE != hFind ) {
      verify( FindClose( hFind ) );
      setInfo( fd );
   }

   return bSuccess;
}

void PropertiesDlg::onDlgCommand(
   int id, HWND hwndCtl, UINT codeNotify )
{
   assert( isGoodPtr( m_pDocument ) );
```

```
switch ( id ) {

case IDC_BROWSEPATH:
   if ( BN_CLICKED == codeNotify ) {
      assert( !m_pDocument->isAccessDenied() );
      if ( !m_pDocument->isAccessDenied() && onBrowse() ) {
         enableDlgItem( IDC_APPLY, TRUE );
      }
   }
   break;

case IDOK:
   if ( BN_CLICKED == codeNotify ) {
      if ( !m_pDocument->isAccessDenied() && applyChanges() ) {
         verify( EndDialog( *this, IDOK ) );
      }
   }
   break;

case IDCANCEL:
   verify( EndDialog( *this, IDCANCEL ) );
   break;

case IDC_FILENAME:
   if ( IsWindowVisible( *this ) && EN_CHANGE == codeNotify ) {
      assert( !m_pDocument->isAccessDenied() );
      if ( !m_pDocument->isAccessDenied() ) {
         enableDlgItem( IDC_APPLY, TRUE );
      }
   }
   break;

case IDC_ARCHIVE:
case IDC_COMPRESSED:
case IDC_READ_ONLY:
case IDC_HIDDEN:
case IDC_SYSTEM:
case IDC_UNICODE:
case IDC_UNIXLINEFEEDS:
   assert( !m_pDocument->isAccessDenied() );
```

```
            if ( BN_CLICKED == codeNotify ) {
                if ( !m_pDocument->isAccessDenied() ) {
                    enableDlgItem( IDC_APPLY, TRUE );
                }
            }
            break;

        case IDC_APPLY:
            if ( BN_CLICKED == codeNotify ) {
                assert( !m_pDocument->isAccessDenied() );
                if ( m_pDocument->isAccessDenied() ) {
                    enableDlgItem( IDC_APPLY, false );
                    MessageBeep( MB_ICONWARNING );
                } else if ( applyChanges() ) {
                    setDlgItemText( IDCANCEL, loadString( IDS_CLOSE ) );
                    if ( GetFocus() == getDlgItem( IDC_APPLY ) ) {
                        assert( IsWindowEnabled( getDlgItem( IDOK ) ) );
                        gotoDlgItem( IDOK );
                    }
                    enableDlgItem( IDC_APPLY, false );
                }
            }
            break;
    }
}
```

Deleting Files

TextEdit's Delete command deletes the current file. Because the unified file model requires a file in order for TextEdit to run, the command closes TextEdit as well.

The Delete command may or may not open the confirmation dialog shown in Figure 14.3. The `ShowDeleteDialog` registry variable defined in `persistence.h` controls this. The user, in turn, controls the registry variable. You can turn it off by unchecking the lower checkbox in Figure 14.3 (the one labeled "Show this dialog the next time you delete a file"). For obvious reasons, you can't turn it back on using the same checkbox. To prevent the user from getting lost, the dialog explains how you can turn it back on. (Note how the functional part of the "confirm file delete" confirmation dialog stops at the horizontal line — what's below is concerned with management of the dialog itself, and has nothing to do with deleting files.)

Figure 14.3 The Delete File dialog. The upper icon is static and helps identify the dialog; the trash can icon is dynamic and changes according to the setting of its corresponding checkbox.

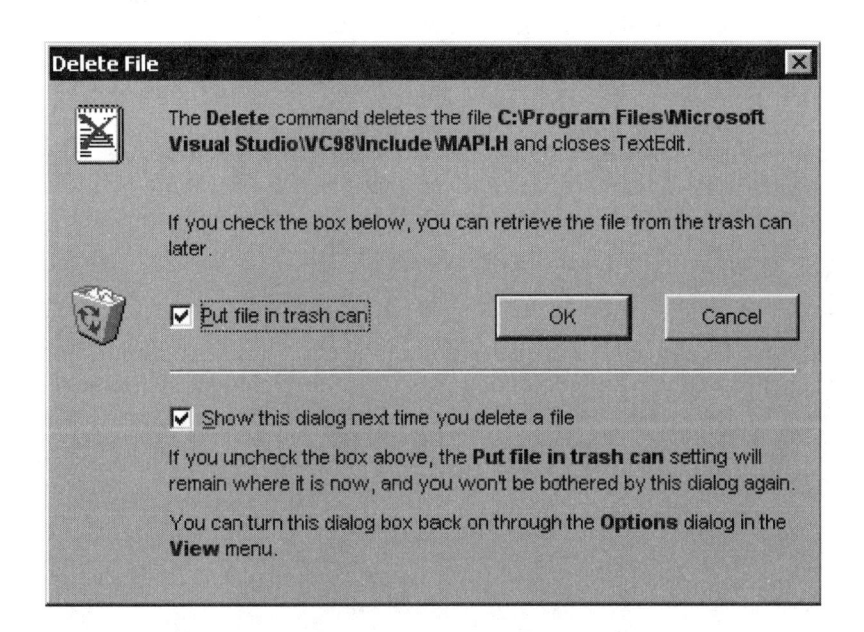

A menu command should have a trailing ellipsis if it invokes a dialog box; otherwise not. The `onInitMenu` message handler (in `mainwnd.h`) handles this by altering the menu text depending on the setting of `ShowDeleteDialog`, as follows:

```
String strDeleteFile = getMenuItemText(
   hmenu, ID_FILE_DELETE );
int iDotPos = strDeleteFile.find( _T( '.' ) );
if ( 0 <= iDotPos ) {
   strDeleteFile.erase( iDotPos );
}
if ( getShowDeleteDialog() ) {
   strDeleteFile.append( _T( "..." ) );
}
setMenuItemText( hmenu, ID_FILE_DELETE, _T( "%1" ),
   strDeleteFile.c_str() );
```

This code fragment checks to see if an ellipsis is present; if so, the ellipsis is removed. If the dialog is to be shown, the ellipsis is appended again. That way, it doesn't matter whether the original menu string contained an ellipsis.

Document::deleteFile physically deletes the file, and removes the file name from the MRU list as well (see Listing 12.4 on page 278). It does not use the DeleteFile function, but relies instead on SHFileOperation. This lets us send the file to the trash can, if the user so desires, just by specifying the FOF_ALLOWUNDO flag. Furthermore, SHFileOperation takes care of the additional confirmation dialog, if any — it follows the user's Explorer settings.

One of the parameters to SHFileOperation is a pointer to an SHFILEOPSTRUCT. The pFrom member of this structure is actually a list of null-terminated file names; the list itself must be doubly null-terminated. (This is an error-prone approach to an API — it did burn me, at least. QED.)

The trash can icon in Figure 14.3 is really two icons — one icon showing a full trash can, another icon showing an empty one. Only one of them is visible at a time, though; this is toggled whenever the user checks or unchecks the "Put file in trash can" checkbox:

```
toggleIcon( IDC_WASTEBASKET, IDC_WASTEBASKETEMPTY,
    0 != Button_GetCheck( getDlgItem( IDC_TRASHCAN ) ) );
```

The icon serves as a visual reinforcement of the setting of the checkbox. In addition to being pretty cool, this is actually useful. The Find dialog uses the same technique. (Discourse continues on page 346.)

Listing 14.3   DeleteDlg.h

```
/*
 * $Header: /Book/DeleteDlg.h 6     3.07.99 17:46 Petter $
 */

#pragma once

#include "String.h"
#include "Dialog.h"
#include "persistence.h"

class DeleteDlg : public Dialog {
private:
    String m_strFile;

protected:
    virtual BOOL onInitDialog( HWND hwndFocus, LPARAM lParam );
    virtual void onDlgCommand( int id, HWND hwndCtl, UINT codeNotify );
    virtual UINT getResourceID( void ) const;

public:
    DeleteDlg( const String& strFile );
};
```

Listing 14.4 `DeleteDlg.cpp`

```cpp
/*
 * $Header: /Book/DeleteDlg.cpp 10    3.07.99 17:46 Petter $
 */

#include "precomp.h"
#include "resource.h"
#include "formatMessage.h"
#include "winUtils.h"
#include "DeleteDlg.h"
#include "HTML.h"
#include "persistence.h"

BOOL DeleteDlg::onInitDialog( HWND hwndFocus, LPARAM lParam ) {

   const String strFmt = getDlgItemText( IDC_INFO );
   const String strInfo = formatMessage( strFmt, m_strFile.c_str() );
   setDlgItemText( IDC_INFO, strInfo );
   subclassHTML( getDlgItem( IDC_INFO ) );
   subclassHTML( getDlgItem( IDC_TIP ) );

   const bool bSendToWasteBasket = 0 != getSendToWasteBasket();
   Button_SetCheck(
      getDlgItem( IDC_TRASHCAN ), bSendToWasteBasket ? 1 : 0 );
   toggleIcon(
      IDC_WASTEBASKET, IDC_WASTEBASKETEMPTY, bSendToWasteBasket );

   // This is always true if we're shoing the dialog!
   Button_SetCheck( getDlgItem( IDC_SHOWDELETEDIALOG ), true);

   return TRUE; // ...since we didn't set the focus.
}

void DeleteDlg::onDlgCommand(
   int id, HWND hwndCtl, UINT codeNotify )
{
   switch ( id ) {
   case IDC_TRASHCAN:
      if ( BN_CLICKED == codeNotify ) {
```

```
            toggleIcon( IDC_WASTEBASKET, IDC_WASTEBASKETEMPTY,
                0 != Button_GetCheck( getDlgItem( IDC_TRASHCAN ) ) );
        }
        break;

    case IDOK:
        if ( BN_CLICKED == codeNotify ) {
            setSendToWasteBasket( Button_GetCheck(
                getDlgItem( IDC_TRASHCAN ) ) ? 1 : 0 );
            setShowDeleteDialog( Button_GetCheck(
                getDlgItem( IDC_SHOWDELETEDIALOG ) ) ? 1 : 0 );
        }

        //*** FALL THROUGH

    case IDCANCEL:
        if ( BN_CLICKED == codeNotify ) {
            verify( EndDialog( *this, id ) );
        }
        break;

    }
}

UINT DeleteDlg::getResourceID( void ) const {
    return IDD_DELETE;
}

DeleteDlg::DeleteDlg( const String& strFile )
    : m_strFile( strFile )
{
}
```

The Open File Dialog

The Open File and Save File common dialogs are little Explorers in their own right. Figure 14.4 shows TextEdit's Open File dialog in action. As you can see, it has four extra controls — one static label, one edit control used to show a preview of the selected file, one icon to show the type of the selected file, and one checkbox that lets you open the file in a new window.

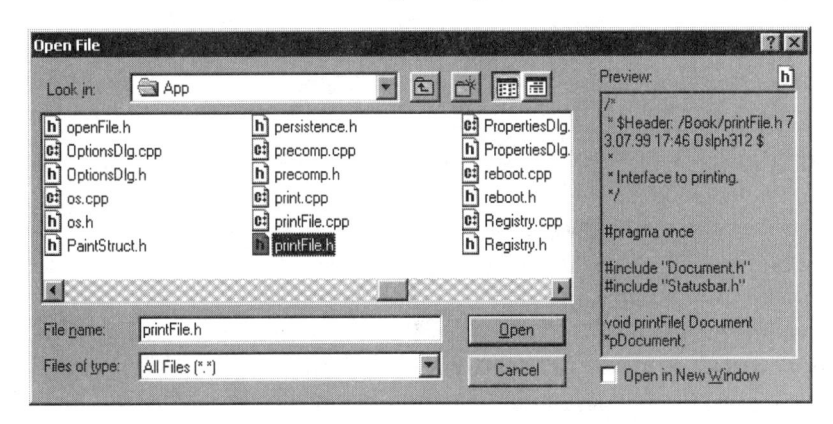

Figure 14.4 The Open File dialog. The extra controls on the right come from the dialog template `IDD_PREVIEW_CHILD`.

You change the look of most common dialogs by specifying a resource template that replaces the default dialog. The Open and Save dialogs are exceptions; you specify, instead, the template of a child dialog that is added to the system-supplied dialog. The template must have the `WS_CHILD` style bit set, and it should include a static control with the ID `stc32`. This is a placeholder for the system-supplied dialog, and tells `GetOpenFileName` and `GetSaveFileName` how to place the child dialog in relation to predefined controls. Figure 14.5 shows the child dialog (`IDD_PREVIEW_CHILD`); its relationship to Figure 14.4 should be clear.

Figure 14.5 The Open File Child dialog. The `STATIC` control labeled `stc32` is a placeholder for the standard contents of the Open File dialog.

The Open File Common Dialog Bug

The Win32 Open File common dialog has a curious bug — at least it does under Windows NT 4.0. It is not even close to being a showstopper, but it is nevertheless a bug. To manifest the bug, do the following:

1. Start the Control Panel Display applet and select the Appearance tab. Select the standard Windows color scheme and click the Apply button.
2. Start Notepad and select the File Open command.
3. Without closing Notepad's Open File dialog box, go back to the Display applet, select the High Contrast Black color scheme and click the Apply button again.

The expected result is for the file list in the Open File dialog to take on the characteristics of the High Contrast Black color scheme, namely a black background with white, boldface text. The background, however, remains white. The font remains black, and its boldness does not increase noticeably.

To verify that this is indeed a bug, and not just some weird feature, close Notepad's Open File dialog and open it again — it has now taken on the expected look.

If you try the same trick with the Visual Studio editor rather than Notepad, the story is the same. If you try the same trick with Microsoft Word, though, the story is slightly different — Word's Open File dialog does handle the color change, but not the font change. In other words: close, but no cigar.

My first thought was that the list view had a bug, but that turned out not to be the case. If you tell the list view that the color scheme has changed, it will change its looks to match the new scheme.

When the color scheme changes, Windows broadcasts a `WM_SYSCOLORCHANGE` message to all top-level windows. The Open File common dialog receives the `WM_SYSCOLORCHANGE` message, but fails to pass it on to the list view. According to the SDK documentation, it should have done so: "Top level windows that use common controls must forward the `WM_SYSCOLORCHANGE` message to the controls; otherwise, the controls will not be notified of the color change."

What about the font change? When the font changes, Windows broadcasts a `WM_SETTINGCHANGE` (formerly `WM_WININICHANGE`) message to all top-level windows. Again, the Open File dialog receives the message, but fails to pass it on. The documentation for `WM_SETTINGCHANGE` does not mention common controls, but if you fail to pass on the message, the font does not change.

To solve the problem, it is not enough to add a hook function to the Open File dialog. Because `WM_SYSCOLORCHANGE` messages and `WM_WININICHANGE` messages aren't sent to the hook function, we must subclass the dialog itself. An `Instansubclasser` called `s_commonDlgSubclasser`, defined in `openDlgCommon.cpp`, is applied when the hook function receives the `CDN_INITDONE` notification, and ensures that the list view gets the required messages.

Filter Strings

The file `openDlgCommon.cpp` defines everything the Open and Save dialogs have in common. Aside from fixing the problem described in the sidebar "Open File Common Dialog Bug," the code here is mostly concerned with handling filter strings — the strings that go into the combo box labeled "File Type" in Figure 14.4. As we shall see, this is a rather convoluted business.

The `lpstrFilter` member of the `OPENFILENAME` structure points to a string defining the predefined filter entries. ("Predefined?" I hear you ask. Well, there is a member named `lpstrCustomFilter` as well, which I'll get back to in a moment.) Each combo box entry is defined by two strings — the text that appears in the drop-down list, and the corresponding wildcard pattern. Each of these sub-strings is null-terminated. For example:

```
Batch Files\0*.bat;*.cmd\0
```

To get multiple entries, you just string several of these together, e.g.:

```
Batch Files\0*.bat;*.cmd\0All Files\0*.*\0
```

A final null terminates the whole assemblage, so that there are two nulls at the end.

There is a problem with this: the filter strings are stored in a string table resource (`IDS_FILEFILTERS`), so that the UI texts may be translated without recompiling the program. Because the null terminator is just that, a terminator, handling strings with embedded nulls is inconvenient. To get around this, the text in the string table uses vertical bars rather than nulls; part of the `IDS_FILEFILTERS` string table entry looks like this:

```
Batch Files|*.bat;*.cmd|All Files|*.*|
```

The bars are translated to nulls in the `getFilterList` function.

So much for `lpstrFilter`. Another member of `OPENFILENAME`, `nFilterIndex`, determines which combo box entry is selected. You can set it before opening the dialog; after the dialog has closed, `nFilterIndex` reflects any changes the used may have made.

This index is not zero-based, but one-based. This has to do with the `lpstrCustomFilter` member of `OPENFILENAME`. Before opening the dialog, I point this to a buffer (`szCustomFilter`) and supply the length of that buffer in the `nMaxCustFilter` member. Now, if the user types a wild-card pattern (e.g., "letter*.txt") rather than selecting one from the drop-down, `szCustomFilter` will reflect this after the dialog has closed. By saving the contents of `szCustomFilter`, we can add "letter*.txt" to the drop-down list the next time the dialog is invoked. That's why nFilterIndex is not zero-based; zero means "select the custom filter supplied in `lpstrCustomFilter`."

To complicate things even more, TextEdit checks to see if the custom pattern matches one of the predefined patterns; if so, the index of the predefined pattern is saved, rather than zero.

As I said, a convoluted business. A custom pattern is formatted with the `IDS_CUSTOM` string, which gives us file type entries like this:

```
Custom (letter*.txt)
```

(Discourse continues on page 357.)

Listing 14.5   openDlgCommon.cpp

```cpp
/*
 * $Header: /Book/openDlgCommon.cpp 6      5.09.99 13:07 Petter $
 *
 * Common stuff for all Open/Save dialogs:
 *
 * - Handles system color and font changes for the list view
 * - Sets Arial font in file name edit control
 *   if FIX_EDIT_FONT is defined.
 */

#include "precomp.h"
#include "trace.h"
#include "Exception.h"
#include "InstanceSubclasser.h"
#include "fileUtils.h"
#include "winUtils.h"
#include "utils.h"
#include "persistence.h"
#include "resource.h"

#define FIX_EDIT_FONT (defined( _UNICODE ) && 0)

#if FIX_EDIT_FONT
PRIVATE HFONT s_hfont = 0;
PRIVATE HFONT s_hfontSaved = 0;
#endif

#ifdef _DEBUG
PRIVATE int s_nRefCount = 0; // Assuming only one at a time
#endif

PRIVATE LRESULT CALLBACK commonDlgSubclassing(
    HWND hwnd, UINT msg, WPARAM wParam, LPARAM lParam );

PRIVATE InstanceSubclasser
    s_commonDlgSubclasser( commonDlgSubclassing );

PRIVATE inline void onSysColorChange( HWND hwnd ) {
```

```
    HWND hwndList = GetDlgItem( hwnd, lst2 );
    assert( IsWindow( hwndList ) );
    FORWARD_WM_SYSCOLORCHANGE( hwndList, SNDMSG );
}

PRIVATE inline void onSettingChange( HWND hwnd, LPCTSTR pszSection ) {

    HWND hwndList = GetDlgItem( hwnd, lst2 );
    assert( IsWindow( hwndList ) );
    FORWARD_WM_WININICHANGE( hwndList, 0, SNDMSG );
}

PRIVATE inline void onDestroy( HWND hwnd ) {

    assert( IsWindow( hwnd ) );
    UINT id = reinterpret_cast< UINT >(
        s_commonDlgSubclasser.getUserData( hwnd ) );
    savePosition( hwnd, id );

#if FIX_EDIT_FONT

    HWND hwndEdit = GetDlgItem( hwnd, edt1 );
    assert( IsWindow( hwndEdit ) );
    if ( IsWindow( hwndEdit ) ) {
        if ( 0 != s_hfontSaved ) {
            SetWindowFont( hwndEdit, s_hfontSaved, false );
            if ( 0 != s_hfont ) {
                DeleteFont( s_hfont );
            }
        }
    }

#endif // FIX_EDIT_FONT

    assert( 0 == --s_nRefCount );
}
```

```
/**
 * This function exists merely to wrap the
 * return statement in the HANDLE_MSG macro.
 */
PRIVATE LRESULT CALLBACK _commonDlgSubclassing(
   HWND hwnd, UINT msg, WPARAM wParam, LPARAM lParam )
{
   assert( IsWindow( hwnd ) );
   switch ( msg ) {
   HANDLE_MSG( hwnd, WM_SYSCOLORCHANGE, onSysColorChange );
   HANDLE_MSG( hwnd, WM_SETTINGCHANGE , onSettingChange  );
   HANDLE_MSG( hwnd, WM_DESTROY       , onDestroy        );
   }
   return 0;
}


PRIVATE LRESULT CALLBACK commonDlgSubclassing(
   HWND hwnd, UINT msg, WPARAM wParam, LPARAM lParam )
{
   assert( IsWindow( hwnd ) );
   _commonDlgSubclassing( hwnd, msg, wParam, lParam );
   return s_commonDlgSubclasser.callOldProc(
      hwnd, msg, wParam, lParam );
}


/**
 * Call this on CDN_INITDONE.
 */
void subclassOpenDlgCommon( HWND hwndChildDlg, UINT id ) {

   assert( 1 == ++s_nRefCount );

   HWND hwndOpenDlg = GetParent( hwndChildDlg );
   assert( IsWindow( hwndOpenDlg ) );
   restorePosition( hwndOpenDlg, id );
   SNDMSG( hwndChildDlg, DM_SETDEFID, IDOK, 0 );

#if FIX_EDIT_FONT
```

```
      s_hfont = s_hfontSaved = 0;
      HWND hwndEdit = GetDlgItem( hwndOpenDlg, edt1 );
      assert( IsWindow( hwndEdit ) );
      if ( IsWindow( hwndEdit ) ) {
         s_hfontSaved = GetWindowFont( hwndEdit );
         if ( 0 != s_hfontSaved ) {
            LOGFONT logFont = { 0 };
            verify( GetObject(
               s_hfontSaved, sizeof logFont, &logFont ) );
            _tcscpy( logFont.lfFaceName, _T( "Arial" ) );
            s_hfont = CreateFontIndirect( &logFont );
            if ( 0 != s_hfont ) {
               SetWindowFont( hwndEdit, s_hfont, false );
            }
         }
      }

#endif // FIX_EDIT_FONT

   // If this subclassing fails, we can live with the consequences:
   try {
      verify( s_commonDlgSubclasser.subclass(
         hwndOpenDlg, reinterpret_cast< void * >( id ) ) );
   }
   catch ( const SubclassException& x ) {
      trace( _T( "%s\n" ), x.what() );
   }
}

PRIVATE LPCTSTR getFilterList( void ) {

   static TCHAR szFilters[ 600 ] = { 0 };
   if ( 0 != szFilters[ 0 ] ) {
      return szFilters; //** FUNCTION EXIT POINT
   }

   LPTSTR pszPtr = szFilters;
   String strFilters = loadString( IDS_FILEFILTERS );
```

```cpp
for ( ;; ) {
   int iBreak = strFilters.find( _T( '|' ) );
   if ( iBreak <= 0 ) {
      break; //*** LOOP EXIT POINT
   }
   String strDescription = strFilters.substr( 0, iBreak );
   strFilters.erase( 0, iBreak + 1 );

   iBreak = strFilters.find( _T( '|' ) );
   assert( 0 < iBreak );
   if ( iBreak <= 0 ) {
      break; //*** LOOP EXIT POINT
   }
   String strExtensions = strFilters.substr( 0, iBreak );
   strFilters.erase( 0, iBreak + 1 );

   // Check if we would overflow the szFilters buffer.
   // If we would, just cut off at this point.
   const int nNewLength =
      strDescription.length() + 2 * strExtensions.length() + 6;
   if ( szFilters + dim( szFilters ) <= pszPtr + nNewLength ) {
      trace( _T( "Filter string too long adding [%s]\n" ),
         strDescription.c_str() );
      break; //*** LOOP EXIT POINT
   }

   // We're home safe; append the filter:
   wsprintf( pszPtr, _T( "%s (%s)" ),
      strDescription.c_str(),
      strExtensions.c_str() );
   pszPtr += _tcsclen( pszPtr ) + 1;
   _tcscpy( pszPtr, strExtensions.c_str() );
   pszPtr += _tcsclen( pszPtr ) + 1;
}

assert( pszPtr < szFilters + dim( szFilters ) );
*pszPtr = 0;
trace( _T( "Filter length = %d\n" ), pszPtr - szFilters );
return szFilters;
}
```

```
PRIVATE bool getOpenOrSaveFileName(
   HWND hwndParent, UINT uiTitleString, LPOFNHOOKPROC fnHook,
   LPTSTR pszFileName, UINT cb,
   UINT uiChildDlg, DWORD dwFlags, bool bSave )
{
   assert( isGoodStringPtr( pszFileName ) );

   int nFilterIndex = getFilterIndex();
   if ( nFilterIndex < 0 ) {
      nFilterIndex = 1;
   }
   String strCustomFilter = getCustomFilter();
   TCHAR szCustomFilter[ MAX_PATH ] = { 0 };
   if ( !strCustomFilter.empty() ) {
      LPTSTR pszPtr = szCustomFilter;
      const String strFmt = loadString( IDS_CUSTOM );
      wsprintf( pszPtr, strFmt.c_str(), strCustomFilter.c_str() );
      pszPtr += _tcsclen( pszPtr ) + 1;
      _tcscpy( pszPtr, strCustomFilter.c_str() );
   }

   const String strTitle = loadString( uiTitleString );
   OPENFILENAME openFileName = {
      sizeof( OPENFILENAME ), hwndParent,
      getModuleHandle(), getFilterList(),
      szCustomFilter, dim( szCustomFilter ), nFilterIndex,
      pszFileName, cb, 0, 0, 0, strTitle.c_str(),
      OFN_EXPLORER | OFN_ENABLETEMPLATE | OFN_HIDEREADONLY,
      0, 0, getDefaultExtension() + 1, // Don't want dot...
      0, fnHook, MAKEINTRESOURCE( uiChildDlg ),
   };
   openFileName.Flags |= dwFlags;
   if ( 0 != fnHook ) {
      openFileName.Flags |= OFN_ENABLEHOOK;
   }
#if defined( _DEBUG ) && defined( OFN_ENABLESIZING )
   openFileName.Flags |= OFN_ENABLESIZING;
#endif
```

```
   if ( HWND_DESKTOP != hwndParent ) {
      FORWARD_WM_COMMAND(
         hwndParent, ID_COMMAND_RESETSTATUSBAR, 0, 0, SNDMSG );
   }

   const BOOL bOK = bSave ? GetSaveFileName( &openFileName )
                          : GetOpenFileName( &openFileName );
   if ( bOK ) {
      LPTSTR pszNewCustomFilter =
         szCustomFilter + _tcsclen( szCustomFilter ) + 1;
      if ( 0 != *pszNewCustomFilter ) {
         openFileName.nFilterIndex = 0;
         LPCTSTR pszPtr = getFilterList();
         for ( int iFilter = 0; ; ++iFilter ) {
            pszPtr += _tcsclen( pszPtr ) + 1;
            if ( 0 == *pszPtr ) {
               break; //*** LOOP EXIT POINT
            }
            if ( 0 == _tcsicmp( pszNewCustomFilter, pszPtr ) ) {
               openFileName.nFilterIndex = iFilter + 1;
               *pszNewCustomFilter = 0;
               break; //*** LOOP EXIT POINT
            }
            pszPtr += _tcsclen( pszPtr ) + 1;
         }
      }
      setFilterIndex( openFileName.nFilterIndex );
      setCustomFilter( pszNewCustomFilter );
   } else {

      // Debugging tip:
      // This illustrates one way of forcing an exception:
#if 0
      const DWORD dwErr = CDERR_FINDRESFAILURE;
#else
      const DWORD dwErr = CommDlgExtendedError();
#endif
```

```
      if ( ERROR_SUCCESS == dwErr ) {
         ; // The user hit cancel; OK.
      } else {
         throw CommonDialogException( dwErr );
      }
   }

   return 0 != bOK;
}

bool getOpenFileName( HWND hwndParent, UINT uiTitleString,
   LPOFNHOOKPROC fnHook, LPTSTR pszFileName, UINT cb,
   UINT uiChildDlg, DWORD dwFlags )
{
   return getOpenOrSaveFileName( hwndParent, uiTitleString,
      fnHook, pszFileName, cb, uiChildDlg, dwFlags, false );
}

bool getSaveFileName(  HWND hwndParent, UINT uiTitleString,
   LPOFNHOOKPROC fnHook, LPTSTR pszFileName, UINT cb,
   UINT uiChildDlg, DWORD dwFlags )
{
   return getOpenOrSaveFileName( hwndParent, uiTitleString,
      fnHook, pszFileName, cb, uiChildDlg, dwFlags, true );
}
```

The Preview Window

Showing the preview window in the dialog of Figure 14.4 is simplicity itself. I set the `lpTemplateName` member of `OPENFILENAME` to `IDD_PREVIEW_CHILD` and the `hInstance` member to TextEdit's module handle, and voila! I have a preview window.

Looks aren't everything, though. A preview window without a preview is useless; the preview window needs to know what is happening elsewhere in the dialog.

To begin with, I customize the behavior of the dialog by pointing `lpfnHook` to `openFileHookProc`. This lets the common dialog send `WM_NOTIFY` messages to notify TextEdit of various happenings, with codes such as `CDN_INITDONE`, `CDN_FILEOK`, `CDN_SELCHANGE`, `CDN_FOLDERCHANGE`, and `CDN_TYPECHANGE`. The latter three indicate that the selected file may have changed; they result in a call to the `updatePreview` function. (Not directly, mind you; I start a timer that, when it fires, calls `updatePreview`. This is to avoid repeated updates of the preview window when the user is using the arrow keys to zoom through a list of files.)

To get the currently selected file, the `updatePreview` function sends a `CDM_GETFILEPATH` message to the Open dialog. If the file is a link, this message returns the unresolved link name rather than the file the link references, so `updatePreview` must call `resolveName`. If I have a valid file name at this point, I display the head of the file and update the little icon in the upper right corner; if not, the variable `s_bValid` is set to false. This variable is checked in the `WM_CTLCOLORSTATIC` handler, so that the preview window gets a gray background when the file name is invalid.

One thing is missing from this picture: the hook function is notified only when the file name changes as a result of selection in the list of files; it is not notified when the file name changes as a result of typing in the file name field. To catch those `EN_*` notifications, it is necessary to subclass the Open dialog itself.

It is possible that the hook function was meant to be a sufficient vehicle for customizing the dialog's behavior. It doesn't quite make the grade.

Listing 14.6 openFile.cpp

```
/*
 * $Header: /Book/openFile.cpp 19    3.07.99 17:46 Petter $
 *
 * This module handles the "Open File" dialog box.
 * Would it be appropriate to reset file time stamps after preview?
 */

#include "precomp.h"
#include "openFile.h"
#include "os.h"
#include "trace.h"
#include "Exception.h"
#include "AutoArray.h"
#include "AutoHandle.h"
#include "InstanceSubclasser.h"
#include "openDlgCommon.h"
#include "resolveName.h"
#include "winUtils.h"
#include "utils.h"
#include "persistence.h"
#include "resource.h"

PRIVATE bool s_bValid = false;
PRIVATE bool s_bReadOnly = false;
PRIVATE bool s_bNewWindow = false;

// LATER: Really ought to fix Unix line feeds in preview.
PRIVATE void showPreview( HANDLE hIn, HWND hwndPreview ) {
```

```
        CHAR szContents[ 4096 ] = { 0 };
        DWORD dwBytesRead = 0;
        const BOOL bOK = ReadFile( hIn, szContents,
            sizeof szContents - sizeof( WCHAR ), &dwBytesRead, 0 );
        if ( bOK ) {
            assert( dwBytesRead < sizeof szContents - 1 );
            if ( isTextUnicode( szContents, dwBytesRead, 0 ) ) {
                // NOTE: isTextUnicode always returns false under Win95.
                assert( isWindowsNT() );
                LPWSTR pszwContents =
                    reinterpret_cast< LPWSTR >( szContents );
                pszwContents[ dwBytesRead / sizeof( WCHAR ) ] = 0;
                SetWindowTextW( hwndPreview, pszwContents );
            } else {
                szContents[ dwBytesRead ] = 0;
                SetWindowTextA( hwndPreview, szContents );
            }
        }
    }

    PRIVATE void updatePreview( HWND hwndOpenDlg, HWND hwndPreview ) {

        trace( _T( "updatePreview\n" ) );

        assert( IsWindow( hwndOpenDlg ) );
        assert( IsWindow( hwndPreview ) );

        SetWindowText( hwndPreview, _T( "" ) );
        PATHNAME szFile = { 0 };
        s_bValid = false;
        const LRESULT lResult = SNDMSG(
            hwndOpenDlg, CDM_GETFILEPATH, dim( szFile ), (LPARAM) szFile );
        HICON hicon = 0;
        if ( 0 < lResult ) {
            const bool isShortcut = resolveName( szFile, szFile );
            AutoHandle hIn( CreateFile( szFile, GENERIC_READ,
                FILE_SHARE_READ | FILE_SHARE_WRITE,
                0, OPEN_EXISTING, 0, 0 ) );
```

```
      s_bValid = INVALID_HANDLE_VALUE != hIn;
      if ( s_bValid ) {
         showPreview( hIn, hwndPreview );

         BY_HANDLE_FILE_INFORMATION bhFileInfo = { 0 };
         s_bReadOnly =
            !GetFileInformationByHandle( hIn, &bhFileInfo ) ||
            ( bhFileInfo.dwFileAttributes & FILE_ATTRIBUTE_READONLY );

         SHFILEINFO fileInfo = { 0 };
         UINT uiFlags = SHGFI_ICON | SHGFI_SMALLICON;
         if ( isShortcut ) {
            uiFlags |= SHGFI_LINKOVERLAY;
         }
         SHGetFileInfo( szFile, 0,
            &fileInfo, sizeof fileInfo, uiFlags );
         hicon = fileInfo.hIcon;
      }
   }

   HWND hwndIcon =
      GetDlgItem( GetParent( hwndPreview ), IDC_FILEICON );
   Static_SetIcon( hwndIcon, hicon );
}

PRIVATE const UINT uiPreviewTimer = 1;

PRIVATE void setPreviewTimer( HWND hwndSubDlg ) {

   assert( IsWindow( hwndSubDlg ) );

   int nDelay = 0;
   SystemParametersInfo( SPI_GETKEYBOARDDELAY, 0, &nDelay, 0 );
   assert( 0 <= nDelay && nDelay <= 3 );
   nDelay &= 0x3;
   const int nPreviewTimeout = 250 * (1 + nDelay) + 100;
   SetTimer( hwndSubDlg, uiPreviewTimer, nPreviewTimeout, 0 );
}
```

```
PRIVATE LRESULT CALLBACK OpenDlgSubclassWndProc(
   HWND hwnd, UINT msg, WPARAM wParam, LPARAM lParam );
PRIVATE LRESULT CALLBACK PreviewSubclassWndProc(
   HWND hwnd, UINT msg, WPARAM wParam, LPARAM lParam );

PRIVATE InstanceSubclasser s_openDlgSub( OpenDlgSubclassWndProc );
PRIVATE InstanceSubclasser s_previewSub( PreviewSubclassWndProc );

/**
 * This is used to subclass the preview edit in order to catch
 * the enter key. Default buttons and subdialogs don't mesh well.
 */
PRIVATE LRESULT CALLBACK PreviewSubclassWndProc(
   HWND hwnd, UINT msg, WPARAM wParam, LPARAM lParam )
{
   const LRESULT lResult =
      s_previewSub.callOldProc( hwnd, msg, wParam, lParam );
   if ( WM_KEYDOWN == msg && VK_RETURN == wParam ) {
      HWND hwndOpenDlg =
         s_previewSub.getUserDataAsHwnd( hwnd );
      assert( hwndOpenDlg == GetParent( GetParent( hwnd ) ) );
      FORWARD_WM_COMMAND( hwndOpenDlg,
         IDOK, 0, BN_CLICKED, PostMessage );
   }
   return lResult;
}


/**
 * This is used to subclass the common open dialog in order to
 * catch notifications from the file name edit control.
 * When it changes, we want a chance to update the preview.
 */
PRIVATE LRESULT CALLBACK OpenDlgSubclassWndProc(
   HWND hwnd, UINT msg, WPARAM wParam, LPARAM lParam )
{
   const LRESULT lResult =
      s_openDlgSub.callOldProc( hwnd, msg, wParam, lParam );
   if ( WM_COMMAND == msg                                 &&
      edt1       == GET_WM_COMMAND_ID ( wParam, lParam ) &&
```

```
            EN_CHANGE == GET_WM_COMMAND_CMD( wParam, lParam ) )
      {
         trace( _T( "EN_CHANGE\n" ) );
         HWND hwndSubDlg = s_openDlgSub.getUserDataAsHwnd( hwnd );
         assert( IsWindow( hwndSubDlg ) );
         setPreviewTimer( hwndSubDlg );
      }
      return lResult;
}

PRIVATE void positionPreview( HWND hwndChildDlg ) {

   HWND hwndOpenDlg = GetParent( hwndChildDlg );
   assert( IsWindow( hwndOpenDlg ) );
   assert( IsWindow( hwndChildDlg ) );

   HWND hwndPreview = GetDlgItem( hwndChildDlg, IDC_PREVIEW );
   assert( IsWindow( hwndChildDlg ) );

   HWND hwndNewWindow = GetDlgItem( hwndChildDlg, IDC_NEW_WINDOW );
   assert( IsWindow( hwndNewWindow ) );

   HWND hwndCancel = GetDlgItem( hwndOpenDlg, IDCANCEL );
   assert( IsWindow( hwndCancel ) );

   const Rect rcCancel = getWindowRectInParent( hwndCancel );
   Rect rcNewWindow = getWindowRectInParent( hwndNewWindow );
   const int nDelta = rcCancel.bottom - rcNewWindow.bottom;
   OffsetRect( &rcNewWindow, 0, nDelta );
   moveWindow( hwndNewWindow, &rcNewWindow );

   Rect rcPreview = getWindowRectInParent( hwndPreview );
   rcPreview.bottom = rcNewWindow.top - 4;
   moveWindow( hwndPreview, &rcPreview );

   HWND hwndIcon = GetDlgItem( hwndChildDlg, IDC_FILEICON );
   const int cx = GetSystemMetrics( SM_CXSMICON );
   const int cy = GetSystemMetrics( SM_CYSMICON );
   rcPreview.left = rcPreview.right - cx;
   rcPreview.bottom = rcPreview.top - 2;
```

```
      rcPreview.top -= cy + 2;
      moveWindow( hwndIcon, &rcPreview );
   }


PRIVATE inline HBRUSH ofnHook_OnCtlColor(
   HWND hwnd, HDC hdc, HWND hwndChild, int type )
{
   if ( GetDlgItem( hwnd, IDC_PREVIEW ) == hwndChild ) {
      const bool bNormal = s_bValid && !s_bReadOnly;
      SetTextColor( hdc, GetSysColor( COLOR_WINDOWTEXT ) );
      SetBkColor( hdc, GetSysColor(
         bNormal ? COLOR_WINDOW : COLOR_3DFACE ) );
      return
         GetSysColorBrush( bNormal ? COLOR_WINDOW : COLOR_3DFACE );
   }
   return 0;
}


PRIVATE inline void ofnHook_OnTimer( HWND hwnd, UINT id ) {
   trace( _T( "WM_TIMER %d\n" ), id );
   KillTimer( hwnd, id );
   HWND hwndPreview = GetDlgItem( hwnd, IDC_PREVIEW );
   assert( IsWindow( hwndPreview ) );
   updatePreview( GetParent( hwnd ), hwndPreview );
}


PRIVATE inline void onInitDone( HWND hwndChildDlg ) {

   subclassOpenDlgCommon( hwndChildDlg, IDD_PREVIEW_CHILD );
   positionPreview( hwndChildDlg );

   // If these subclassings fail, we can live with the consequences:
   try {
      HWND hwndOpenDlg = GetParent( hwndChildDlg );
      HWND hwndPreview = GetDlgItem( hwndChildDlg, IDC_PREVIEW );
      verify( s_openDlgSub.subclass(
         hwndOpenDlg, hwndChildDlg ) );
      verify( s_previewSub.subclass(
         hwndPreview, hwndOpenDlg ) );
   }
```

```
      catch ( const SubclassException& x ) {
         trace( _T( "%s\n" ), x.what() );
      }

      if ( !s_bNewWindow ) {
         HWND hwndNewWindow = GetDlgItem( hwndChildDlg, IDC_NEW_WINDOW );
         assert( IsWindow( hwndNewWindow ) );
         Button_SetCheck( hwndNewWindow, true );
         EnableWindow( hwndNewWindow, false );
      }
}

PRIVATE inline LRESULT ofnHook_OnNotify(
   HWND hwnd, int id, LPNMHDR pNMHDR )
{
   //const OFNOTIFY *pofn = reinterpret_cast< OFNOTIFY * >( lParam );
   assert( 0 != pNMHDR );
   trace( _T( "notify %d %d\n" ), pNMHDR->idFrom, pNMHDR->code );

   switch ( pNMHDR->code ) {

   case CDN_INITDONE:
      onInitDone( hwnd );
      break;

   case CDN_FILEOK:
      s_bNewWindow = 0 != Button_GetCheck(
         GetDlgItem( hwnd, IDC_NEW_WINDOW ) );
      //*** FALL THROUGH

   case CDN_SELCHANGE:
   case CDN_FOLDERCHANGE:
   case CDN_TYPECHANGE:
      trace( _T( "starting timer\n" ) );
      setPreviewTimer( hwnd );
      break;

   default:
      break;
   }
```

```
      return 0;
}

PRIVATE inline void ofnHook_OnCommand(
   HWND hwnd, int id, HWND hwndCtl, UINT codeNotify )
{
   if ( ( IDOK == id || IDCANCEL == id ) &&
        BN_CLICKED == codeNotify )
   {
      FORWARD_WM_COMMAND(
         GetParent( hwnd ), id, hwndCtl, codeNotify, PostMessage );
   }
}

PRIVATE UINT CALLBACK openFileHookProc(
   HWND hwndSubDlg, UINT msg, WPARAM wParam, LPARAM lParam )
{
   switch ( msg ) {
   HANDLE_MSG( hwndSubDlg, WM_CTLCOLORSTATIC, ofnHook_OnCtlColor );
   HANDLE_MSG( hwndSubDlg, WM_TIMER         , ofnHook_OnTimer    );
   HANDLE_MSG( hwndSubDlg, WM_NOTIFY        , ofnHook_OnNotify   );
   HANDLE_MSG( hwndSubDlg, WM_COMMAND       , ofnHook_OnCommand  );
   }

   return FALSE;
}

bool openFile(
   const HWND hwndParent, LPTSTR pszName, int cb,
   bool *pbNewWindow,
   bool bMustExist )
   throw( CommonDialogException )
{
   s_bNewWindow = false;
   if ( 0 != pbNewWindow ) {
      assert( isGoodPtr( pbNewWindow ) );
      s_bNewWindow = *pbNewWindow;
   }
```

```
    const bool bOK = getOpenFileName(
        hwndParent,
        bMustExist ? IDS_OPENFILE : IDS_OPENORCREATEFILE,
        openFileHookProc, pszName, cb, IDD_PREVIEW_CHILD,
        bMustExist ? OFN_FILEMUSTEXIST : 0 );
    if ( 0 != pbNewWindow && *pbNewWindow ) {
        *pbNewWindow = s_bNewWindow;
    }
    return bOK;
}
```

Chapter 15

Search and Replace

Windows offers a common dialog for straight searching and for search and replace. I have a strong dislike for this dialog. I dislike the modelessness of it, I dislike the simple edit field for the search string, and I dislike the dim-witted way it paints a default border on a disabled button (see Figure 15.1). Above all, I dislike the API, which is an invitation to spread related functionality around all the dark corners of a program.

Figure 15.1   The common Find dialog. Note the disabled default button, and cringe.

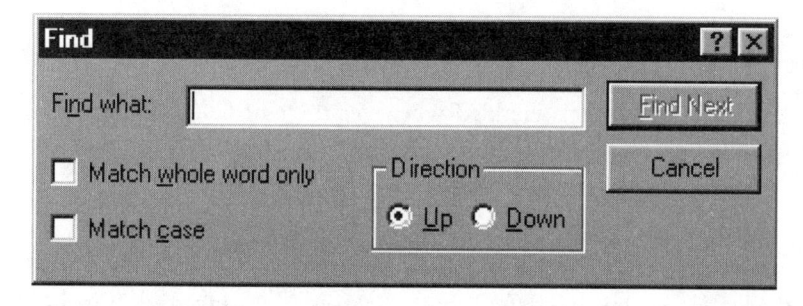

Given such strong feelings, you won't be surprised when I tell you that TextEdit doesn't use the common dialog for search and replace. You can see TextEdit's Find dialog, implemented by the class `FindDlg`, in Figure 15.2. It looks quite similar to the common dialog, but there are differences more than skin deep.

Figure 15.2 The TextEdit Find dialog. Although the presence of the drop-down list is the most obvious difference from the previous dialog, some of the less obvious differences are much more important.

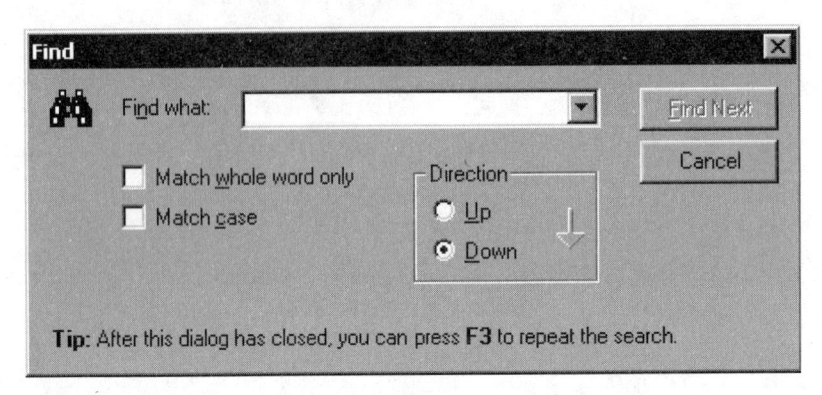

`FindDlg` **is modal.** A modal dialog can only search for one string, whereas a modeless dialog can repeat a search any number of times before you close the dialog. To overcome this limitation, TextEdit has a Find Next command that repeats the last search. To make the existence of this command obvious, it is mentioned rather prominently on the face of the dialog.

`FindDlg` **has a drop-down list associated with the edit field.** The list remembers previous search strings, so that the user can just pick them from the list. `FindDlg` has even enlisted the help of the Windows registry, to preserve these strings across TextEdit sessions (as well as across coexisting TextEdit instances).

`FindDlg` **handles enabling and disabling of the default button carefully.** No dim-wittedness here! The presence of the drop-down list calls for extra care in the handling of defaultness; I'll get back to that shortly.

`FindDlg` **has a simple API and takes care of almost all housekeeping itself.** This is partly a benefit of its modality, of course, which does tend to simplify things.

Default Button Handling

The default button, labeled Find Next, is enabled whenever the edit field contains text and disabled whenever the edit field is empty. The `enableOK` method in `FindDlg` takes care of enabling and disabling it. At the same time, it sets or removes the default border around the button, an important detail that the common Find dialog — and innumerable other dialogs — ignore.

There is one additional complication: what if the drop-down list is open? If the user hits return at this point, the list closes, but the default button action is not invoked. It is, in other words, unacceptable for the Find Next button to have a default border while the drop-down list is showing, no matter how many characters are in the text field.

One solution to this user interface glitch would be to catch the Enter key and actually invoke the default button immediately after closing the drop-down list. I discarded this solution for two reasons: in the first place, the implementation is more convoluted than you might think at first glance — handling `CNB_CLOSEUP` is not enough. (Can you see why?) In the second place, most drop-down lists don't behave like that (although some do), so it would have introduced a quite unnecessary user interface inconsistency.

Actually implementing this functionality was more of a puzzle than I had expected, chiefly because the combobox notifications are peculiar. The `CBN_DROPDOWN` notification is sent before the list opens, while its opposite number, the `CBN_CLOSEUP` notification, is sent after the list has closed. In other words, the list is always closed at notification time. This precludes an elegant, common solution for all cases, in which I wouldn't care whether the message was `CBN_DROPDOWN` or `CBN_CLOSEUP`. Instead, I would just ask the combobox by sending it the `CB_GETDROPPEDSTATE` message (using the `ComboBox_GetDroppedState` macro from `windowsx.h`).

At this point, it occurred to me that this problem is not specific to `FindDlg`, but completely general. I removed all this code from `FindDlg`, and instead used global subclassing (as described in Chapter 4) to subclass the dialog window class. The result is in `dlgSubclasser.cpp`, and has a couple of interesting properties:

- No header file is associated with this file; it has, in a manner of speaking, no interface. The mere existence of the `dlgSubclasser` static variable is enough to initialize the subclassing.
- The subclassing works on all dialogs within TextEdit, including "system" dialogs such as Printer Properties.

Listing 15.1 dlgSubclasser.cpp

```cpp
/*
 * $Header: /Book/dlgSubclasser.cpp 13    3.07.99 17:46 Petter $
 *
 * Subclassing of dialogs to handle default button
 * "defaultness" on combo box drop-down.
 * No include file required; static initialization does it all.
 */

#include "precomp.h"
#include "winUtils.h"
#include "GlobalSubclasser.h"

PRIVATE LRESULT CALLBACK
    dlgSubclassWndProc( HWND, UINT, WPARAM, LPARAM );

PRIVATE GlobalSubclasser
    dlgSubclasser( WC_DIALOG, dlgSubclassWndProc );

inline bool isCombo( HWND hwnd ) {
    TCHAR szClassName[ 100 ] = { 0 };
```

```
      GetClassName( hwnd, szClassName, dim( szClassName ) );
   return 0 == _tcsicmp( szClassName, _T( "ComboBox" ) ) ||
          0 == _tcsicmp( szClassName, WC_COMBOBOXEX      ) ;
}

PRIVATE inline void onCommand(
   HWND hwnd, int id, HWND hwndCtl, UINT codeNotify )
{
   if ( CBN_DROPDOWN == codeNotify || CBN_CLOSEUP == codeNotify ) {
      if ( isCombo( hwndCtl ) ) {
         HWND hwndDefault = getDefaultButton( hwnd );
         if ( IsWindow( hwndDefault ) ) {
            if ( CBN_DROPDOWN == codeNotify ) {
               setButtonStyle( hwndDefault, BS_PUSHBUTTON );
            } else if ( IsWindowEnabled( hwndDefault ) ) {
               setButtonStyle( hwndDefault, BS_DEFPUSHBUTTON );
            }
         }
      }
   }
}

PRIVATE inline LRESULT internal_dlgSubclassWndProc(
   HWND hwnd, UINT msg, WPARAM wParam, LPARAM lParam )
{
   switch ( msg ) {
   HANDLE_MSG( hwnd, WM_COMMAND, onCommand );
   }
   return 0;
}

PRIVATE LRESULT CALLBACK dlgSubclassWndProc(
   HWND hwnd, UINT msg, WPARAM wParam, LPARAM lParam )
{
   const LRESULT lResult =
      dlgSubclasser.callOldProc( hwnd, msg, wParam, lParam );
   internal_dlgSubclassWndProc( hwnd, msg, wParam, lParam );
   return lResult;
}
```

Initializing the Dialog

But I digress. Let's get back to `FindDlg`. What, if anything, should appear in the "Find what" field when the dialog appears? TextEdit's functionality in this area is patterned on Visual C++. Perhaps I feel this is "right" merely because I'm used to it, but I don't really think so. I'm equally used to Microsoft Word, but find its search and replace feature cumbersome compared with that of Visual C++.

If any text is selected when the user requests the search dialog, the selection is used as the initial search string. If no text is selected, the current word is used. If the caret is on white space, the previous search string is used, if any. If this is the first search ever, the "Find what" field comes up empty.

If the selection spans multiple lines, the selection is truncated at the first line boundary. It's not that I have anything against line boundaries; they just don't go too well with single-line edit boxes.

Another aspect of dialog initialization is often overlooked — its position. It's not very nice if the dialog, when it appears, covers up the selected text, for example. For that reason, `FindDlg` has a member function called `positionOutsideSelection` that positions the dialog so as not to cover the selection. This is important for dialogs whose functionality applies to the text itself. It is of no interest to, for example, the File Open dialog, which deals with files rather than their contents.

As for all other dialogs, `Dialog::dispatchDlgMsg` takes care of the initial placement, including the remembered position. When `FindDlg::onInitDialog` takes over, it uses the `positionOutsideSelection` method to do final adjustments. If the dialog doesn't overlap the selected text, fine, I'm done. In this context, there is always "selected text," because if there isn't any, I simply want to avoid the caret position. If the dialog obscures the caret or the selection, the method tries to move the dialog down below the selection. If there isn't enough room on the screen, it tries to move up instead. If that doesn't work either, it moves in the direction that obscures the least amount of selection, making sure that the whole dialog is inside the screen.

Persistence

`FindDlg` has a memory. We've already seen how it remembers its position; it also remembers the ten most recently used search strings, the status of the "Match whole word only" and "Match case" checkboxes, and the search direction (up or down).

The list of recently used search strings is read from the registry by the `loadStrings` method and saved to the registry by the `saveStrings` method. This "historical combobox" has a close kinship with the list of recently used files discussed in Chapter 10, but is actually simpler in its implementation. How so? In addition to being a GUI component, a drop-down list box (or any list box, for that matter) can also be thought of as part of your data structure. Not only can you put strings into it; you can get them out again as well. Here's another design principle:

"Don't duplicate data storage."

If your program maintains a list of strings, and a list box maintains a putatively identical list of strings, it is, for one thing, wasteful. (This not an issue in our case, but sometimes it is.) More important than waste is that dual storage affords inconsistencies an opportunity to creep in. If you make a habit out of violating this principle, it will turn around and bite you, sooner rather than later.

The historical combobox is simpler than the MRU file list simply because I do not duplicate data storage. The drop-down list, in its role as a respected member of the TextEdit data structure, takes care of the strings for us.

One final detail, while I'm on the subject of comboboxes: the CB_FINDSTRINGEXACT message, which checks the strings in the drop-down list to find, if possible, an exact match, is not case-sensitive. I built the function findStringExact on top of CB_FINDSTRINGEXACT (or rather, on top of the ComboBox_FindStringExact macro) to get case sensitivity.

Text Not Found

When Notepad fails to find the text you're searching for, it displays a message box, as depicted in Figure 15.3. Notepad is in good company using a message box for this; others include Word for Windows (Figure 15.4) and Visual C++ (Figure 15.5).

Figure 15.3   Notepad didn't find "Glory Hallelujah!"

Figure 15.4   Microsoft Word fails to find "Glory Hallelujah!" The message box doesn't tell you *what* Word failed to find.

These message boxes are perfect examples of what Alan Cooper terms "excise" — user interface elements that contribute nothing towards fulfilling the user's goals. If a message box were the only way the program could possibly communicate the failure of the search, we would have to accept this excise as necessary. It isn't, though. TextEdit displays the information in the search dialog itself, as depicted in Figure 15.6.

Figure 15.5 Visual C++ fares no better.

Figure 15.6 Glory be! TextEdit can't find "Glory Hallelujah!" either.

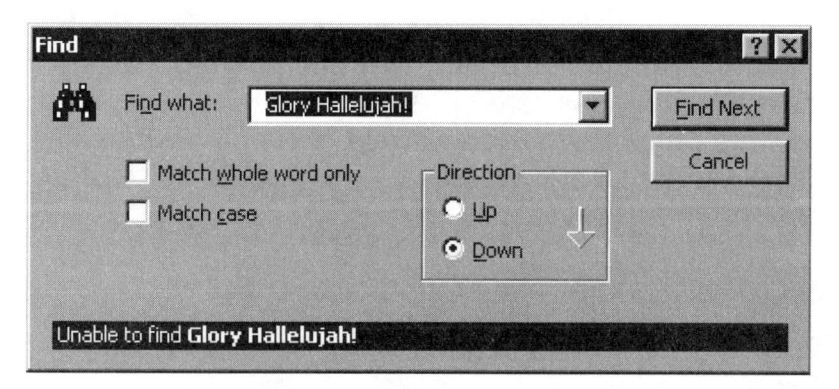

This little trick saves the user one action — keystroke or mouse click — every time some text is not found. Over the course of a long lifetime, this sort of thing adds up.

The Relationship between Dialog and Main Window

In a world of perfect software design, there would be almost no coupling between the Find dialog and the main window. The main window would need the ability to invoke the Find dialog, of course, as well as some means of getting back a search string (or a cancellation), but the Find dialog would live, perfectly encapsulated, off in its own fenced-off little universe, with no knowledge of the outside world.

This kind of thing is nice for programmers, but usually less so for end users. Therefore, there is considerable interaction between the Find dialog and the main window. The dialog must talk to the main edit widget if it wants to avoid obscuring the selected text, and it must also be able to execute a search while the dialog is still open, so that a failed search can be reported without closing the dialog. (This is why `FindDlg` has a pointer to the `Editor` object.)

Replacing Text

`FindDlg` handles both search and replace. These functions use different dialog templates, but the same dialog function. To differentiate between the two modes, `FindDlg` has a flag named `m_isReplace`.

I decided to use the same dialog function for these two dialogs on the assumption that there was considerable functional overlap. While this is true, it may still have been a mistake; the Replace dialog is much more complex than the Find dialog, particularly in terms of user interaction. The code in `FindDlg.cpp` is littered with `if ( m_isReplace )` conditionals, and this is unfortunate.

The Visual C++ Replace Dialog

Before I describe the TextEdit Replace dialog, I'd like to discuss its counterpart in Visual C++. I investigated this dialog quite thoroughly in preparation for my own design and was left with a surreal feeling of having visited a Salvador Dali landscape, where the normal laws of logic don't apply.

Figure 15.7 The Visual C++ Replace dialog without "iString" selected in the text window. Because "iString" is not selected, Find Next is the default. No replacement is even possible and if you click on Replace, it will do a Find Next, in spite of its label.

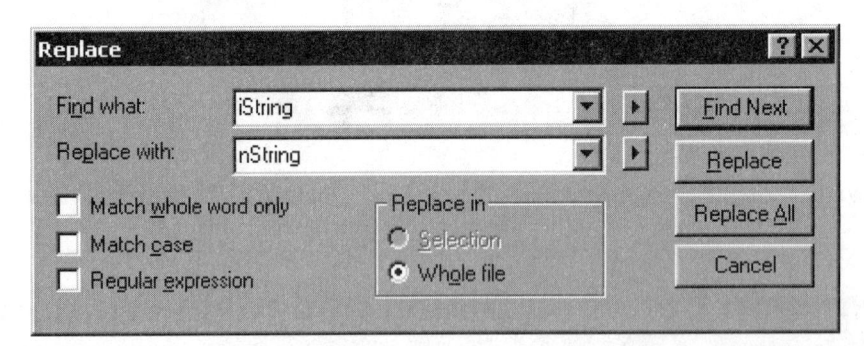

Figure 15.7 shows the VC++ Replace dialog in action. At this point, the Find Next button is the default button and no text is selected in the editor. If I hit return, the first occurrence of "iString" will be selected in the editor, and the Replace button becomes the default button, as depicted in Figure 15.8.

So far, so good. But consider — no replacement is ever performed unless text matching the "Find what" field is selected in the editor. Nevertheless, the Replace button was enabled back in Figure 15.7, where no text was selected in the editor. What, then, does the Replace button do when it doesn't replace anything? Answer: it is equivalent to the Find Next button! True, the Replace button has an implicit Find Next built into it when it actually performs a replacement, but I balk at clicking Replace to perform Find Next, and nothing else.

Even stranger, if I delete the text in the Find what field, all three buttons (Find Next, Replace, and Replace All) remain enabled. I can't for the life of me figure out what meaningful actions the buttons could possibly perform, and, as it turns out, none of them do anything whatsoever.

Figure 15.8 The Visual C++ Replace dialog with "iString" selected in the text window. The Replace button is now the default.

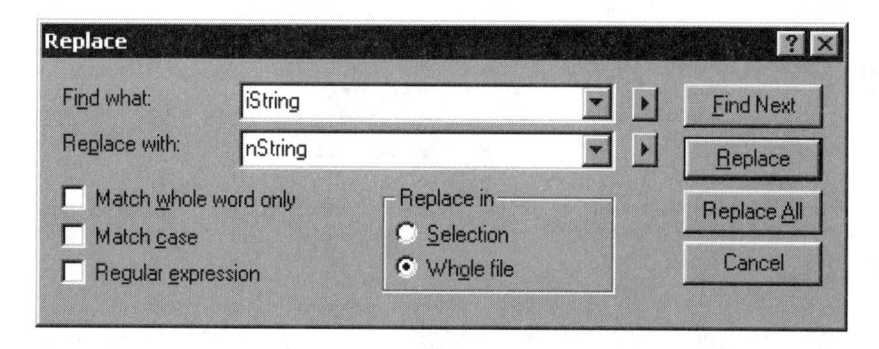

This contrasts with the VC++ Find dialog, where the Find Next button is disabled when I delete the text in the Find what field. Here, on the other hand, the Find Next button retains its default looks even when disabled, exactly as Notepad's corresponding button did in Figure 15.1.

It's a common convention to change the text of a dialog's Cancel button to "Close" whenever a change has been made that can't be reversed from within the dialog. (There are those, including Alan Cooper, that maintain that this is Bad. I have mislaid my guru's license and decline to comment.) The VC++ Replace dialog changes the button caption to "Close" after performing a replacement, which is reasonable. It also changes the button caption to "Close" after performing a search, even though the text is unchanged! What were they thinking?

All that said, I must nevertheless admit that I've never had difficulties with the VC++ Replace dialog. In spite of having used it for years, I didn't consciously notice its surreal aspects until I started work on TextEdit. Still, because the VC++ user interface is so superb in general, it saddens me all the more that the designers didn't take the necessary thought and time to get these details right.

The TextEdit Replace Dialog

The TextEdit Replace dialog is shown in Figure 15.9. It bears a passing resemblance to the C++ Replace dialog; in particular, all the push buttons are identical.

In Figure 15.9, the text "Pocket" is not selected in the editor. Thus, no replacement is possible, and the Replace button is disabled.

Figure 15.9 The TextEdit Replace dialog without "Pocket" selected in the edit widget. In contrast to the Visual C++ dialog in Figure 15.7, the Replace button is disabled.

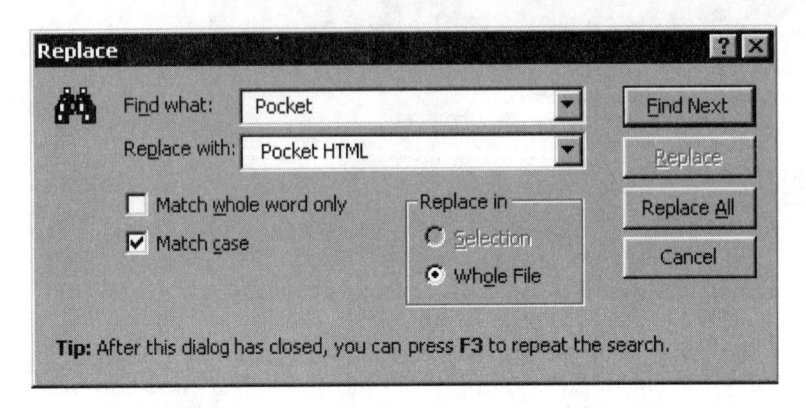

In Figure 15.10, the user has hit Find Next and the text "Pocket" has been selected in the editor. The Replace button has been enabled and it has become the default button as well. The TextEdit Replace button, by the way, has an implicit Find Next built into it, just like Visual C++. Because we now have a selection, the "Replace in Selection" radio button has been enabled.

Figure 15.10 The TextEdit Replace dialog with "Pocket" selected in the edit widget. Its behavior now equals that of the Visual C++ dialog in Figure 15.8.

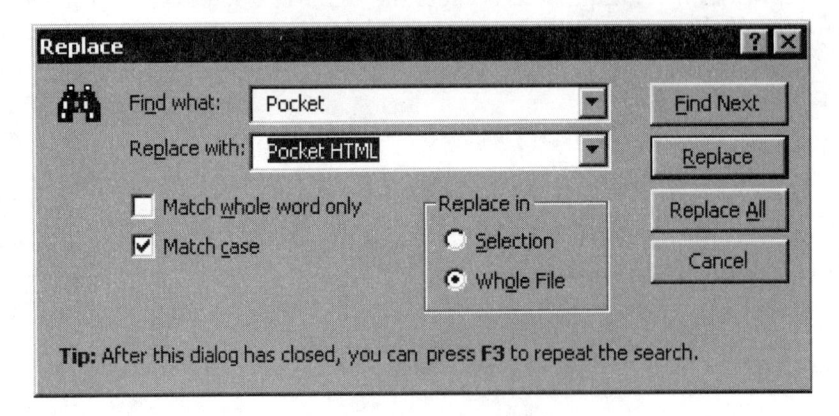

In Figure 15.11, the user has checked "Replace in Selection." In this case, Replace All is the only available action.

Figure 15.11 The TextEdit Replace dialog with "Replace in Selection" selected. Replace All is the only possible action.

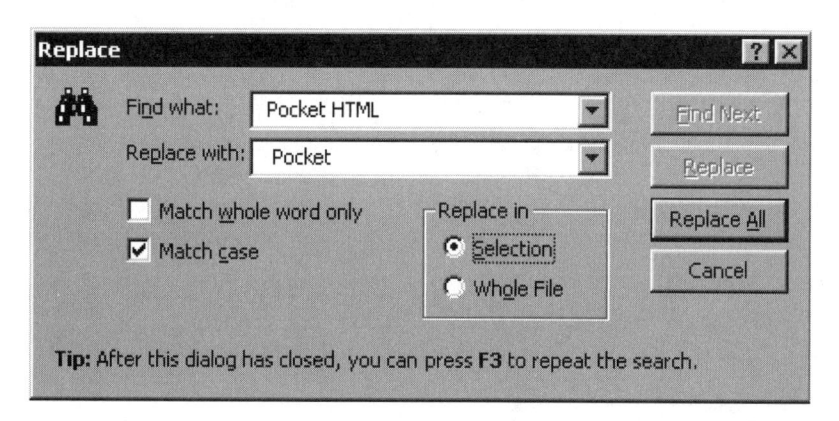

User interaction with the Replace dialog is considerably more complicated than the interaction with the plain Find dialog. In particular, check out the `adjustButtons` method in FindDlg.cpp; it does considerably more work when the `m_isReplace` flag is set.

Listing 15.2 FindDlg.cpp

```
/*
 * $Header: /Book/FindDlg.cpp 17     20.08.99 16:33 Petter $
 *
 * LATER: Real MRU for search strings; include strings
 * searched by Ctrl+F3 also.
 * TODO: Problem with typing when drop-down is open!
 */

#include "precomp.h"
#include "FindDlg.h"
#include "InstanceSubclasser.h"
#include "HTML.h"
#include "resource.h"
#include "formatMessage.h"
#include "winUtils.h"
#include "persistence.h"
#include "utils.h"

PRIVATE inline int findStringExact(
    HWND hwndCombo, const String& strSearch )
```

```
{
   return findStringExact( hwndCombo, strSearch.c_str() );
}

String FindDlg::getComboContents( HWND hwndCtl, bool bSelChange ) {

   assert( isGoodPtr( this ) );
   assert( IsWindow( hwndCtl ) ); // isCombo too?

   const int nSelection = ComboBox_GetCurSel( hwndCtl );
   TCHAR szContents[ MAX_TEXT_LENGTH + 1 ] = { 0 };

   if ( bSelChange && CB_ERR != nSelection ) {
      assert( ComboBox_GetLBTextLen(
         hwndCtl, nSelection ) < dim( szContents ) );
      ComboBox_GetLBText( hwndCtl, nSelection, szContents );
   } else {
      assert( ComboBox_GetTextLength( hwndCtl ) < dim( szContents ) );
      ComboBox_GetText( hwndCtl, szContents, dim( szContents ) );
   }

   return szContents;
}

String FindDlg::getComboContentsAndSetSelection( HWND hwndCtl ) {

   assert( isGoodPtr( this ) );
   assert( IsWindow( hwndCtl ) );

   String strContents;
   if ( 0 < ComboBox_GetCount( hwndCtl ) ) {
      ComboBox_SetCurSel( hwndCtl, 0 );
      strContents = getComboContents( hwndCtl, true );
   } else {
      ComboBox_SetCurSel( hwndCtl, -1 );
   }
   return strContents;
}
```

```
void FindDlg::addComboString( HWND hwndCtl, const String& str ) {

   assert( IsWindow( hwndCtl ) );

   const int nCurrentIndex = findStringExact( hwndCtl, str );
   if ( 0 <= nCurrentIndex ) {
      ComboBox_DeleteString( hwndCtl, nCurrentIndex );
   }
   ComboBox_InsertString( hwndCtl, 0, str.c_str() );
   while ( MAX_STRINGS < ComboBox_GetCount( hwndCtl ) ) {
      ComboBox_DeleteString( hwndCtl, MAX_STRINGS );
   }
   ComboBox_SetCurSel( hwndCtl, 0 );
}

void FindDlg::loadStrings( void ) {

   assert( isGoodPtr( this ) );
   HWND hwndSearchPattern = getDlgItem( IDC_SEARCHPATTERN );
   assert( IsWindow( hwndSearchPattern ) );
   for ( int iString = 0; iString < MAX_STRINGS; ++iString ) {
      const String str = getPattern( iString );
      if ( str.empty() ) {
         break;
      }
      ComboBox_AddString( hwndSearchPattern, str.c_str() );
   }

   if ( m_isReplace ) {
      HWND hwndReplacement = getDlgItem( IDC_REPLACEMENT );
      assert( IsWindow( hwndReplacement ) );
      for ( iString = 0; iString < MAX_STRINGS; ++iString ) {
         const String str = getReplacement( iString );
         if ( str.empty() ) {
            break; //*** LOOP EXIT POINT
         }
         ComboBox_AddString( hwndReplacement, str.c_str() );
      }
      if ( 0 < iString ) {
```

```
            ComboBox_SetCurSel( hwndReplacement, 0 );
        }
    }
}

/**
 * CB_FINDSTRINGEXACT is not case sensitive, hence this function,
 * which makes sure that the we have a case sensitive match.
 * CB_FINDSTRINGEXACT wraps around, which is why we need nPrevIndex.
 */
PRIVATE int findStringExact( HWND hwndCombo, LPCTSTR pszSearch ) {

    int nPrevIndex = -1;
    int nIndex = -1;
    while ( 0 <= (nIndex =
        ComboBox_FindStringExact( hwndCombo, nIndex, pszSearch ) ) )
    {
        TCHAR szString[ FindDlg::MAX_TEXT_LENGTH + 1 ] = { 0 };
        assert( ComboBox_GetLBTextLen(
            hwndCombo, nIndex ) < dim( szString ) );
        ComboBox_GetLBText( hwndCombo, nIndex, szString );
        if ( 0 == _tcscmp( szString, pszSearch ) ) {
            break; //*** LOOP EXIT POINT
        }
        if ( nIndex <= nPrevIndex ) {
            nIndex = -1;
            break; //*** LOOP EXIT POINT
        }
        nPrevIndex = nIndex;
    }

    return nIndex;
}

void FindDlg::saveStrings( bool bSaveReplacements ) {

    assert( isGoodPtr( this ) );
    HWND hwndSearchPattern = getDlgItem( IDC_SEARCHPATTERN );
    addComboString( hwndSearchPattern, m_strSearchPattern );
```

```
      const int nCount =
         __min( MAX_STRINGS, ComboBox_GetCount( hwndSearchPattern ) );
      for ( int iString = 0; iString < nCount; ++iString ) {
         TCHAR szString[ MAX_TEXT_LENGTH + 1 ] = { 0 };
         assert( ComboBox_GetLBTextLen(
            hwndSearchPattern, iString ) < dim( szString ) );
         ComboBox_GetLBText( hwndSearchPattern, iString, szString );
         setPattern( iString, szString );
      }

      if ( bSaveReplacements ) {
         assert( m_isReplace );
         HWND hwndReplacement = getDlgItem( IDC_REPLACEMENT );
         addComboString( hwndReplacement, m_strReplacePattern );

         const int nCount =
            __min( MAX_STRINGS, ComboBox_GetCount( hwndReplacement ) );
         int nString = 0;
         for ( iString = 0; iString < nCount; ++iString ) {
            TCHAR szString[ MAX_TEXT_LENGTH + 1 ] = { 0 };
            const int nLength =
               ComboBox_GetLBTextLen( hwndReplacement, iString );
            assert( nLength < dim( szString ) );
            if ( 0 < nLength ) { // Don't want empty replacement strings.
               ComboBox_GetLBText( hwndReplacement, iString, szString );
               setReplacement( nString, szString );
               ++nString;
            }
         }
      }
   }
}

void FindDlg::positionOutsideSelection( void ) {

   assert( isGoodPtr( this ) );
   assert( isGoodPtr( m_pEditor ) );
   AbstractEditWnd *pEditWnd = m_pEditor->getEditWnd();
   int nStart = 0;
```

```cpp
    int nEnd = 0;
    pEditWnd->getSel( &nStart, &nEnd );

    DWORD dwStart = pEditWnd->sendMessage( EM_POSFROMCHAR, nStart );
    DWORD dwEnd   = pEditWnd->sendMessage( EM_POSFROMCHAR, nEnd   );

    RECT rcSel = {
        LOWORD( dwStart ), HIWORD( dwStart ),
        LOWORD( dwEnd   ), HIWORD( dwEnd   ),
    };

    rcSel.bottom += abs( m_pEditor->getLogFont()->lfHeight );
    verify( MapWindowPoints( *pEditWnd, HWND_DESKTOP,
        reinterpret_cast< LPPOINT >( &rcSel ), 2 ) );

    Rect rcDlg = getWindowRect( *this );
    if ( rcSel.right <= rcDlg.left || rcDlg.right <= rcSel.left ) {
        return;
    }
    if ( rcSel.bottom <= rcDlg.top || rcDlg.bottom <= rcSel.top ) {
        return;
    }

    Rect rcScreen;
    verify( SystemParametersInfo( SPI_GETWORKAREA, 0, &rcScreen, 0 ) );

    int nDeltaDown = rcSel.bottom - rcDlg.top;
    int nDeltaUp   = rcDlg.bottom - rcSel.top;

    const bool isRoomBelow =
        rcDlg.bottom + nDeltaDown < rcScreen.bottom;
    const bool isRoomAbove = rcScreen.top < rcDlg.top + nDeltaUp;

    if ( isRoomBelow ) {
        rcDlg.top += nDeltaDown;
    } else if ( isRoomAbove ) {
        rcDlg.top -= nDeltaUp;
    } else if ( nDeltaUp < nDeltaDown ) {
        rcDlg.top += rcScreen.bottom - rcDlg.bottom;
```

```
   } else {
      rcDlg.top += rcScreen.bottom - rcDlg.bottom;
   }

   moveWindow( *this, rcDlg.left, rcDlg.top );
}

BOOL FindDlg::onInitDialog( HWND hwndFocus, LPARAM lParam ) {

   assert( isGoodPtr( this ) );
   positionOutsideSelection();
   HWND hwndSearchPattern = getDlgItem( IDC_SEARCHPATTERN );

   ComboBox_ResetContent( hwndSearchPattern );
   ComboBox_SetExtendedUI( hwndSearchPattern, true );
   ComboBox_LimitText( hwndSearchPattern, MAX_TEXT_LENGTH );

   Button_SetCheck(
      getDlgItem( IDC_MATCH_WHOLE_WORD ), getMatchWholeWord() );
   Button_SetCheck(
      getDlgItem( IDC_MATCH_CASE       ), getMatchCase      () );

   m_strOriginalTip = getDlgItemText( IDC_SEARCH_TIP );
   subclassHTML( getDlgItem( IDC_SEARCH_TIP ) );

   loadStrings();

   if ( m_strSearchPattern.empty() ) {
      m_strSearchPattern =
         getComboContentsAndSetSelection( hwndSearchPattern );
   } else {
      const int nCurrentIndex = findStringExact(
         hwndSearchPattern, m_strSearchPattern );
      if ( 0 <= nCurrentIndex ) {
         ComboBox_SetCurSel( hwndSearchPattern, nCurrentIndex );
      } else {
         ComboBox_SetText(
            hwndSearchPattern, m_strSearchPattern.c_str() );
      }
   }
```

```cpp
   if ( m_isReplace ) {
      HWND hwndReplacement = getDlgItem( IDC_REPLACEMENT );
      ComboBox_SetExtendedUI( hwndReplacement, true );
      ComboBox_LimitText( hwndReplacement, MAX_TEXT_LENGTH );

      m_strReplacePattern =
         getComboContentsAndSetSelection( hwndReplacement );

      assert( isGoodPtr( m_pEditor ) );
      const AbstractEditWnd *pEditWnd = m_pEditor->getEditWnd();
      enableDlgItem( IDC_SELECTION, pEditWnd->getSel() );
      verify( CheckRadioButton( *this,
         IDC_SELECTION, IDC_WHOLE_FILE, IDC_WHOLE_FILE ) );
   } else {
      toggleIcon( IDC_ARROW_UP, IDC_ARROW_DOWN, getBackwards() );
      verify( CheckRadioButton( *this,
         IDC_UP, IDC_DOWN, getBackwards() ? IDC_UP : IDC_DOWN ) );
   }

   adjustButtons();

   return TRUE; // ...since we did NOT set the focus.
}

void FindDlg::adjustButtons( void ) {

   assert( isGoodPtr( this ) );
   HWND hwndFind = getDlgItem( IDC_SEARCHPATTERN );
   bool bClosed = 0 == ComboBox_GetDroppedState( hwndFind );
   if ( bClosed && m_isReplace ) {
      HWND hwndReplacement = getDlgItem( IDC_REPLACEMENT );
      bClosed = 0 == ComboBox_GetDroppedState( hwndReplacement );
   }

   HWND hwndOK = getDlgItem( IDOK );
   HWND hwndReplace = m_isReplace ? getDlgItem( IDC_REPLACE ) : 0;
   HWND hwndReplaceAll =
      m_isReplace ? getDlgItem( IDC_REPLACE_ALL ) : 0;
```

```cpp
   const HWND hwndFocus = GetFocus();
   if ( m_isReplace ) {
      assert( isGoodPtr( m_pEditor ) );
      const AbstractEditWnd *pEditWnd = m_pEditor->getEditWnd();
      const bool hasSelection = pEditWnd->getSel();
      if ( !hasSelection ) {
         m_bReplaceInSelection = false;
         verify( CheckRadioButton( *this,
            IDC_SELECTION, IDC_WHOLE_FILE, IDC_WHOLE_FILE ) );
         if ( hwndFocus == getDlgItem( IDC_SELECTION ) ) {
            gotoDlgItem( IDC_WHOLE_FILE );
         }
      }
      enableDlgItem( IDC_SELECTION, hasSelection );
   }

   if ( m_bReplaceInSelection ) {
      if ( hwndFocus == hwndOK || hwndFocus == hwndReplace ) {
         gotoDlgItem( IDC_REPLACE_ALL );
      }
      EnableWindow( hwndOK, false );
      EnableWindow( hwndReplace, false );
      EnableWindow( hwndReplaceAll, true );
      sendMessage( DM_SETDEFID, IDC_REPLACE_ALL );
      setButtonStyle( hwndReplaceAll,
         bClosed ? BS_DEFPUSHBUTTON : BS_PUSHBUTTON );
      return; //*** FUNCTION EXIT POINT
   }

   const bool canSearch = !m_strSearchPattern.empty();
   bool canReplace = m_isReplace && canSearch;
   if ( m_isReplace ) {
      String strSelection;
      assert( isGoodPtr( m_pEditor ) );
      const AbstractEditWnd *pEditWnd = m_pEditor->getEditWnd();
      pEditWnd->getSel( &strSelection );
      bool bSearchPatternMatchesSelection = false;
      if ( getMatchCase() ) {
```

```
            bSearchPatternMatchesSelection =
                0 == m_strSearchPattern.compare( strSelection );
        } else {
            bSearchPatternMatchesSelection = 0 == _tcsicmp(
                m_strSearchPattern.c_str(), strSelection.c_str() );
        }
        if ( !bSearchPatternMatchesSelection ) {
            canReplace = false;
        }
    }

    if ( m_isReplace ) {
        EnableWindow( hwndReplace, canReplace );
        EnableWindow( hwndReplaceAll, canSearch );
        sendMessage( DM_SETDEFID, canReplace ? IDC_REPLACE : IDOK );
        setButtonStyle( hwndReplace,
            canReplace && bClosed ? BS_DEFPUSHBUTTON : BS_PUSHBUTTON );
    }

    EnableWindow( hwndOK, canSearch );
    setButtonStyle( hwndOK, canSearch && !canReplace && bClosed
        ? BS_DEFPUSHBUTTON : BS_PUSHBUTTON );
}

void FindDlg::onComboChanged( HWND hwndCtl, UINT codeNotify ) {

    assert( isGoodPtr( this ) );
    assert( IsWindow( hwndCtl ) );

    switch ( codeNotify ) {
    case CBN_EDITCHANGE:
    case CBN_SELCHANGE:
        {
            const int nSelection = ComboBox_GetCurSel( hwndCtl );
            const String strContents =
                getComboContents( hwndCtl, CBN_SELCHANGE == codeNotify );
            if ( getDlgItem( IDC_REPLACEMENT ) == hwndCtl ) {
                m_strReplacePattern = strContents;
            } else if ( getDlgItem( IDC_SEARCHPATTERN ) == hwndCtl ) {
                m_strSearchPattern = strContents;
```

```
            } else {
                assert( false ); // Should never get here.
            }
            trace( _T( "%s: %d %s\n" ),
                CBN_SELCHANGE == codeNotify
                    ? _T( "CBN_SELCHANGE" ) : _T( "CBN_EDITCHANGE" ),
                nSelection, strContents.c_str() );
        }
        adjustButtons();
        break;

    case CBN_CLOSEUP:
        {
            const int nSelection = ComboBox_GetCurSel( hwndCtl );
            const String strContents =
                getComboContents( hwndCtl, CBN_SELCHANGE == codeNotify );
            trace( _T( "CBN_CLOSEUP: %d %s\n" ),
                nSelection, strContents.c_str() );
        }
        break;

    case CBN_SELENDOK:
        {
            const int nSelection = ComboBox_GetCurSel( hwndCtl );
            const String strContents =
                getComboContents( hwndCtl, CBN_SELCHANGE == codeNotify );
            trace( _T( "CBNCBN_SELENDOK: %d %s\n" ),
                nSelection, strContents.c_str() );
        }
        break;

    case CBN_SELENDCANCEL:
        {
            const int nSelection = ComboBox_GetCurSel( hwndCtl );
            const String strContents =
                getComboContents( hwndCtl, CBN_SELCHANGE == codeNotify );
            trace( _T( "CBN_SELENDCANCEL: %d %s\n" ),
                nSelection, strContents.c_str() );
        }
        break;
```

```
      default:
        {
            const int nSelection = ComboBox_GetCurSel( hwndCtl );
            const String strContents =
                getComboContents( hwndCtl, CBN_SELCHANGE == codeNotify );
            trace( _T( "[%d]: %d %s\n" ),
                codeNotify, nSelection, strContents.c_str() );
        }
    }

    // NOTE: Without this, we have flashing!
    if ( 0 != m_strOriginalTip.compare(
       getDlgItemText( IDC_SEARCH_TIP ) ) )
    {
       setDlgItemText( IDC_SEARCH_TIP, m_strOriginalTip );
       removeHighlight( getDlgItem( IDC_SEARCH_TIP ) );
    }
}

void FindDlg::onFindNext( void ) {

    assert( isGoodPtr( this ) );
    m_uiRetCode = IDOK;
    saveStrings( false );
    setMatchWholeWord(
       0 != Button_GetCheck( getDlgItem( IDC_MATCH_WHOLE_WORD ) ) );
    setMatchCase     (
       0 != Button_GetCheck( getDlgItem( IDC_MATCH_CASE       ) ) );
    if ( !m_isReplace ) {
       setBackwards( 0 != Button_GetCheck( getDlgItem( IDC_UP ) ) );
    }

    assert( isGoodPtr( m_pEditor ) );
    if ( !m_pEditor->searchAndSelect( m_strSearchPattern ) ) {
       // 1. Do things that will result in
       //    IDC_SEARCHPATTERN notifications...
       gotoDlgItem( IDC_SEARCHPATTERN );
       SNDMSG( getDlgItem( IDC_SEARCHPATTERN ), EM_SETSEL, 0, -1 );
```

```cpp
        // ...and 2. Set the error stuff. Order is important!
        setHighlight( getDlgItem( IDC_SEARCH_TIP ) );
        const String strMessage = formatMessage(
           IDS_STRING_NOT_FOUND, m_strSearchPattern.c_str() );
        setDlgItemText( IDC_SEARCH_TIP, strMessage );
        MessageBeep( MB_ICONWARNING );
    } else if ( m_isReplace ) {
        positionOutsideSelection();
        adjustButtons();
    } else {
        verify( EndDialog( *this, m_uiRetCode ) );
    }
}

void FindDlg::onReplace( void ) {

    assert( isGoodPtr( this ) );
    m_uiRetCode = IDOK;
    saveStrings( true );
    assert( isGoodPtr( m_pEditor ) );
    AbstractEditWnd *pEditWnd = m_pEditor->getEditWnd();
    assert( pEditWnd->getSel() );
    pEditWnd->replaceSel( m_strReplacePattern.c_str() );
    setDlgItemText( IDCANCEL, loadString( IDS_CLOSE ) );
    if ( m_pEditor->searchAndSelect( m_strSearchPattern ) ) {
        positionOutsideSelection();
    } else {
        // 1. Do things that will result in
        //    IDC_SEARCHPATTERN notifications...
        gotoDlgItem( IDC_SEARCHPATTERN );
        SNDMSG( getDlgItem( IDC_SEARCHPATTERN ), EM_SETSEL, 0, -1 );

        // ...and 2. Set the error stuff.
        setHighlight( getDlgItem( IDC_SEARCH_TIP ) );
        const String strMessage = formatMessage(
           IDS_STRING_NOT_FOUND, m_strSearchPattern.c_str() );
        setDlgItemText( IDC_SEARCH_TIP, strMessage );
        MessageBeep( MB_ICONWARNING );
    }
```

```
      adjustButtons();
}

/**
 * QUESTION: Disable everything for the duration?
 * Would really require active Cancel button.
 */
void FindDlg::onReplaceAll( void ) {

   assert( isGoodPtr( this ) );
   removeHighlight( getDlgItem( IDC_SEARCH_TIP ) );
   saveStrings( true );
   int nReplacements = 0;
   assert( isGoodPtr( m_pEditor ) );
   AbstractEditWnd *pEditWnd = m_pEditor->getEditWnd();
   if ( m_bReplaceInSelection ) {
      assert( pEditWnd->getSel() );
      nReplacements = pEditWnd->replaceInSelection(
         m_strSearchPattern, m_strReplacePattern,
         getMatchWholeWord(), getMatchCase() );
   } else {
      int nStart = 0;
      pEditWnd->getSel( &nStart );
      pEditWnd->setSel( 0, 0 );
      bool bWrap = false;
      while ( m_pEditor->searchAndSelect(
         m_strSearchPattern, &bWrap ) )
      {
         if ( bWrap ) {
            break;
         }
         assert( pEditWnd->getSel() );
         pEditWnd->replaceSel( m_strReplacePattern.c_str() );
         ++nReplacements;
         if ( GetAsyncKeyState( VK_ESCAPE ) < 0 ) {
            break; // In case of endless loop
         }
      }
      if ( 0 == nReplacements ) {
```

```cpp
            pEditWnd->setSel( nStart, nStart );
        }
    }

    const String strMessage = formatMessage(
        1 == nReplacements ? IDS_REPLACEMENTS1 : IDS_REPLACEMENTS,
        nReplacements );
    setDlgItemText( IDC_SEARCH_TIP, strMessage );
    setDlgItemText( IDCANCEL, loadString( IDS_CLOSE ) );
    adjustButtons();
    sendMessage( DM_SETDEFID, IDCANCEL );
}

void FindDlg::onDlgCommand( int id, HWND hwndCtl, UINT codeNotify ) {

    assert( isGoodPtr( this ) );
    switch ( id ) {
    case IDC_DOWN:
    case IDC_UP:
        assert( !m_isReplace );
        if ( BN_CLICKED == codeNotify ) {
            const bool isBackwards =
                0 != Button_GetCheck( getDlgItem( IDC_UP ) );
            toggleIcon( IDC_ARROW_UP, IDC_ARROW_DOWN, isBackwards );
        }
        break;

    case IDOK:
        if ( BN_CLICKED == codeNotify ) {
            onFindNext();
        }
        break;

    case IDCANCEL:
        if ( BN_CLICKED == codeNotify ) {
            verify( EndDialog( *this, m_uiRetCode ) );
        }
        break;
```

```cpp
      case IDC_REPLACE:
         if ( BN_CLICKED == codeNotify ) {
            onReplace();
         }
         break;

      case IDC_REPLACE_ALL:
         if ( BN_CLICKED == codeNotify ) {
            onReplaceAll();
         }
         break;

      case IDC_SEARCHPATTERN:
      case IDC_REPLACEMENT:
         onComboChanged( hwndCtl, codeNotify );
         break;

      case IDC_MATCH_WHOLE_WORD:
      case IDC_MATCH_CASE:
         setMatchWholeWord(
            0 != Button_GetCheck( getDlgItem( IDC_MATCH_WHOLE_WORD ) ) );
         setMatchCase     (
            0 != Button_GetCheck( getDlgItem( IDC_MATCH_CASE       ) ) );
         if ( BN_CLICKED == codeNotify ) {
            adjustButtons();
         }
         break;

      case IDC_SELECTION:
      case IDC_WHOLE_FILE:
         m_bReplaceInSelection = IDC_SELECTION == id;
         adjustButtons();
      }
}

UINT FindDlg::getResourceID( void ) const {

   return m_isReplace ? IDD_EDITREPLACE : IDD_EDITFIND;
}
```

```
FindDlg::FindDlg(
    Editor *pEditor, const String &strSearchPattern, bool isReplace )

    : m_pEditor( pEditor )
    , m_isReplace( isReplace )
    , m_uiRetCode( IDCANCEL )
    , m_bReplaceInSelection( false )
{
    assert( isGoodPtr( this ) );
    assert( isGoodPtr( m_pEditor ) );

    const int nNewLine =
        strSearchPattern.find_first_of( _T( "\r\n" ) );
    if ( 0 <= nNewLine ) {
        m_strSearchPattern = strSearchPattern.substr( 0, nNewLine );
    } else {
        m_strSearchPattern = strSearchPattern;
    }
    if ( MAX_TEXT_LENGTH < m_strSearchPattern.length() ) {
        m_strSearchPattern =
            m_strSearchPattern.substr( 0, MAX_TEXT_LENGTH );
    }
}
```

Chapter 16

Printing

In one sense, printing under Windows is similar to displaying stuff on the screen: you use GDI commands to draw text and graphics in a display context. You don't obtain (or release) a printer display context the same way you obtain a screen display context, but once you have that display context, you use the same familiar set of GDI functions.

In another sense, printing under Windows is different from displaying stuff on the screen. Even if we disregard, for a moment, the task of obtaining the printer display context, we still have to deal with pagination, margins, headers and footers, nothing of which applies to the screen. Besides, the edit window does the screen rendering for TextEdit in any case. On the printer, we have to render the text ourselves. (Actually, the rich edit control does understand something of printing, even though TextEdit doesn't use this capability. The poor edit control, however, doesn't understand much of anything.)

I'll start with the print-related dialogs and describe the actual printing afterwards. But first of all...

DEVMODE and DEVNAMES

A `DEVMODE` data structure contains information about device initialization and environment of a printer. Both the page setup and print dialogs use the `getDevMode` and `setDevMode` functions defined in `devMode.cpp`. The main point of this module is to provide persistent storage for the selected paper size, printer resolution, and device orientation (landscape or portrait).

A `DEVNAMES` data structure contains strings that identify the driver, device, and output port names for a printer. Both the page setup and print dialogs use the `getDevNames` and

Chapter 16: Printing

setDevNames functions defined in devNames.cpp. The main point of this module is to provide persistent storage for these strings.

The DEVNAMES structure is a nasty, variable-length thing, where you have to figure out the position of the strings from the offsets:

```
typedef struct tagDEVNAMES {
    WORD wDriverOffset;
    WORD wDeviceOffset;
    WORD wOutputOffset;
    WORD wDefault;
} DEVNAMES;
```

The documentation fails to mention whether the strings should be ANSI or Unicode; testing reveals them to be LPTSTRs. (Discourse continues on page 400.)

Listing 16.1   devMode.cpp

```
/*
 * $Header: /Book/devMode.cpp 8     5.09.99 13:06 Petter $
 *
 * Consider including this, or some of it, in Document class?
 * Would give document-specific printer setup.
 */

#include "precomp.h"
#include "persistence.h"
#include "devMode.h"

DEFINE_PERSISTENT_INT(    "Printer", Orientation, DMORIENT_PORTRAIT );
DEFINE_PERSISTENT_INT(    "Printer", Paper       , 0                );
DEFINE_PERSISTENT_INT(    "Printer", Resolution  , 0                );
DEFINE_PERSISTENT_STRING( "Printer", DeviceName  , ""               );

HGLOBAL getDevMode( void ) {

    HGLOBAL hDevMode = GlobalAlloc( GHND, sizeof( DEVMODE ) );
    DEVMODE *pDevMode =
        reinterpret_cast< DEVMODE * >( GlobalLock( hDevMode ) );
    if ( 0 == pDevMode ) {
        return 0; // This is fairly OK; will get default initialization.
    }
```

```cpp
   pDevMode->dmSize = sizeof( DEVMODE );

   const String strDeviceName = getDeviceName();
   _tcsncpy( (LPTSTR) pDevMode->dmDeviceName,
      strDeviceName.c_str(), CCHDEVICENAME );

   pDevMode->dmOrientation = getOrientation();
   if ( DMORIENT_PORTRAIT <= pDevMode->dmOrientation &&
       pDevMode->dmOrientation <= DMORIENT_LANDSCAPE )
   {
      pDevMode->dmFields = DM_ORIENTATION;
   }

   pDevMode->dmPaperSize = getPaper();
   if ( DMPAPER_FIRST <= pDevMode->dmPaperSize &&
      pDevMode->dmPaperSize <= DMPAPER_LAST )
   {
      pDevMode->dmFields |= DM_PAPERSIZE;
   }

   pDevMode->dmYResolution = getResolution();
   if ( 0 < pDevMode->dmYResolution ) {
      pDevMode->dmFields |= DM_YRESOLUTION;
   }

   GlobalUnlock( hDevMode );
   return hDevMode;
}

void setDevMode( HGLOBAL hDevMode ) {

   if ( 0 != hDevMode ) {
      DEVMODE *pDevMode =
         reinterpret_cast< DEVMODE * >( GlobalLock( hDevMode ) );
      assert( isGoodPtr( pDevMode ) );
      setDeviceName( (LPTSTR) pDevMode->dmDeviceName );
      if ( pDevMode->dmFields & DM_ORIENTATION) {
         setOrientation( pDevMode->dmOrientation );
      }
```

```
        if ( pDevMode->dmFields & DM_PAPERSIZE ) {
            setPaper( pDevMode->dmPaperSize );
        }
        if ( pDevMode->dmFields & DM_YRESOLUTION ) {
            setResolution( pDevMode->dmYResolution );
        }
        GlobalUnlock( hDevMode );
    }
}
```

Listing 16.2 devNames.cpp

```
/*
 * $Header: /Book/devNames.cpp 11    5.09.99 13:07 Petter $
 *
 * Consider including this, or some of it, in Document class?
 * Would give document-specific printer selection.
 */

#include "precomp.h"
#include "persistence.h"
#include "devNames.h"
#include "trace.h"

DEFINE_PERSISTENT_STRING( "Printer", Driver, "" );
DEFINE_PERSISTENT_STRING( "Printer", Device, "" );
DEFINE_PERSISTENT_STRING( "Printer", Port  , "" );

HGLOBAL getDevNames(
    LPCTSTR pszPrinter, LPCTSTR pszDriver, LPCTSTR pszPort )
{
    String strDriver = getDriver();
    String strDevice = getDevice();
    String strPort   = getPort  ();

    if ( 0 != pszPrinter ) {
        strDevice = pszPrinter;
    }
    if ( 0 != pszDriver ) {
        strDriver = pszDriver;
```

```cpp
      }
      if ( 0 != pszPort ) {
         strPort = pszPort;
      }

      const int nChars =
         strDriver.length() + strDevice.length() + strPort.length();
      if ( 0 == nChars ) {
         return 0; // This is OK; will get default initialization.
      }
      HGLOBAL hDevNames = GlobalAlloc( GHND,
         sizeof DEVNAMES + sizeof( TCHAR ) * ( nChars + 4 ) );
      DEVNAMES *pDevNames =
         reinterpret_cast< DEVNAMES * >( GlobalLock( hDevNames ) );
      if ( 0 == pDevNames ) {
         return 0; // This is OK; will get default initialization.
      }
      trace( _T( "sizeof( DEVNAMES ) = %d\n" ), sizeof( DEVNAMES ) );

      LPTSTR psz = reinterpret_cast< LPTSTR >( pDevNames ) +
         sizeof( DEVNAMES ) / sizeof( TCHAR );
      _tcscpy( psz, strDriver.c_str() );
      pDevNames->wDriverOffset =
         psz - reinterpret_cast< LPTSTR >( pDevNames );

      psz += _tcsclen( psz ) + 1;
      _tcscpy( psz, strDevice.c_str() );
      pDevNames->wDeviceOffset =
         psz - reinterpret_cast< LPTSTR >( pDevNames );

      psz += _tcsclen( psz ) + 1;
      _tcscpy( psz, strPort.c_str() );
      pDevNames->wOutputOffset =
         psz - reinterpret_cast< LPTSTR >( pDevNames );

      GlobalUnlock( hDevNames );
      return hDevNames;
   }

   void setDevNames( HGLOBAL hDevNames ) {
```

```
    if ( 0 != hDevNames ) {
      DEVNAMES *pDevNames =
        reinterpret_cast< DEVNAMES * >( GlobalLock( hDevNames ) );
      LPCTSTR psz = reinterpret_cast< LPCTSTR >( pDevNames ) +
        pDevNames->wDriverOffset;
      setDriver( reinterpret_cast< LPCTSTR >( psz ) );
      psz = reinterpret_cast< LPCTSTR >( pDevNames ) +
        pDevNames->wDeviceOffset;
      setDevice( reinterpret_cast< LPCTSTR >( psz ) );
      psz = reinterpret_cast< LPCTSTR >( pDevNames ) +
        pDevNames->wOutputOffset;
      setPort( reinterpret_cast< LPCTSTR >( psz ) );
      GlobalUnlock( hDevNames );
    }
  }
```

The Page Setup Dialog

TextEdit uses the standard common dialog for page setup. The `setupPage` function is defined in `setupPage.cpp`. The Page Setup dialog is closely related to the Print dialog; the values set during page setup are typically used during printing.

You invoke the standard page setup dialog by calling `PageSetupDlg` with a pointer to a suitably initialized `PAGESETUPDLG` as its lone parameter. The result looks like Figure 16.1.

The common page setup dialog provides for no less than two hook functions: the `PageSetupHook` and the `PagePaintHook`. The code in `setupPage.cpp` uses both, though the `PagePaintHook` is a dummy included only to show how it's done. The default page is good enough for TextEdit, but if I were writing a graphics editor, I might implement custom rendering of the sample page.

Figure 16.1 The Page Setup dialog box.

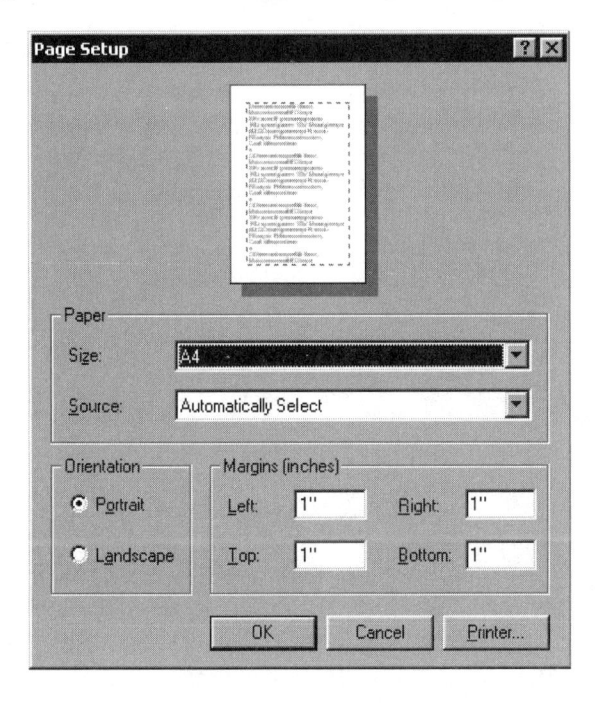

Listing 16.3 setupPage.cpp

```
/*
 * $Header: /Book/setupPage.cpp 12    20.08.99 16:33 Petter $
 */

#include "precomp.h"
#include "AutoGlobalMemoryHandle.h"
#include "setupPage.h"
#include "devMode.h"
#include "devNames.h"
#include "winUtils.h"
#include "persistence.h"
#include "resource.h"


/**
 * This does nothing. Fill in the blanks if you need it.
 */
PRIVATE UINT CALLBACK PagePaintHook(
```

```
   HWND hwnd, UINT msg, WPARAM wParam, LPARAM lParam )
{
   assert( IsWindow( hwnd ) );

   switch ( msg ) {
   case WM_PSD_GREEKTEXTRECT:
      ;
      // FillRect( hdc, prc, GetStockBrush( LTGRAY_BRUSH ) );
      // return 1; // if you don't want the parent dialog to paint:
   }

   return 0;
}

/**
 * Centers the dialog on its parent on opening.
 * Stores position on closing; uses this on later openings.
 */
PRIVATE UINT CALLBACK PageSetupHook(
   HWND hwnd, UINT msg, WPARAM, LPARAM )
{
   assert( IsWindow( hwnd ) );
   if ( WM_INITDIALOG == msg ) {
      restorePosition( hwnd, IDD_PRINT_SETUP );
   } else if ( WM_DESTROY == msg ) {
      savePosition( hwnd, IDD_PRINT_SETUP );
   }
   return 0;
}

void setupPage( HWND hwndParent, Document *pDocument ) {

   assert( IsWindow( hwndParent ) );
   assert( isGoodPtr( pDocument ) );

   PAGESETUPDLG pageSetupDlg = {
      sizeof( PAGESETUPDLG ),
      hwndParent,
      getDevMode(), getDevNames(),
```

```
        PSD_ENABLEPAGESETUPHOOK | PSD_ENABLEPAGEPAINTHOOK,
      { 0, }, { 0, }, { 0, },
      0, 0, PageSetupHook, PagePaintHook,
   };

   const AutoGlobalMemoryHandle a1( pageSetupDlg.hDevMode  );
   const AutoGlobalMemoryHandle a2( pageSetupDlg.hDevNames );

   pageSetupDlg.rtMargin.left   = pDocument->getLeftMargin  ();
   pageSetupDlg.rtMargin.top    = pDocument->getTopMargin   ();
   pageSetupDlg.rtMargin.right  = pDocument->getRightMargin ();
   pageSetupDlg.rtMargin.bottom = pDocument->getBottomMargin();
   if ( 0 < pageSetupDlg.rtMargin.left ) {
      pageSetupDlg.Flags |= PSD_MARGINS;
      if ( pDocument->getMarginsAreMetric() ) {
         pageSetupDlg.Flags |= PSD_INHUNDREDTHSOFMILLIMETERS;
      } else {
         pageSetupDlg.Flags |= PSD_INTHOUSANDTHSOFINCHES;
      }
   }


   if ( HWND_DESKTOP != hwndParent ) {
      FORWARD_WM_COMMAND(
         hwndParent, ID_COMMAND_RESETSTATUSBAR, 0, 0, SNDMSG );
   }

   const BOOL bOK = PageSetupDlg( &pageSetupDlg );
   if ( bOK ) {
      // Orientation and paper, common with printing
      setDevMode ( pageSetupDlg.hDevMode  );
      setDevNames( pageSetupDlg.hDevNames );
      pDocument->setLeftMargin   ( pageSetupDlg.rtMargin.left   );
      pDocument->setTopMargin    ( pageSetupDlg.rtMargin.top    );
      pDocument->setRightMargin  ( pageSetupDlg.rtMargin.right  );
      pDocument->setBottomMargin ( pageSetupDlg.rtMargin.bottom );
      if ( pageSetupDlg.Flags & PSD_INHUNDREDTHSOFMILLIMETERS ) {
         pDocument->setMarginsAreMetric( 1 );
      } else if ( pageSetupDlg.Flags & PSD_INTHOUSANDTHSOFINCHES ) {
```

```
                pDocument->setMarginsAreMetric( 0 );
        }
    }
}
```

The Print Dialog

TextEdit uses the standard common dialog for printing. The `printFile` function is defined in `printFile.cpp`. The Print dialog is closely related to the Page Setup dialog; the values set during page setup are typically used during printing.

You invoke the standard print dialog by calling `PrintDlg` with a pointer to a suitably initialized `PRINTDLG` as its lone parameter. The result looks like Figure 16.2.

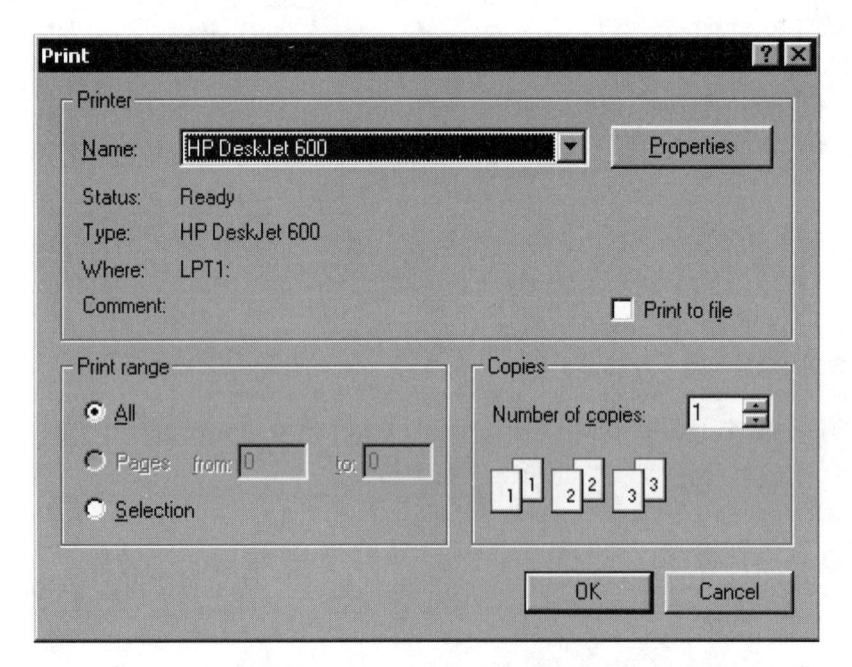

Figure 16.2   The Print dialog box.

When you are certain of running under Windows 2000, you may use `PrintDlgEx` instead, which gives you extended functionality.

The print dialog is special in that it may be the sole manifestation of TextEdit; this happens if TextEdit is started with the `/p` switch. If so, the `WM_INITDIALOG` handler adds the file's title to the dialog title.

The "Selection" radio button must be disabled if no text is selected. Obviously, no text is ever selected when TextEdit is invoked with one of the printer switches.

The printing switches give rise to another complication: what if the file in question is already open in another instance of TextEdit? This is handled in `activateOldInstance`, which activates the old instance, then sends it an `ID_FILE_PRINT` command. This approach is the reason why the parent window of the Print Common dialog is `GetLastActivePopup( m_hwndMain )` rather than plain `m_hwndMain`. There's always the chance that a dialog box is open in the running instance. Two modal dialog boxes parented to the same window is not merely asking for trouble, but insisting on trouble. Only one of them will have a keyboard interface, and as soon as one is killed, the parent is again enabled, with the remaining dialog displaying a distinctly modeless behavior. Better, then, to parent the print dialog to the existing dialog. (Discourse continues on page 409.)

Listing 16.4 `printFile.cpp`

```cpp
/*
 * $Header: /Book/printFile.cpp 14     20.08.99 16:33 Petter $
 */

#include "precomp.h"
#include "AutoArray.h"
#include "Exception.h"
#include "Editor.h"
#include "AutoGlobalMemoryHandle.h"
#include "printFile.h"
#include "winUtils.h"
#include "devMode.h"
#include "devNames.h"
#include "formatMessage.h"
#include "resource.h"
#include <dlgs.h>

#define PD_COMMON_TEXTEDIT (PD_ENABLEPRINTHOOK | PD_RETURNDC)

PRIVATE inline BOOL onInitDialog(
   HWND hwnd, HWND hwndFocus, LPARAM lParam )
{
   PRINTDLG *pPrintDlg = reinterpret_cast< PRINTDLG * >( lParam );
   assert( isGoodPtr( pPrintDlg ) );
   Document *pDocument = reinterpret_cast< Document * >(
      pPrintDlg->lCustData );
   if ( 0 != pDocument ) {
      assert( isGoodPtr( pDocument ) );
      const String strTitle = formatMessage( IDS_PRINT_HEADER,
         pDocument->getTitle().c_str() );
      SetWindowText( hwnd, strTitle.c_str() );
   }
```

```
      restorePosition( hwnd, IDD_PRINT );
   if ( 1 < pPrintDlg->nCopies ) {
      HWND hwndCopies = GetDlgItem( hwnd, edt3 );
      if ( IsWindow( hwndCopies ) ) {
         SetFocus( hwndCopies );
         Edit_SetSel( hwndCopies, 0, -1 );
         return FALSE;
      }
   }
   return TRUE;
}

PRIVATE inline void onDestroy( HWND hwnd ) {

   savePosition( hwnd, IDD_PRINT );
}

UINT CALLBACK PrintHookProc(
   HWND hwnd, UINT msg, WPARAM wParam, LPARAM lParam )
{
   switch ( msg ) {
   HANDLE_MSG( hwnd, WM_INITDIALOG, onInitDialog );
   HANDLE_MSG( hwnd, WM_DESTROY   , onDestroy    );
   }

   return 0;
}

class AutoDC {
private:
   HDC m_hdc;

public:
   AutoDC( HDC hdc ) : m_hdc( hdc ) {
   }
   ~AutoDC() {
      verify( DeleteDC( m_hdc ) );
   }
};
```

```cpp
/**
 * This printFile is used with the /p and /pt command line switches.
 */
void printFile( Document *pDocument,
   LPCTSTR pszPrinter, LPCTSTR pszDriver, LPCTSTR pszPort )
{
   PRINTDLG printDlg = {
      sizeof( PRINTDLG ),
      HWND_DESKTOP, getDevMode(),
      getDevNames( pszPrinter, pszDriver, pszPort ),
      0, PD_COMMON_TEXTEDIT | PD_NOSELECTION,
      0, 0, 0, 0, 1, 0, reinterpret_cast< DWORD >( pDocument ),
      PrintHookProc,
   };

   const AutoGlobalMemoryHandle a1( printDlg.hDevMode  );
   const AutoGlobalMemoryHandle a2( printDlg.hDevNames );

   if ( 0 != pszPrinter ) {
      const DEVMODE *pDevMode = 0;
      if ( 0 != printDlg.hDevMode ) {
         pDevMode = reinterpret_cast< DEVMODE * >(
            GlobalLock( printDlg.hDevMode ) );
      }
      printDlg.hDC = CreateDC( pszDriver, pszPrinter, 0, pDevMode );
      if ( 0 != printDlg.hDevMode ) {
         GlobalUnlock( printDlg.hDevMode );
      }
   } else {
      const BOOL bOK = PrintDlg( &printDlg );
      if ( bOK ) {
         setDevMode ( printDlg.hDevMode  );
         setDevNames( printDlg.hDevNames );
      } else {
         const DWORD dwErr = CommDlgExtendedError();
         if ( ERROR_SUCCESS == dwErr ) {
            return; // The user hit cancel; OK.
         } else {
```

```
                throw CommonDialogException( dwErr );
            }
        }


    }

    if ( 0 == printDlg.hDC ) {
        throwException( _T( "Can't get a printer device context" ) );
    }
    const AutoDC autoDC( printDlg.hDC );
    const AutoString pszText( pDocument->getContents() );
    pDocument->print( printDlg.hDC, pszText );
}

/**
 * This printFile is used for normal editing sessions.
 * # of copies is persistent only within session.
 */
void Editor::printFile( void ) {

    assert( isGoodConstPtr( this ) );
    assert( IsWindow( m_hwndMain ) );

    static int s_nCopies = 1; // Retain per session.

    PRINTDLG printDlg = {
        sizeof( PRINTDLG ),
        GetLastActivePopup( m_hwndMain ),
        getDevMode(), getDevNames(), 0,
        PD_COMMON_TEXTEDIT, 0, 0, 0, 0, s_nCopies, 0, 0, PrintHookProc,
    };

    const AutoGlobalMemoryHandle a1( printDlg.hDevMode  );
    const AutoGlobalMemoryHandle a2( printDlg.hDevNames );

    if ( m_pEditWnd->getSel() ) {
        printDlg.Flags |= PD_SELECTION;
    } else {
        printDlg.Flags |= PD_NOSELECTION;
    }
```

```
    FORWARD_WM_COMMAND(
       m_hwndMain, ID_COMMAND_RESETSTATUSBAR, 0, 0, SNDMSG );

    const BOOL bOK = PrintDlg( &printDlg );
    if ( bOK ) {
       s_nCopies = printDlg.nCopies;
       setDevMode ( printDlg.hDevMode  );
       setDevNames( printDlg.hDevNames );
       if ( 0 == printDlg.hDC ) {
          throwException( _T( "Can't get a printer device context" ) );
       }
       const AutoDC autoDC( printDlg.hDC );
       TemporaryStatusIcon statusIcon( m_pStatusbar, STD_PRINT );
       if ( printDlg.Flags & PD_SELECTION ) {
          String strText;
          assert( m_pEditWnd->getSel( &strText ) );
          m_pDocument->print( printDlg.hDC, strText.c_str() );
       } else {
          AutoString pszText( m_pDocument->getContents() );
          m_pDocument->print( printDlg.hDC, pszText, s_nCopies );
       }
    }
}
```

Text Rendering and Pagination

Actual printing is done by the `print` method in the `Document` class. It calculates the printable area from the margins and printer device context metrics, then goes into a loop where it calls `printSingleCopy` for each requested copy. As usual, a couple of the classes involved have exception safety as their sole purpose: `PrinterDC` and `PrinterDoc`.

The `printSingleCopy` method loops on `getLine`, retrieving lines one by one until it runs out of lines. Each physical line may be broken any number of times if it is too wide to fit on a single line; this occurs no matter what the `WordWrap` setting is. A new page, including a page header, is emitted whenever necessary.

The font used for printing is created by the `createPrintFont` method in the `Document` class. It is the same font used for display, scaled to (approximately) the same physical size.

The `pageHeader` method is responsible for rendering the page header.

Listing 16.5 `print.cpp`

```cpp
/*
 * $Header: /Book/print.cpp 8     20.08.99 16:33 Petter $
 */

#include "precomp.h"
#include "Document.h"
#include "Exception.h"
#include "WaitCursor.h"
#include "persistence.h"
#include "graphics.h"
#include "geometry.h"
#include "utils.h"

HFONT Document::createPrintFont( HDC hdc ) {

   LOGFONT logFont = { 0 };
   if ( getFixedFont() ) {
      _tcscpy( logFont.lfFaceName, getFixedFace().c_str() );
      logFont.lfHeight = devPointsFromPrinterPoints(
         getFixedHeight(), hdc );
      logFont.lfWeight = getFixedWeight();
      logFont.lfItalic = getFixedItalic();
      logFont.lfCharSet = getFixedCharSet();
   } else {
      _tcscpy( logFont.lfFaceName, getProportionalFace().c_str() );
      logFont.lfHeight = devPointsFromPrinterPoints(
         getProportionalHeight(), hdc );
      logFont.lfWeight = getProportionalWeight();
      logFont.lfItalic = getProportionalItalic();
      logFont.lfCharSet = getProportionalCharSet();
   }
   return CreateFontIndirect( &logFont );
}

PRIVATE String getLine( LPCTSTR *ppszText ) {

   assert( isGoodPtr( ppszText ) );
   assert( isGoodStringPtr( *ppszText ) );
```

```
      const int nLength = _tcscspn( *ppszText, _T( "\r\n" ) );
      String strLine( *ppszText, nLength );
      *ppszText += nLength;
      if ( _T( '\r' ) == **ppszText ) {
         ++*ppszText;
      }
      if ( _T( '\n' ) == **ppszText ) {
         ++*ppszText;
      }

      return strLine;
}

class PrinterDC {
private:
   HDC   m_hdc;
   HFONT m_hfont;
   int   m_nSavedContext;

public:
   void restore() {
      SelectFont( m_hdc, m_hfont );
      SetTextAlign( m_hdc, TA_TOP | TA_LEFT );
   };

   PrinterDC( HDC hdc, HFONT hfont )
      : m_hdc( hdc )
      , m_hfont( hfont )
      , m_nSavedContext( SaveDC( hdc ) )
   {
      assert( 0 != m_hdc );
      assert( 0 != m_hfont );
      assert( 0 != m_nSavedContext );
      restore();
   };

   ~PrinterDC() {
      verify( RestoreDC( m_hdc, m_nSavedContext ) );
```

```
         verify( DeleteFont( m_hfont ) );
      };

      operator HDC() const {
         return m_hdc;
      };
};

class PrinterDoc {
private:
   HDC m_hdc;

public:
   PrinterDoc( HDC hdc, const String& strTitle ) : m_hdc( hdc ) {

      DOCINFO docInfo = {
         sizeof( DOCINFO ),
         strTitle.c_str(),
      };

      const int nPrintJobId = StartDoc( hdc, &docInfo );
      if ( nPrintJobId <= 0 ) {
         throwException(
            _T( "Unable to print document (StartDoc failed)" ) );
      }
   };

   ~PrinterDoc() {
      if ( EndDoc( m_hdc ) <= 0 ) {
         trace( _T( "EndDoc failed (%u)\n" ), GetLastError() );
      }
   }
};

PRIVATE void pageHeader(
   PrinterDC& printerDC, const String strHeader, int *pnPage,
   const RECT& rcPrintArea, LPPOINT pptCurrPos )
{
   assert( isGoodPtr( pnPage ) );
```

```
pptCurrPos->y = rcPrintArea.top;
if ( 0 != *pnPage ) {
   if ( EndPage( printerDC ) <= 0 ) {
      throwException( _T( "EndPage failed" ) );
   }
}
if ( StartPage( printerDC ) <= 0 ) {
   throwException( _T( "StartPage failed" ) );
}

// Because of Win95, which resets the DC on StartPage.
printerDC.restore();
++*pnPage;

const COLORREF crSaved =
   SetBkColor( printerDC, RGB( 226, 226, 226 ) );
const int nSavedBkMode = SetBkMode( printerDC, TRANSPARENT );

SIZE size;
verify( GetTextExtentPoint32(
   printerDC, strHeader.c_str(), strHeader.length(), &size ) );

RECT rcHeader = rcPrintArea;
rcHeader.bottom = rcHeader.top + size.cy;
const COLORREF crHeaderBk = RGB( 192, 192, 192 );
fillSolidRect( printerDC, &rcHeader, crHeaderBk );

verify( DrawText( printerDC, strHeader.c_str(), -1,
   &rcHeader, DT_LEFT | DT_VCENTER | DT_NOPREFIX ) );

TCHAR szPage[ 10 ] = { 0 };
wsprintf( szPage, _T( "%d" ), *pnPage );
verify( DrawText( printerDC, szPage, -1,
   &rcHeader, DT_RIGHT | DT_VCENTER | DT_NOPREFIX ) );

SetBkMode( printerDC, nSavedBkMode );
SetBkColor( printerDC, crSaved );
```

```
      pptCurrPos->y += MulDiv( size.cy, 3, 2 );
}

void printSingleCopy( PrinterDC& printerDC, const RECT& rcPrintArea,
   LPCTSTR pszText, const String strHeader, int nTabs )
{
   TEXTMETRIC tm = { 0 };
   if ( !GetTextMetrics( printerDC, &tm ) ) {
      throwException( _T( "Failure in GetTextMetrics" ) );
   }
   const int nLineHeight = tm.tmHeight + tm.tmExternalLeading;

   SIZE sizeSpace;
   GetTextExtentPoint32( printerDC, _T( " " ), 1, &sizeSpace );
   const int nPixelsPerTab = nTabs * sizeSpace.cx;

   Point ptCurrPos( rcPrintArea.left, rcPrintArea.top );
   int nPage = 0;
   pageHeader(
      printerDC, strHeader, &nPage, rcPrintArea, &ptCurrPos );

   while ( 0 != *pszText ) {
      String strLine = getLine( &pszText );
      ptCurrPos.x = rcPrintArea.left;
      while ( !strLine.empty() ) {
         int nSpace = strLine.find_first_of( _T( " \t" ) );
         if ( 0 == nSpace ) {
            if ( _T( '\t' ) == strLine[ 0 ] ) {
               int nOffset = ptCurrPos.x - rcPrintArea.left;
               nOffset = (nOffset + nPixelsPerTab) / nPixelsPerTab;
               nOffset *= nPixelsPerTab;
               ptCurrPos.x = rcPrintArea.left + nOffset;
            } else {
               assert( _T( ' ' ) == strLine[ 0 ] );
               ptCurrPos.x += sizeSpace.cx;
            }
            strLine.erase( 0, 1 );
         } else {
            if ( nSpace < 0 ) {
```

```
                    nSpace = strLine.length();
                }
                assert( 0 < nSpace );
                String strWord( strLine.substr( 0, nSpace ) );
                strLine.erase( 0, nSpace );
                SIZE size;
                GetTextExtentPoint32(
                    printerDC, strWord.c_str(), strWord.length(), &size );
                if ( rcPrintArea.right < ptCurrPos.x + size.cx ) {
                    ptCurrPos.x = rcPrintArea.left;
                    ptCurrPos.y += nLineHeight;
                    if ( rcPrintArea.bottom < ptCurrPos.y + nLineHeight ) {
                        pageHeader( printerDC,
                            strHeader, &nPage, rcPrintArea, &ptCurrPos );
                    }
                }
                verify( TextOut( printerDC, ptCurrPos.x, ptCurrPos.y,
                    strWord.c_str(), strWord.length() ) );
                ptCurrPos.x += size.cx;
            }
        }
        ptCurrPos.y += nLineHeight;
        if ( rcPrintArea.bottom < ptCurrPos.y + nLineHeight ) {
            if ( 0 != *pszText ) {
                pageHeader( printerDC,
                    strHeader, &nPage, rcPrintArea, &ptCurrPos );
            }
        }
    }

    if ( EndPage( printerDC ) <= 0 ) {
        throwException( _T( "EndPage failed" ) );
    }
}

/**
 * NOTE: Both MS-DOS and Unix-style line feeds are OK for pszText.
 */
void Document::print( HDC hdc, LPCTSTR pszText, int nCopies ) {
```

```
assertValid();
assert( isGoodStringPtr( pszText ) );
WaitCursor waitCursor( _T( "print.ani" ) );

const int nLogPixelsX      = GetDeviceCaps( hdc, LOGPIXELSX      );
const int nLogPixelsY      = GetDeviceCaps( hdc, LOGPIXELSY      );
const int nPhysicalOffsetX = GetDeviceCaps( hdc, PHYSICALOFFSETX );
const int nPhysicalOffsetY = GetDeviceCaps( hdc, PHYSICALOFFSETY );
const int nPhysicalWidth   = GetDeviceCaps( hdc, PHYSICALWIDTH   );
const int nPhysicalHeight  = GetDeviceCaps( hdc, PHYSICALHEIGHT  );

const int nUnitsPerInch = getMarginsAreMetric() ? 2540 : 1000;
assert( 0 != nUnitsPerInch );

int nLeftMargin   =
   MulDiv( getLeftMargin  (), nLogPixelsX, nUnitsPerInch );
int nTopMargin    =
   MulDiv( getTopMargin   (), nLogPixelsY, nUnitsPerInch );
int nRightMargin  =
   MulDiv( getRightMargin (), nLogPixelsX, nUnitsPerInch );
int nBottomMargin =
   MulDiv( getBottomMargin(), nLogPixelsY, nUnitsPerInch );

// One-inch defaults:
if ( 0 == nLeftMargin ) {
   nLeftMargin = nRightMargin = nLogPixelsX;
   nTopMargin = nBottomMargin = nLogPixelsY;
}

// Adjust to physical offsets:
nLeftMargin   = __max( nPhysicalOffsetX, nLeftMargin   );
nTopMargin    = __max( nPhysicalOffsetY, nTopMargin    );
nRightMargin  = __max( nPhysicalOffsetX, nRightMargin  );
nBottomMargin = __max( nPhysicalOffsetY, nBottomMargin );

const RECT rcPrintArea = {
   nLeftMargin - nPhysicalOffsetX,
   nTopMargin  - nPhysicalOffsetY,
```

```
        nPhysicalWidth  - nRightMargin  - nPhysicalOffsetX,
        nPhysicalHeight - nBottomMargin - nPhysicalOffsetY,
    };

    PrinterDoc printerDoc( hdc, getTitle() );
    PrinterDC printerDC( hdc, createPrintFont( hdc ) );

    for ( int iCopy = 0; iCopy < nCopies; ++iCopy ) {
        printSingleCopy(
            printerDC, rcPrintArea, pszText, getTitle(), getTabs() );
    }
}
```

Chapter 17

Changing Fonts

TextEdit allows the user to select one proportional font and one fixed-width font. These selections are global across all instances of TextEdit, but it is quick to switch between proportional and fixed-width font, and the selected font is retained for individual files and for file types.

The TextEdit Font Dialog is an example of implementation problems overpowering user requirements, a problem I talked about in Chapter 2. My original plan called for a single dialog for font customization, looking something like Figure 17.1.

Figure 17.1 The Font dialog that never was. Is there a bug in `WM_CHOOSEFONT_SETLOGFONT,` or am I all thumbs?

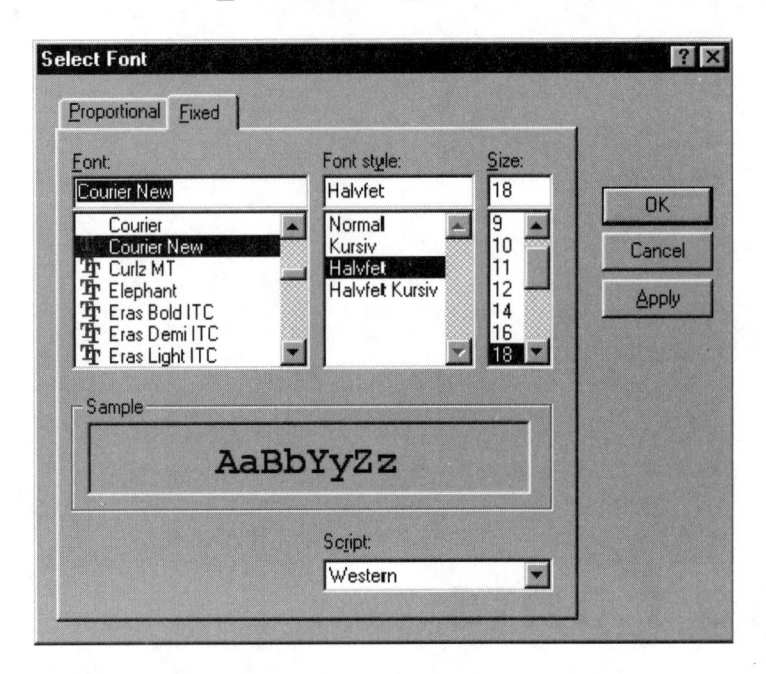

Figure 17.1 is based on the Font common dialog; I merely added a tab control. I figured that judicious use of the `WM_CHOOSEFONT_SETLOGFONT` and `WM_CHOOSEFONT_GETLOGFONT` messages in response to tab clicks would serve to change the dialog's contents appropriately.

This solution would have been ever so much nicer than having two separate dialogs, but it never happened. The catch? `WM_CHOOSEFONT_SETLOGFONT` does not, as near as I can figure out, work. To realize the design in Figure 17.1, I would've had to implement a font selection dialog from scratch. While this is certainly possible, it is considerably more work than customizing a common dialog. Besides, it's best to stick with common dialogs whenever possible. If you don't, the next Windows release may leave you in the dust.

At any rate, I ended up putting font selection into the Options dialog (see Figure 13.2), with a font selection dialog box available from two different push buttons. The font selection dialogs are also available by double clicking on the Fixed Font or Proportional Font buttons in the tool bar, or through the `Ctrl+Shift+F` accelerator.

Subclassing the Font Common Dialog

Changing the looks of the common Font Selection dialog is a matter of creating a replacement dialog template, an approach quite different from that used with the Open and Save dialogs. The standard template supplied by Microsoft is shown in Listing 17.1, `FONT.DLG`; TextEdit's dialog template (`IDD_FONT`) is based on this. All I did was hide some unneeded controls and change the size of the sample display to fully utilize the vacated space.

Listing 17.1 FONT.DLG

```
/*++

Copyright (c) 1990-1997, Microsoft Corporation  All rights reserved.
Module Name:
    font.dlg

Abstract:
    This module contains the resource descriptions for the Win32
    font common dialogs.
--*/


//
// Font Dialogs.
//

FORMATDLGORD31 DIALOG 13, 54, 263, 196
STYLE DS_MODALFRAME | WS_POPUP | WS_CAPTION | WS_SYSMENU |
      DS_CONTEXTHELP | DS_3DLOOK
CAPTION "Font"
FONT 8, "MS Shell Dlg"
BEGIN
    LTEXT           "&Font:", stc1, 7, 7, 40, 9
    COMBOBOX        cmb1, 7, 16, 98, 76, CBS_SIMPLE |
                    CBS_AUTOHSCROLL | CBS_SORT | WS_VSCROLL |
                    WS_TABSTOP | CBS_HASSTRINGS |
                    CBS_OWNERDRAWFIXED | CBS_DISABLENOSCROLL
    LTEXT           "Font st&yle:", stc2, 110, 7, 44, 9
    COMBOBOX        cmb2, 110, 16, 62, 76, CBS_SIMPLE | WS_VSCROLL |
                    CBS_DISABLENOSCROLL | WS_TABSTOP
    LTEXT           "&Size:", stc3, 177, 7, 30, 9
    COMBOBOX        cmb3, 177, 16, 27, 76, CBS_SIMPLE | WS_VSCROLL |
                    WS_TABSTOP | CBS_HASSTRINGS | CBS_OWNERDRAWFIXED |
                    CBS_SORT | CBS_DISABLENOSCROLL
    DEFPUSHBUTTON   "OK", IDOK, 210, 16, 45, 14, WS_GROUP
    PUSHBUTTON      "Cancel", IDCANCEL, 210, 32, 45, 14, WS_GROUP
    PUSHBUTTON      "&Apply", psh3, 210, 48, 45, 14, WS_GROUP
    PUSHBUTTON      "&Help", pshHelp, 210, 64, 45, 14, WS_GROUP
    GROUPBOX        "Effects", grp1, 7, 97, 98, 72, WS_GROUP
    AUTOCHECKBOX    "Stri&keout", chx1, 13, 110, 49, 10, WS_TABSTOP
```

```
    AUTOCHECKBOX   "&Underline", chx2, 13, 123, 51, 10
    LTEXT          "&Color:", stc4, 13, 136, 30, 9
    COMBOBOX       cmb4, 13, 146, 82, 100,
                   CBS_DROPDOWNLIST | CBS_OWNERDRAWFIXED |
                   CBS_AUTOHSCROLL | CBS_HASSTRINGS | WS_BORDER |
                   WS_VSCROLL | WS_TABSTOP
    GROUPBOX       "Sample", grp2, 110, 97, 94, 43, WS_GROUP
    CTEXT          "AaBbYyZz", stc5, 118, 111, 77, 23,
                   SS_NOPREFIX | NOT WS_VISIBLE
    LTEXT          "", stc6, 7, 176, 196, 20, SS_NOPREFIX |
                   NOT WS_GROUP
    LTEXT          "Sc&ript:", stc7, 110, 147, 30, 9
    COMBOBOX       cmb5, 110, 157, 94, 30, CBS_DROPDOWNLIST |
                   CBS_OWNERDRAWFIXED | CBS_AUTOHSCROLL |
                   CBS_HASSTRINGS | WS_BORDER | WS_VSCROLL | WS_TABSTOP
END
```

Note the script selection combo box in the dialog. This means that we must save the `lfCharSet` member of the `LOGFONT` structure between invocations. With Unicode, this doesn't matter, but with ANSI, it does. (More about this in Chapter 18.)

All TextEdit must do to show the font selection dialog is call the `selectFont` function, passing a pointer to a `LOGFONT` structure. If the user uses OK to dismiss the dialog, any changes to the font are reflected in the `LOGFONT` structure upon return.

The font dialog is invoked with the Options dialog as its parent if you click either of its Change buttons. It is invoked with the main window as its parent if you double-click one of the two font buttons on the toolbar or use the Ctrl+Shift+F accelerator. In the latter case, the font selection dialog is subject to the same positioning persistence as all other TextEdit dialogs, i.e., it will reappear where you last put it, relative to the main window. In the former case, though, the dialog is placed flush below either the Fixed Font or Proportional Font sample widgets, depending on which Change button you clicked. This reinforces the connection between the dialog and the sample widget, and reduces your chance of getting confused about whether you're modifying the fixed or the proportional font. This is indeed a minor detail, but every little bit helps.

A pointer to the rectangle of the sample widget is passed in the `prcAvoid` parameter to `selectFont`; this, in turn, is passed to the `FontHookProc` in the `lCustData` member of the `CHOOSEFONT` structure. All callers except the Options dialog pass null instead.

The `Editor` class has responsibility for the fonts used in the editor; it is the responsibility of `selectFont`'s callers to get and set the fonts, as demonstrated by this excerpt from `mainwnd.h`:

```
PRIVATE void onViewSetFixedFont( HWND hwnd ) {

   LOGFONT logFont = *getEditor( hwnd )->getLogFont( true );
   if ( selectFont( hwnd, &logFont, 0, CF_FIXEDPITCHONLY ) ) {
      getEditor( hwnd )->setLogFont( &logFont, true );
```

```
      }
   }

   PRIVATE void onViewSetProportionalFont( HWND hwnd ) {

      LOGFONT logFont = *getEditor( hwnd )->getLogFont( false );
      if ( selectFont( hwnd, &logFont ) ) {
         getEditor( hwnd )->setLogFont( &logFont, false );
      }
   }

   PRIVATE void onViewSetFont( HWND hwnd ) { // Ctrl+Shift+F

      if ( getEditor( hwnd )->hasFixedFont() ) {
         onViewSetFixedFont( hwnd );
      } else {
         onViewSetProportionalFont( hwnd );
      }
   }
```

Listing 17.2   FontDlg.cpp

```
/*
 * $Header: /Book/FontDlg.cpp 11    3.07.99 17:46 Petter $
 */

#include "precomp.h"
#include "Editor.h"
#include "resource.h"
#include "utils.h"
#include "winUtils.h"
#include "FontDlg.h"

UINT CALLBACK FontHookProc(
   HWND hwnd, UINT msg, WPARAM wParam, LPARAM lParam )
{
   static bool s_wasPositioned = false;

   if ( WM_INITDIALOG == msg ) {
      const CHOOSEFONT *pChooseFont =
```

```cpp
            reinterpret_cast< const CHOOSEFONT * >( lParam );
        assert( isGoodConstPtr( pChooseFont ) );
        centerDialog( hwnd );

        const Rect *prcAvoid =
            reinterpret_cast< const Rect * >( pChooseFont->lCustData );
        s_wasPositioned = 0 != prcAvoid;
        if ( s_wasPositioned ) {
            SetWindowPos( hwnd, 0, prcAvoid->left, prcAvoid->bottom,
                0, 0, SWP_NOZORDER | SWP_NOSIZE | SWP_NOACTIVATE );
            adjustToScreen( hwnd );
        } else {
            restorePosition( hwnd, IDD_FONT );
        }
        return TRUE;
    } else if ( WM_DESTROY == msg ) {
        if ( !s_wasPositioned ) {
            savePosition( hwnd, IDD_FONT );
        }
    }
    return 0;
}

bool selectFont( HWND hwndParent, LOGFONT *pLogFont,
    const Rect *prcAvoid, DWORD dwExtraFlags )
{
    const DWORD chooseFontFlags =
        CF_SCREENFONTS | CF_ENABLEHOOK | CF_ENABLETEMPLATE |
        CF_INITTOLOGFONTSTRUCT | CF_FORCEFONTEXIST;

    CHOOSEFONT chooseFont = {
        sizeof( CHOOSEFONT ), hwndParent, 0, pLogFont, 0,
        chooseFontFlags | dwExtraFlags,
    };
    chooseFont.lpfnHook = FontHookProc;
    chooseFont.lpTemplateName = MAKEINTRESOURCE( IDD_FONT );
    chooseFont.hInstance = getModuleHandle();
    chooseFont.lCustData = reinterpret_cast< LPARAM >( prcAvoid );
    return 0 != ChooseFont( &chooseFont );
}
```

Chapter 18

Going Abroad

Even though I'm running the US edition of Windows NT 4 Workstation, I can nevertheless create files with Greek names; my file system is NTFS, so file names are Unicode. The question is, "Can I display those file names?" The answer is, "It depends."

Figure 18.1 Γρεεκ Φιλε.**log (Greek File.log — English written using the Greek alphabet. An even Greeker file name would be** Εκθεσι Ελληνικον.**log.) The file name is Unicode, the program is Unicode, and the Unicode title font contains the required Greek characters.**

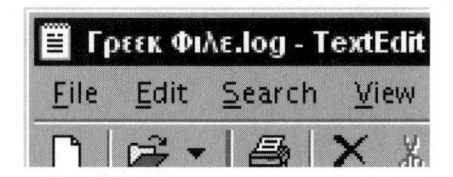

Figure 18.1 shows a screen from a Unicode build of TextEdit, using a font (Tahoma) that contains the Greek Unicode characters (0x0370-0x03cf). In Figure 18.2, I've switched to MS Sans Serif, which does not, and the Greek characters can't be displayed. A default character — a black rectangle — is displayed instead. It would be a different matter if Greek were installed as the system default language. In that case, a different code page of MS Sans Serif

would be installed, and character codes between 128 and 255 would be used to display the Greek characters, even though the file name characters are actually from the Greek Unicode page. The Unicode character code for uppercase alpha, for example, is 0x0391; it obviously can't be represented in an 8-bit code.

Figure 18.2   A truly Greek file name. (Apologies to all Greeks. This is Chinese to you, of course.) In this case, the problem lies with the MS Sans Serif font.

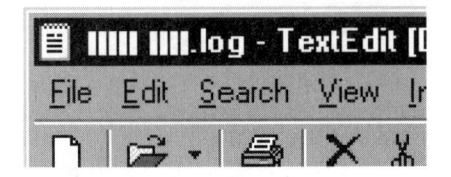

Figure 18.3 shows a Tahoma menu. Note item 2, a beautiful rendition of a Greek file name. Even more interesting are items 5 and 6, leftovers from an ANSI build. They show how difficult life can be for an ANSI application on a Unicode file system. The `WideCharToMultiByte` function has mapped the Gamma, Epsilon, and Phi characters with a modicum of success. The rest were deemed untranslatable, and thus replaced by the default character. Because I didn't specify a default character, the default default character was used, and because this doubly default character is a question mark, the file name is more than merely wrong: the question mark is a wild-card character, so the file name is illegal.

Figure 18.3   Tahoma menu in Unicode build. Items 5 and 6 show how badly Unicode-to-ANSI translations can screw things up.

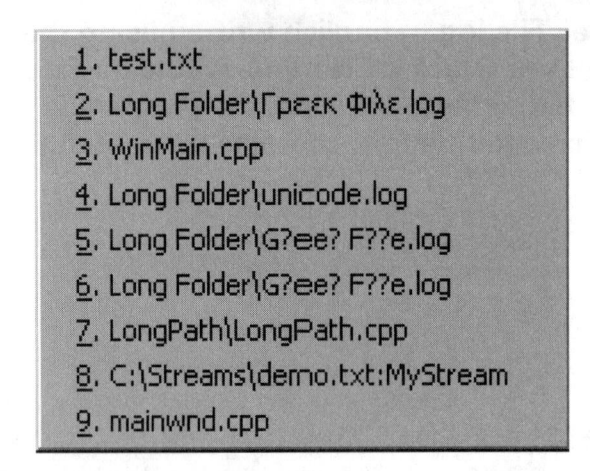

The moral is that Windows NT is a Unicode system to the core and best served by Unicode applications using Unicode fonts. The problem with that, though, is that we'd all like to create a single executable to run under both Windows 9x and Windows NT. ANSI applications on NT run into the "G?ee? F??e" problem from Figure 18.3, and creating a Unicode application that runs well on Windows 9x is a major undertaking — you must build an architectural layer that wraps all string-related APIs. The `getPathFromIDList` set of functions in `utils.cpp` gives you an idea about what this entails.

Resource Files

One reason for the existence of resource files as separate from the code is to permit translations between languages without touching the code itself. To create a German TextEdit version, all you have to do is translate the resources into German and relink the application.

That much has been true since the early days of Win16. Win32 introduced language tags for resources. This allows you to have any number of copies of, say, a dialog box, all with the same identifier, provided they have different language tags. Consider this resource script:

```
LANGUAGE LANG_ENGLISH, SUBLANG_ENGLISH_US
STRINGTABLE DISCARDABLE
{
   IDS_VERSION          "Version:"
   ...
   IDS_STRING_NOT_FOUND "Unable to find <b>%1</b>"
}

LANGUAGE LANG_NORWEGIAN, SUBLANG_NORWEGIAN_BOKMAL
STRINGTABLE DISCARDABLE
{
   IDS_VERSION          "Versjon:"
   ...
   IDS_STRING_NOT_FOUND "Fant ikke <b>%1</b>"
}
```

What happens if you call `loadString( IDS_VERSION )`? If you're running Windows NT, the current thread locale decides. The current thread locale, in turn, is by default initialized to the user locale selected in the Regional Settings Control Panel applet. If you're running Windows 95, the system default locale decides — Windows 95 does not support thread locales or user locales.

If a resource doesn't exist in the desired language, the system has several fallback positions. The search order is as follows:

1. Primary language/sublanguage
2. Primary language/any sublanguage
3. Language neutral
4. English
5. Any

If the current locale is French, the `loadString` example returns the US English resource, according to rule 4 above. If the current locale is Norwegian Nynorsk (rather than Norwegian

Bokmål), the example returns the Norwegian resource because there's a match in the primary language, and rule 2 applies. If there were only one string table resource, tagged with `LANG_SWAHILI`, you would get the Swahili string no matter what the current locale (rule 5).

Windows NT allows you to change the user default language on the fly from the Control Panel. If this happens, a `WM_SETTINGCHANGE` message is broadcast, allowing us to change the application's language on the fly. The main window's `onSettingChange` function, in `mainwnd.cpp`, contains the following code fragment:

```
// Switch languages, if indicated:
const LCID lcid = GetUserDefaultLCID();
if ( GetThreadLocale() != lcid ) {
    assert( isWindowsNT() );
    verify( SetThreadLocale( lcid ) );
    verify( DestroyMenu( GetMenu( hwnd ) ) );
    SetMenu( hwnd, LoadMenu( getModuleHandle(),
        MAKEINTRESOURCE( IDR_MENU ) ) );
    verify( DrawMenuBar( hwnd ) );
    getEditor( hwnd )->loadAcceleratorTable();
}
```

Presto, language change! The important part is to reload the menu and the accelerator table. Dialog resources are loaded anew each time the dialog is invoked. Any dialog box that's open at the time of the language switch will, unfortunately, remain in the old language until the next time it is invoked. I'm not going to tackle that problem, though; I feel that I'm approaching a point of diminishing returns.

You can switch languages programmatically, too, by calling the `SetThreadLocale` function. The options dialog (`OptionsDlg.cpp`) has an example of this; it lets you select the desired language from a combo box. Under Windows 9x, however, this combo box is disabled. Although `SetThreadLocale` is present in all versions of the Windows API, it has no effect under Windows 9x. The best you can do under Windows 9x is to change the system default locale, then reboot the system.

To change languages on the fly under Windows 9x, your best approach is to put all the resources into a DLL, then create differently-named versions of this DLL for each supported language. With such an approach, the call

```
LoadMenu( getModuleHandle(), ... );
```

above would change to something like

```
LoadMenu( getResourceModuleHandle(), ... );
```

where `getResourceModuleHandle` would return the module handle of the DLL matching the currently selected language.

If I haven't said so before, I'll say it now: Windows NT is a *much*, much better operating system than Windows 9x.

Formatting Messages

Traditional C programming relies on the `printf` family of functions to format messages. Thus, one writes:

```
wsprintf( szMsg, "File %s not found", szFile );
```

Now, if this string were hard-coded, a translation into German would entail changing that line of code, then recompiling:

```
wsprintf( szMsg, "Datei %s nicht gefunden", szFile );
```

To avoid this, we store the string in a string table. Translation no longer requires recompilation, and the code might look like this:

```
wsprintf( szMsg, loadString( IDS_FILE_NOT_FOUND ).c_str(), szFile );
```

This is better, but one problem remains. When you use `wsprintf` (or any of its relatives), the order of the arguments is fixed. This is not a problem in the example above, but is sometimes a problem in translations involving two or more inserts, where argument reordering may be preferable, or even required.

The Win32 API offers an alternative called `FormatMessage`. This very capable function lets you vary the order of the inserts; rather than specifying %s and %d, it wants %1!s! and %2!d!, which lets you switch the first and second inserts in the formatting string, or even repeat an insert. It can retrieve descriptive text for Windows errors, and allocate the buffer for it if you so wish. This paragon of flexibility can do everything but tie your shoelaces.

The functions defined in `formatMessage.cpp` wraps `FormatMessage` in functions that take `printf`-style variable-length argument lists. One of them takes a resource string ID rather than a string.

Listing 18.1 formatMessage.cpp

```
/*
 * $Header: /Book/formatMessage.cpp 11    5.09.99 13:07 Petter $
 *
 * Defines the formatMessage functions and their
 * companion, the formatMessageV function.
 */

#include "precomp.h"
#include "formatMessage.h"
#include "utils.h"

#define MAX_LENGTH 1000

/**
 * Formats a message using the FormatMessage function,
```

```
 * with a formatting string. Note that the formatting
 * string contains %1, %2, ... rather than printf-style
 * format specifiers. You can still specify a printf-style
 * format by enclosing it in a pair of exclamation marks
 * and putting it behind the number, e.g. %1!d! for a digit.
 * The default is !s!, signifying a string.
 */
String __cdecl formatMessage( const String strFmt, ... ) {

    va_list vl;
    va_start( vl, strFmt );
    const String strMessage = formatMessageV( strFmt, vl );
    va_end( vl );

    return strMessage;
}

/**
 * Formats a message using the FormatMessage function,
 * with a formatting string loaded from the string table.
 * See the other formatMessage for further comments.
 */
String __cdecl formatMessage( UINT uiFmtID, ... ) {

    const String strFmt = loadString( uiFmtID );
    va_list vl;
    va_start( vl, uiFmtID );
    const String strMessage = formatMessageV( strFmt, vl );
    va_end( vl );

    return strMessage;
}

/**
 * Formats a message using the FormatMessage function,
 * with a formatting string. This is the real workhorse,
 * used by both formatMessage functions.
 */
String formatMessageV( const String& strFmt, va_list vl ) {
```

```
    // This buffer *must* be empty in case strFmt is empty!
    TCHAR sz[ MAX_LENGTH ] = { 0 };
    FormatMessage( FORMAT_MESSAGE_FROM_STRING,
        strFmt.c_str(), 0, 0, sz, dim( sz ), &vl );
    return sz;
}
```

Initialize the Output String!

The `formatMessageV` function is the real workhorse. It defines text buffer that `FormatMessage` will fill:

```
TCHAR sz[ MAX_LENGTH ] = { 0 };
```

Note that this initializes the buffer to an empty string. All string declarations in TextEdit are initialized in the same manner, but in this case, it is particularly important. If the format specification string is empty, `FormatMessage` does nothing to the output string — it does not even empty it. If it were uninitialized, the best that could happen would be the return of a garbage string. As for the worst that could happen, the sky is the limit: if the uninitialized array doesn't contain a terminator somewhere, the String constructor (called when the function returns) will continue to read beyond the end of the array.

Beware of References!

The `formatMessage` function with a string argument was originally defined as follows:

```
String __cdecl formatMessage( LPCTSTR pszFmt, ... );
```

This was fine, except that most places that called the function had a formatting `String` rather than a formatting `LPCTSTR`, and the code was littered with calls to `String::c_str`, there being no conversion operator available. Why not, I thought, change the formal parameter to a `const String&`, and avoid the conversion hassle? Any calls to `formatMessage` that actually used an `LPCTSTR` would be OK because a suitable `String` constructor is available to convert the `LPCTSTR` to a `String`.

In innocent ignorance, I changed `formatMessage` to the following:

```
String __cdecl formatMessage( const String& strFmt, ... ) {

    va_list vl;
    va_start( vl, strFmt );
    const String strMessage = formatMessageV( strFmt, vl );
    va_end( vl );

    return strMessage;
}
```

It promptly blew up. It took me a long debugging session to figure out what the problem was; can you see it?

The culprit is the application of the `va_start` macro to a reference. The `strFmt` reference argument is actually a pointer to a String object, but there's no way to get the address of the pointer value. The address operator retrieves the address of the `strFmt` String object, while `va_start` needs the address of the pointer to the `strFmt` object that is actually passed on the stack. The compiler can't catch this, of course, and the `va_list` gets screwed up something horribly.

Solving the problem was then a simple trade-off between efficiency (an `LPCTSTR` parameter) and readability at the point of call (a `String` parameter). For TextEdit, I chose readability, and changed `formatMessage` to this:

```
String __cdecl formatMessage( const String strFmt, ... ) {
```

The string is now passed by value, and must therefore be copied. Inefficient, yes, but TextEdit doesn't format messages frequently enough to make it much of an issue.

Formatting Numbers

TextEdit displays numbers in several places: in the status bar, it displays the current line and column; in the Properties dialog, it displays file sizes in three different ways.

Consider the number 1834597891. This is a nice, big number and difficult to grasp it is, too. Quick, how big is it? Is it more or less than one billion?

The easy way to format a number for display is to use `printf( "%d", 1834597891 )`, which gives the result you just saw. What we want is 1,834,597,891 — perhaps. In the US, the comma is used to separate groups of thousands; in Europe, it is more common to use a period (1.834.597.891), reserving the comma for the decimal point. In Norway, we like to use spaces instead, and to really confuse the issue, some locations don't even group by thousands, or even by the same number of digits for each group.

To find out what the correct format is, we have the `GetLocaleInfo` function to help us. If you call it with `LOCALE_STHOUSAND` as the second parameter, it will return a string containing the thousands separator. For example, if you're using the US locale, this code snippet will set `szThousandSep` to ",":

```
TCHAR szThousandSep[ 10 ] = { 0 };
GetLocaleInfo( LOCALE_USER_DEFAULT, LOCALE_STHOUSAND,
    szThousandSep, dim( szThousandSep ) ) );
```

If you call `GetLocaleInfo` with `LOCALE_SGROUPING` as the second parameter, it will return a string describing how you should group the digits. The grouping string contains digits separated by semicolons; the final digit should be zero. As soon as the zero has been reached, the last group size given should be repeated ad infinitum. A couple of examples will make this clear: "3;0" specifies groups of three digits, while "3;2;0" specifies one group of three digits, then groups of two from there on.

The `formatNumber` function (in Listing 18.2, `formatNumber.cpp`) takes all this into account when formatting numbers. The one implementation issue worth mentioning is that the string is built backwards and then reversed at the end. This could lead us astray if a thousand separator string of more than one character came along. To protect against such a potential mishap, the thousands separator string is itself reversed before we start applying it.

Listing 18.2 `formatNumber.cpp`

```
/*
 * $Header: /Book/formatNumber.cpp 8     5.09.99 13:07 Petter $
 *
 * Defines the formatNumber function.
 */

#include "precomp.h"
#include "formatNumber.h"
#include "utils.h"
#include "trace.h"

/**
 * Does not support negative numbers.
 * If you need a more efficient implementation,
 * perform the GetLocaleInfo and initialization
 * only on startup and locale changes.
 * If you don't need a more efficient implementation,
 * this way is better, because it is simpler.
 * See also: GetNumberFormat
 */
String formatNumber( int nValue ) {

    assert( 0 <= nValue );

    const int MAX_GROUPINGS = 10;

    // Win16:
    // GetProfileString( "intl", "sThousand", ",",
    //     szThousandSep, sizeof szThousandSep );

    TCHAR szThousandSep[ MAX_GROUPINGS ] = { 0 };
    verify( GetLocaleInfo( LOCALE_USER_DEFAULT, LOCALE_STHOUSAND,
        szThousandSep, dim( szThousandSep ) ) );
    _tcsrev( szThousandSep ); // We will reverse the string later.
```

```
   TCHAR szGrouping[ 100 ] = { 0 };
   verify( GetLocaleInfo( LOCALE_USER_DEFAULT, LOCALE_SGROUPING,
      szGrouping, dim( szGrouping ) ) );

   int anGrouping[ 10 ] = { 0 };
   int nGroupings = 0;
   for ( TCHAR *psz = szGrouping;
         0 != *psz && _T( '0' ) != *psz;
         psz = charNext( psz ) )
   {
      if ( _istdigit( *psz ) ) {
         assert( nGroupings < dim( anGrouping ) );
         if ( dim( anGrouping ) <= nGroupings ) {
            trace( _T(
               "more than %d digit groupings; ignoring the rest\n" ),
               dim( anGrouping ) );
            break; //*** LOOP EXIT POINT
         }
         anGrouping[ nGroupings++ ] = *psz - _T( '0' );
      } else {
         assert( _T( ';' ) == *psz );
      }
   }

   if ( 0 == nGroupings ) {
      anGrouping[ 0 ] = 3;
      nGroupings = 1;
   }

#if 0 // Testing
   nGroupings = 3;
   anGrouping[ 0 ] = 3;
   anGrouping[ 1 ] = 1;
   anGrouping[ 2 ] = 2;
#endif

#ifdef _DEBUG
   for ( int iGrouping = 0; iGrouping < nGroupings; ++iGrouping ) {
      assert( 0 != anGrouping[ iGrouping ] );
   }
```

```
#endif

    TCHAR szValue[ 100 ] = { 0 };
    psz = szValue;
    int nGroup = 0;
    int nDigitsInGroup = anGrouping[ nGroup ];

    for ( ;; ) {
       *psz++ = (TCHAR)(_T( '0' ) + nValue % 10);
       if ( (nValue /= 10) <= 0 ) {
          break; //*** LOOP EXIT POINT
       }
       if ( --nDigitsInGroup <= 0 ) {
          _tcscpy( psz, szThousandSep );
          psz += _tcsclen( psz );
          if ( nGroup < nGroupings - 1 ) {
             ++nGroup;
          }
          nDigitsInGroup = anGrouping[ nGroup ];
       }
    }

    // The string is now backwards, so switch:
    _tcsrev( szValue );
    return szValue;
}
```

By now, you will have figured out that the number 1834597891 is larger than one billion. The TextEdit Properties dialog displays file sizes in two formats, one of which would be 1.8 GB for our example (or 1,8 GB in some parts of the world). This bit of formatting is performed by a Windows function from SHLWAPI called StrFormatByteSize; it is used in PropertiesDlg::setInfo (PropertiesDlg.cpp).

GetNumberFormat is another Windows function useful for number formatting. I would have used it in formatNumber except that, by default, GetNumberFormat adds decimals to the output string. Overriding the default behavior involves filling in a NUMBERFMT structure, and suddenly the use of GetNumberFormat is more trouble than it is worth. In addition, the NUMBERFMT structure has a structural problem: it has but a single Grouping member (of type UINT) to handle digit groupings. In other words, GetNumberFormat does not support differently sized groupings.

Formatting Dates, and Money, and...

I have already covered most of the formatting that TextEdit does — TextEdit is a light formatter. The Properties dialog needs to display time stamps though. Their formatting is handled by the `formatFileTime` function, defined in `PropertiesDlg.cpp`:

```
PRIVATE String formatFileTime( const FILETIME& ft ) {

   FILETIME local = ft;
   verify( FileTimeToLocalFileTime( &ft, &local ) );

   SYSTEMTIME st;
   verify( FileTimeToSystemTime( &local, &st ) );

   TCHAR szTime[ 100 ] = { 0 };
   GetTimeFormat(
      LOCALE_USER_DEFAULT, 0, &st, 0, szTime, dim( szTime ) );

   TCHAR szDate[ 100 ] = { 0 };
   GetDateFormat( LOCALE_USER_DEFAULT,
      DATE_LONGDATE, &st, 0, szDate, dim( szDate ) );

   return formatMessage( _T( "%1 %2" ), szDate, szTime );
}
```

Formatting Dates, and Money, and...

Most commercial applications do more, dealing as they do with dates, money, calendars, phone numbers, units of measurement, and a host of other stuff that varies from locale to locale. Just to give you an idea of the things you must consider, here is a list of the possible values for the second argument to `GetLocalInfo`:

```
LOCALE_ILANGUAGE, LOCALE_SLANGUAGE, LOCALE_SENGLANGUAGE,
LOCALE_SABBREVLANGNAME, LOCALE_SNATIVELANGNAME, LOCALE_SSORTNAME,
LOCALE_ICOUNTRY, LOCALE_SCOUNTRY, LOCALE_SENGCOUNTRY, LOCALE_SABBREVCTRYNAME,
LOCALE_SNATIVECTRYNAME, LOCALE_IDEFAULTLANGUAGE, LOCALE_IDEFAULTCOUNTRY,
LOCALE_IDEFAULTANSICODEPAGE, LOCALE_IDEFAULTOEMCODEPAGE,
LOCALE_IDEFAULTCODEPAGE, LOCALE_IDEFAULTEBCDICCODEPAGE, LOCALE_SLIST,
LOCALE_IMEASURE, LOCALE_SDECIMAL, LOCALE_STHOUSAND, LOCALE_SGROUPING,
LOCALE_IDIGITS, LOCALE_ILZERO, LOCALE_INEGNUMBER, LOCALE_SNATIVEDIGITS,
LOCALE_SENGCURRNAME, LOCALE_SNATIVECURRNAME, LOCALE_SCURRENCY,
LOCALE_SINTLSYMBOL, LOCALE_SMONDECIMALSEP, LOCALE_SMONTHOUSANDSEP,
LOCALE_SMONGROUPING, LOCALE_ICURRDIGITS, LOCALE_IINTLCURRDIGITS,
LOCALE_ICURRENCY, LOCALE_INEGCURR, LOCALE_SDATE, LOCALE_STIME,
LOCALE_STIMEFORMAT, LOCALE_SYEARMONTH, LOCALE_SSHORTDATE, LOCALE_SLONGDATE,
LOCALE_IDATE, LOCALE_ILDATE, LOCALE_ITIME, LOCALE_ICENTURY, LOCALE_ITLZERO,
LOCALE_IDAYLZERO, LOCALE_IMONLZERO, LOCALE_S1159, LOCALE_S2359,
LOCALE_ICALENDARTYPE, LOCALE_IOPTIONALCALENDAR, LOCALE_IFIRSTDAYOFWEEK,
LOCALE_IFIRSTWEEKOFYEAR, LOCALE_SDAYNAME1
```
through `LOCALE_SDAYNAME7`, `LOCALE_SABBREVDAYNAME1` through `LOCALE_SABBREVDAYNAME7`, `LOCALE_SMONTHNAME1` through `LOCALE_SMONTHNAME13`, `LOCALE_SABBREVMONTHNAME1` through
```
LOCALE_SABBREVMONTHNAME13, LOCALE_SPOSITIVESIGN, LOCALE_SNEGATIVESIGN,
LOCALE_IPOSSIGNPOSN, LOCALE_INEGSIGNPOSN, LOCALE_IPOSSYMPRECEDES,
LOCALE_IPOSSEPBYSPACE, LOCALE_INEGSYMPRECEDES, LOCALE_INEGSEPBYSPACE,
LOCALE_IPAPERSIZE
```

Whew! This is not a reference book, but I couldn't resist throwing in that list, just to give you a flavor of what software translation can entail. All this, and we haven't even begun to consider the implications of different cultural conventions!

(Did you notice `LOCALE_SMONTHNAME13`, by the way? No, it's not a misprint.)

Chapter 19

Meanwhile, in the Background

Multi-threading is used for many different purposes. In a server application, a typical purpose is to service multiple requests in parallel, while in a client application, a typical purpose is to perform background processing while keeping the user interface responsive.

An alternative approach to client-side background processing is idle-time processing. Under 16-bit Windows, this is the only possibility, as Win16 doesn't have preemptive multi-tasking (except between virtual machines, which is of little help within a single application).

The best choice depends on the characteristics of the background processing. If your task is easily broken into small chunks, and it is easy to maintain the task's internal state between the execution of chunks, idle-time processing may be a good choice. If not, threads may be a better choice.

The problem with multi-threading is that it can be difficult. To begin with, a whole slew of bugs is associated with multi-threading, including unprotected access to shared resources, synchronization between threads, deadlocks, and race conditions. Moreover, multi-threading bugs are hard to debug. For example, a multi-threaded program that works without fail on a single-processor machine may well fail without fail on a multi-processor machine, when the threads get the opportunity to really run at the same time, instead of merely being scheduled one at a time. A multi-threaded program that hasn't been tested on a multi-processor machine should be regarded as untested.

In the case of memory management, excellent tools can help you find memory leaks, reads and writes outside allocated boundaries, reading from uninitialized memory and so on. No similar magic exists in the case of multi-threading; the best you can do is to apply the KISS principle (Keep It Simple, Stupid!) in full force — keep things as simple as you possibly can.

The Windows NT Explorer contains a lovely example of multi-threading. When you open a directory (excuse me, a folder), the Explorer displays an icon for each file. Many icons are cached in the system image list, but the Explorer always displays icon or cursor files with the actual icon in the file. No icons are associated with .ico or .cur files in general. Getting hold of all those icons may take a long time, particularly if the folder is on a floppy or similarly slow medium. What the Explorer does is to display all the files immediately with a generic Windows icon, then update the icons at its leisure, remaining responsive to user input.

(Never having seen the source code for the Windows NT Explorer, I must admit that I do not *know* that this feature is implemented using threads. But I suspect it is. My Task Manager shows EXPLORER.EXE running no less than eleven threads right now, so the thing is certainly multithreaded.)

Threads in TextEdit

There are several possible uses for background threads in TextEdit — automatic background saving, background printing, or continuous monitoring of the disk. It would even be conceivable to run each concurrent TextEdit instance as a separate UI thread within the same single process.

Keeping the KISS principle in mind, I ended up with no background threads whatsoever in TextEdit proper. Triggering automatic background saving from a timer is smooth enough. TextEdit does have worker threads, but they only make an appearance during setup, not during normal operation. The purpose of searchPreviousThread, uninstallThread and installThread is to let the user interface of SetupDlg remain responsive while potentially time-consuming tasks are going on. I shall get back to SetupDlg in the next chapter.

Starting Threads

The Win32 API gives you the CreateThread function. You should never use this function directly if you make calls to the C runtime library from multiple threads. Instead, you should use the CRT functions _beginthread or _beginthreadex. This allocates resources for the CRT on a per-thread basis, ensuring that different threads don't trample each other's data. The strtok function is a good example of a problem function — because it must retain state between invocations, each thread needs its own storage for this.

In TextEdit, this is wrapped in beginThread and endThread, defined in Listing 19.1, threads.h.

Listing 19.1 `threads.h`

```c
/*
 * $Header: /Book/threads.h 4     3.07.99 17:46 Petter $
 */

#pragma once

#include "Exception.h"

#ifndef _MT
   #error "No threads in single-threaded app"
#endif

typedef UINT (__stdcall *THREADFUNC) (void *);

inline HANDLE beginThread( THREADFUNC pfnThreadFunc, LPVOID pData )
   throw( WinException )
{
   UINT uiID = 0;
   const HANDLE hThread = reinterpret_cast< HANDLE >(
      _beginthreadex( 0, 0, pfnThreadFunc, pData, 0, &uiID ) );
   if ( 0 == hThread ) {
      throwException( _T( "Unable to start thread" ) );
   }
   return hThread;
}

inline void endThread( UINT uiRetCode ) {
   _endthreadex( uiRetCode );
}
```

Communication Between Threads

The threads in `SetupDlg` communicate with the dialog's UI thread by sending or posting messages. Message posting, being asynchronous, is usually a safer bet than message sending, but consider this code fragment in `SetupDlg`'s `installThread` function:

```
try {
   pSetupDlg->install();
}
catch ( const Exception& x ) {
   pSetupDlg->sendMessage( WM_APP, INSTALL_FAILED,
      reinterpret_cast< LPARAM >( x.what() ) );
}
```

On the receiving end of this `sendMessage` call, the UI thread needs to get hold of the string passed in `LPARAM`. If the message were posted, the string would almost certainly be invalid by the time the UI thread got around to handling it. One possibility would be to copy the string to a static buffer. Because this creates reentrancy problems, it is bad as a general solution.

The problem with using `sendMessage` lies in the UI thread's response to the message. Among other things, it calls `cleanupThread`, which calls `WaitForSingleObject` on the background thread handle. Because the thread is currently in `SendMessage`, waiting for a response, it will not terminate any time soon. We have a deadlock situation until `WaitForSingleObject` times out.

One solution would be to split the message in two — one message for setting the string, another to indicate that the worker thread is done and about to die. The first would be sent, the second would be posted.

Another solution — the one actually used — is to employ `ReplyMessage`. On the receiving end, the UI thread first grabs the string, then calls `ReplyMessage` and finally `cleanupThread`:

```
case INSTALL_FAILED:
   ...
   setDlgItemText(
      IDC_MESSAGE2, reinterpret_cast< LPCTSTR >( lParam ) );
   ReplyMessage( 0 );
   ...
   cleanupThread();
   break;
```

After the `ReplyMessage` call, the worker thread's call to `sendMessage` returns and the worker thread is free to continue to termination. Thus, `cleanupThread` avoids the deadlock.

Chapter 20

Setup, and Down Again

Installation and setup of TextEdit is less of a chore than installation and setup of, say, Microsoft Office. TextEdit is distributed as a single file, rather than umpteen zillion. Still, a number of issues must be dealt with, including version control, registry entries, shortcuts to the application, and how to uninstall cleanly.

There are many ways to install programs under Windows, including manual file copying, batch files, various Windows APIs and the Windows 98/Windows 2000 installer. There is also a large number of installation-creating products that help you automate the process.

The TextEdit installation is hand coded, mainly because I want to show you some of what's happening behind the scenes.

In its installation incarnation, TextEdit looks like Figure 20.1 when it starts.

Figure 20.1 **TextEdit Setup in action. This is the standard TextEdit executable, started with the** `/setup` **switch.**

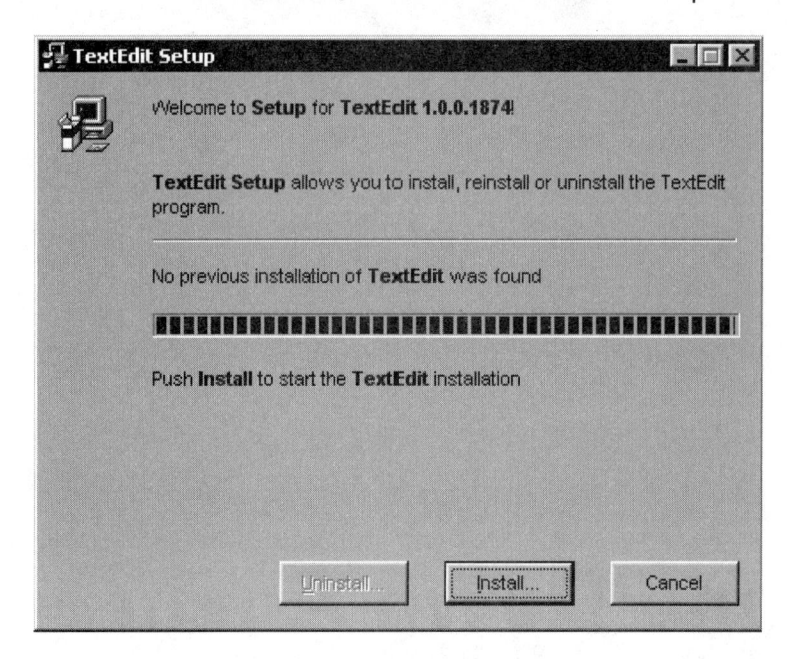

Here are two ways to let TextEdit know that it should be an installer rather than a text editor:

- Start TextEdit with the `/setup` switch
- Rename the executable to `setup.exe` or `install.exe`

Installation leaves traces in the registry, under the key `HKEY_LOCAL_MACHINE\Software\Andersen Consulting\TextEdit\InstallPath`. TextEdit checks this registry key each time it starts. If nothing is there, it runs setup. If something is there, and TextEdit was started without arguments, it compares version numbers. If the running instance is newer than the installed instance, TextEdit asks the user whether an upgrade is in order. This is all handled by the `isSetup` function in `init.cpp`.

To start setup automatically on insertion of a CD, create a file named `autorun.inf` on the CD, with the following contents:

```
[autorun]
open=setup.exe
icon=setup.exe,5
```

The first thing the setup dialog does is check for a previous installation. If it finds one, it compares the version number of the installed file with that of the running executable. If the installed file is newer than the running executable, the `m_isOlderThanPrevious` member of `SetupDlg` is set to `true`, and the Cancel button of Figure 20.1 is made the default button. If the user nevertheless clicks the Install button, a warning pops up.

Installation

Invoking the Install button in Figure 20.1 starts the installation. The first step is customization, handled by `InstallDlg1`, as shown in Figure 20.2.

Figure 20.2 **The Installation dialog. The check marks in the list are communicated back to** `SetupDlg` **through the** `FileType` **class.**

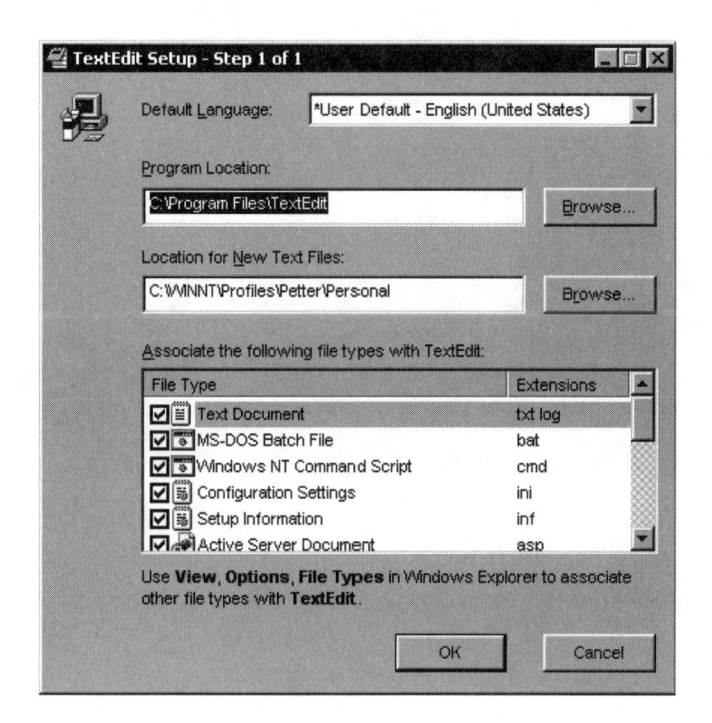

The customization dialog lets you customize the installation by overriding the default values for data directory and program directory and by selecting the file types that TextEdit should be associated with. It also lets you select the UI language (if you're running under Windows NT); both the language and the data directory settings can be changed later through the Options dialog.

The `FileType` class handles everything related to file types. Each `FileType` instance describes one class of files and the array `FileType::sm_aFileType` lists all file types we know about.

Three standard actions are usually associated with data files: Open (the default action), Edit, and Print. These appear on the context menu when the data file is right-clicked in the explorer. Not all action/file type combinations are created equal though. For a text document, Open means the same as Edit. For a batch file, Open means Execute. For an HTML document, Open means view it in a browser, and Edit probably means to edit it in a WYSIWYG HTML editor such as the Microsoft FrontPage editor.

For each document type, TextEdit knows whether Edit is the default action, whether Edit means "edit the source," and whether TextEdit should handle printing. In the cases where a program other than TextEdit is the natural choice for any of these actions, as is the case with HTML files, we simply add a new command to the context menu, "Edit with TextEdit."

The `FileType` class has a member named `m_bInclude`; the user controls its value through the list box check marks in Figure 20.2. (Discourse continues on page 459.)

Listing 20.1 FileType.h

```
/*
 * $Header: /Book/FileType.h 3     3.07.99 17:46 Petter $
 */

#pragma once

#include "String.h"

class FileType {
private:
    String m_strExtension;
    String m_strClass;
    bool   m_isEditDefault;
    bool   m_bEdit;
    bool   m_bPrint;
    bool   m_bInclude;

    FileType( LPCTSTR pszExtension,
        bool isEditDefault, bool bEdit, bool bPrint );
    void setCommand( LPCTSTR pszPath,
        LPCTSTR pszFmt, LPCTSTR pszName = 0 );
    void removeCommand( LPCTSTR pszPath, LPCTSTR pszFmt );

    LPCTSTR getClass    ( void ) const;
    bool isEditDefault( void ) const;
    bool useEdit      ( void ) const;
    bool shouldInclude( void ) const;
    bool shouldPrint  ( void ) const;

    static FileType sm_aFileType[];
    static String   sm_strCommand;

public:
    LPCTSTR getExtension( void ) const;
```

```cpp
    bool       exists      ( void ) const;

    void    registerType ( void );
    void  unregisterType ( void );

    static int getNumFileTypes( void );
    static FileType *getFileType( int nIndex );
    static void include( LPCTSTR pszExt, bool bInclude );
    static void setCommand( const String& strCommand );
};

inline LPCTSTR FileType::getExtension( void ) const {

    return m_strExtension.c_str();
}

inline LPCTSTR FileType::getClass( void ) const {

    return m_strClass.c_str();
}

inline bool FileType::isEditDefault( void ) const {

    return m_isEditDefault;
}

inline bool FileType::useEdit( void ) const {

    return m_bEdit;
}

inline bool FileType::shouldPrint( void ) const {

    return m_bPrint;
}

inline bool FileType::shouldInclude( void ) const {

    return m_bInclude;
}
```

Listing 20.2 FileType.cpp

```cpp
/*
 * $Header: /Book/FileType.cpp 5      5.09.99 13:07 Petter $
 */

#include "precomp.h"
#include "FileType.h"
#include "Registry.h"
#include "formatMessage.h"
#include "utils.h"
#include "resource.h"

FileType::FileType( LPCTSTR pszExt,
   bool isEditDefault, bool bEdit, bool bPrint )
   : m_strExtension( pszExt )
   , m_strClass( Registry::getString( HKEY_CLASSES_ROOT, pszExt ) )
   , m_isEditDefault( isEditDefault )
   , m_bEdit( bEdit )
   , m_bInclude( true )
   , m_bPrint( bPrint )
{
   const int nNumEntries = getNumFileTypes();
   for ( int iType = 0; iType < nNumEntries; ++iType ) {
      FileType *pOther = getFileType( iType );
      if ( pOther == this || !exists() ) {
         break; //*** LOOP EXIT POINT
      }
      if ( 0 == m_strClass.compare( pOther->m_strClass ) ) {
         pOther->m_strExtension += _T( " " );
         pOther->m_strExtension += m_strExtension.substr( 1 );
         m_strExtension.erase();
         m_strClass    .erase();
      }
   }
}

String FileType::sm_strCommand;

FileType FileType::sm_aFileType[] = {
```

```
    //              isEditDefault  bEdit  bPrint
   FileType( _T( ".txt"  ), true , true , true  ),
   FileType( _T( ".bat"  ), false, true , true  ),
   FileType( _T( ".cmd"  ), false, true , true  ),
   FileType( _T( ".ini"  ), false, true , true  ),
   FileType( _T( ".inf"  ), false, true , true  ),
   FileType( _T( ".asp"  ), false, false, false ),
   FileType( _T( ".htm"  ), false, false, false ),
   FileType( _T( ".html" ), false, false, false ),
   FileType( _T( ".log"  ), true , true , true  ),
   FileType( _T( ".cpp"  ), true , true , true  ),
   FileType( _T( ".cxx"  ), true , true , true  ),
   FileType( _T( ".c"    ), true , true , true  ),
   FileType( _T( ".h"    ), true , true , true  ),
   FileType( _T( ".hxx"  ), true , true , true  ),
   FileType( _T( ".hpp"  ), true , true , true  ),
   FileType( _T( ".jav"  ), true , true , true  ),
   FileType( _T( ".java" ), true , true , true  ),
   FileType( _T( ".reg"  ), false, true , true  ),
   FileType( _T( ".asc"  ), true , true , true  ),
   FileType( _T( ".asm"  ), true , true , true  ),
};

int FileType::getNumFileTypes( void ) {

   return dim( sm_aFileType );
}

FileType *FileType::getFileType( int nIndex ) {

   assert( 0 <= nIndex && nIndex < dim( sm_aFileType ) );
   return &sm_aFileType[ nIndex ];
}

bool FileType::exists( void ) const {

   return !m_strClass.empty();
}
```

```cpp
void FileType::include( LPCTSTR pszExt, bool bInclude ) {

   for ( int iType = 0; iType < dim( sm_aFileType ); ++iType ) {
      const LPCTSTR pszThis = sm_aFileType[ iType ].getExtension();
      if ( 0 == _tcsicmp( pszThis + 1, pszExt ) ) {
         sm_aFileType[ iType ].m_bInclude = bInclude;
         break; //*** LOOP EXIT POINT
      }
   }
}

void FileType::setCommand( const String& strCommand ) {

   sm_strCommand = strCommand;
}

#define SHELL_ROOT       _T( "%1\\shell" )
#define SHELL_PATH       SHELL_ROOT _T( "\\%2" )
#define EDITWITHTEXTEDIT _T( "EditWithTextEdit" )

void FileType::setCommand(
   LPCTSTR pszPath, LPCTSTR pszFmt, LPCTSTR pszName )
{
   assert( !sm_strCommand.empty() );
   const LPCTSTR pszClass = getClass();
   String strPath =
      formatMessage( SHELL_PATH, pszClass, pszPath );
   const String strCurrent = Registry::getString( HKEY_CLASSES_ROOT,
      strPath.c_str(), _T( "" ), _T( "" ) );
   if ( strCurrent.empty() ) {
      if ( 0 == pszName || 0 == _tcslen( pszName ) ) {
         Registry::deleteEntry(
            HKEY_CLASSES_ROOT, strPath.c_str(), _T( "" ) );
      } else {
         Registry::setString(
            HKEY_CLASSES_ROOT, strPath.c_str(), _T( "" ), pszName );
      }
   }
   strPath += _T( "\\command" );
```

```cpp
    Registry::setString( HKEY_CLASSES_ROOT, strPath.c_str(),
        _T( "" ), pszFmt, sm_strCommand.c_str() );
}

#include "trace.h"
void FileType::removeCommand( LPCTSTR pszPath, LPCTSTR pszFmt ) {

    assert( !sm_strCommand.empty() );
    const LPCTSTR pszClass = getClass();
    String strPath = formatMessage(
        SHELL_PATH _T( "\\command" ), pszClass, pszPath );
    const String strCurrent = Registry::getString( HKEY_CLASSES_ROOT,
        strPath.c_str(), _T( "" ) );
    if ( strCurrent.find( sm_strCommand ) < strCurrent.length() ) {
        Registry::setString( HKEY_CLASSES_ROOT, strPath.c_str(),
            _T( "" ), pszFmt, _T( "NOTEPAD.EXE" ) );
    }
    trace( _T( "%s\n" ), strCurrent.c_str() );
}

void FileType::registerType( void ) {

    if ( shouldInclude() ) {
        if ( isEditDefault() ) {
            setCommand( _T( "open" ), _T( "\"%1\" \"%%1\"" ) );
        } else if ( useEdit() ) {
            setCommand( _T( "edit" ), _T( "\"%1\" \"%%1\"" ) );
        }
        if ( shouldPrint() ) {
            setCommand( _T( "print" ), _T( "\"%1\" -p \"%%1\"" ) );
            setCommand( _T( "printto" ),
                _T( "\"%1\" -pt \"%%1\" \"%%2\" \"%%3\" \"%%4\"" ) );
        }
    } else {
        unregisterType();
    }

    const String strMenuCommand = loadString( IDS_EDIT_WITH_TEXTEDIT );
    setCommand( EDITWITHTEXTEDIT,
```

```
      _T( "\"%1\" \"%%1\"" ), strMenuCommand.c_str() );
}

void FileType::unregisterType( void ) {

   String strPath =
      formatMessage( SHELL_PATH, getClass(), EDITWITHTEXTEDIT );
   Registry::deleteEntry( HKEY_CLASSES_ROOT, strPath.c_str() );

   strPath =
      formatMessage( SHELL_ROOT, getClass(), EDITWITHTEXTEDIT );
   const String strCurrent = Registry::getString( HKEY_CLASSES_ROOT,
      strPath.c_str(), _T( "" ) );
   if ( strCurrent.find( EDITWITHTEXTEDIT ) < strCurrent.length() ) {
      Registry::deleteEntry(
         HKEY_CLASSES_ROOT, strPath.c_str(), _T( "" ) );
   }

   removeCommand( _T( "open" ), _T( "\"%1\" \"%%1\"" ) );
   removeCommand( _T( "edit" ), _T( "\"%1\" \"%%1\"" ) );
   removeCommand( _T( "print" ), _T( "\"%1\" -p \"%%1\"" ) );
   removeCommand( _T( "printto" ),
      _T( "\"%1\" -pt \"%%1\" \"%%2\" \"%%3\" \"%%4\"" ) );
}
```

Listing 20.3 `InstallDlg1.cpp`

```
/*
 * $Header: /Book/InstallDlg1.cpp 12    5.09.99 13:07 Petter $
 */

#include "precomp.h"
#include "VersionInfo.h"
#include "Exception.h"
#include "Registry.h"
#include "HTML.h"
#include "InstallDlg1.h"
#include "AutoShellObject.h"
#include "FileType.h"
#include "formatMessage.h"
```

```
#include "menuUtils.h"
#include "setup.h"
#include "persistence.h"
#include "language.h"
#include "geometry.h"
#include "utils.h"
#include "fileUtils.h"
#include "winUtils.h"
#include "resource.h"
#include "trace.h"

UINT InstallDlg1::getResourceID( void ) const {
   return IDD_INSTALL_1;
}

BOOL InstallDlg1::DlgProc( UINT msg, WPARAM wParam, LPARAM lParam ) {

   // Putting this here results in its getting called
   // more often than necessary. But my, how convenient!
   HMENU hmenu = GetSystemMenu( *this, false );
   enableMenuItem( hmenu, SC_RESTORE, 0 != IsIconic( *this ) );

   return Dialog::DlgProc( msg, wParam, lParam );
}

BOOL InstallDlg1::onInitDialog( HWND hwndFocus, LPARAM lParam ) {

   initLanguageComboBox( *this );

   HMENU hmenu = GetSystemMenu( *this, false );
   DeleteMenu( hmenu, SC_MAXIMIZE, MF_BYCOMMAND );
   DeleteMenu( hmenu, SC_SIZE    , MF_BYCOMMAND );
   enableMenuItem( hmenu, SC_RESTORE, false );

   const HICON hicon =
      LoadIcon( m_hinst, MAKEINTRESOURCE( IDI_TEXTEDIT1 ) );
   sendMessage( WM_SETICON, ICON_SMALL,
      reinterpret_cast< LPARAM >( hicon ) );
   sendMessage( WM_SETICON, ICON_BIG,
      reinterpret_cast< LPARAM >( hicon ) );
```

```cpp
   subclassHTML( getDlgItem( IDC_TIP ) );

   setDlgItemText( IDC_PATH, m_strInstallDir );
   SetFocus( getDlgItem( IDC_PATH ) );
   SendDlgItemMessage( *this, IDC_PATH, EM_SETSEL, 0, -1 );

   setDlgItemText( IDC_DOC_PATH, m_strDataDir );
   setupList();

   return false; // Don't let dialog manager set the focus.
}

#define ListView_CheckItem( hwnd, item ) \
   ListView_SetItemState( hwnd, item, 2 << 12, LVIS_STATEIMAGEMASK)

void InstallDlg1::getList( void ) {

   HWND hwndList = getDlgItem( IDC_FILETYPES );
   assert( IsWindow( hwndList ) );

   const int nItems = ListView_GetItemCount( hwndList );
   for ( int iItem = 0; iItem < nItems; ++iItem ) {
      const bool bInclude =
         0 != ListView_GetCheckState( hwndList, iItem );
      TCHAR sz[ 200 ] = { 0 };
      ListView_GetItemText( hwndList, iItem, 1, sz, dim( sz ) );
      FileType::include( sz, bInclude );
   }
}

void InstallDlg1::setupList( void ) {

   HWND hwndList = getDlgItem( IDC_FILETYPES );
   assert( IsWindow( hwndList ) );

   DWORD dwExStyle = ListView_GetExtendedListViewStyle( hwndList );
   ListView_SetExtendedListViewStyle( hwndList,
      dwExStyle | LVS_EX_CHECKBOXES | LVS_EX_FULLROWSELECT );
```

```
const Rect rcClient = getClientRect( hwndList );
const int w = rcClient.width() - GetSystemMetrics( SM_CXVSCROLL );
const int cx0 = MulDiv( w, 3, 4 );

String str = loadString( IDS_FILE_TYPE );
LV_COLUMN lvColumn = {
   LVCF_FMT | LVCF_SUBITEM | LVCF_TEXT | LVCF_WIDTH,
   LVCFMT_LEFT, cx0,
   const_cast< LPTSTR >( str.c_str() ),
   0, /* image */ 0, /* order */ 0,
};
ListView_InsertColumn( hwndList, 0, &lvColumn );

str = loadString( IDS_EXTENSIONS );
lvColumn.pszText = const_cast< LPTSTR >( str.c_str() );
lvColumn.cx = w - cx0;
ListView_InsertColumn( hwndList, 1, &lvColumn );

SHFILEINFO fileInfo = { 0 };
HIMAGELIST hSysImageList = reinterpret_cast< HIMAGELIST >(
   SHGetFileInfo( _T( ".txt" ), FILE_ATTRIBUTE_NORMAL,
      &fileInfo, sizeof fileInfo,
      SHGFI_SYSICONINDEX | SHGFI_USEFILEATTRIBUTES |
      SHGFI_SMALLICON ) );
ListView_SetImageList( hwndList, hSysImageList, LVSIL_SMALL );

const int nTypes = FileType::getNumFileTypes();
for ( int iType = 0; iType < nTypes; ++iType ) {

   const FileType *pFileType = FileType::getFileType( iType );
   if ( 0 == pFileType || !pFileType->exists() ) {
      continue; //*** LOOP CONTINUATION
   }
   assert( isGoodConstPtr( pFileType ) );

   const UINT uiFlags =
      SHGFI_USEFILEATTRIBUTES |
      SHGFI_ICON              |
      SHGFI_SMALLICON         |
      SHGFI_TYPENAME          ;
```

```
        PATHNAME szExt = { 0 };
        _tcscpy( szExt, pFileType->getExtension() );
        LPTSTR pszSpace = _tcschr( szExt, _T( ' ' ) );
        if ( 0 != pszSpace ) {
            *pszSpace = 0;
        }
        SHGetFileInfo( szExt, FILE_ATTRIBUTE_NORMAL,
            &fileInfo, sizeof fileInfo, uiFlags );

        const int nItems = ListView_GetItemCount( hwndList );
        LV_ITEM lvItem = {
            LVIF_TEXT | LVIF_IMAGE | LVIF_STATE, nItems,
            0, 0 == nItems ? (LVIS_FOCUSED | LVIS_SELECTED) : 0, 0,
            fileInfo.szTypeName, _tcsclen( fileInfo.szTypeName ),
            fileInfo.iIcon, (LPARAM) 0,
        };
        ListView_InsertItem( hwndList, &lvItem );
        ListView_CheckItem( hwndList, nItems );

        LPCTSTR pszExt = pFileType->getExtension() + 1;
        lvItem.mask = LVIF_TEXT;
        lvItem.iSubItem = 1;
        lvItem.pszText = const_cast< LPTSTR >( pszExt );
        lvItem.cchTextMax = _tcsclen( pszExt );
        ListView_SetItem( hwndList, &lvItem );
    }
}


/**
 * Callback function for SHBrowseForFolder. It is used to
 * a) set the initial directory, and
 * b) ensure that the defaultness of the OK button is OK.
 */
PRIVATE int CALLBACK BrowseCallbackProc(
    HWND hwnd, UINT msg, LPARAM, LPARAM lpData )
{
    if ( BFFM_INITIALIZED == msg ) {
        SNDMSG( hwnd, BFFM_SETSELECTION, TRUE, lpData );
    } else if ( BFFM_SELCHANGED == msg ) {
```

```
      HWND hwndOK = GetDlgItem( hwnd, IDOK );
      if ( IsWindowEnabled( hwndOK ) ) {
         setButtonStyle( hwndOK, BS_DEFPUSHBUTTON );
      } else {
         setButtonStyle( hwndOK, BS_PUSHBUTTON );
      }
   }

   return 0;
}

void InstallDlg1::onBrowse( UINT id, LPCTSTR pszTitle ) {

   const String strDefault = getDlgItemText( id );
   PATHNAME szPath = { 0 };

   // The pszDisplayName member of BROWSEINFO returns, for example,
   // "(C:)" or "3_ Floppy (A:)" instead of "C:\" or "A:\", so it's
   // not used. szPath is used as a placeholder to avoid declaring
   // an additional string.

   // A little bit of confusion here -- the lParam member of bi
   // reappears as the lpData (rather than the lParam) parameter
   // to BrowseCallbackProc.
   BROWSEINFO bi = {
      *this, /* root */ 0, szPath, pszTitle,
      BIF_RETURNONLYFSDIRS, BrowseCallbackProc,
      reinterpret_cast< LPARAM >( strDefault.c_str() ),
   };

   AutoShellObject< ITEMIDLIST >
      pItemIdList( SHBrowseForFolder( &bi ) );
   if ( (LPITEMIDLIST) 0 != pItemIdList ) {
      if ( SHGetPathFromIDList( pItemIdList, szPath ) ) {
         String strPath( szPath );
         if ( IDC_PATH == id ) {
            appendProgramName( &strPath );
         }
         setDlgItemText( id, strPath.c_str() );
```

```
            SendDlgItemMessage( *this, id, EM_SETSEL, 0, -1 );
            gotoDlgItem( id );
        }
    }
}

void InstallDlg1::onDlgCommand(
    int id, HWND hwndCtl, UINT codeNotify )
{
    switch ( id ) {
    case IDC_BROWSE:
        onBrowse( IDC_PATH, loadString( IDS_CHOOSE_FOLDER ).c_str() );
        break;

    case IDC_BROWSEDOCPATH:
        onBrowse( IDC_DOC_PATH,
            loadString( IDS_CHOOSE_DATA_FOLDER ).c_str() );
        break;

    case IDC_INSTALL:
        m_strInstallDir = getDlgItemText( IDC_PATH     );
        m_strDataDir    = getDlgItemText( IDC_DOC_PATH );
        getList();
        exitLanguageComboBox( *this );

        //*** FALL THROUGH

    case IDCANCEL:
        ListView_SetImageList(
            getDlgItem( IDC_FILETYPES ), 0, LVSIL_SMALL );
        verify( EndDialog( *this, id ) );
        break;
    }
}

InstallDlg1::InstallDlg1( HINSTANCE hinst,
    const String& strInstallDir, const String& strDataDir )
    : m_hinst       ( hinst        )
```

```
    , m_strInstallDir( strInstallDir )
    , m_strDataDir   ( strDataDir    )
{
}
```

Copying Files

Once the customization dialog has been OK'd, the setup dialog starts `installThread`, which in turn executes `SetupDlg`'s `install` member function, the true workhorse of the installation process. This method

- creates the application directory,
- copies the executable there,
- extracts the help files (see below),
- registers itself appropriately for all file types,
- creates shortcuts to the installed executable in the Programs section of the Start menu and in the user's `SendTo` folder (see below)
- and, finally, stores the installation path in the registry.

The `registerFileForDeletion` function is the interface to a registry-based repository of names of files that should be deleted on uninstall. The file names are stored under the key

```
HKEY_LOCAL_MACHINE\SOFTWARE\Andersen Consulting\TextEdit\Uninstall
```

The uninstall process enumerates the values under this key and deletes the files.

From Resources to Files

The TextEdit setup program is a single executable file, identical to the everyday TextEdit executable. From where, then, do we install the help files? The help files are embedded in the executable in the form of custom resources. In the resource script, we have the following two lines:

```
IDR_CNT_FILE FILE DISCARDABLE "Help\\TextEdit.cnt"
IDR_HLP_FILE FILE DISCARDABLE "Help\\TextEdit.hlp"
```

The `copyResource` function in `SetupDlg.cpp` uses the resource access API to copy a resource from the executable into a file. After you execute the following code, `pData` points to the first byte of `TEXTEDIT.HLP`:

```
HRSRC hrsrc = FindResource(
    0, MAKEINTRESOURCE( IDR_HLP_FILE ), _T( "FILE" ) );
HGLOBAL hRes = LoadResource( 0, hrsrc );
LPVOID pData = LockResource( hRes );
```

When you're done with `pData`, the following code frees up the resource:

```
UnlockResource( hrsrc );
FreeResource( hrsrc );
```

...or does it? According to the documentation, `UnlockResource` is deprecated in Win32. Its definition bears this out — it's a macro that simply evaluates its argument. A dummy, in other words.

According to the documentation, `FreeResource` is also obsolete. In this case, however, the header file (`winbase.h`) serves up a function prototype rather than a dummy macro, so the obsolescence is less obvious. The documentation goes on to say that, in the case of accelerator tables, bitmaps, cursors, icons and menus, you should call the corresponding destructor function (`DestroyAcceleratorTable`, `DeleteObject`, `DestroyCursor`, `DestroyIcon` and `DestroyMenu`) when you're done with them.

If you're supposed to free standard resources, why not custom resources? It seems likely that the documentation is wrong or incomplete on this point. Resource access is, in any case, badly documented, and I've found it difficult to get a clear picture of the design underlying the API.

Shortcuts in the Shell

Creating shortcuts is a rather painful process involving two COM interfaces, `IShellLink` and `IPersistFile`. I've wrapped the whole thing in the `addShortcut` function in `SetupDlg.cpp`. The interface to this function is unsuited for a general `addShortCut` utility function, as it can only add shortcuts to one of the "special folder locations," and the name of the shortcut is determined by the `FileDescription` entry in the file's version resource.

Uninstall

You uninstall TextEdit by starting it with the `/setup` switch. This invokes TextEdit in the general setup mode, which includes the uninstall function. It takes care of deleting the program file, deleting any directories created, cleaning up the registry, removing desktop shortcuts and removing start-menu shortcuts. I'll get to the details as soon as we've given some thought to the user.

The user does not know about the `/setup` switch. How, then, does she invoke uninstall? One possibility is to provide a shortcut in the start menu or on the desktop. This approach has been used by many applications in the past, but is no longer recommended by Microsoft and I agree. The start menu overfloweth as it is; no need to add more clutter.

The currently recommended approach is to use the Add/Remove Programs applet in the Control Panel (see Figure 20.3). The title of this dialog is passing strange, by the way — why "Properties?" And, when the keyboard focus is in the list of removable software, why isn't the Add/Remove button the default button?

Figure 20.3 The Add/Remove Programs Control Panel applet. Given that the keyboard focus is in the list, why isn't the Add/Remove button the default? Eh?

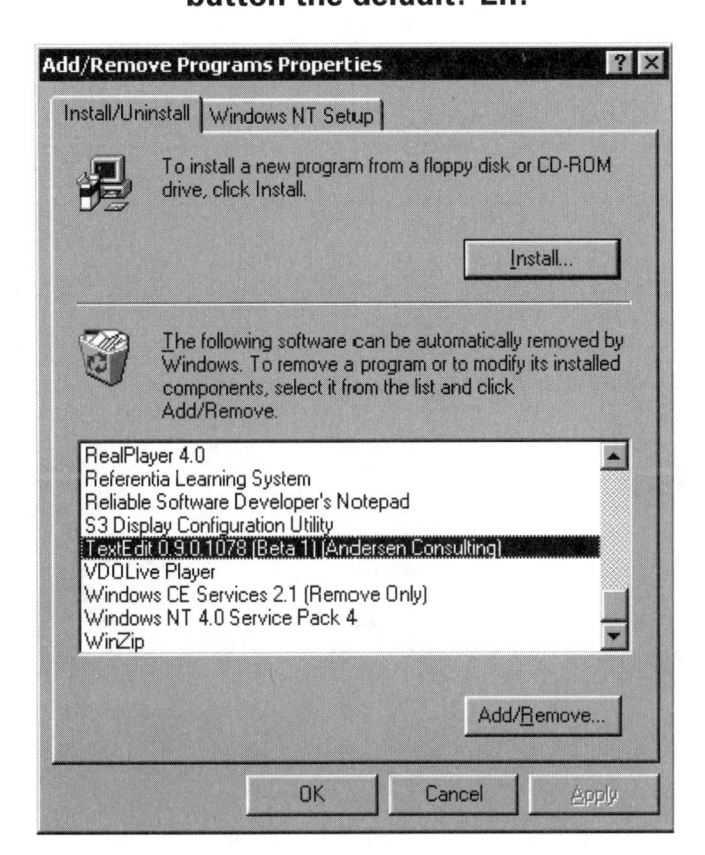

Getting TextEdit into the list of removable programs is easy; we just have to add two entries to the registry, as follows:

Under the key

```
HKEY_LOCAL_MACHINE\SOFTWARE\Microsoft\
   Windows\CurrentVersion\Uninstall
```

we create a new key for our application. It happens to be named TextEdit, but it doesn't really matter what it's called, it just needs to be unique. The name displayed in the list in Figure 20.3 is taken from one of the values under that key, named `DisplayName`. The other value is named `UninstallString`, and should contain the uninstall command: `<program-path>\TextEdit.exe /setup`.

Note that the Add/Remove button in Figure 20.3 has an ellipsis after it, and that the text above the list includes "…remove a program *or modify its installed components.*" This means that uninstall may not barge ahead with its job; the least it must do is to ask the user if she really wants to do this potentially horrible thing. I once tried to modify the way a program was set up by clicking the Add/Remove button. The program softly and silently vanished away, and I got very upset. Believe me, you don't want to put your users through such a painful ordeal.

Both the `install` function and its inverse, `uninstall`, can be found in `SetupDlg.cpp`. (Discourse continues on page 480.)

Listing 20.4 SetupDlg.cpp

```cpp
/*
 * $Header: /Book/SetupDlg.cpp 15     5.09.99 13:07 Petter $
 *
 * Handles the setup dialog box, as well as actual install/uninstall.
 * TODO: Check free disk space.
 */

#include "precomp.h"
#include <winver.h>
#include "Help/map.hh"
#include "formatMessage.h"
#include "SetupDlg.h"
#include "AutoHandle.h"
#include "AutoComReference.h"
#include "AutoShellObject.h"
#include "VersionInfo.h"
#include "Exception.h"
#include "Registry.h"
#include "AboutDlg.h"
#include "InstallDlg1.h"
#include "HTML.h"
#include "FileType.h"
#include "language.h"
#include "createNewFile.h"
#include "menuUtils.h"
#include "winUtils.h"
#include "fileUtils.h"
#include "resource.h"
#include "setup.h"
#include "persistence.h"
#include "threads.h"
#include "utils.h"
#include "os.h"
#include "trace.h"
```

```
// Resource IDs in SHELL32.DLL:

#define IDAVI_SEARCH    150
#define IDAVI_FILECOPY  161
#define IDAVI_FILENUKE  164

#define SHOW_PROGRESS( step ) \
    SendMessage( hwndProgress, PBM_SETPOS, step, 0 )

PRIVATE void registerFileForDeletion( const String& strFile ) {

    Registry::setString(
        HKEY_LOCAL_MACHINE, _T( "Uninstall" ), strFile.c_str() );
}

void SetupDlg::deleteResource( UINT uiID, DWORD dwBytes ) {

    /*
     * LATER:
     * This does nothing at the moment. Might consider using the
     * BeginUpdateResource/UpdateResource/EndUpdateResource API
     * to trim the size of the installed executable; the help
     * files are already extracted when this is called.
     * These functions only work under Windows NT, though.
     */
}

void SetupDlg::copyResource( UINT uiID, const String& strFile ) {

    HRSRC hrsrc =
        FindResource( 0, MAKEINTRESOURCE( uiID ), _T( "FILE" ) );
    DWORD dwBytes = SizeofResource( 0, hrsrc );
    HGLOBAL hRes = LoadResource( 0, hrsrc );
    LPVOID pData = LockResource( hRes );

    AutoHandle hFile( CreateFile( strFile.c_str(),
        GENERIC_WRITE, FILE_SHARE_NONE, 0, CREATE_ALWAYS, 0, 0 ) );
    if ( INVALID_HANDLE_VALUE == hFile ) {
        throwException( _T( "Unable to copy help files" ) );
```

```
      }
      DWORD dwBytesWritten = 0;
      verify( WriteFile( hFile, pData, dwBytes, &dwBytesWritten, 0 ) );
      assert( dwBytes == dwBytesWritten );

      UnlockResource( hrsrc ); // Obsolete!
      FreeResource  ( hrsrc ); // Obsolete?
      deleteResource( uiID, dwBytes );

      Sleep( 150 );
      registerFileForDeletion( strFile );
   }

   void SetupDlg::startAnimation( UINT uiAviId ) {

   #ifndef Animate_OpenEx
      #define Animate_OpenEx( hwnd, hInst, szName ) \
         (BOOL)SNDMSG( hwnd, ACM_OPEN,              \
            (WPARAM) hInst, (LPARAM)(LPTSTR)( szName ) )
   #endif // Animate_OpenEx

      hideDlgItem( IDC_MESSAGE2 );
      showDlgItem( IDC_ANIMATE );

      HWND hwndAnimate = getDlgItem( IDC_ANIMATE );
      Animate_OpenEx(
         hwndAnimate, m_hShell32, MAKEINTRESOURCE( uiAviId ) );
      Animate_Seek( hwndAnimate, 0 );
      Animate_Play( hwndAnimate, 0, -1, -1 );
   }

   void SetupDlg::stopAnimation( void ) {

      hideDlgItem( IDC_ANIMATE );

      HWND hwndAnimate = getDlgItem( IDC_ANIMATE );
      Animate_Stop( hwndAnimate );
      Animate_Seek( hwndAnimate, 0 );
```

```
      showDlgItem( IDC_MESSAGE2 );
}


void SetupDlg::cleanupThread( void ) {
   if ( 0 != m_hThread ) {
      const DWORD dwResult = WaitForSingleObject( m_hThread, 5000 );
      if ( WAIT_OBJECT_0 != dwResult ) {
         trace( _T( "WaitForSingleObject( %d ) failed: %s" ),
            m_hThread, WinException().what() );
      }
      verify( CloseHandle( m_hThread ) );
      m_hThread = 0;
   }
}

String SetupDlg::getHelpFile( void ) const {
   return formatMessage( _T( "%1\\TextEdit.hlp" ),
      m_strInstallDir.c_str() );
}

UINT __stdcall SetupDlg::searchPreviousThread( LPVOID p ) {

   SetupDlg *pSetupDlg = reinterpret_cast< SetupDlg * >( p );
   assert( isGoodPtr( pSetupDlg ) );

   try {
      pSetupDlg->searchPrevious();
   }
   catch ( const Exception& x ) {
      pSetupDlg->sendMessage( WM_APP, SEARCH_FAILED,
         reinterpret_cast< LPARAM >( x.what() ) );
   }
   return 0;
}

UINT __stdcall SetupDlg::installThread( LPVOID p ) {

   SetupDlg *pSetupDlg = reinterpret_cast< SetupDlg * >( p );
   assert( 0 != pSetupDlg );
```

```cpp
   HRESULT hres = coInitialize();
   if ( SUCCEEDED( hres ) ) {
      try {
         pSetupDlg->install();
      }
      catch ( const Exception& x ) {
         pSetupDlg->sendMessage( WM_APP, INSTALL_FAILED,
            reinterpret_cast< LPARAM >( x.what() ) );
      }

      CoUninitialize();
   } else {
      const LPCTSTR pszMessage =
         _T( "Cannot initialize COM.\nSorry, I give up." );
      pSetupDlg->sendMessage( WM_APP, INSTALL_FAILED,
         reinterpret_cast< LPARAM >( pszMessage ) );
   }
   return 0;
}

UINT __stdcall SetupDlg::uninstallThread( LPVOID p ) {

   SetupDlg *pSetupDlg = reinterpret_cast< SetupDlg * >( p );
   assert( 0 != pSetupDlg );

   try {
      pSetupDlg->uninstall();
   }
   catch ( const Exception& x ) {
      pSetupDlg->sendMessage( WM_APP, UNINSTALL_FAILED,
         reinterpret_cast< LPARAM >( x.what() ) );
   }
   return 0;
}

void SetupDlg::searchPrevious( void ) {

   sendMessage( WM_APP, START_SEARCH, 0 );
```

```cpp
HWND hwndProgress = getDlgItem( IDC_PROGRESS );
SendMessage( hwndProgress, PBM_SETRANGE, 0, MAKELPARAM( 0, 2 ) );
SHOW_PROGRESS( 0 );
Sleep( 150 );

m_strExePath = getInstallPath();
WIN32_FIND_DATA fd = { 0 };
HANDLE hFind = FindFirstFile( m_strExePath.c_str(), &fd );
m_hasPrevious = INVALID_HANDLE_VALUE != hFind;
if ( m_hasPrevious ) {
   verify( FindClose( hFind ) );
   const VersionInfo viOld( m_strExePath.c_str() );
   assert( viOld.isValid() );
   m_hasPrevious = viOld.isValid();
   if ( m_hasPrevious ) {
      m_strVersion =
         viOld.getStringFileInfo( _T( "FileVersion" ) );
      DWORD dwVersionLoOld = 0;
      DWORD dwVersionHiOld = 0;
      verify( viOld.getFileVersion(
         &dwVersionLoOld, &dwVersionHiOld ) );
      const VersionInfo viNew( getModuleHandle() );
      assert( viNew.isValid() );
      DWORD dwVersionLoNew = 0;
      DWORD dwVersionHiNew = 0;
      verify( viNew.getFileVersion(
         &dwVersionLoNew, &dwVersionHiNew ) );
      m_isOlderThanPrevious =
         dwVersionHiNew < dwVersionHiOld ? true  :
         dwVersionHiOld < dwVersionHiNew ? false :
         dwVersionLoNew < dwVersionLoOld ;
   }
}
Sleep( 150 );
SHOW_PROGRESS( 1 );
Sleep( 150 );
SHOW_PROGRESS( 2 );
```

```
      if ( !m_isCancelled ) {
         sendMessage( WM_APP, DONE_SEARCH, 0 );
      }
   }
}

PRIVATE void addShortcut( int nFolder, const String &strProgPath ) {

   String strLinkPath = getSpecialFolderLocation( nFolder );
   if ( !strLinkPath.empty() ) {

      // Program name: Get title from version resource
      LPCTSTR pszTitle = _T( "TextEdit" );
      const VersionInfo vi( getModuleHandle() );
      if ( vi.isValid() ) {
         pszTitle = vi.getStringFileInfo( _T( "FileDescription" ) );
         assert( 0 != pszTitle );
         if ( 0 == _tcscmp( pszTitle, _T( "?" ) ) ) {
            trace( _T( "addShortcuts: Unable to retrieve " )
               _T( "program title; using default\n" ) );
            pszTitle = _T( "TextEdit" );
         }
      } else {
         trace( _T( "Unable to retrieve version info\n" ) );
      }

      addPathSeparator( &strLinkPath );
      strLinkPath += formatMessage(
         _T( "%1.lnk" ), pszTitle );

      AutoComReference< IShellLink >
         psl( CLSID_ShellLink, IID_IShellLink );
      AutoComReference< IPersistFile > ppf( IID_IPersistFile, psl );
      PATHNAMEW wszLink = { 0 };
#ifdef UNICODE
      _tcscpy( wszLink, strLinkPath.c_str() );
#else
      multiByteToWideChar( strLinkPath.c_str(), wszLink );
#endif
      trace( _T( "Creating link: %ws\n" ), wszLink );
      verify( SUCCEEDED( psl->SetPath( strProgPath.c_str() ) ) );
```

```cpp
         verify( SUCCEEDED( psl->SetIconLocation(
            strProgPath.c_str(), 0 ) ) );
         verify( SUCCEEDED( ppf->Save( wszLink, true ) ) );
         registerFileForDeletion( strLinkPath );
      }
   }

void SetupDlg::install( void ) {

   sendMessage( WM_APP, START_INSTALL, 0 );
   setNewLanguage( getLanguage() );


   HWND hwndProgress = getDlgItem( IDC_PROGRESS );
   SendMessage( hwndProgress, PBM_SETRANGE, 0, MAKELPARAM( 0, 4 ) );
   SHOW_PROGRESS( 1 );


   CreateDirectory( m_strInstallDir.c_str(), 0 );
   DWORD dwErr = GetLastError();
   if ( NOERROR != dwErr && ERROR_ALREADY_EXISTS != dwErr ) {
      throwException(
         _T( "Unable to create program directory.<p>" ) );
   }
   if ( NOERROR == dwErr ) {
      SHChangeNotify(
         SHCNE_MKDIR, SHCNF_PATH, m_strInstallDir.c_str(), 0 );
   }


   const String strSetupPath = getModuleFileName();

   // NOTE: Check version! VerInstallFile, VerFindFile?
   m_strExePath = formatMessage(
      _T( "%1\\TextEdit.exe" ), m_strInstallDir.c_str() );

   // NOTE: CopyFileEx not supported on Windows 95
   const BOOL bOK = CopyFile( strSetupPath.c_str(),
      m_strExePath.c_str(), /* fail if exists */ false );
   if ( !bOK ) {
      throwException( _T( "Unable to copy program file.<p>" ) );
   }
```

```cpp
      SHOW_PROGRESS( 2 );
      copyResource( IDR_HLP_FILE,
         formatMessage( _T( "%1\\TextEdit.hlp" ),
         m_strInstallDir.c_str() ) );
      SHOW_PROGRESS( 3 );
      copyResource( IDR_CNT_FILE,
         formatMessage( _T( "%1\\TextEdit.cnt" ),
         m_strInstallDir.c_str() ) );
      SHOW_PROGRESS( 4 );

      SHChangeNotify(
         SHCNE_UPDATEDIR, SHCNF_PATH, strSetupPath.c_str(), 0 );

      FileType::setCommand( m_strExePath );
      const int nTypes = FileType::getNumFileTypes();
      for ( int iType = 0; iType < nTypes; ++iType ) {
         FileType *pFileType = FileType::getFileType( iType );
         pFileType->registerType();
      }

      try {
         addShortcut( CSIDL_PROGRAMS, m_strExePath );
         addShortcut( CSIDL_SENDTO  , m_strExePath );
      }
      catch ( const ComException& x ) {
         trace( _T( "ComException in addShortcuts" ), x.what() );
         messageBox( *this, MB_OK | MB_ICONWARNING,
            _T( "Couldn't create start menu shortcut:\n%1" ), x.what() );
      }

      SHChangeNotify( SHCNE_FREESPACE, SHCNF_PATH,
         getRootDir( strSetupPath ).c_str(), 0 );
      if ( !m_isCancelled ) {
         sendMessage( WM_APP, DONE_INSTALL, 0 );
      }

      setInstallPath( m_strExePath );
}
```

```cpp
bool SetupDlg::deleteFile( LPCTSTR pszFile ) {

    const String strPath = formatMessage( _T( "%1\\%2" ),
        m_strInstallDir.c_str(), pszFile );
    return 0 != DeleteFile( strPath.c_str() );
}

void SetupDlg::uninstall( void ) {

    sendMessage( WM_APP, START_UNINSTALL, 0 );

    HWND hwndProgress = getDlgItem( IDC_PROGRESS );

    // Remove program and help files

    WinHelp( *this, getHelpFile().c_str(), HELP_QUIT, 0 );

    SendMessage( hwndProgress, PBM_SETRANGE, 0, MAKELPARAM( 0, 8 ) );
    SHOW_PROGRESS( 0 );

    const bool bDeleted = deleteFile( _T( "TextEdit.exe" ) );
    DWORD dwErr = GetLastError();
    assert( bDeleted || ERROR_ACCESS_DENIED == dwErr );
    Sleep( 150 );
    SHOW_PROGRESS( 1 );

    deleteFile( _T( "TextEdit.hlp" ) );
    Sleep( 150 );
    SHOW_PROGRESS( 2 );

    deleteFile( _T( "TextEdit.cnt" ) );
    Sleep( 150 );
    SHOW_PROGRESS( 3 );

    deleteFile( _T( "TextEdit.gid" ) );
    Sleep( 150 );
    SHOW_PROGRESS( 4 );
```

```
deleteFile( _T( "TextEdit.fts" ) );
Sleep( 150 );
SHOW_PROGRESS( 5 );


// Remove all shortcuts on desktop and on start menu.
// Some files in the uninstall list have already been deleted.
String strFileToDelete;
DWORD dwIndex = 0;
while ( Registry::enumValues( HKEY_LOCAL_MACHINE,
   _T( "Uninstall" ), dwIndex++, &strFileToDelete ) )
{
   DeleteFile( strFileToDelete.c_str() );
}
Registry::deleteEntry( HKEY_LOCAL_MACHINE, _T( "Uninstall" ) );

Sleep( 150 );
SHOW_PROGRESS( 6 );


bool bDirRemoved = 0 != RemoveDirectory( m_strInstallDir.c_str() );
dwErr = GetLastError();
assert( bDirRemoved ||
   ERROR_ACCESS_DENIED == dwErr ||
   ERROR_DIR_NOT_EMPTY == dwErr );
Sleep( 150 );
SHOW_PROGRESS( 7 );


// Remove uninstall strings in registry:
Registry::deleteEntry( HKEY_LOCAL_MACHINE, UNINSTALL_PATH );
Sleep( 150 );
SHOW_PROGRESS( 8 );


// Remove RunOnce strings in registry:
Registry::deleteEntry( HKEY_CURRENT_USER,
   RUNONCE_PATH, _T( "TextEdit Restart" ) );


// Remove user data in registry -- for all users!
Registry::deleteEntry( HKEY_CURRENT_USER, _T( "" ) );


// Remove application data in registry.
Registry::deleteEntry( HKEY_LOCAL_MACHINE, _T( "" ) );
```

```cpp
   // Remove all registry commands:
   FileType::setCommand( m_strExePath );
   const int nTypes = FileType::getNumFileTypes();
   for ( int iType = 0; iType < nTypes; ++iType ) {
      FileType *pFileType = FileType::getFileType( iType );
      pFileType->unregisterType();
   }

   bool bDelayedDelete = false;
   bool bDelayedDirRemove = false;
   if ( !bDeleted ) {
      bDelayedDelete = delayedRemove( m_strInstallDir );
   }
   if ( !bDirRemoved ) {
      bDelayedDirRemove = delayedRemove( m_strInstallDir.c_str() );
   }
   m_bDelayedRemove = bDelayedDirRemove || bDelayedDelete;

   SHChangeNotify( SHCNE_UPDATEDIR, SHCNF_PATH,
      m_strInstallDir.c_str(), 0 );
   SHChangeNotify( SHCNE_FREESPACE, SHCNF_PATH,
      m_strInstallDir.c_str(), 0 );

   if ( !m_isCancelled ) {
      sendMessage( WM_APP, DONE_UNINSTALL );
   }
}

inline void SetupDlg::setMessage( const String& strMessage ) {

   setDlgItemText( IDC_MESSAGE, strMessage.c_str() );
}

inline void SetupDlg::setMessage( UINT uiString ) {

   setMessage( loadString( uiString ) );
}
```

Chapter 20: Setup, and Down Again

```
UINT SetupDlg::getResourceID( void ) const {

   return IDD_SETUP;
}

int SetupDlg::getDefaultButtonID( void ) const {

   if ( m_hasPrevious ) {
      return m_isOlderThanPrevious ? IDCANCEL : IDC_INSTALL;
   }
   return IDC_INSTALL;
}

BOOL SetupDlg::DlgProc( UINT msg, WPARAM wParam, LPARAM lParam ) {

   assert( (ID_HELP_ABOUT & 0xF) == 0 );
   if ( WM_SYSCOMMAND == msg && (wParam & 0xFFF0) == ID_HELP_ABOUT ) {
      AboutDlg( *this );
      return TRUE;
   }

   if ( WM_APP != msg ) {

      // Putting this here results in its getting called
      // more often than necessary. But my, how convenient!
      HMENU hmenu = GetSystemMenu( *this, false );
      enableMenuItem( hmenu, SC_RESTORE, 0 != IsIconic( *this ) );

      return Dialog::DlgProc( msg, wParam, lParam );
   }

   switch ( wParam ) {
   case START_SEARCH:
      startAnimation( IDAVI_SEARCH );
      setMessage( IDS_INSTALL_SEARCH );
      break;

   case DONE_SEARCH:
      ReplyMessage( 0 );
```

```
         stopAnimation();
         if ( m_hasPrevious ) {
            setMessage( formatMessage(
               IDS_INSTALL_FOUND, m_strVersion.c_str() ) );
            setDlgItemText( IDC_MESSAGE2, IDS_INSTALL_UNINSTALL );
            enableDlgItem( IDC_UNINSTALL, true );
         } else {
            setMessage( IDS_INSTALL_NOT_FOUND );
            setDlgItemText( IDC_MESSAGE2, IDS_INSTALL );
         }
         enableDlgItem( IDC_INSTALL, true );
         sendMessage( DM_SETDEFID, getDefaultButtonID() );
         gotoDlgItem( getDefaultButtonID() );
         cleanupThread();
         break;

      case START_UNINSTALL:
         ReplyMessage( 0 );
         startAnimation( IDAVI_FILENUKE );
         sendMessage( DM_SETDEFID, IDCANCEL );
         gotoDlgItem( IDCANCEL );
         DestroyWindow( getDlgItem( IDC_UNINSTALL ) );
         DestroyWindow( getDlgItem( IDC_INSTALL   ) );
         setMessage( IDS_DELETING );
         setDlgItemText( IDC_MESSAGE2, _T( "" ) );
         break;

      case DONE_UNINSTALL:
         ReplyMessage( 0 );
         stopAnimation();
         cleanupThread();
         m_uiResult = IDC_UNINSTALL;
         setMessage( IDS_DELETED );
         if ( m_bDelayedRemove ) {
            setDlgItemText( IDC_MESSAGE2, IDS_DELAYED_REMOVE );
         } else {
            setDlgItemText( IDC_MESSAGE2, _T( "" ) );
         }
         setDlgItemText( IDCANCEL, IDS_CLOSE );
         break;
```

```
        case START_INSTALL:
            ReplyMessage( 0 );
            startAnimation( IDAVI_FILECOPY );
            sendMessage( DM_SETDEFID, IDCANCEL );
            gotoDlgItem( IDCANCEL );
            DestroyWindow( getDlgItem( IDC_UNINSTALL ) );
            DestroyWindow( getDlgItem( IDC_INSTALL   ) );
            setMessage( IDS_INSTALL_COPYING );
            setDlgItemText( IDC_MESSAGE2, _T( "" ) );
            break;

        case DONE_INSTALL:
            ReplyMessage( 0 );
            stopAnimation();
            cleanupThread();
            m_uiResult = IDC_INSTALL;
            setMessage( IDS_INSTALL_SUCCESS );
            setDlgItemText( IDC_MESSAGE2, IDS_UNINSTALL_HINT );
            setDlgItemText( IDCANCEL, IDS_CLOSE );
            break;

        case SEARCH_FAILED:
        case UNINSTALL_FAILED:
        case INSTALL_FAILED:
            stopAnimation();
            setMessage( IDS_INSTALL_FAILED );
            setDlgItemText(
                IDC_MESSAGE2, reinterpret_cast< LPCTSTR >( lParam ) );
            ReplyMessage( 0 );
            setDlgItemText( IDCANCEL, IDS_CLOSE );
            cleanupThread();
            break;
    }

    return TRUE;
}

PRIVATE inline void fixSystemMenu( HMENU hmenu ) {
```

```cpp
        DeleteMenu( hmenu, SC_MAXIMIZE, MF_BYCOMMAND );
        DeleteMenu( hmenu, SC_SIZE    , MF_BYCOMMAND );
        appendSeparator( hmenu );
        appendMenuItem(
            hmenu, ID_HELP_ABOUT, loadString( IDS_ABOUT ).c_str() );
    }

    BOOL SetupDlg::onInitDialog( HWND hwndFocus, LPARAM lParam ) {

        fixSystemMenu( GetSystemMenu( *this, false ) );

        const HICON hicon =
            LoadIcon( getModuleHandle(), MAKEINTRESOURCE( IDI_SETUP ) );
        sendMessage(
            WM_SETICON, ICON_SMALL, reinterpret_cast< LPARAM >( hicon ) );
        sendMessage(
            WM_SETICON, ICON_BIG  , reinterpret_cast< LPARAM >( hicon ) );

        const VersionInfo vi( getModuleHandle() );
        const LPCTSTR pszVersion =
            vi.getStringFileInfo( _T( "FileVersion" ) );
        assert( 0 != pszVersion );
        const String strFmt = getDlgItemText( IDC_SETUP_TITLE );
        setDlgItemText( IDC_SETUP_TITLE,
            formatMessage( strFmt, pszVersion ) );

        subclassHTML( getDlgItem( IDC_SETUP_TITLE ) );
        subclassHTML( getDlgItem( IDC_MESSAGE     ) );
        subclassHTML( getDlgItem( IDC_MESSAGE2    ) );

        m_hThread = beginThread( searchPreviousThread, this );

        sendMessage( DM_SETDEFID, IDCANCEL );
        SetFocus( getDlgItem( IDCANCEL ) );
        return FALSE; // Don't let dialog manager set the focus; we did it.
    }

    void SetupDlg::onDlgCommand( int id, HWND hwndCtl, UINT codeNotify ) {
```

```cpp
    switch ( id ) {
    case IDC_UNINSTALL:
      {
        const UINT uiResult = messageBox( *this,
          MB_YESNO | MB_ICONQUESTION | MB_DEFBUTTON2,
          IDS_UNINSTALL_WARNING );
        if ( IDYES == uiResult ) {
          m_hThread = beginThread( uninstallThread, this );
        }
      }
      break;

    case IDC_INSTALL:
      {
        if ( m_isOlderThanPrevious ) {
          const UINT uiAnswer = messageBox( *this,
            MB_OKCANCEL | MB_DEFBUTTON2 | MB_ICONQUESTION,
            IDS_VERSION_WARNING );
          if ( IDOK != uiAnswer ) {
            gotoDlgItem( IDCANCEL );
            break; //*** BREAK POINT
          }
        }
        InstallDlg1 installDlg1( getModuleHandle(),
          m_strInstallDir, m_strDataDir );
        const UINT uiRetCode = dynamic_cast< Dialog * >(
          &installDlg1 )->doModal( *this );
        if ( IDC_INSTALL == uiRetCode ) {
          m_strInstallDir = installDlg1.getInstallDir();
          m_strDataDir    = installDlg1.getDataDir   ();
          m_strExePath = formatMessage(
            _T( "%1\\TextEdit.exe" ), m_strInstallDir.c_str() );
          setInstallPath ( m_strExePath.c_str() );
          setDocumentPath( m_strDataDir.c_str() );
          m_hThread = beginThread( installThread, this );
        }
      }
      break;
```

```cpp
      case IDCANCEL:
         m_isCancelled = true;
         Sleep( 0 );
         cleanupThread();
         verify( EndDialog( *this, m_uiResult ) );
         break;
      }
}

SetupDlg::SetupDlg( bool bInstall )
   : m_hThread( 0 )
   , m_bInstall( bInstall )
   , m_strVersion( _T( "" ) )
   , m_isCancelled( false )
   , m_hasPrevious( false )
   , m_isOlderThanPrevious( false )
   , m_uiResult( IDCANCEL )
   , m_hShell32( LoadLibrary( _T( "shell32" ) ) )
{
   m_isCancelled = false;

   m_strInstallDir = getInstallPath();
   if ( m_strInstallDir.empty() ) {
      m_strInstallDir = Registry::getString(
         HKEY_LOCAL_MACHINE,
         _T( "SOFTWARE\\Microsoft\\Windows\\CurrentVersion" ),
         _T( "ProgramFilesDir" ), _T( "C:\\" ) );
   }
   appendProgramName( &m_strInstallDir );

   m_strDataDir = getDocumentPath();
   if ( m_strDataDir.empty() ) {
      m_strDataDir = getDefaultPath();
   }
   if ( m_strDataDir.empty() ) {
      m_strDataDir = m_strInstallDir; // Not too billiant.
   }
}
```

```
SetupDlg::~SetupDlg() {
    FreeLibrary( m_hShell32 );
}
```

While setup does check the versions of the executables involved, it does no such things with the help files. This is because the help files embedded in the exe file are by definition the ones that belong to that version of the program.

Mea Culpa...

In Chapter 2, I told you that the best user interfaces are invisible. Anything that does not contribute towards the user's goals is, therefore, suspect.

In truth, SetupDlg violates that principle. I admit it; I dragged in those animations because they are cool, not because they serve any essential purpose. If these operations really were time-consuming, it would be a different matter, but they're not — I had to put in extra Sleep statements to give the user time to see the animations!

Under normal circumstances, I would have thrown out the extravaganzas. Given the time I spent fiddling with this, though, I felt it would be a shame to keep the results from my readers. If you need to do time-consuming stuff, this code may come in handy.

Chapter 21

The End of the Road

This is it. We've reached the end of the road; TextEdit is done. At least, version 1 of TextEdit is done. There are many things I'd like to change and there are many features that I'd like to add. In spite of blemishes and imperfections, however, I think the overall design and implementation of TextEdit illustrate my basic arguments. My intention with this book has not been to present TextEdit as an example of a perfect Windows program, but rather to make you think. About this, for example:

- Error handling and error reporting must be integrated into the application architecture from the beginning. Even then, it is a difficult subject, and the unified file model complicates it still more.
- Defensive programming takes longer. It also gets you to your goal faster. Paradox!
- The details matter. They matter so much as to make black-box object-oriented programming very, very difficult. I contend that low-level systems programming can't be truly object-oriented and any attempt to describe an operating system as object-oriented is, at best, marketing fluff.
- If you keep the user's best interest in mind, you'll end up doing lots more work. Your users may end up wearing expressions of delighted surprise.
- The Unified File Model is — I believe — superior to the standard model. As computers become household appliances, we need to adopt stern measures of simplicity and usability.

- I admit to some suspense as to how the unified file model will actually fare; the industry has decades of conditioning to turn around. TextEdit is an experiment and the jury is still deliberating.

Let me close with some thoughts and ideas on how TextEdit could be improved. This includes additional functionality as well as improvements in the architecture and user interface, all mixed up.

- Forward/backward buttons á la browser (work within a single TextEdit session).
- Look at files across Internet protocols such as HTTP or FTP.
- Regular expressions for search and replace. Don't reinvent the wheel; there are several good, free implementations on the Net.
- Indent/outdent selection.
- Mail integration: File/SendTo/Mail Recipient, Fax Recipient.
- Copy to Floppy command.
- Improve loading speed for large files. Load and display the first page (or one I/O page, typically 64KB), then read the rest at our leisure. The second-best solution is to update the window, finish reading and update the edit widget before starting any interaction; the waiting time before useful interaction would be the same as now. The best solution is more complicated to implement: load the remainder of the document in a background thread, and allow whatever limited interaction possible until the total document has been loaded.
- Additional shell property page that displays Unicode/Linefeeds/preview.
- Customizable headers and footers for printing.
- Insert menu, with commands to insert Date and Time, perhaps whole files.
- Bookmarks.
- Properties dialog, file name edit field: filter out illegal file name characters. This also requires that you intercept clipboard pasting, as discussed in Chapter 4.
- Improve the File Not Found dialog — put the name of the offending file in an edit field rather than a static and add the MRU as a drop-down list.
- Brace and parentheses matching; cool for programmers such as thee and me and nobody else need know about it.
- Option to keep paragraphs together during printing.
- Spell checker.
- Word count — as part of properties page perhaps.
- Sensitivity to power status.
- Overtype mode, toggled by `INS` key. Requires edit subclassing (or a different edit control), plus display on the status bar.
- Splitter windows, at least vertically.
- An alternative to Window Maximize that makes the window as large as necessary, but no larger.
- Corollary: for first-time viewing of a file, make an intelligent decision on window size and placement based on content rather than the Windows default values.

- Track changes (view differences between current file and another).
- A "goto line number" command-line parameter, allowing integration with other programs in the form of links. Additional parameters are possible. Implementing OLE Automation is a thought, although not an entirely happy-making one.
- Initialize different default font and tab setting for different types of source code documents. Most people will usually view source code will a fixed font, for example; assembly listings traditionally require eight spaces per tab.
- File names are handled sloppily. If the value of MAX_PATH ever grows, we'll have to recompile. A more bullet-proof solution would be to inspect the volume.
- Event log integration on Windows NT.
- Single process, multiple UI threads, rather than one process for each instance.
- More robust setup. TextEdit makes some assumptions about its environment that may sometimes be wrong.
- Setup/customization: position the "Browse for Folder" dialogs under their corresponding edit fields so that it's easier to see where they belong.
- Unicode version that runs well under Windows 9x (non-trivial!).
- Using NTFS streams.
- Try default extensions one by one when open file fails.
- Fix typing in combobox when the drop-down list is open.
- File New: add a "select file type" dialog box?

Some of these are easy, and some are hard. It is never right, however, to just barge in and implement whatever seems easiest or most fun or interesting to implement.

First, make a list of priorities, of guiding principles that will help you select appropriate features. If you do this in the spirit of TextEdit, rock-solid robustness takes precedence over flashy gimmicks, for example.

Next, do the detailed design for the selected features, striving for a conceptually unified whole. If you elect to replace the MRU list with browser-type forward/backward buttons, for example, you should also consider an address field for the file name.

Then, and only then, should you start thinking about the implementation.

In this book, I've tried to emphasize the importance of doing things properly, of getting the details right. But no matter how good your intentions, you can't always do what you like. The marketplace imposes its own constraints, including competitors' feature sets, impending ship dates, and escalating costs. Striking the proper path through this terrain is a difficult balancing act. I do hope, though, that the industry as a whole will start to veer ever so slightly towards a stance of greater responsibility towards the end user. Perhaps the market forces will start to work that way, too, as the global economy comes to rely more heavily upon the correct functioning of software, and ever more software users — and software buyers! — come to realize that efficient flow of information is more important than dancing deodorants.

Do the world a favor. Help lead the way.

Chapter 21: The End of the Road

Appendix A

TextEdit Command Index

Command	Description	Location	Accelerator
New Window	Creates a new window (with a new document)	File Menu	Ctrl+Shift+N
New	Creates a new document.	File Menu, Toolbar	Ctrl+N
Open...	Displays the Open File dialog	File Menu, Toolbar	Ctrl+O
Save	Saves current document	Invisible	Ctrl+S
Properties...	Displays File Properties dialog box	File Menu	Alt+Enter
Move/Rename...	Displays Move/Rename dialog box	File Menu	
Make Copy	Creates a copy of the document being edited, then starts editing the copy	File Menu	
Delete	Deletes the file and closes TextEdit	File Menu	
Delete...	Displays the Delete File dialog box	File Menu	
Abandon Changes	Reverts to start-of-editing-session version of document	File Menu	
Page Setup...	Displays the Page Setup dialog box	File Menu	

Appendix A: TextEdit Command Index

Command	Description	Location	Accelerator
Print...	Opens the print dialog box	File Menu, Toolbar	Ctrl+P
Close	Saves current document, if necessary, and exits the program	File Menu	Alt+F4
MRU file list	Opens the selected recently used file.	File Menu, Toolbar	Ctrl+F6 for file #2
Undo	Reverses the last editing action.	Edit Menu, Toolbar	Ctrl+Z
Redo	Redoes the last undone action.	Edit Menu, Toolbar	Ctrl+Y
Cut	Moves selection to clipboard	Edit Menu, Toolbar	Ctrl+X Shift+Del
Copy	Copies selection to clipboard	Edit Menu, Toolbar	Ctrl+C Ctrl+Ins
Paste	Pastes clipboard contents into the text at the current caret position, replacing selected text, if any	Edit Menu, Toolbar	Ctrl+V Shift+Ins
Delete	Deletes selected text, if any, otherwise deletes character to the right of caret, if any	Edit Menu, Toolbar	Del
Select All	Selects all text in document	Edit Menu	Ctrl+A
Find...	Opens the Find dialog box	Search Menu, Toolbar	Ctrl+F
Find Next	Finds next occurrence of a string	Search Menu	F3
Find Previous	Finds previous occurrence of a string	Search Menu	Shift+F3
Find Selection	Finds next occurrence of selected text, if any, otherwise next occurrence of current word	Search Menu	Ctrl+F3
Find previous occurrence of selection	Finds previous occurrence of selected text, if any, otherwise previous occurrence of current word	Invisible	Ctrl+Shift+F3
Replace...	Opens the Replace dialog box	Search Menu	Ctrl+H
Tool Bar	Shows or hides the tool bar	View Menu	
Status Bar	Shows or hides the status bar	View Menu	
Word Wrap	Toggles word wrap on or off	View Menu, Toolbar	Ctrl+W

Command	Description	Location	Accelerator
Fixed Font	Sets fixed font	View Menu, Toolbar	
Proportional Font	Sets proportional font	View Menu, Toolbar	
Toggle Font	Switches between fixed and proportional font.	Invisible	Ctrl+Alt+F
Change Font	Lets you change the typeface of the current (i.e., fixed or proportional) font	Invisible	Ctrl+Shift+F double-click either font button in tool bar
Options...	Opens the Options dialog box, which lets you change fonts, language and whether to show the Delete dialog next time you delete a file	View Menu	
Contents	Shows help contents	Help Menu	F1
Keyboard	Shows keyboard command list	Help Menu	
Web Home Page	Opens the R&D Books web site (http://www.rdbooks.com) in your browser	Help Menu	
About TextEdit...	Displays the About dialog box	Help Menu	
Toggle Read Only	Toggles the read-only attribute of the current file	Toolbar	Alt+R

Appendix B

Bibliography and Recommended Reading

In addition to the books referenced in the text, this bibliography lists a few other books and publications that I consider good and useful. Some of them have had a strong influence on how I think about software design.

Looking over this list, I'm struck by one common feature of the books: their permeating attitude that you must understand what you're doing, that it's important to get the details right, that the whole exercise is worth while. Some of them provide a wealth of technical detail as well, but so does a good reference manual. The underlying philosophy of design and programming is what wins me over.

Arlov, Laura: *GUI Design for Dummies*. IDG Books Worldwide 1997.
  Despite the dummy title, this is an excellent introduction to usability and the design of graphical user interfaces, full of valuable hints for the practicing designer.

Cooper, Alan: *About Face: The Essentials of User Interface Design*. IDG Books Worldwide 1995.
  This book covers a wide range of UI topics, from high-level conceptual models down to minute details of mouse interaction. Even if you don't agree with everything Cooper says, you will to find much of value here.

Edson, Dave: *Dave's Book of Top Ten Lists for Great Windows Programming.* M&T Books 1995.

This is a collection of articles on Windows programming. The material on Windows 3.x is a bit dated, unless you're stuck doing 16-bit programming, but that's only a minor part of the book. Edson ranges wide and far across the Windows landscape, giving a good overview of what's out there.

Gamma, Erich; Richard Helm, Ralph Johnson, and John Vlissides: *Design Patterns: Elements of Reusable Object-Oriented Software.* Addison-Wesley 1995.

Design patterns for software development are codified rules of thumb that solve recurring and often general problems. In the inimitable words of Martin Fowler, "Some idea, found to be useful in a practical context, which will probably be useful in other contexts."

This book catalogues simple and elegant solutions that have developed and evolved over time. Don't leave home without it.

Koenig, Andrew: *C Traps and Pitfalls.* Addison-Wesley 1988.

Much of this book concern pitfalls in pre-ANSI C, which does date it a bit. It still contains valuable tips, though, and it is saturated with a pervading sense of the necessity to understand what you're doing.

The following (perfectly portable) expression gives a flavor of the book; it evaluates to the hexadecimal character corresponding to x:

```
"0123456789ABCDEF" [ x & 0xf ]
```

Maguire, Steve: *Writing Solid Code.* Microsoft Press 1994.

This book is devoted to exterminating bugs by eliminating bad habits and encouraging good ones. Maguire's approach is anecdotal, entertaining, and thought-provoking.

McConnel, Steve: *Code Complete.* Microsoft Press 1993.

This is the most comprehensive overview of software construction that I know. To quote the author, "The research and programming experience collected in this book will help you create high-quality software and do your work more quickly and with fewer problems."

If you don't own this book, run out and buy it.

Microsoft Systems Journal. **Miller Freeman.** [http://www.msj.com]

This magazine is devoted to evangelizing the plethora of hot, new technologies that flows from Redmond. It has much well-presented technical detail and is recommended reading if you work on the bleeding edge of Windows technology.

Petzold, Charles and Paul Yao: *Programming Windows 95.* Microsoft Press 1996.

I maintain an army of random monkeys that bang away at my keyboard when I'm not using it. One of them came up with this:

Programming Windows is simple
When Petzold is at your side,
To smooth over every pimple
And polish your program's hide.

I can't improve on that; I only want to add that my 1996 edition is not the latest Petzold. The latest Petzold is much heavier than mine and requires an industrial-strength wheelbarrow just to get it home from the bookstore.

Richter, Jeffrey: *Advanced Windows Programming (Third Edition).* **Microsoft Press 1996.**
True to its title, this book is a deep dive into the Windows API. It does an excellent and comprehensive job of describing kernel objects, processes, threads, fibers, multithreading, synchronization objects, asynchronous I/O, virtual memory and more. Much more, in fact.

Tognazzini, Bruce: *Tog on Software Design.* **Addison-Wesley 1996.**
This is a collection of design essays from one of the pioneers behind the Apple Macintosh and the creator of Sun Microsystem's Starfire vision. I'm particularly fond of his catalog of surrealistic error messages such as these:

Unable to save file. Save anyway (y or n)?

No keyboard found. Hit F1 to continue.

Need I say more?

***Windows Developer's Journal.* Miller Freeman.** [http://www.wdj.com]
Windows Developer's Journal is devoted to practical solutions for the working Windows programmer. It differs from Microsoft Systems Journal in being independent of Microsoft, and in having a quite different editorial focus to begin with. WDJ is my favorite software magazine.

(Because I write regularly for WDJ, you may suspect a bias on my part. But it's not my favorite magazine because I write for it; I write for it because it is my favorite magazine.)

Index

Symbols
#define 22
/boot switch 129
/edit switch 129
/last switch 129
/max switch 129
/min switch 129
/p switch 129, 404
/pt switch 129
/setup switch 129, 444

Numerics
16-bit Windows 4, 439

A
AboutDlg 309
AbstractEditWindow 65–66
AbstractEditWnd 67, 71, 82
AbstractEditWndProc 148
abstraction 31
activateOldInstance 125, 188, 404
Add/Remove Programs (Control Panel Applet) 460–461
addShortcut 460
adjust 150
adjustButtons 377
adjustToScreen 301
applyChanges 325, 331
__argc 130
ArgumentList 21, 130
__argv 130
Arlov, Laura 10, 489
assert 21–22
assert.h 22
atoi 94
AutoArray 25, 28
AutoArray.h 27
AutoHandle 28, 272
AutoHandle.h 29–30, 88
automatic pointers 24
AutoPtr 25
auto_ptr 25
AutoPtr.h 25–26
autorun.inf 444

B
backward compatibility 4
BeginPaint 28
beginThread 440
_beginthread 440
_beginthreadex 440

blob 225
BM_SETSTYLE 325
BN_CLICKED 38, 40, 324–325
branching 121
BS_DEFPUSHBUTTON 325
bubble sort 19–20, 276
BUTTON window class 325

C

C Runtime Library (CRT) 96, 130, 440
C++ xv–xvi, 5–6, 23, 25, 35, 54–55, 66, 88, 94–95, 106–107
CallWindowProc 37–38, 40
CancelException 96, 272
__catch 107
CB_FINDSTRINGEXACT 372
CB_GETDROPPEDSTATE 369
CBN_CLOSEUP 369
CBN_DROPDOWN 369
CCmdTarget 7
CDN_FILEOK 357
CDN_FOLDERCHANGE 357
CDN_INITDONE 348, 357
CDN_SELCHANGE 357
CDN_TYPECHANGE 357
CDocument 7
centerDialog 231
CF_FIXEDPITCHONLY 422
CFile class 95
changeFont 325
changing the UI language on the fly 428
CHOOSEFONT 422
cl 36
class cloning 36, 41, 369
class libraries 6
cleanupThread 442
ClientDC 29
clipboard 180–181
    commands 180
    viewer chain 181–182
Clone.cpp (example program) 41
cmd.exe 118–119
CNB_CLOSEUP 369
code stubs 54
coding style xv–xvi
ComboBox_FindStringExact 372

ComboBox_GetDroppedState 369
COMCTL32.DLL 148, 166
command index 485
command.com 118–119
command-line pipes 127–128
common.h 22, 87–88
compactPath 315
compressFile 330
conceptual models 4, 10, 13–14, 112
const 22–23
const_cast 23
construction
    two-stage 95
containsMenuItem 184
Control Panel 223, 231, 255, 348, 428, 460
Cooper, Alan 10, 14, 372, 375, 489
copyFile 272, 275
copyResource (function) 459
create 82
createNewFile 112, 128
createNewFile.cpp 112
createPrintFont 409
CreateProcess 112, 119
CreateThread 440
CreateWindow 32, 299
CreateWindowEx 299
CRT (C Runtime Library) 96, 130
CSIDL_APPDATA 261
CSIDL_PERSONAL 112
Ctrl+C 70
Ctrl+Enter 326
Ctrl+V 70
Ctrl+X 70
current thread locale 427
cursors 265
custom resources 459–460
customization
    See Chapter 10
customizing the installation 445
Customizing Windows
    See Chapter 10
CView 7
CWaitCursor 263
CWnd 55

D

DATE_LONGDATE 436
DefDlgProc 299–300
DEFINE_PERSISTENT_BOOL 244–245
DEFINE_PERSISTENT_DOC_INT 248
DEFINE_PERSISTENT_STRING_EX 245
DefWindowProc 32–33
delete 24–25
DeleteDlg.cpp 345
DeleteDlg.h 344
DeleteFile 344
DeleteObject 460
designing for users
    See Chapter 2
DestroyAcceleratorTable 460
DestroyCursor 460
DestroyIcon 460
DestroyMenu 428, 460
DestroyWindow 33, 40
destructors 6, 23, 25, 54, 95
DeviceIoControl 330
DEVMODE 395
devMode.cpp 395
DEVNAMES 395
devNames.cpp 396
DIALOG 37
Dialog 107, 300, 302, 304
DialogBox 40–41, 299
DialogBoxParam 300
dim 88
dir 127
dispatchDlgMsg 300–301, 371
DispatchMessage 32, 70
DlgProc 300
dlgSubclasser 369
DLGWINDOWEXTRA 299
DM_SETDEFID 325, 327
Document 77, 270, 278
Document class 67, 76, 248, 270, 277, 409
doModal 300
doPaint (function) 314
DragAcceptFiles 128
DragFinish 128–129, 182
DragQueryFile 128–129, 182
DrawMenuBar 428
DRIVE_NO_ROOT_DIR 270

DS_CENTER 37, 301
DS_MODALFRAME 37
DS_NOFAILCREATE 41

E

EditListener 66, 71
Editor 373
Editor class 66, 184, 422
Editor::run 70
EDITTEXT 37
EditWnd 82
Edson, Dave 490
EM_SETPARAFORMAT 83
EM_SETTABSTOPS 83
enableDlgItem 326
encapsulation 20–21, 31–32, 47
EN_CHANGE 66
EndDialog 38, 40, 325
EndPaint 28
endThread 440
EN_KILLFOCUS 327
EN_SETFOCUS 327
EOF 94
ERROR_ACCESS_DENIED 272
ERROR_FILE_NOT_FOUND 272
ERROR_INVALID_NAME 272
ERROR_SHARING_VIOLATION 272
ERROR_WRITE_PROTECT 270–271
ES_NUMBER 36
ES_WANTRETURN 326
Exception class 96
exceptions 23–25, 93
    vs. return codes 93
    See also Chapter 6
exitLanguageComboBox 325
explicit (C++ keyword) 28

F

FAT 261, 331
file I/O 263, 269
FileMapping 29, 272–274
FileNotFoundDlg 272
FILETIME 436
FileTimeToLocalFileTime 436
FileTimeToSystemTime 436

FileType 445–446, 448
fileUtils.cpp 270, 272, 330–331
fillSysColorSolidRect 315
filter strings 349
FilterIndex 234
final 23, 107
__finally 107
finally 25
FindClose 22
FindDlg 310, 315, 377, 396, 398, 401, 405
FindFileFirst 119
FindFileNext 119
FindFirstFile 22, 119
FindResource 459
findStringExact 372
FOF_ALLOWUNDO 344
FONT.DLG 421
FontDlg 423
FontHookProc 422
formatFileTime 436
FormatMessage 429
formatMessage 429, 431–432, 436
formatMessage.cpp 429
formatMessageV 431
formatNumber 432–433, 435
FORWARD_WM_CHANGECBCHAIN 181
FORWARD_WM_DRAWCLIPBOARD 181
fragmentation xiii
FromHandle (CWnd method) 55

G

Gamma, Erich et al., 490
garbage collection 6, 23
get (auto_ptr method) 25
getArg (argumentList method) 21
getAutoSaveTime 270
getchar 94
GetClassLong 43
getContents 275
GetCursorPos 264
GetDateFormat 436
GetDC 18–19
getDevMode 395
getDevNames 395
getDlgItem 325
getDlgItemText 325

GetDriveType 270
getDriveType 270
getEditor 129, 189, 422–423, 428
GetFileInformationByHandle 275
getFilterIndex 234
getFilterList 349
GetFocus 325
GetLastActivePopup 404
GetLastError 107, 271–272
GetLocaleInfo 432
GetLocalInfo **argument list** 437
getLogFont 423
getLongFileName 270
GetLongPathName 119
getLongPathName 119
getLongPathName.cpp 120
GetMenu 428
getMenuDescription 184
getMenuItemDescription 184
getMenuItemText 343
GetMessage 32–33, 70
GetModuleFileName 107
getModuleFileName 107, 256
getModuleHandle 428
getNewFile 272
GetNumberFormat 435
GetOpenFileName 40, 347
getOrgContents 275
GetParent 301
getPathFromIDList 427
getPathFromIdListA 20
GetProp 46
getResourceID 302
getResourceModuleHandle 428
GetSaveFileName 347
getShowDeleteDialog 343
getSpecialFolderLocation 261
GetStockObject 225
GetSysColor 224
GetSystemMetrics 224
GetTempFileName 269, 271
getTempFileName 275
GetThreadLocale 428
GetTimeFormat 436
getToken 313
getToken (**function**) 314

GetUserDefaultLCID 428
GetVersionEx 21
GetVolumeInformation 331
GetWindowOrg 95
GetWindowOrgEx 95
getWindowRectInParent 301
GetWindowText xvi, 24
getWindowText 24
GetWindowTextA xvi
GetWindowTextLength 24
GetWindowTextW xvi
GetWindowTitle 230
global subclassing 36, 39–40, 43, 369
GlobalSubclasser 43
GlobSub 39, 43
GlobSub.cpp (example program) 40
gotoDlgItem 326
Grouping (member of NUMBERFMT) 435
guiding principles 17, 95, 106–107
GWL_USERDATA 46
GWL_WNDPROC 36

H

HANDLE 28
HANDLE_MSG 179
handlers.cpp 108
HANDLE_WM_MENUSELECT 183
hasFixedFont 423
HCURSOR 263
High Contrast Black 348
HINSTANCE 32
hInstance 357
HKEY_CURRENT_USER 232
HKEY_LOCAL_MACHINE (registry key) 461
HTML 313–315, 445
    static control 313
HTML.cpp 167, 316
HTML.h 315
HWND 31, 35, 54
HWND_DESKTOP 32, 301

I

ID_ACCEL_FINDNEXT 179
IDCANCEL 37, 300
IDC_ARROW 263

IDC_COMMENTS 310
IDC_COMMERCIAL 310
ID_COMMAND_PROPSCHANGED 331
IDD_FONT 420
IDD_PREVIEW_CHILD 347, 357
ID_EDIT_FIND 180
ID_EDIT_FINDNEXT 179
ID_FILE_DELETE 343
ID_FILE_NEW 184
ID_FILE_PRINT 404
IDOK 37, 300, 327
IDS_CUSTOM 349
IDS_FILEFILTERS 349
IDS_FILE_NOT_FOUND 429
ID_TABPLACEHOLDER 150
iff 180
inheritance 31–32
init 67, 148
init.cpp 148, 444
initReboot (function) 256
_initstdio 96
_initterm 96
insert (String method) 277
install (SetupDlg method) 459, 462
install.exe 129, 444
InstallDlg1 445, 452
InstallDlg1.cpp 452
installThread 440, 442, 459
instance subclassing 36, 46, 149
InstanceSubclasser 47, 54–55
Instansubclasser 348
InstSub.cpp (example program) 38
InstSub.rc (resource file listing) 37
INTERNET_MAX_PATH_LENGTH 88
INTERNET_MAX_SCHEME_LENGTH 88
INTERNET_MAX_URL_LENGTH 88
InvalidateCursor 264
InvalidateRect 264
IPersistFile 460
IsDialogMessage 70, 299, 325
isGoodStringPtr 270
IShellLink 121
isSetup 444
isToolbarDialogMessage 70
isValid (method in VersionInfo) 96
IsWindowEnabled 325

isWindowsNT 21, 428
isWriteProtectedDisk 270–271

J
Java 5–6, 23, 32

K
Koenig, Andrew 490

L
LANG_ENGLISH 427
LANG_NORWEGIAN 427
LANG_SWAHILI 428
LANGUAGE (resource statement) 427
LCID 428
lCustData 422
loadAcceleratorTable 428
LoadCursor 263–265
LoadMenu 428
LoadResource 459
loadString 149, 427
loadStrings 371
loadToolTip 149
LOCALE_ICALENDARTYPE 437
LOCALE_ICENTURY 437
LOCALE_ICOUNTRY 437
LOCALE_ICURRDIGITS 437
LOCALE_ICURRENCY 437
LOCALE_IDATE 437
LOCALE_IDAYLZERO 437
LOCALE_IDEFAULTANSICODEPAGE 437
LOCALE_IDEFAULTCODEPAGE 437
LOCALE_IDEFAULTCOUNTRY 437
LOCALE_IDEFAULTEBCDICCODEPAGE 437
LOCALE_IDEFAULTLANGUAGE 437
LOCALE_IDEFAULTOEMCODEPAGE 437
LOCALE_IDIGITS 437
LOCALE_IFIRSTDAYOFWEEK 437
LOCALE_IFIRSTWEEKOFYEAR 437
LOCALE_IINTLCURRDIGITS 437
LOCALE_ILANGUAGE 437
LOCALE_ILDATE 437
LOCALE_ILZERO 437
LOCALE_IMEASURE 437
LOCALE_IMONLZERO 437
LOCALE_INEGCURR 437
LOCALE_INEGNUMBER 437
LOCALE_INEGSEPBYSPACE 437
LOCALE_INEGSIGNPOSN 437
LOCALE_INEGSYMPRECEDES 437
LOCALE_IOPTIONALCALENDAR 437
LOCALE_IPAPERSIZE 437
LOCALE_IPOSSEPBYSPACE 437
LOCALE_IPOSSIGNPOSN 437
LOCALE_IPOSSYMPRECEDES 437
LOCALE_ITIME 437
LOCALE_ITLZERO 437
LOCALE_S1159 437
LOCALE_S2359 437
LOCALE_SABBREVCTRYNAME 437
LOCALE_SABBREVDAYNAME1 437
LOCALE_SABBREVDAYNAME7 437
LOCALE_SABBREVLANGNAME 437
LOCALE_SABBREVMONTHNAME1 437
LOCALE_SABBREVMONTHNAME13 437
LOCALE_SCOUNTRY 437
LOCALE_SCURRENCY 437
LOCALE_SDATE 437
LOCALE_SDAYNAME1 437
LOCALE_SDAYNAME7 437
LOCALE_SDECIMAL 437
LOCALE_SENGCOUNTRY 437
LOCALE_SENGCURRNAME 437
LOCALE_SENGLANGUAGE 437
LOCALE_SGROUPING 432, 437
LOCALE_SINTLSYMBOL 437
LOCALE_SLANGUAGE 437
LOCALE_SLIST 437
LOCALE_SLONGDATE 437
LOCALE_SMONDECIMALSEP 437
LOCALE_SMONGROUPING 437
LOCALE_SMONTHNAME1 437
LOCALE_SMONTHNAME13 437
LOCALE_SMONTHOUSANDSEP 437
LOCALE_SNATIVECTRYNAME 437
LOCALE_SNATIVECURRNAME 437
LOCALE_SNATIVEDIGITS 437
LOCALE_SNATIVELANGNAME 437
LOCALE_SNEGATIVESIGN 437
LOCALE_SPOSITIVESIGN 437

LOCALE_SSHORTDATE 437
LOCALE_SSORTNAME 437
LOCALE_STHOUSAND 432, 437
LOCALE_STIME 437
LOCALE_STIMEFORMAT 437
LOCALE_SYEARMONTH 437
LOCALE_USER_DEFAULT 436
LockResource 459
LOGFONT 225, 422–423
LOGFONTA 225
LOGFONTW 225
LOGFONTWIN95REG 225
longjmp 95
LPARAM 33
lpfnHook 357
lpstrCustomFilter 349
lpstrFilter 349
LPSTR_TEXTCALLBACK 149
lpTemplateName 357
LRESULT 40
lstrcpy 180
LTEXT 37

M

Maguire, Steve 19, 490
main 130
maintainability 20
mainwnd.cpp 66, 189–190, 277, 428
mainwnd.h 343
MAINWND_EXTRABYTES 189
MainWndProc 66
MAKEINTRESOURCE 428
malloc 94, 106
MapWindowPoints 301
MAX_PATH 20, 87–88, 483
m_bBinary 277
m_bInclude 446
MB_NOFOCUS 326
McConnel, Steve xvi, 490
memory management 6
memory-mapped files 272
mental model 13
MENU_CLOSING 183
MenuFont 189, 225–226
MenuFont.cpp 225
MenuHelp 184

menuUtils.cpp 185
menuUtils.h 184
MessageBox 111, 326
method xvi, 23, 32, 54–55, 71, 95–96, 275, 277, 300
MFC xv, 6–7, 55, 95, 167, 263
Microsoft Systems Journal 490
Microsoft Visual C++ xvi
Microsoft Word 5, 65, 348, 371–372
m_isOlderThanPrevious 444
m_isReplace 373
models
    conceptual 13
modes
    in the user interface 9
modifyAttribs 330
moveWindow 301
MRU 248, 250
MRU (Most Recently Used) 248
msctls_statusbar32 166
m_strFileName 270
multiByteToWideChar 20
multi-threading 439–440
mutable (C++ keyword) 23

N

NDEBUG 22
nFilterIndex 349
nMaxCustFilter 349
Notepad 3–4, 83, 112, 116–117, 119, 124–125, 348, 372, 375
NullPointerException 96
NUMBERFMT (structure) 435
NumericEdit 41

O

object-orientation 5, 31, 33
object-oriented programming
    and Windows 31
offsetof 21
onAccessViolation 180
onChange 66
onChangeCBChain 181
onCommand 300
onCreate 148, 277

onDivideByZero 180
onDlgCommand 300, 325
onDrawClipboard 181
onEditFindNext 179–180
onErrSpace 66
onGetDispInfo 149
onInitDialog 309, 331
onInitMenu 183, 343
onMaxText 66
onMenuSelect 106, 184
onOutOfMemory 180
onPaint (function) 314
onPosChange 66, 181
onSettingChange 225, 230, 428
onStackOverflow 180
onSysColorChange 225
onViewSetFixedFont 422–423
onViewSetFont 423
onViewSetProportionalFont 423
Open File common dialog bug 348
openDlgCommon.cpp 348, 350
openFile 71, 129, 272, 329
openFile (method in Document) 272
openFile.cpp 358
openFileHookProc 357
OPENFILENAME 40, 349, 357
operator new 106
operator_new 106
optimization 22–23, 275–277
options 129–130, 324
OS/2 148, 184
OSVERSIONINFO 21

P

pageHeader 409
PagePaintHook 400
PAGESETUPDLG 400
PageSetupDlg 400
PageSetupHook 400
paintHTML 167, 313
paintHTML (function) 314
PAINTSTRUCT 28
PaintStruct 28
PATHNAME 87, 128, 271
PATHNAMEA 87
PATHNAMEW 87

persistence.h 234, 245, 342
persistent variables 76, 182, 234, 244–245
Petzold, Charles 490
pFrom (member of SHFILEOPSTRUCT) 344
PHTML_SINGLE_LINE 314
platform changes 4
Pocket HTML control 315
pointer arithmetic 6
PointMap 301
polymorphism 31, 33
portability 20
positionOutsideSelection 371
PostQuitMessage 33
prcAvoid 422
Presentation Manager 184
print 129, 445
print 409
print.cpp 410
PRINTDLG 404
PrintDlg 404
PrintDlgEx 404
PrinterDC 409
PrinterDoc 409
printf 429, 432
printFile 71, 404
printSingleCopy 409
printto 118
PRIVATE 88
program initialization 96
programming
    defensively 31, 481
    guiding principles 17
    languages 5–6, 23, 33
PropertiesDlg 325
PropertiesDlg.cpp 31, 332
PropertiesDlg.h 332
pszCmdLine 111–112, 116–118, 130

Q

Quicksort 19–20, 276

R

rc 36
ReadFile 272
reboot (option) 256

reboot.cpp 257
recalcParts 167
refreshToolbar 148
REG_DWORD 232
RegisterClass 32
registerFileForDeletion 459
Registry 234, 236, 248
REG_SZ 232
reinterpret_cast 442
ReleaseDC 18–19
removeHighlight 315
ReplyMessage 442
reset 148
reset (method in AutoPtr) 25
resolveName 121, 125, 134
resources
    custom resources 459–460
restore (method in WaitCursor) 264
restoreOriginal 71
restorePosition 301
return codes 94–95
    vs. exceptions 93
reusability 20
RICHED20.DLL 82
RichEditWnd 82
Richter, Jeffrey 491
robustness 11, 19
run (method in Editor) 70, 106
RunOnce 255–256
RUNONCE_PATH 256

S

safety 20
save 71, 275
save (method in Document) 277
saveFile 329
savePosition 301
saveStrings 371
SBT_OWNERDRAW 167
s_commonDlgSubclasser 348
SDI (Single Document Interface) 116, 128, 147, 182
search and replace 71, 367, 482
searchAndSelect 71
searchPreviousThread 440
SEH (Structured Exception Handling) 95, 107

selectFont 422–423
sendMessage 442
SendTo folder 118
setargv.obj 119
SetClassLong 39, 43
SetCursor 263–265
SetCursorPos 264
setDevMode 395
setDevNames 396
setDlgItemText 325, 442
setDocumentPath 325
SetErrorMode 271
SetFileAttributes 330
setFilterIndex 234
SetFocus 326
setFonts 309
setHighlight 315
setInfo 309
setjmp 95
setLogFont 422–423
SetMenu 428
setMenuItemText 343
_set_new_handler 106
_set_new_mode 106
setRunning 275
setShowDeleteDialog 325
setString 256
SetThreadLocale 428
setup.exe 129, 444
Setup.exe.lnk 129
setup.h 256
SetupDlg 440, 442, 444, 459, 462, 480
SetupDlg.cpp 459, 462
setupPage (function) 400
SetWindowFont 309
SetWindowLong 36–38, 40, 46
SHAddToRecentDocs 248
shell integration 111
SHFileOperation 344
SHFILEOPSTRUCT 344
SHGetPathFromIDListA 20
SHGetSpecialFolderLocation 112
SHLWAPI 435
shortcuts 121
ShowDeleteDialog 342
SilentErrorMode 271

Single Document Interface (SDI) 147
`sizeof` 88
`Sleep` 480
`sm_aFileType` 445
smart pointers 25
speed 19
stack unwinding 23
standard C++ library 86
Standard Template Library (STL) 25
standards 12
`startInstance` 129, 183
`STATIC` 309, 347
`static` 88
static storage 47
status bar 3, 11, 71, 106, 147–149, 166, 184, 189, 224–225, 231, 314, 432
`StatusBar` 315
`Statusbar` 167, 170
`Statusbar` class 167
`StatusBarParts` 166
`stc32` 347
`std::map` 301
`std::string` 86
STL (Standard Template Library) 25
`StrFormatByteSize` 435
`STRICT` 17
`String` 43, 86
`String.h` header file 86
`STRINGTABLE` (resource statement) 427
`strtok` 440
Structured Exception Handling (SEH) 95, 107
style
    coding xv
`subclassHTML` 310
subclassing 35–37, 42–43, 46–47
    common dialogs 347
    global 39
    instance 36
    the font common dialog 420
`SubclassWindow` 36
`SUBLANG_ENGLISH_US` 427
`SUBLANG_NORWEGIAN_BOKMAL` 427
`SUBSYSTEM` linker switch 118, 130
superclassing 36
`supportsCompression` 331
switches 118, 123, 129–130, 404
    `/edit` 82
    `/p` 404
    `/setup` 444, 460
`SYSTEMTIME` 436

T

`_T` 88
target platform selection 4
`TBBUTTON` 150
`TB_GETTOOLTIPS` 149
`TBSTYLE_TOOLTIPS` 149
`_tcscpy` 180
`TemporaryStatusIcon` 29
testability 20
`TestClass` 180
testing
    usability 13
`TEXTEDIT.HLP` 459
`TextOut` 314
`thePointMap` 301
`threads.h` 440
TIFFs 260
Tognazzini, Bruce 14, 491
`Toolbar` 47, 66, 150, 153, 166
`Toolbar` class 148
`ToolbarWindow32` 148
`TOOLINFO` 149
`TranslateAccelerator` 70
`TranslateMessage` 70
`__try` 107
`_tsplitpath` 271
`TTF_CENTERTIP` 149
`TTF_IDISHWND` 149
`TTF_SUBCLASS` 149
`TTF_TRANSPARENT` 149
`TTM_ADDTOOL` 149
`TTN_GETDISPINFO` 149
two-stage construction 95

U

UI thread 440, 442
unhooking 47
`_UNICODE` 86
`UNICODE` 225

Unicode 4, 37, 76, 88, 96, 275, 329, 331, 422, 425–426, 483
unified file model 14, 125, 342, 481–482
uninstall 460
uninstall (function) 462
uninstallThread 440
UNIX 9, 129
update 275, 277
updatePreview 357
usability testing 12–14
user interface 10, 180, 255, 326–327, 368–369, 375, 439–440
  standards 12
user locale 427
user-centered design 9
utils.cpp 20, 149, 427

V

va_end 431
va_list 431
va_start 431–432
VB
  See Visual Basic 6
verify 22, 428
VER_PLATFORM_WIN32_NT 21
VersionInfo 96, 107, 309
vi (text editor) 9
virtual functions 54–55
Visual Basic xv, 5–6

W

wait cursor 263
WaitCursor 93, 264–265
WaitForSingleObject 442
while 19
WideCharToMultiByte 426
wildargs.obj 119
Win16 4, 118, 127, 179, 264, 427, 439
Win32 4, 28, 107, 111, 121, 127, 179, 264, 348, 427, 429, 440, 460
winbase.h 460
window
  class 32
  properties 32, 315
  styles 300–301, 325–326

Window class 55, 148, 166, 300
WINDOWS 118–119
Windows 2000 4, 119, 404, 443
Windows 95 4, 225, 427
Windows 98 4, 119, 443
Windows CE 4
Windows Developer's Journal 491
Windows Explorer 5, 111, 189, 230, 256, 329–330
Windows Logo program 12
Windows NT 4, 37, 46, 118, 182, 225, 257, 348, 425–428, 440, 445, 483
windowsx.h 36, 179, 309, 369
winerror.h 107
WinException 96, 107, 272
wingdi.h 225
wininet.h 88
WinMain 32, 39–40, 67, 96, 106, 111–112
WinMainCRTStartup 96
WIN_PATH 256
winUtils.cpp 231, 301
WM_APP 188
WM_CHANGECBCHAIN 181
WM_CHAR 38, 40
WM_CHOOSEFONT_GETLOGFONT 420
WM_CHOOSEFONT_SETLOGFONT 420
WM_CLOSE 33
WM_COMMAND 31, 37, 179, 300, 326–327
WM_CREATE 148
WM_CTLCOLORSTATIC 358
WM_DESTROY 33, 47, 315
WM_DRAWCLIPBOARD 181–182
WM_DRAWITEM 167
WM_DROPFILES 128, 182
WM_ENDSESSION 256–257
WM_ENTERSIZEMOVE 182
WM_ERASE 315
WM_EXITSIZEMOVE 182
WM_GETDLGCODE 149, 300, 325
WM_GETTEXT 33
WM_INITDIALOG 36, 38, 40, 301, 404
WM_INITMENU 180, 183
WM_KILLFOCUS 149
WM_MENUSELECT 183–184
WM_NCDESTROY 38, 40, 47
WM_NOTIFY 149, 189, 357

WM_PAINT 314–315
WM_QUERYENDSESSION 257
WM_SETCURSOR 264
WM_SETFOCUS 149
WM_SETFONT 309
WM_SETTEXT 315
WM_SETTINGCHANGE 189, 225, 230, 348, 428
WM_SIZE 36, 149, 167, 189
WM_SYSCOLORCHANGE 189, 225, 348
WM_WININICHANGE 348
WNDCLASS 32
WNDPROC 32, 38, 40, 54
Word for Windows 5, 327, 372
WordStar 5
WPARAM 33
WriteFile 272
WS_CHILD 347
WS_OVERLAPPEDWINDOW 32
wsprintf 429
WS_TABSTOP 300
wstring 86
WS_VISIBLE 32
wWinMain 96
wWinMainCRTStartup 96

Y

Yao, Paul 490

Get the working code, tools & techniques **GUARANTEED** to make you a better C & C++ programmer!

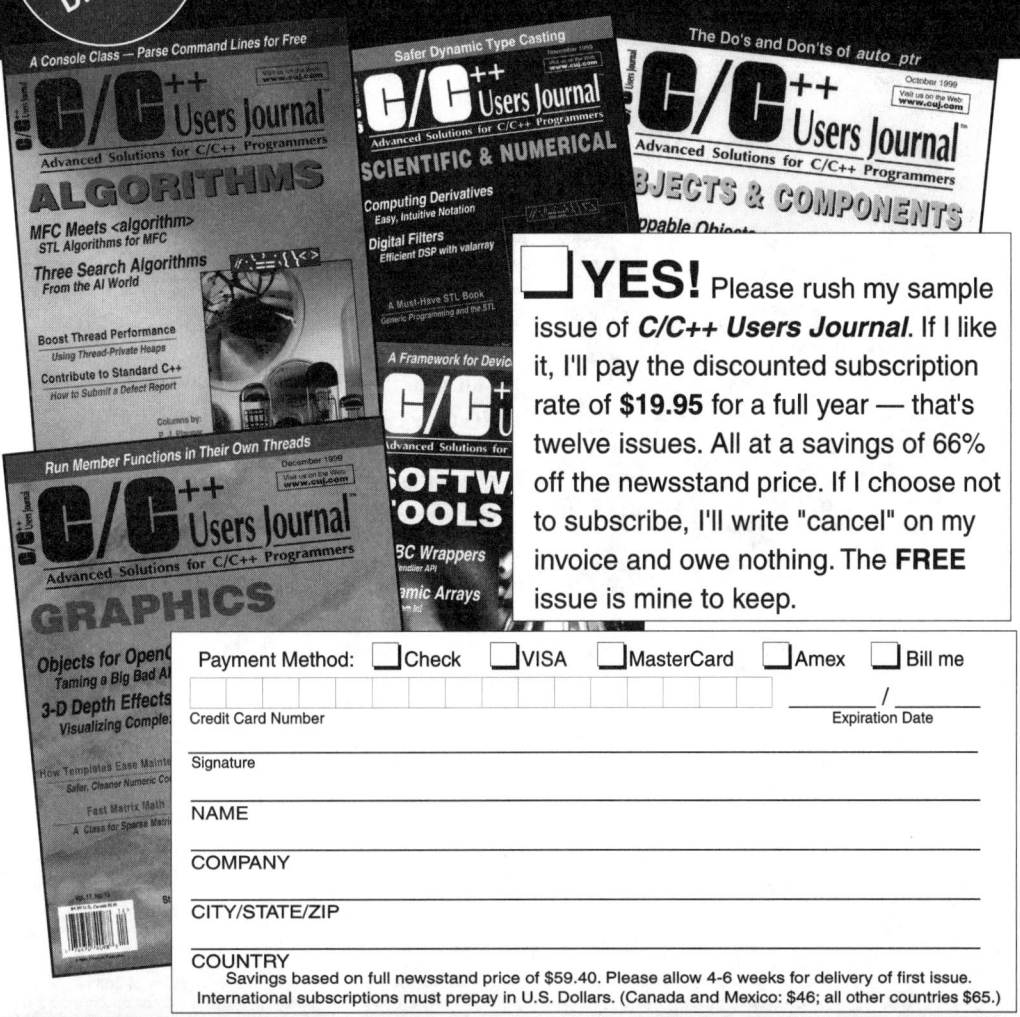

Special Book Buyer Discount!

☐ **YES!** Please rush my sample issue of *C/C++ Users Journal*. If I like it, I'll pay the discounted subscription rate of **$19.95** for a full year — that's twelve issues. All at a savings of 66% off the newsstand price. If I choose not to subscribe, I'll write "cancel" on my invoice and owe nothing. The **FREE** issue is mine to keep.

Payment Method: ☐ Check ☐ VISA ☐ MasterCard ☐ Amex ☐ Bill me

_____ ____ / ____
Credit Card Number   Expiration Date

Signature _____

NAME _____

COMPANY _____

CITY/STATE/ZIP _____

COUNTRY _____

Savings based on full newsstand price of $59.40. Please allow 4-6 weeks for delivery of first issue. International subscriptions must prepay in U.S. Dollars. (Canada and Mexico: $46; all other countries $65.)

Mail to: **C/C++ Users Journal**
P.O. Box 52582
Boulder, CO 80322-2582

For *faster* service, call **800-365-1364**
or **FAX** this card to **303-661-1181**

5RDG

Get the Independent Source for Accurate Windows Programming Information!

Special Book Buyer Discount!

☐ **YES!** Please rush my sample issue of *Windows Developer's Journal* to examine without obligation. If I like it, I'll pay the discounted subscription rate of **$19.95** for a full year — that's twelve issues. All at a savings of 66% off the newsstand price. If I choose not to subscribe, I'll write "cancel" on my invoice and owe nothing. The **FREE** issue is mine to keep.

Payment Method: ☐ Check ☐ VISA ☐ MasterCard ☐ Amex ☐ Bill me

Credit Card Number _____ Expiration Date ___/___

Signature _____

NAME _____

COMPANY _____

CITY/STATE/ZIP _____

COUNTRY _____

Savings based on full newsstand price of $59.40. Please allow 4-6 weeks for delivery of first issue. International subscriptions must prepay in U.S. Dollars. (Canada and Mexico: $45; all other countries $64.)

Mail to: **Windows Developer's Journal**
P.O. Box 56565
Boulder, CO 80322-6565

For *faster* service, call **800-365-1425**
or **FAX** this card to **303-661-1181**

5RDF

Visual C++ MFC Programming by Example
by John E. Swanke

RD3003   **$49.95**

Learn by example how to extend MFC to create more sophisticated and powerful applications. First you learn the in's and out's of messaging, which is the single most important concept to understanding how MFC works. Then the author presents 85 user interface examples, each fully annotated and ready to insert into applications. "Any half dozen of the 85 examples is likely to save you more than a couple of hours of research." Ron Burk *Windows Developer's Journal.* CD-ROM and MFC Quick Reference Guide included, 624 pp, ISBN 0-87930-544-4

VC++ MFC Extensions by Example
by John E. Swanke

Extend MFC to create more sophisticated and powerful applications. You get 67 examples — each fully annotated and ready to insert into applications. This book features a menu of advanced techniques across the entire range of Windows functions that complement the author's earlier title, *Visual C++ MFC Programming by Example.* The CD contains working projects in Visual C++ V5.0 & V6.0 and the author's own *SampleWizard* utility that facilitates adding these examples into users' applications. CD and MFC Quick Reference Guide included, 528 pp, ISBN 0-87930-588-6

RD3250   **$49.95**

Find R&D Books in your local bookstore.

Order direct 800-500-6875
fax 408-848-5784

e-mail: rd@rushorder.com
http://www.rdbooks.com

Automating Windows with Perl
by Scott McMahan

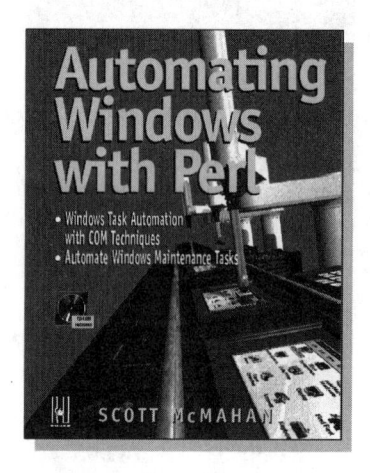

Perl is the perfect language for achieving Automation in MSWindows. With it, you can control Win32 systems processes without immediate user interaction. You learn how to use Perl scripts with the COM techniques of Office '97 to automate tasks such as processing complex documents. System and network programmers can also learn how to automate Windows maintenance tasks such as automating backups. CD-ROM included, 272pp, ISBN 0-87930-589-4

RD2737 $34.95

Supercharge MFC
by Jeffrey Galbraith

Achieve User Interface functionality not yet offered by Microsoft! Extend MFC with the author's revolutionary use of C++ subclassing to achieve pseudo-multiple inheritance. You get a sophisticated message handler that can be used with any window — eliminating the need for complicated MFC message maps. If MFC objects should do the work, it lets the message pass through; if the developer wants customized class extensions to do the work, then the C++ wrappers handle the messages themselves. CD-ROM included, 544pp, ISBN 0-87930-569-X

RD3056 $49.95

R&D BOOKS

Find R&D Books in your local bookstore.

Order direct 800-500-6875
fax 408-848-5784

e-mail: rd@rushorder.com
http://www.rdbooks.com

Writing Windows WDM Device Drivers

by Chris Cant

Master the new Windows Driver Model (WDM) that is the common hardware interface for Windows 98 and Windows 2000. You get overview of driver development, including hardware and software interface issues, appropriate application of driver types, and descriptions of where drivers fit in the new 'layer' model of WDM. Instructions on writing device drivers, including installation and debugging, are demonstrated with code provided on the companion CD-ROM. 568pp, ISBN 0-87930-565-7

RD3121 $49.95

Print Programming in Windows

by Jeff Potts

Finally — output solutions for specialized printers! Learn why off-the-shelf Windows printing products don't always work and how to resolve the exceptions of printing in a Windows environment. Make program modifications in C or Visual Basic to print to any of the specialized printers found in industry and business today, such as bar code printers, label printers, pin-fed printers for multi-forms, and special document printers. Covers all species of Windows from 3.X through 98 and NT. Disk included, 230 pp, ISBN 0-87930-585-1

RD3120 $29.95

Find R&D Books in your local bookstore.

Order Direct 800-500-6875
fax 408-848-5784

email: rd@rushorder.com
http://www.rdbooks.com

What's on the CD-ROM?

The CD-ROM that accompanies **Programming Industrial Strength Windows** contains the full 20,000 lines of source code that make up TextEdit, the author's text editor that replaces Notepad. You may use the code as you see fit in your own programming endeavors including commercial purposes. Note that any customized version of TextEdit must be clearly marked as such.

TextEdit was developed using version 6 of Microsoft Visual C++. While the text reflects that fact on occasion, the book is meant to be compiler-independent. In particular, it is not a book about Visual C++.

For more information on TextEdit, differences from Notepad, keyboard shortcuts, and so on, consult the `TextEdit.rtf` file on the CD.